American College of Physicians

# MKSAP® 15

Medical Knowledge Self-Assessment Program®

*Pulmonary and Critical Care Medicine*

# Pulmonary and Critical Care Medicine

## Contributors

**Scott F. Davies, MD, FACP, Book Editor**[1]
Professor of Medicine
University of Minnesota
Chief of Medicine
Hennepin County Medical Center
Minneapolis, Minnesota

**Richard S. Eisenstaedt, MD, FACP, Associate Editor**[2]
Clinical Professor of Medicine
Temple University School of Medicine
Chair, Department of Medicine
Abington Memorial Hospital
Abington, Pennsylvania

**Marie R. Baldisseri, MD, FCCM**[2]
Associate Professor of Critical Care Medicine
Department of Critical Care Medicine
University of Pittsburgh School of Medicine
Pittsburgh, Pennsylvania

**Craig E. Daniels, MD**[2]
Assistant Professor of Medicine
Section Head, Critical Care Medicine
Division of Pulmonary & Critical Care Medicine
Mayo Clinic
Rochester, Minnesota

**E. Wesley Ely, MD, MPH, FACP**[2]
Professor of Medicine
Allergy, Pulmonary and Critical Care
Health Services Research Center
Associate Director of Aging Research, VA GRECC
Vanderbilt University School of Medicine
Health Services Research Center
Nashville, Tennessee

**Stanley B. Fiel, MD, FACP, FCCP**[2]
Professor of Medicine
Mt. Sinai School of Medicine
Regional Chairman, Department of Medicine/Atlantic
   Health
The deNeufville Professor and Chairman
Department of Medicine
Morristown Memorial Hospital
Morristown, New Jersey

**Nizar N. Jarjour, MD, FACP, FCCP**[2]
Professor and Head
Section of Allergy, Pulmonary and Critical Care
Department of Medicine
University of Wisconsin School of Medicine and Public
   Health
Madison, Wisconsin

**Robert Kempainen, MD**[2]
Associate Professor of Medicine
University of Minnesota
Hennepin County Medical Center
Minneapolis, Minnesota

**David E. Midthun, MD, FACP**[2]
Professor of Medicine
Consultant, Division of Pulmonary and Critical Care
   Medicine
Mayo Clinic
Rochester, Minnesota

**Timothy Morris, MD**[2]
Professor of Medicine
Clinical Service Chief
Division of Pulmonary and Critical Care Medicine
University of California, San Diego
San Diego, California

## Consulting Authors

**E. Brigitte Gottschall, MD, MSPH**[1]
Assistant Professor
Division of Environmental and Occupational Health
   Sciences
National Jewish Health
University of Colorado Denver School of Medicine
Denver, Colorado

**Teofilo Lee-Chiong, MD**[2]
Head, Division of Sleep Medicine
Department of Medicine
Associate Professor of Medicine
National Jewish Health
University of Colorado Denver School of Medicine
Denver, Colorado

**E. Wesley Ely, MD, MPH, FACP**
*Research Grants/Contracts*
Pfizer, Lilly, Hospira, Aspect
*Honoraria*
Lilly, Hospira, Pfizer
*Speakers Bureau*
Lilly, Hospira, Pfizer

**Stanley B. Fiel, MD, FACP, FCCP**
*Research Grants/Contracts*
Novartis, Genetech, Gilead, Transave, Cystic Fibrosis
    Foundation
*Speakers Bureau*
GlaxoSmithKline, Boehringer Ingelheim, Novartis, Pfizer
*Consultantship*
Novartis, GlaxoSmithKline

**Nora Goldschlager, MD, MACP**
*Honoraria*
St. Jude Medical

**Nizar N. Jarjour, MD, FACP, FCCP**
*Research Grants/Contracts*
GlaxoSmithKline, Dey, Genentech, Merck
*Consultantship*
Genentech, GlaxoSmithKline, Asthmatx
*Honoraria*
Merck, Novartis

**Robert Kempainen, MD**
*Research Grants/Contracts*
Hill-Rom, Inc.

**Teofilo Lee-Chiong, MD**
*Research Grants/Contracts*
Respironics, Restore, Cephalon, Takeda, Saunders, Wiley,
    Elsevier, Oxford University Press, Lippincott Williams
    and Wilkins
*Consultantship*
Saunders, Elsevier, Covidien
*Speakers Bureau*
GlaxoSmithKline

**David E. Midthun, MD, FACP**
*Royalties*
UpToDate
*Honoraria*
ACP (PIER)

**Timothy Morris, MD**
*Research Grants/Contracts*
Agen Biomedical, Ltd.

**Trish M. Perl, MD**
*Research Grants/Contracts*
3M, Sage, Astellas
*Honoraria*
Merck, GlaxoSmithKline, 3M, Baxter
*Consultantship*
IHI

**Ileana L. Piña, MD**
*Speakers Bureau*
AstraZeneca, Sanofi-Aventis, Innovia, Merck, Solvay,
    Novartis

**Steven A. Sahn, MD, FACP**
*Research Grants/Contracts*
Novartis, AstraZeneca, Intermune, Boehringer Ingelheim,
    Actelion, Gilead, Centocor, NIH IPFnet
*Royalties*
UpToDate
*Honoraria*
ACCP (PCCU)
*Consultantship*
Intermune, Pilot, LAM Foundation
*Speakers Bureau*
Intermune, Boehringer Ingelheim, Pilot

**Jean-Louis Vincent, MD**
*Research Grants/Contracts*
Abbott, AM Pharma, Apex, Artisan-Asahi, AstraZeneca,
    Biosite, Biotest, BioMerieux, Brahms, Covidien,
    DaiichiSanyo, Discovery, Drager, Edwards Lifesciences,
    Eli Lilly, Esai, Ferring, GlaxoSmithKline, Hutchinson,
    Intercell, Merck, Novartis, NovaLung, Novo Nordisk,
    Organon, Pfizer, Philips, PICIS, Roche Diagnostics,
    Spectral, Takeda, Teva, Tyco, Vasamed, Wyeth Lederle,
    Zeneus
*Honoraria*
Eli Lilly, Edwards Lifesciences, Esai, GlaxoSmithKline,
    Novartis, Novo Nordisk, Pfizer
*Consultantship*
AM Pharma, Apex, Artisan-Asahi, AstraZeneca, Biosite,
    BioMerieux, Covidien, Edwards Lifesciences, Eli Lilly,
    Esai, Ferring, GlaxoSmithKline, Instrumentation Labs,
    Intercell, Merck, Novartis, Novo Nordisk, Organon,
    Pfizer, Philips, Roche Diagnostics, Spacelabs, Spectral,
    Takeda, Wyeth Lederle
*Speakers Bureau*
Eli Lilly, Edwards Lifesciences, Esai, GlaxoSmithKline,
    Novartis, Novo Nordisk, Pfizer

**Steven E. Weinberger, MD, FACP**
*Stock Options/Holdings*
Abbott, GlaxoSmithKline

## Acknowledgments

The American College of Physicians (ACP) gratefully acknowledges the special contributions to the development and production of the 15th edition of the Medical Knowledge Self-Assessment Program® (MKSAP 15) of Scott Thomas Hurd (Senior Systems Analyst/Developer), Ricki Jo Kauffman (Manager, Systems Development), Michael Ripca (Technical Administrator/Graphics Designer), and Lisa Torrieri (Graphic Designer). The Digital version (CD-ROM and Online components) was developed within the ACP's Interactive Product Development Department by Steven Spadt (Director), Christopher Forrest (Senior Software Developer), Ryan Hinkel (Senior Software Developer), John McKnight (Software Developer), Sean O'Donnell (Senior Software Developer), and Brian Sweigard (Senior Software Developer). Computer scoring and reporting are being performed by ACT, Inc., Iowa City, Iowa. The College also wishes to acknowledge that many other persons, too numerous to mention, have contributed to the production of this program. Without their dedicated efforts, this program would not have been possible.

## Continuing Medical Education

The American College of Physicians is accredited by the Accreditation Council for Continuing Medical Education (ACCME) to provide continuing medical education for physicians.

The American College of Physicians designates this educational activity for a maximum of 166 *AMA PRA Category 1 Credits*™. Physicians should only claim credit commensurate with the extent of their participation in the activity.

*AMA PRA Category 1 Credit*™ is available from July 31, 2009, to July 31, 2012.

## Learning Objectives

The learning objectives of MKSAP 15 are to:
- Close gaps between actual care in your practice and preferred standards of care, based on best evidence
- Diagnose disease states that are less common and sometimes overlooked and confusing
- Improve management of comorbidities that can complicate patient care
- Determine when to refer patients for surgery or care by subspecialists
- Pass the ABIM certification examination
- Pass the ABIM maintenance of certification examination

## Target Audience

- General internists and primary care physicians
- Subspecialists who need to remain up-to-date in internal medicine
- Residents preparing for the certifying examination in internal medicine
- Physicians preparing for maintenance of certification in internal medicine (recertification)

## How to Submit for CME Credits

To earn CME credits, complete a MKSAP 15 answer sheet. Use the enclosed, self-addressed envelope to mail your completed answer sheet(s) to the MKSAP Processing Center for scoring. Remember to provide your MKSAP 15 order and ACP ID numbers in the appropriate spaces on the answer sheet. The order and ACP ID numbers are printed on your mailing label. If you have not received these numbers with your MKSAP 15 purchase, you will need to acquire them to earn CME credits. E-mail ACP's customer service center at custserv@acponline.org. In the subject line, write "MKSAP 15 order/ACP ID numbers." In the body of the e-mail, make sure you include your e-mail address as well as your full name, address, city, state, ZIP code, country, and telephone number. Also identify where you have made your MKSAP 15 purchase. You will receive your MKSAP 15 order and ACP ID numbers by e-mail within 72 business hours.

## Disclosure Policy

It is the policy of the American College of Physicians (ACP) to ensure balance, independence, objectivity, and scientific rigor in all its educational activities. To this end, and consistent with the policies of the ACP and the Accreditation Council for Continuing Medical Education (ACCME), contributors to all ACP continuing medical education activities are required to disclose all relevant financial relationships with any entity producing, marketing, re-selling, or distributing health care goods or services consumed by, or used on, patients. Contributors are required to use generic names in the discussion of therapeutic options and are required to identify any unapproved, off-label, or investigative use of commercial products or devices. Where a trade name is used, all available trade names for the same product type are also included. If trade-name products manufactured by companies with whom contributors have relationships are discussed, contributors are asked to provide evidence-based citations in support of the discussion. The information is reviewed by the committee responsible for producing this text. If necessary, adjustments to topics or contributors' roles in content development are made to balance the discussion. Further, all readers of this text are asked to evaluate the content for evidence of commercial bias so that future decisions about content and contributors can be made in light of this information.

## Resolution of Conflicts

To resolve all conflicts of interest and influences of vested interests, the ACP precluded members of the content-creation committee from deciding on any content issues that involved generic or trade-name products associated with proprietary entities with which these committee members had relationships. In addition, content was based on best evidence and updated clinical care guidelines, when such evidence and guidelines were available. Contributors' disclosure information can be found with the list of contributors' names and those of ACP principal staff listed in the beginning of this book.

## Educational Disclaimer

The editors and publisher of MKSAP 15 recognize that the development of new material offers many opportunities for error. Despite our best efforts, some errors may persist in print. Drug dosage schedules are, we believe, accurate and in accordance with current standards. Readers are advised, however, to ensure that the recommended dosages in MKSAP 15 concur with the information provided in the product information material. This is especially important in cases of new, infrequently used, or highly toxic drugs. Application of the information in MKSAP 15 remains the professional responsibility of the practitioner.

The primary purpose of MKSAP 15 is educational. Information presented, as well as publications, technologies, products, and/or services discussed, is intended to inform subscribers about the knowledge, techniques, and experiences of the contributors. A diversity of professional opinion exists, and the views of the contributors are their own and not those of the ACP. Inclusion of any material in the program does not constitute endorsement or recommendation by the ACP. The ACP does not warrant the safety, reliability, accuracy, completeness, or usefulness of and disclaims any and all liability for damages and claims that may result from the use of information, publications, technologies, products, and/or services discussed in this program.

## Publisher's Information

## Unauthorized Use of This Book Is Against the Law

MKSAP 15 ISBN: 978-1-934465-25-7
Pulmonary and Critical Care Medicine ISBN: 978-1-934465-35-6

Printed in the United States of America.

For order information in the U.S. or Canada call 800-523-1546, extension 2600. All other countries call 215-351-2600. Fax inquiries to 215-351-2799 or e-mail to custserv@acponline.org.

## Errata and Norm Tables

Errata for MKSAP 15 will be posted at http://mksap.acponline.org/errata as new information becomes known to the editors.

MKSAP 15 Performance Interpretation Guidelines with Norm Tables, available December 31, 2010, will reflect the knowledge of physicians who have completed the self-assessment tests before the program was published. These physicians took the tests without being able to refer to the syllabus, answers, and critiques. For your convenience, the tables are available in a printable PDF file at http://mksap.acponline.org/normtables.

# Table of Contents

# Pulmonary and Critical Care Medicine

## Asthma

Asthma is a chronic inflammatory disease of the airways characterized by variable and recurrent respiratory symptoms, including cough, chest tightness, shortness of breath, and wheezing. The disease involves underlying airway inflammation and hyperresponsiveness (an increased sensitivity of the airways to an inhaled bronchoconstrictor agonist, a steeper slope of the dose-response curve, and a greater maximal response to the agonist) and manifests as airway obstruction that is reversible, either spontaneously or with treatment and that can be confirmed with pulmonary function testing. Some stimuli (specific allergens) cause an early asthmatic response (15- to 30-minute onset and lasting 1 to 2 hours) and a late response (3- to 8-hour onset and lasting up to 24 hours), whereas other stimuli, such as exercise, cause an early, but not a late, response. Repeated exposure to allergic stimuli can lead to increasing inflammation and worsening obstruction.

## Epidemiology and Natural History

Asthma is one of the most common chronic conditions, affecting at least 5% of the adult population in the United States. The prevalence of asthma has increased worldwide in recent years, especially in industrialized countries; the reasons for this increase are unclear. In the United States, minority groups and the poor have a higher prevalence of asthma and higher morbidity and mortality from the disease. Although the number of deaths from asthma has decreased over the past few years, there are still 4000 deaths from asthma annually in the United States, many of which may be preventable. Asthma is diagnosed most commonly in children, but adult-onset asthma also occurs. Allergies are common in childhood-onset asthma but are somewhat less so in adult-onset disease. Asthma has a hereditary basis, but it appears to be a complicated process with multiple involved genes and likely gene-environment interactions. The most important environmental factors appear to be airborne allergens and viral infections. Diet, tobacco smoke, and air pollutants may also contribute to the development of asthma in susceptible persons. Airway obstruction in asthma is typically reversible, but the normal decline in lung function with aging appears to be slightly accelerated in patients with asthma, especially in patients who are also smokers.

## Pathogenesis

The central features of airway histopathology in asthma include infiltration of inflammatory cells, edema, subepithelial fibrosis, mucous gland and goblet cell hyperplasia, and increased airway smooth muscle mass (**Figure 1**). These findings are most prominent in patients with more severe disease, but they also occur in patients with mild to moderate disease, even when stable and relatively controlled.

Eosinophils are the most commonly detected inflammatory cells in patients with active disease, especially patients with an allergic component to their disease. Eosinophils in the sputum are associated with increased airway hyperresponsiveness and propensity toward exacerbations, although, at this time, examination of sputum for eosinophils is of limited clinical utility in patients with stable asthma. Most patients with sputum eosinophilia respond to treatment with corticosteroids. Interleukin-5 (IL-5) is involved in the development, activation, and survival of eosinophils, and there is significant interest in the potential therapeutic use of a monoclonal antibody against IL-5 in asthma. Although early trials of IL-5 in patients with asthma have not shown significant improvement, recent studies focusing on patients with more severe asthma and significant airway eosinophilia have shown encouraging results, with improved quality of life and reduced frequency of asthma exacerbations.

Neutrophils contribute significantly to the pathogenesis of persistent asthma, especially severe persistent asthma, or viral disease–induced asthma exacerbations. If neutrophils are present, the disease tends to be less reversible with inhaled

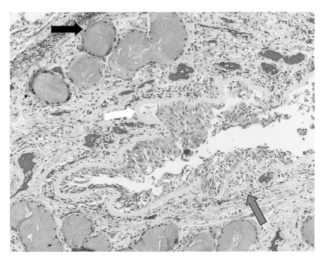

**FIGURE 1.**
**Lung tissue specimen of a patient who died of asthma.**
The specimen shows significant mucus gland hyperplasia (*black arrow*), sub-basement membrane thickening (*white arrow*), and disruption of the elastic fibers (*red arrow*).

bronchodilators, less responsive to corticosteroid therapy, and associated with reduced lung function. There are no medications that specifically target this neutrophilic phenotype of asthma. However, there is limited evidence that macrolide antibiotics and 5-lipoxygenase inhibitors may be effective in treating neutrophilic asthma. During asthma exacerbations, the numbers of lymphocytes and their level of activation are increased, with a subtype of T helper cells known as Th2 cells predominating. Th2 cells generate higher quantities of IL-4, which is important in the production of IgE, and IL-5, which is essential for promotion of eosinophilic inflammation. Immunosuppressive therapy that targets lymphocytes (for example, cyclosporine and methotrexate) has been tried in patients with asthma with limited benefits and significant side effects. Macrophages play a role in airway inflammation, probably participating in host defense and antigen presentation, with the potential to promote inflammation but also under other circumstances to down-regulate inflammation. The release of stored mediators (histamine and tryptase) as well as newly generated mediators (leukotrienes and cytokines) from mast cells plays a role in the development of early and late responses to inhaled allergens.

Finally, most patients with asthma show structural alteration in the airway, including subepithelial fibrosis, increased muscle mass, angiogenesis, and mucous gland hyperplasia. These changes, collectively known as airway remodeling, probably contribute to increased airway obstruction, decreased reversibility, and increased morbidity. However, it has been suggested that some of the remodeling features are likely to be detrimental (for example, increased smooth muscle mass, mucous gland hyperplasia), whereas other features may be protective against excessive bronchoconstriction (for example, subepithelial fibrosis, which leads to increased airway stiffness and reduces the tendency toward airway closure). The cause of airway remodeling is unknown, but chronic unchecked airway inflammation is believed to be an important component.

---

**KEY POINTS**

- Airway inflammation is an important underlying feature of asthma.
- In asthma, uncontrolled, long-standing inflammation may lead to permanent structural changes known as airway remodeling.

## Clinical Evaluation

### Symptoms and Signs
Patients with asthma typically present with recurrent cough, wheezing, chest tightness, and shortness of breath. The cough is typically productive. Other significant causes of airway obstruction leading to wheezing must be considered both in the initial diagnosis and if there is no clear response to initial therapy (**Table 1**).

The symptoms of asthma can be intermittent, seasonal, or persistent. Symptoms vary diurnally, being worse at night and in the early morning. Precipitating and aggravating factors include exercise, environmental allergens, viral respiratory tract infections, cold air, stress, and many comorbid conditions (for example, sinusitis, rhinitis, gastroesophageal reflux disease, and obstructive sleep apnea). Most asthma exacerbations resolve spontaneously or in response to therapy, and the response is often complete. Clinical examination is important for evaluation of associated conditions (nasal polyps, rhinitis, or sinusitis) and to assess the signs of airway obstruction (wheezing, use of accessory muscles to breathe, hyperinflation). Although none of these symptoms and signs is diagnostic of asthma, the combination of these findings in a patient with a history of allergy or family history of asthma along with the exclusion of alternative diagnoses makes the diagnosis of asthma very likely.

### Pulmonary Function Testing
Patients with suspected asthma should be evaluated with spirometry to confirm airway obstruction and to assess its reversibility. Spirometry is recommended in the initial evaluation of patients with suspected asthma and should be considered during follow-up evaluations. With the availability of hand-held spirometers, pulmonary function can be accurately evaluated in most office settings. The $FEV_1/FVC$ ratio is typically greater than 75% in normal adults; a lower ratio indicates the presence of obstruction. Significant reversibility of obstruction is indicated by a 12% or greater improvement in $FEV_1$ after administration of a short-acting inhaled $\beta_2$-agonist (**Figure 2**).

Peak flow meters can be used at home for serial measurement of lung function and to assess the relationship of lung function to symptoms. In patients with poor perception of airway obstruction, monitoring peak expiratory flow rate (PEFR) may help detect the loss of asthma control. When peak flow meters are used for managing asthma in outpatient settings, the highest value of PEFR obtained during a 2-week

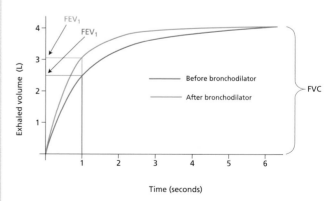

**FIGURE 2.**
Spirometry before and after an inhaled bronchodilator showing reversible airway obstruction.

**TABLE 1** Differential Diagnosis of Asthma

| Condition | Comments |
|---|---|
| Chronic obstructive pulmonary disease | Less reversibility of airflow obstruction; associated with a history of tobacco use. May coexist with asthma in adults. |
| Vocal cord dysfunction | Abrupt onset of severe symptoms, often with rapid improvement. Monophonic wheezing heard loudest during either inspiration or expiration. The preferred diagnostic test is direct visualization of the vocal cords during symptoms or flow volume loops. May closely mimic asthma, particularly in young adults. |
| Heart failure | Spirometry may or may not be normal. Wheezing may be a sentinel manifestation of heart failure. Consider heart failure when there is not prompt improvement with asthma therapy. Always a consideration for persons with underlying cardiac disease. |
| Bronchiectasis | Voluminous sputum production, often purulent, sometimes blood tinged. Suspect when physical examination shows clubbing or crackles with wheezing or with peribronchial thickening on chest radiograph. |
| Pulmonary infiltration with eosinophilia syndromes | Wheezing may occur in ABPA, eosinophilic pneumonia, and Churg-Strauss syndrome. Note that in uncomplicated asthma, chest radiograph is normal. Findings of infiltrates, striking peripheral blood eosinophilia, and constitutional symptoms, such as fever and weight loss, suggest chronic eosinophilic pneumonia. Asthma with eosinophilia, markedly high serum IgE levels, and intermittent pulmonary infiltrates is characteristic of ABPA. Upper airway and sinus disease, difficult-to-treat asthma, and multisystem organ dysfunction suggest Churg-Strauss syndrome. |
| Mechanical airway obstruction | Respiratory noises may be more pronounced in the inspiratory or expiratory phase of respiration, depending on location of obstruction. Diagnosed by flow volume loops. |
| Cystic fibrosis | Associated with thick, purulent sputum containing bacteria and gastrointestinal symptoms due to pancreatic insufficiency. Recurrent respiratory tract infections may be present without gastrointestinal or other systemic involvement. |

ABPA = allergic bronchopulmonary aspergillosis.

period of stability is regarded as a patient's personal best. Obtaining subsequent values within 20% of the personal best suggests that the disease is stable. PEFR reduction of 20% to 50% from personal best indicates a moderate increase in airway obstruction, whereas a greater than 50% reduction suggests severe airway obstruction. Patients who are poor perceivers of airway obstruction or who have more severe asthma symptoms may benefit from regular home monitoring using peak flow meters. Other measures of pulmonary function, such as measurements of lung volumes and DLCO, are typically not needed for the evaluation of asthma; however, they can be used in the initial evaluation of patients with suspected asthma to help exclude other conditions, such as interstitial lung diseases and emphysema, which, unlike asthma, are associated with decrease in DLCO.

In patients who have symptoms suggestive of asthma but normal spirometry, bronchoprovocation with methacholine can help establish the presence of airway hyperresponsiveness. Methacholine is administered by inhalation in increasing concentrations through a dosimeter-activated nebulizer. Spirometry is obtained after inhalation of each dose of methacholine to determine the effect on $FEV_1$. Increasing doses of methacholine are given until there is a 20% or greater reduction in $FEV_1$. The dose-response curve is used to calculate the methacholine concentration leading to a 20% reduction in $FEV_1$, which is referred to as the provocative concentration 20% ($PC_{20}$). In normal persons, the $PC_{20}$ is typically greater than 16 mg/mL; most patients with asthma have a $PC_{20}$ of less than 8 mg/mL. Cigarette smoking, chronic obstructive pulmonary disease, allergic rhinitis, and recent viral respiratory tract infection can lead to increased airway hyperresponsiveness and a positive methacholine challenge test. Therefore, the best clinical use of the methacholine challenge test is to exclude asthma in patients who have atypical symptoms because it has a high negative predictive value. However, a positive test should be correlated with other features of asthma before reaching a clinical diagnosis. Additional testing is recommended for patients who have atopic manifestations, such as rhinitis, or who describe association of their symptoms with certain exposures or seasons. The results of allergy skin tests can help explain symptoms, guide immunotherapy, and target avoidance and allergen control measures. Allergy evaluation should also be considered in patients with asthma who require more than minimal medication to control their disease. When skin testing cannot be obtained because of confounding medications that cannot be discontinued, a radioallergosorbent test can be used to measure allergen-specific serum IgE levels.

Measurement of exhaled nitric oxide is sometimes used as an indirect method of assessing airway inflammation in asthma. It is noninvasive, easy to do, and reproducible. In several studies, increased exhaled nitric oxide has been shown to correlate with asthma exacerbation and with eosinophilic inflammation. Inhaled corticosteroids decrease the levels of exhaled nitric oxide so predictably that measurement of nitric oxide levels can be used to test adherence with inhaled corticosteroids. An approach to asthma management based on measurement of exhaled nitric oxide has been proposed, but there are no randomized clinical trials that support this approach.

Measurement of sputum eosinophils also has been proposed as a means of evaluating disease activity and propensity toward exacerbations. Reducing the level of sputum eosinophils and maintaining them at normal range have been shown to improve asthma control and reduce exacerbations; however, obtaining sputum samples and reliably measuring sputum eosinophils can be difficult, and this approach is largely limited to some specialty clinics and research settings.

**KEY POINTS**

- Spirometry should be performed in patients with suspected asthma to confirm the presence of airway obstruction and reversibility.
- Measurement of peak expiratory flow rates can be used to monitor airway obstruction at home and to assess the relationship between symptoms and airway obstruction.
- Allergy evaluation should be considered in patients with asthma who require more than minimal medication to control their disease.
- The methacholine challenge test has a high negative predictive value for asthma, and a negative test can therefore be used to exclude asthma.

## Asthma Syndromes

### Occupational Asthma

Patients with asthma should be asked about their workplace exposures, particularly to irritants, sensitizing chemicals, and allergens. Asthma related to the work environment can be based on allergic sensitization or nonallergic mechanisms. Asthma symptoms may not occur during or immediately after exposure to the offending agent. Resolution or significant improvement in symptoms during weekends and vacations is an important but not universal feature of occupational asthma. Patients with occupational asthma may show improvement in lung function, symptoms, and airway hyperresponsiveness over time, provided that they have no subsequent exposure to the offending agent.

### Reactive Airways Dysfunction Syndrome

Exposure to high levels of irritants (for example, chlorine gas, bleach, or ammonia) can result in significant airway injury, which can lead to persistent airway inflammation and dysfunction with airway hyperresponsiveness and obstruction. After a single exposure, typically accidental, the patient may develop chronic and persistent cough, shortness of breath, and chest tightness. This is known as the reactive airways dysfunction syndrome (RADS). The symptoms of RADS may subside with time but can persist for years in some patients. Like patients with occupational asthma, patients with RADS may show improvement over time, provided that they have no subsequent exposure to the offending agent.

### Virus-induced Asthma

Infection with rhinovirus, influenza virus, and respiratory syncytial virus has been associated with asthma exacerbation. Rhinovirus is the most common infectious cause of asthma. Although it is mostly limited to the upper airway, the virus has been recovered from the lower airway in patients with colds. Direct lower airway infection and promotion of airway inflammation have been proposed as potential mechanisms for virus-induced asthma. Typically, asthma exacerbations occur 2 to 4 days after the onset of the cold and can range from mild to very severe exacerbations. When mild, these exacerbations can be treated with inhaled corticosteroids and long-acting $\beta_2$-agonists; however, severe exacerbations require therapy with systemic corticosteroids. Whether doubling (or quadrupling) the dose of inhaled corticosteroids is as effective as using systemic corticosteroids is not known at this time.

### Cough-variant Asthma

In a subset of patients with asthma, cough can be the predominant or, at times, the only symptom. This syndrome is called cough-variant asthma, and it needs to be distinguished from other causes of chronic cough, such as rhinitis or gastroesophageal reflux disease. Patients with cough-variant asthma typically have airway hyperresponsiveness on methacholine challenge testing and can show evidence of obstruction on spirometry, with improvement after inhaled bronchodilators (see MKSAP 15 General Internal Medicine).

Treatment of cough-variant asthma is similar to treatment of asthma in general; however, in a subset of patients, cough can be very difficult to control despite the appropriate use of anti-asthma medications. A comprehensive management plan for all provoking factors is essential to achieving control in these patients.

### Asthma and Gastroesophageal Reflux Disease

Gastroesophageal reflux disease (GERD) is common in patients with asthma and can lead to chronic cough resembling that of cough-variant asthma or may result in worsening asthma control and severity. Patients with refractory asthma should be evaluated for GERD (see MKSAP 15 Gastroenterology and Hepatology). Although heartburn is a common symptom in GERD, many patients do not have typical symptoms and can be asymptomatic. Therefore, in patients with difficult-to-control asthma, lifestyle modifications and a trial of acid suppression with a proton pump inhibitor should be considered. Acid suppression neutralizes the acidity of the gastric juices but does not prevent reflux. Therefore, patients with GERD and asthma should be encouraged to adopt lifestyle changes to reduce reflux, including avoiding meals close to bedtime, avoiding certain foods, and elevating the head of the bed. If GERD is still suspected, a 24-hour esophageal pH monitoring study should be considered.

### Allergic Bronchopulmonary Aspergillosis

In patients with difficult-to-control asthma and a history of recurrent pulmonary infiltrates, allergic bronchopulmonary aspergillosis (ABPA) should be considered. The ubiquitous fungus *Aspergillus fumigatus* can grow in the bronchial secretions of patients with asthma or cystic fibrosis. The organism does not invade tissue, but it results in immune-mediated allergic inflammation, with subsequent damage to the bronchial wall and development of proximal bronchiectasis that can be best demonstrated on high-resolution CT scan of the chest. Affected patients typically have eosinophilia, elevated serum levels of circulating IgE (total and specific IgE against *A. fumigatus*), and a positive skin test for *Aspergillus*. The treatment of ABPA is similar to that of asthma in general, but the initial therapy involves systemic corticosteroids until the disease is controlled; the corticosteroid dosage is then tapered, and IgE levels are monitored. Untreated, ABPA can result in permanent lung damage and fibrosis.

### Exercise-induced Bronchospasm

Exercise-induced bronchospasm (EIB) can develop in most patients with asthma if they do high-intensity exercise. The occurrence of EIB is related to the degree of ventilation with significant contribution of cooling and drying of the airways. The symptoms typically occur during or shortly after exercise, peak within 5 to 10 minutes after stopping the activity, and resolve in less than 30 minutes. The disorder can be confused with vocal cord dysfunction, which can also be induced by exercise. Exercise challenge testing helps confirm the diagnosis. Typically, a 15% reduction in $FEV_1$ after intense exercise is compatible with the diagnosis.

Affected patients do not have to limit their participation in sports or other physical activities. Approximately 10% of the athletes on the U.S. Olympic teams in recent years had EIB. The bronchospasm can be prevented by adequate warm-up before exercise, by wearing a mask or scarf over the mouth in cold weather, or by therapy with short- or long-acting $\beta_2$-agonists or leukotriene antagonists. Short-acting $\beta_2$-agonists

given 10 to 15 minutes before exercise can prevent EIB for up to 3 hours. In some patients, EIB is the only manifestation of asthma, and such patients require treatment with intermittent short-acting inhaled $\beta_2$-agonists before exercise without regular use of long-term controller therapy.

### Vocal Cord Dysfunction

Vocal cord dysfunction (VCD) simulates asthma and manifests as recurrent wheezing and stridor. Symptoms can occur suddenly without a clear cause or in response to irritants, exercise, or stress; VCD can occur in patients with or without asthma. Patients with VCD can have exercise-induced symptoms that are difficult to distinguish from exercise-induced bronchospasm, and both conditions can occur in competitive athletes. Recognizing VCD is important because it is treated differently from asthma; unrecognized, it can lead to unnecessary treatment with high-dose inhaled or systemic corticosteroids. The diagnosis can be confirmed by flow volume loops when the patient is symptomatic, which show an inspiratory cut-off (**Figure 3**), or laryngoscopy, which shows abnormal adduction of the vocal cords. Treatment involves speech therapy, behavior modification, and patient education. During an acute attack, inhalation of a helium-oxygen mixture and continuous positive airway pressure can relieve the symptoms of VCD.

### Aspirin-sensitive Asthma

Up to 20% of adults with asthma develop bronchoconstriction after taking aspirin or other NSAIDs. Patients with asthma, especially those with poorly controlled disease, should be asked about the use of these analgesics and advised to avoid taking them. Patients who must use aspirin should be

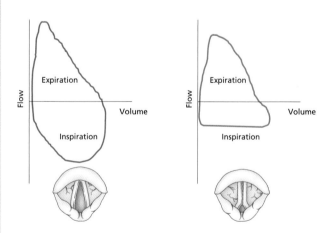

**FIGURE 3.**
**Flow volume loops in vocal cord dysfunction.**
Flow volume loops showing maximum inspiratory and expiratory flow-volume relationships in a patient with vocal cord dysfunction during asymptomatic (*left*) and symptomatic (*right*) periods. Note also the marked adduction of the vocal cords with severe reduction of the glottic aperture during a symptomatic period (*right*) of airway obstruction.

referred for desensitization. The mechanism for aspirin-induced asthma involves increased leukotriene levels, and, as such, patients with mild disease may benefit from the use of leukotriene modifying agents (montelukast, zafirlukast) as part of their asthma treatment.

### KEY POINTS

- Exposure to high levels of irritants (for example, chlorine gas, bleach, or ammonia) can result in significant airway injury, which can lead to persistent airway inflammation and dysfunction with airway hyper-responsiveness and obstruction.

- In patients with difficult-to-control asthma, lifestyle modifications and a trial of acid suppression with a proton pump inhibitor for potential gastroesophageal reflux disease should be considered.

- Patients with allergic bronchopulmonary aspergillosis typically have eosinophilia, elevated serum levels of circulating IgE (total and specific IgE against *Aspergillus fumigatus*), and a positive skin test for *Aspergillus*.

- The diagnosis of vocal cord dysfunction can be confirmed by flow volume loops when the patient is symptomatic, which show an inspiratory cut-off, or laryngoscopy, which shows abnormal adduction of the vocal cords.

## Management of Asthma

The goal of therapy for asthma is to reduce impairment and risk (**Table 2**). Impairment is based on the frequency of daytime symptoms, nighttime symptoms, need for the use of a rescue inhaler, limitation in activity, and lung function. Risk is based on the frequency of asthma exacerbation, which can occur even in patients with limited symptoms and relatively preserved lung functions between exacerbations. Asthma is classified according to the degree of impairment and risk as intermittent or persistent, and persistent asthma is further classified as mild, moderate, or severe (**Table 3**).

A stepwise approach to managing asthma is recommended to gain and maintain control of the disease and to limit impairment and risks (**Figure 4**).

### Pharmacotherapy for Asthma

Therapy by metered-dose inhaler with various agents is essential in asthma. The proper technique for using the various inhalers is necessary for an adequate therapeutic response. Patients should be shown the proper technique for using inhalers, and any patients with poorly controlled disease should be evaluated for the proper inhaler technique.

**TABLE 2** Goals of Therapy for Control of Asthma

| **Reduce Impairment** |
| --- |
| Prevent chronic and troublesome symptoms (coughing or breathlessness during the day, night, or after exertion) |
| Require infrequent use (<2 days a week) of inhaled short-acting $\beta_2$-agonist for quick relief of symptoms (not including prevention of exercise-induced bronchospasm) |
| Maintain (near) normal pulmonary function |
| Maintain normal activity levels (including exercise and other physical activity and attendance at school or work) |
| Meet patients' and families' expectations of and satisfaction with asthma care |
| **Reduce Risk** |
| Prevent recurrent exacerbations of asthma and minimize the need for emergency department visits or hospitalizations |
| Prevent loss of lung function |
| Provide optimal pharmacotherapy with minimal or no adverse effects of therapy |

Reproduced with permission from U.S. Department of Health and Human Services, National Institutes of Health. Expert Panel Report 3 (EPR-3): Guidelines for the Diagnosis and Management of Asthma–Summary Report 2007. www.nhlbi.nih.gov/guidelines/asthma/asthsumm.pdf. Published October, 2007. Accessed July 15, 2009.

### $\beta_2$-Agonists

All patients with asthma should be treated with a bronchodilator. Short-acting $\beta_2$-agonists (for example, albuterol) are the most effective bronchodilators; they have a rapid onset of action and effectively relieve bronchoconstriction and protect against exercise- and cold air–induced asthma. Using $\beta_2$-agonists by metered-dose inhaler is an effective means of drug delivery to the lung. Some patients may have difficulty mastering inhaler technique, particularity older patients and those with musculoskeletal or neurologic disorders. In such patients, inhalation aids or other modes of delivery should be considered.

Short-acting $\beta_2$-agonists should be used as needed rather than on a regular scheduled basis. Long-acting $\beta_2$-agonists (salmeterol and formoterol) provide bronchodilation for up to 12 hours and prevent exercise-induced asthma. Formoterol has a rapid onset of action; salmeterol has a relatively slow onset. Adding long-acting $\beta_2$-agonist inhalers in patients whose disease is not controlled on low- to medium-dose inhaled corticosteroids is superior to doubling the dose of inhaled corticosteroids with regard to improving symptom control and reducing exacerbations. Long-acting $\beta_2$-agonists control asthma symptoms but have no anti-inflammatory effects. Because airway inflammation is a major component of the pathophysiology of asthma, long-acting $\beta_2$-agonists should not be used as single-agent therapy in asthma because this can lead to masking inflammation and worsening of asthma control with increased risk for asthma-related complications.

Inhaled $\beta_2$-agonists are well tolerated in most patients; side effects may include tremor, arrhythmias, and

**TABLE 3** Classification of Asthma Severity

| Components of Severity | Intermittent | Persistent | | |
| --- | --- | --- | --- | --- |
| | | **Mild** | **Moderate** | **Severe** |
| **Impairment**[a] | | | | |
| Symptoms | ≤2 days/week | >2 days/week but not daily | Daily | Throughout the day |
| Nighttime awakenings | ≤2 ×/month | 3-4 ×/month | >1 ×/week but not nightly | Often 7 ×/week |
| SABA use for symptom control (not prevention of EIB) | ≤2 days/week | >2 days/week but not more than 1 ×/d | Daily | Several times a day |
| Interference with normal activity | None | Minor limitation | Some limitation | Extremely limited |
| Lung function | Normal $FEV_1$ between exacerbations $FEV_1$ >80% of predicted $FEV_1$/FVC normal | $FEV_1$ >80% of predicted $FEV_1$/FVC normal | $FEV_1$ >60% but <80% of predicted $FEV_1$/FVC reduced 5% | $FEV_1$ <60% of predicted $FEV_1$/FVC reduced >5% |
| **Risk** | | | | |
| Exacerbations (consider frequency and severity)[b,c] | 0-2/year | | >2/year | |
| Recommended step for initiating treatment (see Figure 4 for treatment steps)[d] | Step 1 | Step 2 | Step 3; consider short courses of systemic corticosteroids | Step 4 or 5; consider short courses of systemic corticosteroids |

EIB = exercise-induced bronchospasm; SABA = short-acting β-agonist.

[a]Normal $FEV_1$/FVC: 8-19 years old, 85%; 20-39 years old, 80%; 40-59 years old, 75%; 60-80 years old, 70%.

[b]Frequency and severity may fluctuate over time for patients in any severity category.

[c]Relative annual risk for exacerbations may be related to $FEV_1$.

[d]In 2 to 6 weeks, evaluate the level of asthma control that is achieved and adjust therapy accordingly.

Reproduced with permission from U.S. Department of Health and Human Services, National Institutes of Health. Expert Panel Report 3 (EPR-3): Guidelines for the Diagnosis and Management of Asthma–Summary Report 2007. www.nhlbi.nih.gov/guidelines/asthma/asthsumm.pdf. Published October, 2007. Accessed July 15, 2009.

hypokalemia. The safety of β₂-agonists in asthma has been questioned in some studies over the past two decades. Findings from these studies are now believed to reflect the use of nonselective β₂-agonists, which are no longer available, or excessive use of β₂-agonists in the absence of anti-inflammatory therapy, which reflects inadequate treatment of severe and unstable asthma rather than an effect of β₂-agonists themselves.

More recently, questions were raised about the safety of β₂-agonists in a subgroup of patients with asthma who are homozygous for arginine (Arg/Arg) rather than glycine at position 16 of the β₂-adrenergic receptor. Studies done by the Asthma Clinical Research Network suggested that this polymorphism in the receptor could lead to an unfavorable response to a short-acting β₂-agonist when used regularly but not when used as needed. A similar study that randomized patients based on their genotype to use of long-acting β₂-agonists or placebo showed no significant increase in asthma morbidity related to the use of long-acting β₂-agonists. A large study of 26,000 patients with asthma who were randomized to salmeterol versus placebo (Salmeterol Multi-center Asthma Research Trial, SMART) revealed a small increase in asthma-related deaths and/or life-threatening experiences in patients receiving salmeterol. This effect occurred largely in the black population. As a result of this study, the U.S. Food and Drug Administration (FDA) issued an advisory with regard to increased risk for asthma-related complications with regular use of long-acting β₂-agonists. It is now recommended that long-acting β₂-agonists be used as a controller therapy in patients who remain symptomatic despite the use of inhaled corticosteroids, which are the first-line controller therapy in persistent asthma. Long acting β₂-agonists should not be used without concomitant anti-inflammatory therapy with inhaled corticosteroids.

## Inhaled Corticosteroids

Inhaled corticosteroids exert an anti-inflammatory effect by reducing the number of mast cells, eosinophils, and lymphocytes and by reducing cell activation. As such, they reduce generation of cytokines by airway cells and block the late allergic response to allergens. Corticosteroids can also up-regulate β-adrenergic receptor function, thereby enhancing the effectiveness of β₂-agonists. The regular use of inhaled corticosteroids in patients with asthma improves lung function, decreases airway hyperresponsiveness, reduces asthma exacerbations, and reduces asthma-related mortality.

**Persistant asthma: Daily medication**
Consult with asthma specialist if step 4 care or higher is required
Consider consultation at step 3

**Intermittent asthma**

**Step 1**

*Preferred:*
SABA PRN

**Step 2**

*Preferred:*
Low-dose ICS

*Alternative:*
Cromolyn, LTRA, Nedocromil, or Theophylline

**Step 3**

*Preferred:*
Low-dose ICS + LABA or Medium-dose ICS

*Alternative:*
Low-dose ICS + LTRA, Theophylline, or Zileuton

**Step 4**

*Preferred:*
Medium-dose ICS + LABA

*Alternative:*
Medium-dose ICS + either LTRA, Theophylline, or Zileuton

**Step 5**

*Preferred:*
High-dose ICS + LABA

AND

Consider Omalizumab for patients who have allergies

**Step 6**

*Preferred:*
High-dose ICS + LABA + oral corticosteroid

AND

Consider Omalizumab for patients who have allergies

Step up if needed

(first check adherence, environmental control, and comorbid conditions)

Assess control

Step down if possible

(and asthma is well controlled at least 3 months)

**Each step: Patient education, environmental control, and management of comorbidities**

Steps 2-4: Consider subcutaneous allergen immunotherapy for patients who have allergic asthma

Quick relief medication for all patients

- SABA as needed for symptoms. Intensity of treatment depends on severity of symptoms: up to 3 treatments at 20-minute intervals as needed. Short course of oral systemic corticosteroids may be needed

- Use SABA >2 days a week for symptom relief (not prevention of EIB); generally indicates inadequate control and the need to step up treatment

**FIGURE 4.**
**Stepwise approach to asthma therapy.**

EIB = exercise-induced bronchospasm; ICS = inhaled corticosteroids; LABA = long-acting β$_2$-agonist; LTRA = leukotriene receptor antagonist; PRN = as needed; SABA = short-acting β$_2$-agonist.

Reproduced with permission from National Heart, Lung, and Blood Institute. Expert Panel Report 3 (EPR-3): Guidelines for the Diagnosis and Management of Asthma–Summary Report 2007.

Most side effects of inhaled corticosteroid therapy are local, such as dysphonia (in part from myopathy of small muscles of phonation), oral thrush, and cough. Regular and careful mouth-rinsing after the use of inhalers and the use of inhalation aid devices can significantly reduce or eliminate the occurrence of these local side effects. When these effects do occur, they can be managed with dose reduction (which often alleviates dysphonia) and topical antifungal therapy for oral thrush. However, some patients cannot tolerate the side effects and require alternative control medications.

The systemic side effects of inhaled corticosteroids are relatively uncommon but do occur in patients on high-dose therapy, particularly long-term, high-dose therapy. These effects include adrenal suppression, reduced growth velocity in children, weight gain, glaucoma, cataracts, osteopenia,

and skin thinning. Therefore, the lowest dose consistent with disease control should always be used. For most end points, the effects of inhaled corticosteroids are relatively flat at high doses. Step-down therapy should be considered at regular intervals, perhaps every 3 months, if the disease is adequately controlled.

**Leukotriene Modifiers**
Initially called the slow reacting substance of anaphylaxis, leukotrienes have important effects in asthma, including vasodilatation, mucus secretion, and inflammation. Leukotriene-modifying drugs include the leukotriene receptor antagonists montelukast and zafirlukast and the 5-lipoxygenase inhibitor zileuton. Because of the need for close monitoring of liver function in patients treated with zileuton and

difficulty in maintaining adherence to therapy with this medication, which is given four times a day, its use has been limited. In patients with asthma, leukotriene modifiers improve lung function, reduce symptoms, improve quality of life, reduce the need for albuterol rescue, and prevent exercise-induced asthma. These agents have only a modest anti-inflammatory effect, particularly compared with that of inhaled corticosteroids. Leukotriene modifiers can be used as an alternative to corticosteroids but are not preferred therapy for persistent asthma.

Patient response to leukotriene modifiers varies significantly, with a subset of patients showing significant response and many others showing limited or no response. These agents may have an added advantage of relieving the allergic response, particularly the early response, as well as providing some relief from other allergic manifestations, such as rhinitis and sinusitis. Leukotriene modifiers may be appropriate for patients with aspirin-sensitive asthma, exercise-induced asthma, and virus-induced wheezing. Leukotriene modifiers have been associated with the development of the Churg-Strauss syndrome in patients with asthma who are tapering the dosage of oral corticosteroids. It is unclear whether this is due to unmasking preexisting Churg-Strauss syndrome or a direct causal relationship of the drug. Recently, neuropsychiatric side effects, including agitation, depression, and suicide, have been reported in patients taking leukotriene modifiers. Therefore, the FDA advised stopping these drugs if patients start experiencing neuropsychiatric symptoms.

### Theophylline

Theophylline is an inhibitor of phosphodiesterase, but it appears to work through other mechanisms, including activation of histone deacetylase and adenosine antagonism. Theophylline is a mild bronchodilator with limited anti-inflammatory effect. Theophylline can inhibit the transcription of proinflammatory genes that regulate the production of cytokines, such as granulocyte-macrophage colony-stimulating factor and interleukin-8 (IL-8). Other possible effects of theophylline include improved respiratory muscle contraction and enhanced respiratory ciliary function. The therapeutic serum concentration of theophylline is between 5 and 12 µg/mL (27.75 and 66.6 µmol/L); such side effects as tremor, palpitations, headache, nausea, and vomiting can occur in the high therapeutic to slightly supratherapeutic range. More serious side effects, such as life-threatening arrhythmias and seizures, can occur at concentrations greater than 20 µg/mL (111 µmol/L). Because of significant drug-drug interaction, these toxic concentrations can be reached in a patient who previously had stable serum theophylline levels but who begins taking an interfering medication, such as a fluoroquinolone antibiotic (for example, ciprofloxacin). Theophylline levels should therefore be monitored regularly and adjusted when patients are given other medications that can interfere with the metabolism of this agent. Because of these side effects, theophylline is not recommended as a first-line therapy for chronic asthma. It should be considered as an add-on option in patients who do not respond adequately to other controller treatments. The use of theophylline in acute asthma exacerbation is not recommended because of its limited added benefit as a bronchodilator and significant risk for toxicity.

### Anti-IgE Antibody

IgE is integral to the allergic response. IgE receptors on basophils and mast cells allow IgE molecules to bind to the surface of these cells. When they encounter a specific allergen, the IgE molecules on the surface of these cells are cross-linked, leading to release of mediators, including histamine, leukotrienes, and proinflammatory cytokines.

Omalizumab, a recombinant monoclonal antibody that binds to the Fc portion of IgE antibody, is approved for use in patients with moderate to severe, persistent allergic asthma. By binding to the free circulating IgE, omalizumab prevents IgE from attaching to its receptors on the surface of basophils and mast cells, thus limiting IgE cross-linking and release of mediators. The amount of anti-IgE antibody given to patients needs to be adjusted based on the patients' weight and circulating serum IgE level so that the majority of free IgE in the serum is bound and therefore unavailable to attach to the surface of basophils and mast cells. Treatment with omalizumab improves asthma control, reduces exacerbations, and lowers the required dose of corticosteroids. Omalizumab is given as a subcutaneous injection every 2 to 4 weeks based on patients' weight and serum IgE levels. There is a small risk for serious anaphylactoid reactions, which have occurred in roughly 1 of 1000 patients. Therefore, treated patients need to be observed for at least 2 hours after the initial three doses and for 1 hour after subsequent treatments. Like other biologic medications, omalizumab is expensive, with therapy costing up to $36,000 per year. Therefore, it should be reserved mainly for patients with severe, poorly controlled asthma who do not respond to other treatments.

## Allergen Immunotherapy and Allergen Avoidance

Immunotherapy can be useful in patients with allergic rhinitis and insect sting hypersensitivity. In patients with specific allergic symptoms, allergen avoidance is recommended. Several studies have assessed the benefits of house dust mite control measures (for example, encasing bedding), but results show limited benefits. Several modifications of immunotherapy are being explored, including sublingual administration that can be given at home and using antigen that has been conjugated with immunostimulatory molecules. These approaches may be as effective as or more effective than traditional subcutaneous injections.

## Alternative and Complementary Therapies

Alternative therapies, such as use of vitamins, relaxation and breathing techniques, acupuncture, homeotherapy, herbal medication, and chiropractic manipulation, have been proposed as therapy for asthma. There is, however, no convincing evidence to support recommending any of these treatments for asthma, and in some cases, such as use of certain herbal therapies, there could be significant potential for harm.

**KEY POINTS**

- The proper technique for using inhalers is necessary for an adequate therapeutic response in asthma; patients should be shown the proper technique, and any patients with poorly controlled disease should be evaluated for proper technique.

- The regular use of inhaled corticosteroids in patients with asthma improves lung function, decreases airway hyperresponsiveness, reduces asthma exacerbations, and reduces asthma-related mortality.

- Adding long-acting $\beta_2$-agonist inhalers in patients whose asthma is not controlled on low- to medium-dose inhaled corticosteroids is more effective than doubling the dose of inhaled corticosteroids.

- Leukotriene modifiers may be appropriate for patients with aspirin-sensitive asthma, exercise-induced asthma, and virus-induced wheezing.

- Because of significant drug-drug interaction, toxic serum concentrations of theophylline can be reached in a patient who previously had stable levels but who begins taking an interfering medication, such as a fluoroquinolone antibiotic.

## Asthma and Pregnancy

Asthma can lead to increased pregnancy-related complications (preeclampsia, low birth weight, premature labor, and infant mortality), most commonly in patients with severe, poorly controlled disease. During pregnancy, asthma may improve, worsen, or remain stable. Patients with asthma who become pregnant should be monitored regularly to evaluate disease activity and to attempt step-down therapy if feasible. The short-acting $\beta_2$-agonist albuterol has an excellent safety profile and is recommended for quick relief of asthma symptoms during pregnancy. Inhaled corticosteroids should be used for long-term control of asthma during pregnancy. All currently available inhaled corticosteroids are considered to be safe during pregnancy. Pregnant patients whose asthma is controlled on an inhaled corticosteroid should continue the same medication during their pregnancy. If another controller medication is required, salmeterol is the recommended long-acting $\beta_2$-agonist because of its length of time on the market, lack of known pregnancy-related side effects, and demonstrated efficacy. Cromolyn sodium, montelukast, zafirlukast,

and theophylline can be used during pregnancy if necessary, but they are considered less preferred alternatives to inhaled corticosteroids. For acute severe asthma exacerbations during pregnancy, oral corticosteroids are recommended, even though a small risk of congenital malformations has been reported. Acute severe asthma can be fatal, and uncontrolled asthma has a more significant effect on the outcome of pregnancy than the potential risk of asthma medications.

**KEY POINTS**

- Inhaled corticosteroids should be used for long-term control of asthma during pregnancy; all currently available inhaled corticosteroids are considered to be safe during pregnancy.

- Uncontrolled asthma has a more significant effect on the outcome of pregnancy than the potential risk of asthma medications.

## Bibliography

Fanta CH. Asthma [erratum in N Engl J Med. 2009;360(16):1685]. N Engl J Med. 2009;360(10):1002-1014. [PMID: 19264689]

Hewitt DJ. Interpretation of the "positive" methacholine challenge. Am J Ind Med. 2008;51(10):769-781. [PMID: 18702111]

Ibrahim WH, Gheriani HA, Almohamed AA, Raza T. Paradoxical vocal cord motion disorder: past, present and future. Postgrad Med J. 2007;83(977):164-172. [PMID: 17344570]

King CS, Moores LK. Clinical asthma syndromes and important asthma mimics. Respir Care. 2008;53(5):568-80. [PMID: 18426611]

Moore WC. Update in asthma 2007. Am J Respir Crit Care Med. 2008;177(10):1068-1073. [PMID: 18460462]

Namazy JA, Schatz M. Current guidelines for the management of asthma during pregnancy. Immunol Allergy Clin North Am. 2006;26(1):93-102. [PMID: 16443145]

National Heart, Lung, and Blood Institute. National Asthma Education and Prevention Program: Expert panel report III: Guidelines for the diagnosis and management of asthma. www.nhlbi.nih.gov/guidelines/asthma/asthgdln.htm. Published Bethesda, MD; 2007. Accessed July 29, 2009.

Parsons JP, Mastronarde JG. Exercise-induced asthma. Curr Opin Pulm Med. 2009;15(1):25-28. [PMID: 19077702]

Pavord ID, Chung KF. Management of chronic cough. Lancet. 2008;371(9621):1375-1384. [PMID: 18424326]

Schatz M, Dombrowski MP. Clinical practice. Asthma in pregnancy. N Engl J Med. 2009;360(18):1862-1869. [PMID: 19403904]

Long-acting beta-2 agonists in asthma. Med Lett Drugs Ther. 2009 Jan 12;51(1303):1-2. [PMID: 19122566]

# Chronic Obstructive Pulmonary Disease

Chronic obstructive pulmonary disease (COPD) is a slowly progressive, variably inflammatory disease of the airways and lung parenchyma that is characterized by a gradual loss of lung function with increasing obstruction to expiratory airflow. The obstruction is due to inflammatory narrowing of the small airways and proteolytic digestion of lung tissue adjacent to these airways. The inflammation, which intensifies as the disease progresses, increases the risk of exacerbations that affect health status, exercise tolerance, and quality of life. The symptoms of COPD become more severe as lung function deteriorates (**Figure 5**).

COPD is also associated with significant extrapulmonary effects, particularly in patients with severe disease. Cachexia is common in patients with severe COPD and is linked with reduced survival, poor functional status, and health-related diminished quality of life. There may be a loss of skeletal muscle mass and weakness as a result of deconditioning, malnutrition, and even programmed cell death (apoptosis). There is also an increased likelihood of osteoporosis and depression. These systemic effects are probably interrelated and multifactorial, including inactivity, systemic inflammation, tissue hypoxia, and oxidative stress. Increased concentrations of inflammatory mediators indicating immune activation also have been found and may mediate some of these systemic effects. These systemic effects add to the respiratory morbidity produced by the underlying pulmonary disease.

The current clinical classification of COPD fails to take into account the heterogeneity of the disease. COPD appears to represent a spectrum of overlapping diseases with important extrapulmonary consequences. A phenotype describes the outward physical manifestations of a particular disease and includes everything that is part of the observable structure, function, or behavior of an individual. In COPD, phenotypic components include frequent exacerbations, cachexia, rapid decline in pulmonary function, airway hyperresponsiveness, impaired exercise tolerance, and emphysema or airways disease. All of these phenotypes have smoking as a common risk factor, but the other risk factors that determine these phenotypes remain poorly understood.

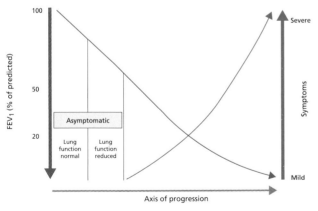

**FIGURE 5.**
**Deterioration of lung function in patients with chronic obstructive pulmonary disease.**
Symptoms generally develop only after a significant decline in FEV$_1$ has occurred; they progress as lung function deteriorates.

## Epidemiology

COPD is more common than once believed, with prevalence in adults older than 40 years estimated at about 10%. An estimated 24 million adults in the United States have symptomatic COPD, 12 million physician-diagnosed and 12 million undiagnosed. The prevalence is greater in men than women and in whites than blacks and increases with age. The 30-year projections for the global increase in COPD from 1990 to 2020 indicate that it is expected to move from fourth to third in terms of morbidity. In 1990, COPD was the twelfth leading cause of disability-adjusted life years lost worldwide and, according to projections, will be the fifth leading cause in 2020, behind ischemic heart disease, major depression, traffic accidents, and cerebrovascular disease. The disease also is associated with several comorbid conditions (accelerated by chronic inflammation and smoking-related toxins, including carcinogens) that significantly affect morbidity and mortality, including cancer, coronary artery disease and other vascular diseases, osteoporosis, and diabetes mellitus.

The Global Burden of Disease Study projected that COPD will rise from sixth to third most common cause of death by 2020. Mortality trends are particularly striking in women. Worldwide COPD deaths in women have been rising steadily since the 1970s, with the number of deaths in women exceeding those in men in the year 2000. The substantial increase in morbidity and mortality is caused by a combination of increased tobacco use and changing global demographics, especially in developing countries; these changing demographics enable more people to survive long enough to develop COPD. In the United States, COPD is currently the fourth leading cause of death and is projected to be the third leading cause of death for both men and women by the year 2020. Among the six leading causes of death in the United States from 1970 through 2003 (heart disease, stroke, cancer, accidents, diabetes mellitus, COPD), mortality rates for heart disease, stroke, cancer, and accidents have declined, whereas deaths from COPD doubled and deaths from diabetes increased by 45%.

COPD is also a costly disease. In developed countries, exacerbations of COPD account for the greatest burden on the health care system. In the United States in 2002, the direct costs of COPD were $18 billion and the indirect costs totaled $14.1 billion.

## Risk Factors

Essentially all risk for COPD results from an interaction between host factors (genetics, airway hyperresponsiveness, lung growth influencing size distribution of small airways, sex, race) and environmental factors (tobacco smoke, passive smoke, marijuana smoke, pollution, occupational dusts/chemicals, socioeconomic status, respiratory infections, and diet) (**Table 4**).

**TABLE 4** Risk Factors for Chronic Obstructive Pulmonary Disease

Genes

Exposure to particles
  Tobacco smoke
  Occupational dusts (organic and inorganic)
  Indoor air pollution

Heating and cooking with biomass fuel in poorly vented buildings
  Outdoor air pollution

Lung growth and development

Oxidative stress

Sex

Age

Socioeconomic status

Nutrition

Comorbidities

Reproduced with permission from Global Strategy for the Diagnosis, Management and Prevention of COPD, Global Initiative for Chronic Obstructive Lung Disease (GOLD) 2007. www.goldcopd.org/Guidelineitem.asp?l1=2&l2=1&intId=2003. Published 2008. Accessed June 15, 2009. Copyright 2008, Medical Communications Resources Inc.

Cigarette smoking is by far the most common risk factor for COPD. Cigarette smokers have a higher prevalence of respiratory symptoms and lung function abnormalities, a greater annual rate of decline in $FEV_1$, and a greater COPD mortality rate than nonsmokers. The risk for COPD in smokers is dose related. Age at starting to smoke, total pack-years smoked, and current smoking status are all predictive of COPD mortality. Smoking cessation is the single most clinically effective—and cost effective—way to prevent COPD, to slow progression of established disease, and to improve survival.

There is significant evidence that supports a hereditary component to the development of COPD. The disease clusters in families, and several studies have demonstrated an increased incidence of COPD in relatives of affected patients compared with controls. COPD is a polygenic disease, of which the best documented genetic influence is hereditary deficiency of $\alpha_1$-antitrypsin (a circulating inhibitor of serine protease) that leads to severe emphysema at a very early age, particularly in smokers. Although other genes have been implicated in COPD pathogenesis (including genes controlling transforming growth factor β1, microsomal epoxide hydroxylase 1, and tumor necrosis factor α), the study of genetic conditions other than $\alpha_1$-antitrypsin deficiency has yielded inconsistent results.

Exposure to various inhaled particles may contribute to the risk for COPD. However, only tobacco smoke and occupational dust and chemicals (vapors, irritants, fumes) are known to cause COPD. Inhaled cigarette smoke and other noxious particles cause lung inflammation, a normal response that appears to be amplified in the subset of smokers who develop COPD. This inflammatory response may damage and thicken small airways and also disrupt normal repair mechanisms (resulting in small airway fibrosis) but also is associated with release of proteases from the inflammatory cells that dissolve some of the adjacent supporting lung tissue that tethers the small airways (resulting in centrilobular emphysema). These pathologic changes lead to progressive expiratory airflow limitation and sometimes to lung volumes in some patients showing increased residual volume (air trapping) and increased total lung capacity (hyperinflation). Hyperinflation flattens the diaphragm and reduces its effectiveness, making use of accessory muscles of breathing more important, and also markedly increases the work of breathing as chest wall compliance decreases. Low DLCO correlates with the degree of emphysema as the capillary bed is reduced by lung parenchyma loss.

**KEY POINT**

- Smoking cessation is the single most clinically effective—and cost effective—way to prevent chronic obstructive pulmonary disease, to slow progression of established disease, and to improve survival.

## Assessment and Monitoring

### Assessment

A clinical diagnosis of COPD should be considered in any patient who has dyspnea, chronic cough or sputum production, and/or a history of risk factors for the disease. The diagnosis of COPD is confirmed and staged by spirometry. Spirometry should be performed after the administration of an adequate dose of an inhaled bronchodilator (for example, salbutamol, 400 µg) in order to minimize variability. Although measurements of postbronchodilator $FEV_1/FVC$ and $FEV_1$ are recommended for the diagnosis and assessment of severity of COPD, respectively, determining the degree of reversibility of airflow limitation (change in $FEV_1$ after administration of bronchodilators or corticosteroids) is no longer recommended for diagnosis, for distinguishing COPD from asthma, or for predicting the response to long-term treatment with bronchodilators or corticosteroids. A postbronchodilator $FEV_1$ less than 80% of predicted and $FEV_1/FVC$ less than 0.70 confirm the presence of airflow limitation that is not fully reversible. The spirometric classification of COPD is summarized in **Table 5**.

### Ongoing Monitoring

Symptoms and measures of airflow limitation should be monitored to determine when and whether therapy should be adjusted and to identify complications. As at the initial assessment, follow-up visits include a physical examination and discussion of symptoms, particularly any new or worsening ones. A patient's decline in lung function is best tracked by periodic spirometry.

**TABLE 5** Spirometric Classification of Chronic Obstructive Pulmonary Disease Severity

| Stage | Spirometry Range |
|---|---|
| Stage I: Mild | $FEV_1/FVC$ <0.70<br>$FEV_1$ ≥80% of predicted |
| Stage II: Moderate | $FEV_1/FVC$ <0.70<br>50% ≤$FEV_1$ <80% of predicted |
| Stage III: Severe | $FEV_1/FVC$ <0.70<br>30% ≤$FEV_1$ <50% of predicted |
| Stage IV: Very Severe | $FEV_1/FVC$ <0.70<br>$FEV_1$ <30% of predicted *or*<br>$FEV_1$ <50% of predicted *plus* chronic respiratory failure |

Reproduced with permission from: Global Strategy for the Diagnosis, Management and Prevention of COPD, Global Initiative for Chronic Obstructive Lung Disease (GOLD) 2007. www.goldcopd.org/Guidelineitem.asp?l1=2&l2=1&intId=2003. Published 2008. Accessed June 15, 2009. Copyright 2009, Medical Communications Resources Inc.

Monitoring to adjust therapy as the disease progresses should focus on doses of medications, adherence to the regimen, inhaler technique, effectiveness of the current therapeutic plan for controlling symptoms, and the side effects of treatment. Inhaled medications are central to the management of COPD; if the patient does not use the inhaler properly, the response to such therapy is not optimal. Therefore, if a patient is not responding to therapy, the inhaler technique should be evaluated before therapy is adjusted.

Patients should be questioned and evaluated for exacerbation frequency and severity, and likely triggers and the patient's psychological well being should be assessed. Increased sputum volume, acutely worsening dyspnea, and the presence of purulent sputum should be noted to monitor and document the incidental and longitudinal changes associated with the presence or risk of debilitating COPD exacerbations. These actions may help the physician in prescribing antibiotics for early symptoms of exacerbation in outpatients and may reduce the need for subsequent hospitalizations.

**KEY POINT**

- A postbronchodilator $FEV_1$ less than 80% of predicted and $FEV_1/FVC$ less than 0.70 confirm the presence of airflow limitation that is not fully reversible and is compatible with chronic obstructive pulmonary disease.

# Management of Stable Disease

The management goals for stable COPD are to slow disease progression, relieve symptoms, improve exercise tolerance and health status, prevent and treat complications and exacerbations, reduce risk factors, and reduce mortality.

## Pharmacologic Therapy

Although no medication has been shown to reduce the progressive decline in lung function in COPD, pharmacologic intervention reduces symptoms, diminishes the frequency and severity of exacerbations, reduces the frequency of hospitalizations, and improves exercise tolerance and health status. Treatment tends to be cumulative, that is, more medications are added as the disease worsens (**Table 6**).

### Bronchodilators

Bronchodilators relax airway smooth muscle and result in an increase in $FEV_1$ (or a change in other spirometric variables). The three types of commonly used bronchodilators are $\beta_2$-agonists, anticholinergic agents, and methylxanthines. They are given either as needed to treat acute symptoms or on a regular basis to prevent or reduce symptoms. In addition to improving lung function, bronchodilators improve exercise performance and are first-line therapy.

$\beta_2$-agonists stimulate $\beta_2$-adrenergic receptors and may be either short- or long-acting.

The short-acting $\beta_2$-agonists (albuterol and levalbuterol) act quickly and are effective for up to 6 hours. Long-acting $\beta_2$-agonists (salmeterol, formoterol, and arformoterol) have a duration of action of 12 hours or more and are first-line maintenance therapy to control symptoms. The most common side effects of $\beta_2$-agonist therapy are increased heart rate and tremor.

Anticholinergic agents block the effect of acetylcholine on muscarinic receptors. Short-acting agents, such as ipratropium, produce effects for 4 to 6 hours; long-acting agents (also known as long-acting muscarinic antagonists), such as tiotropium, produce effects for 24 hours. The primary side effect of the inhaled anticholinergic agents used for COPD is dry mouth. Anticholinergic agents should be used with caution in patients with urinary obstruction and narrow-angle glaucoma.

The mechanism of the methylxanthines (aminophylline and theophylline) is not fully known, but they may act as nonselective inhibitors of phosphodiesterase. The therapeutic effect lasts up to 24 hours, and they are available in both oral and intravenous formulations. Methylxanthines are usually used only after other long-acting bronchodilators have been tried. They have a narrow therapeutic window, and most patients are effectively treated with plasma levels of 5 to 12 μg/mL (27.75 to 66.6 μmol/L). Toxicity is dose-related, and common side effects include headache, insomnia, nausea, and heartburn, as well as a potential for development of arrhythmias and tremor. Methylxanthines are metabolized by cytochrome P450, and drug interactions are common.

Combination bronchodilator therapy using medications with different durations and mechanisms of action may increase the amount of bronchodilation achieved. Combining a $\beta_2$-agonist with an anticholinergic agent and/or a methylxanthine may produce additional and more sustained therapeutic effects.

Short-acting $\beta_2$-agonists are recommended at all stages of COPD for the alleviation of symptoms such as dyspnea and

**TABLE 6** Drug Treatment for Chronic Obstructive Pulmonary Disease

| Agent | Comments |
| --- | --- |
| Inhaled short-acting $\beta_2$-agonists | Bronchodilation. Alleviate symptoms and improve pulmonary function. Generally used as needed |
| Inhaled short-acting anticholinergic agents | Bronchodilation. Alleviate symptoms and improve pulmonary function. Used as scheduled maintenance. Do not combine short- and long-acting anticholinergic drugs. |
| Inhaled long-acting anticholinergic agents | Bronchodilation. Alleviate symptoms and improve pulmonary function. Used as scheduled maintenance. Do not combine short- and long-acting anticholinergic drugs. |
| Inhaled long-acting $\beta_2$-agonists | Bronchodilation. Alleviate symptoms and improve pulmonary function. Used as scheduled maintenance. |
| Oral theophylline, aminophylline | Bronchodilation possibly improves respiratory muscle function. Alleviate symptoms and improve pulmonary function. Aim for serum levels between 5 and 12 µg/mL. Used as scheduled maintenance. Use is intravenous in emergency department situations. |
| Oral $\beta_2$-agonists | Bronchodilation. Alleviate symptoms and improve pulmonary function. Used as scheduled maintenance. Rarely used because of side effects but may be of benefit in patients who cannot use inhalers. |
| $\alpha_1$-Antitrypsin augmentation therapy for AAT deficiency | Antiproteolytic enzyme. Possibly reduces decline in pulmonary function and reduces mortality. Life-long therapy, most effective in patients with $FEV_1$ 35% to 60% of predicted, may be used in patients receiving lung transplants for AAT deficiency; not to be used unless emphysema is present. |
| Inhaled corticosteroids | Anti-inflammatory. Alleviate symptoms and improve pulmonary function. Used as scheduled maintenance. In patients with a history of frequent exacerbations, high doses are best studied. Pulmonary function improved in 10% to 20% of patients but symptoms and exacerbations reduced in a larger percentage. No effect on decline in pulmonary function. |
| Oral corticosteroids | Anti-inflammatory. Alleviate symptoms and improve pulmonary function. Avoid use in stable chronic disease. Intravenous or oral corticosteroids are effective for acute exacerbations. |
| Supplemental oxygen | Improves tissue oxygenation. Improves quality of life; prolongs life. Must qualify for use on basis of arterial $Po_2$ or arterial oxygen hemoglobin saturation level. |
| Antibiotics for acute exacerbations of COPD | May alleviate symptoms and reduce severity of exacerbation. Most exacerbations due to viruses not susceptible to antibiotics. |

ATT = $\alpha_1$-antitrypsin; COPD = chronic obstructive pulmonary disease.

Littner MR. Chronic obstructive pulmonary disease. http://pier.acponline.org/physicians/diseases/d1153. [accessed: 2009 July 29] In: PIER [online database]. Philadelphia, American College of Physicians, 2009.

treatment of exacerbations. Long-acting bronchodilators, such as long-acting $\beta_2$-agonists or tiotropium, are recommended as first-line maintenance therapy when patients require regular and frequent bronchodilatory management, beginning in Global Initiative for Chronic Obstructive Lung Disease (GOLD) stage II and through GOLD stage IV. Either long-acting $\beta_2$-agonists or tiotropium may be initiated first, although anecdotal evidence suggests that tiotropium may be more effective in achieving control of symptoms. If patients require additional bronchodilatory control, long-acting $\beta_2$-agonists may be added to tiotropium or vice versa to optimize bronchodilator therapy. Use of methylxanthines is becoming relegated to use in patients with later COPD stages and for the treatment of acute exacerbations.

### Corticosteroids

The role of corticosteroids in the management of stable COPD is limited; however, regular use of inhaled corticosteroids in patients who experience recurrent exacerbations reduces the frequency of further exacerbations. Inhaled corticosteroids should not be used alone. Combinations of inhaled corticosteroids and long-acting bronchodilators are more effective than either therapy alone in reducing exacerbations and improving health status. The long-term safety of inhaled corticosteroids in COPD is not known. The use of inhaled corticosteroids in the elderly must be carefully monitored because of the risk of adverse effects such as osteopenia, cataracts, hyperglycemia, and pneumonia, all which may be particularly debilitating in elderly patients with compromised health and comorbidities frequently associated with COPD. The use of short-term oral corticosteroids is beneficial only in exacerbations of COPD. Long-term treatment is associated with significant side effects and is not recommended.

### Other Pharmacologic Treatments

Influenza vaccines can reduce serious illness and death in patients with COPD by about 50%. Although the evidence for the efficacy of pneumococcal vaccine in patients with COPD is inconclusive, it is recommended for all such patients. $\alpha_1$-Antitrypsin (AAT) augmentation therapy may be helpful in the rare patients with COPD and severe hereditary AAT deficiency. However, the therapy is expensive and is not indicated for those without the hereditary deficiency.

Antibiotic therapy is most beneficial in treating infectious exacerbations of COPD. Mucolytic (mucokinetic, mucoregulatory) agents provide minor benefit to some patients with viscous sputum, but the widespread use of these agents is not recommended. The regular use of antitussives is not recommended in patients with stable COPD because cough has a significant protective role.

### KEY POINTS

- Inhaled medications are central to the management of chronic obstructive pulmonary disease; if a patient is not responding to therapy, the inhaler technique should be evaluated before therapy is adjusted.

- Influenza and pneumococcal vaccines are recommended for all patients with chronic obstructive pulmonary disease.

## Nonpharmacologic Therapy

### Risk Factor Reduction

Smoking cessation not only improves lung function, it also improves survival. Participants in the Lung Health Study were followed for up to 14.5 years and the data for mortality rates were analyzed in terms of smoking habits. Notably, smoking cessation had a positive impact not only on death from COPD but on death from all causes.

### Pulmonary Rehabilitation

Pulmonary rehabilitation involves a combination of education, nutrition counseling, exercise training, and behavior modification techniques. The exercise component helps to improve endurance, flexibility, and strength in the upper and lower extremities and may require the patient to attend sessions of 30 minutes or more at least 3 times a week for 6 to 8 weeks. Pulmonary rehabilitation generally helps to improve exercise tolerance, decrease dyspnea and fatigue, improve quality of life, and increase patient participation in daily activities. Patients are encouraged to continue pulmonary rehabilitation to ensure sustained benefit.

### Oxygen Therapy

Oxygen therapy is a major component of treatment for patients with very severe COPD (stage IV) and is usually prescribed for patients who have arterial $Po_2$ less than 55 mm Hg or oxygen saturation less than 88% with or without hypercapnia or who exhibit arterial $Po_2$ of 56 to 59 mm Hg or oxygen saturation less than 89% with one or more of the following: pulmonary hypertension, evidence of cor pulmonale or edema as a result of right heart failure, or hematocrit greater than 56%. The duration of treatment should be at least 15 hours a day. The use of long-term oxygen therapy in patients with chronic respiratory failure improves survival and has a beneficial effect on hemodynamics, exercise capacity, and mental status.

### Noninvasive Ventilation

Noninvasive ventilation (using either negative or positive pressure devices) is now widely used to treat acute exacerbations of COPD. In stable patients, it has no effect on improving shortness of breath, exercise tolerance, arterial blood gases, respiratory muscle strength, quality of life, or lung function. However, noninvasive ventilation has positive effects in patients with exacerbations of COPD. Some patients with COPD who retain carbon dioxide have sleep fragmentation from further hypoventilation during sleep, leading to multiple arousals. Noninvasive ventilation at night in selected patients can improve sleep continuity, improve daytime symptoms (reducing sleepiness and exertional dyspnea), and also result in improved awake arterial $Pco_2$ during the day.

### Surgery

Lung volume reduction surgery involves resecting parts of the lung to reduce hyperinflation. This type of surgery makes respiratory muscles more effective by improving their mechanical efficiency and improves expiratory flow rates by increasing the elastic recoil pressure of the lung. Because this procedure is expensive and high-risk, it is recommended only in carefully selected patients. The surgery is most beneficial in patients with severe, predominantly upper lobe disease and a large amount of mildly emphysematous or normal middle and lower lung.

Patients with severe COPD who have had maximal medical treatment, including pulmonary rehabilitation, and have $FEV_1$ greater than 20% of predicted, DLCO greater than 20% of predicted, and predominant upper lobe emphysema are likely to benefit from lung volume reduction surgery.

In one study, patients who had lung volume reduction surgery and medical therapy had longer survival than those who had medical therapy alone. The patients who had surgery also had greater improvement in maximal work capacity and health-related quality of life.

Lung transplantation has been shown to improve quality of life and functional capacity in appropriate patients. Referral criteria for this procedure include $FEV_1$ less than 35% of predicted, arterial $Po_2$ less than 55 to 60 mm Hg, arterial $Pco_2$ greater than 50 mm Hg, and secondary pulmonary hypertension. There are many exclusion criteria, including advanced age and comorbid conditions, and demand for suitable organs outstrips availability.

## Managing Exacerbations

An exacerbation of COPD is defined as an acute event characterized by a change in baseline dyspnea, cough, and/or sputum production beyond normal daily variation. Exacerbations are commonly caused by infection and air pollution. The main symptoms include increased dyspnea often accompanied by wheezing and chest tightness, increased cough and sputum production, change in the color and/or tenacity of sputum, and fever. Various nonspecific signs and symptoms may accompany these findings, such as fatigue, insomnia, depression, and confusion.

Exacerbations cause bronchoconstriction, airway inflammation, increased secretions, and hyperinflation with decreased chest wall compliance, all of which increase the work of breathing. The severity of the exacerbation has been defined only in the context of clinical trials. Mild exacerbations require at-home treatment with short-acting bronchodilators. Moderate exacerbations require treatment with short-acting bronchodilators and systemic corticosteroids and/or antibiotics. Severe exacerbations require treatment with short-acting bronchodilators, systemic corticosteroids, and/or antibiotics along with hospitalization. Clinically, severity of the exacerbation can be suggested by the sputum volume and color and the extent of activity limitation. Even if the cause of the exacerbation is viral, patients with COPD are often colonized with bacteria and therefore require antibiotics. Increases in sputum volume or purulence are evidence of a bacterial cause and may indicate the need for antibiotic therapy. In addition, pulse oximetry and measurement of arterial blood gas levels are used to evaluate the patient's oxygenation and carbon dioxide level. In patients with very severe COPD (stage IV), the most important sign of a severe exacerbation is sometimes a change in mental status, which signals a need for immediate hospital evaluation.

### Home Management

Home care is increasingly common for treating exacerbations of COPD in patients with end-stage disease. Home management usually involves increasing the dose and/or frequency of bronchodilator therapy, preferably including a $\beta_2$-agonist. If not already used, a short-acting anticholinergic agent may be added until symptoms resolve. In exacerbations, systemic corticosteroids shorten recovery time, improve lung function and hypoxemia, and may reduce the risk of early relapse, treatment failure, and subsequent length of hospital stay. Systemic corticosteroids should be considered in addition to bronchodilators if the patient's baseline $FEV_1$ is less than 50% of predicted. Prednisone, 30 to 40 mg/d with a taper over 7 to 10 days, is recommended. Antibiotics are used for patients with some combination of purulent secretions, increased volume of secretions, and/or fever. Commonly used antibiotics include macrolides, sulfa drugs, tetracyclines, penicillins, cephalosporins, and/or fluoroquinolones. Local antibiotic resistance patterns of community-acquired organisms may help direct treatment.

### Hospital Management

Indications for hospital assessment/admission for exacerbations of COPD include a marked increase in the intensity of symptoms, decrease in mental status, onset of new physical signs such as cyanosis or peripheral edema, failure of the exacerbation to respond to initial medical management, the presence of significant comorbidities, frequent exacerbations, newly occurring arrhythmias of diagnostic uncertainty, older age, and/or insufficient home support.

Oxygen therapy is the cornerstone of hospital treatment of exacerbations, with a goal of adequate levels of oxygenation ($Po_2$ greater than 60 mm Hg or oxygen saturation greater than 90%). Arterial blood gas levels should be measured 30 to 60 minutes after oxygen therapy is started to ensure that oxygenation is adequate without carbon dioxide retention or acidosis.

Bronchodilator therapy with short-acting $\beta_2$-agonists is preferred for treating exacerbations. An anticholinergic agent should be added if the patient does not respond promptly to the $\beta_2$-agonist. There are no studies evaluating the use of long-acting $\beta$-agonists with or without corticosteroids during an acute exacerbation.

In addition, systemic (oral or intravenous) corticosteroids are recommended for hospital management of acute exacerbations of COPD. The effective dose is not known, but high doses are associated with a significant risk of side effects. Initial treatment is intravenous methylprednisolone for 72 hours at 125 mg every 6 hours, followed by 2 weeks of an oral taper starting at 60 mg; however, prolonged treatment does not result in greater efficacy and increases the risk of side effects.

There is a significant beneficial effect of using antibiotics in patients who present with increases in dyspnea, sputum volume, and sputum purulence. The predominant bacteria recovered are *Haemophilus influenzae*, *Streptococcus pneumoniae*, and *Moraxella catarrhalis*. Generally, antibiotic regimens for community-acquired infection include coverage with a third-generation cephalosporin in combination with a macrolide or a fluoroquinolone.

Noninvasive intermittent ventilation alleviates respiratory acidosis and decreases respiration rate, severity of dyspnea, and length of hospital stay. More important, mortality is also reduced. The indications for noninvasive ventilation include moderate to severe dyspnea with the use of accessory muscles of breathing and paradoxical abdominal motion, moderate to severe acidosis (pH less than 7.35) and/or hypercapnia ($P_{CO_2}$ greater than 45 mm Hg), and respiration rate greater than 25/min. Exclusion criteria include respiratory arrest, cardiovascular instability (hypotension, arrhythmias, myocardial infarction), change in mental status (lack of cooperation), high aspiration risk, viscous or copious secretions, recent facial or gastroesophageal surgery, craniofacial trauma, fixed nasopharyngeal abnormalities, burns, and extreme obesity.

Invasive mechanical ventilation is indicated for patients who cannot tolerate noninvasive ventilation and those with severe dyspnea with a respiration rate greater than 35/min, life-threatening hypoxia, severe acidosis (pH less than 7.25) and/or hypercapnia ($P_{CO_2}$ greater than 60 mm Hg), respiratory arrest, somnolence or impaired mental status, cardiovascular complications (hypotension, shock), and other complications such as metabolic abnormalities, sepsis, pneumonia, pulmonary embolism, barotrauma, and massive pleural effusion. In patients with very severe disease and a poor prognosis, the decision to begin invasive ventilation is influenced by the likelihood of reversing the precipitating event, the patient's advance directives and current wishes, and the availability of intensive care facilities. When possible, a patient's treatment preferences should be clearly outlined in advance of such acute events but can be altered situationally if the patient is alert and interactive.

## Hospital Discharge and Follow-up

After hospitalization for an acute exacerbation of COPD, patients should be discharged when they no longer require short-acting inhaled $\beta_2$-agonist therapy more frequently than every 4 hours, can walk across the room, and can sleep without frequent awakening by dyspnea. Patients must have been clinically stable and had stable arterial blood gas levels for 12 to 24 hours and understand the correct use of medications. Follow-up and home care arrangements must be completed before discharge, and the patient, family, and physician must be confident that the patient can successfully manage at home. A follow-up visit should occur 4 to 6 weeks after hospital discharge. Subsequent treatment is the same as for stable COPD. If the patient required oxygen in the hospital and still needs it at discharge, follow-up at approximately 2 weeks with evaluation of the oxygen level on ambient air should be done to determine whether supplemental oxygen continues to be necessary. Subsequent follow-up should occur at 2 to 4 weeks based on clinical assessment of the patient.

Aggressive treatment, including long-acting inhaled bronchodilators, inhaled corticosteroids, and combination inhalers as well as pulmonary rehabilitation and education, may help to prevent, or at least delay, future exacerbations and hospitalizations.

**KEY POINTS**

- Exacerbations of chronic obstructive pulmonary disease must be aggressively managed with short-acting $\beta_2$-agonists, short-acting anticholinergic agents, and oxygen therapy if warranted.
- In exacerbations of chronic obstructive pulmonary disease, therapy should include antibiotics to treat the potential infectious triggering event and systemic corticosteroids to manage the airway and parenchymal inflammation resulting in bronchoconstriction.
- The use of noninvasive intermittent ventilation in severe chronic obstructive pulmonary disease exacerbations improves respiratory acidosis and decreases severity of dyspnea and length of hospital stay.

## Bibliography

Agustí AG. Systemic effects of chronic obstructive pulmonary disease. Proc Am Thorac Soc. 2005;2(4):367-370. [PMID: 16267364]

Anthonisen NR, Skeans MA, Wise RA, Manfreda J, Kanner RE, Connett JE; Lung Health Study Research Group. The effects of a smoking cessation intervention on 14.5-year mortality: a randomized clinical trial. Ann Intern Med. 2005;142(4):233-239. [PMID: 15710956]

Chapman KR, Mannino DM, Soriano JB, et al. Epidemiology and costs of chronic obstructive pulmonary disease. Eur Respir J. 2006;27(1):188-207. [PMID: 16387952]

Curtis JL, Freeman CM, Hogg JC. The immunopathogenesis of chronic obstructive pulmonary disease: insights from recent research. Proc Am Thorac Soc. 2007;4(7):512-521. [PMID: 17878463]

Friedlander AL, Lynch D, Dyar LA, Bowler RP. Phenotypes of chronic obstructive pulmonary disease. COPD. 2007;4(4):355-384. [PMID: 18027163]

Global Initiative for Chronic Obstructive Lung Disease (GOLD). Global Strategy for the Diagnosis, Management and Prevention of COPD. www.goldcopd.org. Published 2007. Accessed July 17, 2009.

Halbert RJ, Natoli JL, Gano A, at al. Global burden of COPD: systematic review and meta-analysis. Eur Respir J. 2006;28(3):523-532. [PMID: 16611654]

Jemal A, Ward E, Hao Y, Thun M. Trends in the leading causes of death in the United States, 1970-2002. JAMA. 2005;294(10):1255-1259. [PMID: 16160134]

National Heart, Lung, and Blood Institute. COPD Fact Sheet. www.nih.gov/about/researchresultsforthepublic/COPD.pdf. Published September, 2007. Accessed July 17, 2009

National Heart, Lung, and Blood Institute. Fiscal Year 2006 Fact Book. www.nhlbi.nih.gov/about/factbook-06/toc.htm. Bethesda, Maryland: US Department of Health and Human Services; May 2007. Accessed July 17, 2009.

# Diffuse Parenchymal Lung Disease

Diffuse infiltrates on chest radiograph are a common finding. Although the term *diffuse* suggests widespread involvement of the lungs, the process may not affect the lung uniformly, and some areas may be spared. Diffuse lung disease is a nonspecific radiographic pattern that may be caused by edema, alveolar hemorrhage, infection, inflammation, fibrosis, or neoplasms; this radiographic pattern may also be associated with drug-induced lung disease, environmental or occupational lung disease, systemic and immune diseases, and various interstitial lung diseases.

Diffuse parenchymal lung disease (DPLD) is a descriptive term for diffuse lung diseases that predominantly affect the interstitium or parenchyma of the lung and that share certain radiographic, pathologic, and physiologic features. These diseases are also sometimes referred to as interstitial lung disease and diffuse infiltrative lung disease. Diseases that affect the interstitium of the lung may also involve the alveolar space as well as the airways and are included in certain DPLD classification schemes, depending on the clinical and radiographic presentation.

## Classification and Epidemiology

There are more than one hundred DPLDs; most of them are rare, but the number of diseases makes it difficult to develop a narrow differential diagnosis for a patient with radiographic DPLD. Proposed classification schemes for DPLD have been based on causality, radiographic characteristics, histopathologic features, corticosteroid responsiveness, and chronicity. The variety of published schemes is often a source of confusion. Although each classification scheme has its strengths and weaknesses, one that is helpful to clinicians is based on whether the cause is known or idiopathic (**Table 7**).

The most commonly encountered classification scheme for DPLDs was published in 2001 as a consensus statement of the American Thoracic Society and the European Respiratory Society. Although this group of disorders is termed idiopathic interstitial pneumonias, several are associated with a known cause. These disorders are functionally grouped together because a definitive diagnosis commonly requires a surgical lung biopsy demonstrating specific histopathologic features (**Table 8**). Clinical correlation of the patient's exposure history and exclusion of underlying disease processes are required to exclude known causes of the histopathologic finding. For example, idiopathic pulmonary fibrosis is associated with the histopathologic pattern of usual interstitial pneumonia, a pattern also found in connective tissue disease–associated DPLD, radiation-induced lung disease, and, occasionally, hypersensitivity pneumonitis.

**TABLE 7** Classification of the Diffuse Parenchymal Lung Diseases

**Known Causes**

| |
|---|
| Connective tissue disease–associated (for example, rheumatoid arthritis, polymyositis, scleroderma) |
| Hypersensitivity pneumonitis (for example, farmer's lung, hot tub lung, bird fancier's lung) |
| Pneumoconioses (for example, asbestosis, silicosis, coal worker's pneumoconiosis) |
| Drug-induced (for example, chemotherapeutic agents, amiodarone, nitrofurantoin) |
| Smoking-related |
| Pulmonary Langerhans cell histiocytosis |
| Respiratory bronchiolitis interstitial lung disease |
| Desquamative interstitial pneumonia |
| Acute eosinophilic pneumonia |
| Radiation-induced |
| Toxic inhalation–induced (for example, cocaine, zinc chloride [smoke bomb], ammonia) |

**Unknown Causes**

| |
|---|
| Idiopathic pulmonary fibrosis |
| Sarcoidosis |
| Other idiopathic interstitial pneumonias |
| Cryptogenic organizing pneumonia |
| Nonspecific interstitial pneumonia |
| Lymphocytic interstitial pneumonia |
| Acute interstitial pneumonia |
| Eosinophilic pneumonias |
| Pulmonary vasculitides |
| Pulmonary lymphangioleiomyomatosis |
| Pulmonary alveolar proteinosis |
| Many other rare disorders |

Reproduced with permission from Ryu JH, Daniels CE, Hartman TE, Yi ES. Diagnosis of interstitial lung diseases. Mayo Clin Proc. 2007;82(8):976-986. [PMID: 17673067] Copyright 2009 Mayo Foundation for Medical Education and Research.

## Diagnostic Approach and Evaluation

Because of the many diagnostic possibilities in patients with dyspnea or cough and the radiographic finding of diffuse lung disease, it is most useful to approach the diagnosis of DPLD by evaluating the clinical context, temporal pattern of the disease, and radiographic abnormalities (**Table 9**).

### Clinical Context

The incidence of specific DPLDs depends on such patient factors as age, sex, smoking status, environmental or occupational exposure, medications, and medical history. Elderly patients and young patients tend to develop different DPLDs based on age alone. The incidence of idiopathic pulmonary

**TABLE 8 Classification of Idiopathic Interstitial Pneumonias by Histopathologic Features[a]**

| Histologic Pattern | Clinical-Radiologic-Pathologic Diagnosis |
|---|---|
| Usual interstitial pneumonia | Idiopathic pulmonary fibrosis/cryptogenic fibrosing alveolitis |
| Nonspecific interstitial pneumonia | Nonspecific interstitial pneumonia (provisional)[b] |
| Organizing pneumonia | Cryptogenic organizing pneumonia[c] |
| Diffuse alveolar damage | Acute interstitial pneumonia |
| Respiratory bronchiolitis | Respiratory bronchiolitis interstitial lung disease |
| Lymphoid interstitial pneumonia | Lymphoid interstitial pneumonia |

[a]Some cases are unclassifiable for various reasons.

[b]This group represents a heterogeneous group with poorly characterized clinical and radiologic features that needs further study.

[c]Cryptogenic organizing pneumonia is the preferred term, but it is synonymous with bronchiolitis obliterans organizing pneumonia.

Reproduced with permission from American Thoracic Society/European Respiratory Society International Multidisciplinary Consensus Classification of the Idiopathic Interstitial Pneumonias. This joint statement of the American Thoracic Society (ATS) and the European Respiratory Society (ERS) was adopted by the ATS board of directors, June 2001 and by the ERS Executive Committee, June 2001 [erratum in Am J Respir Crit Care Med. 2002;166(3):426]. Am J Respir Crit Care Med. 2002;165(2):277-304. [PMID: 11790668] Copyright 2002, American Thoracic Society.

**TABLE 9 Diagnostic Approach to Patients with Diffuse Parenchymal Lung Disease**

History
  Demographics
  Pulmonary and extrapulmonary manifestations
  Temporal course of symptoms
  Smoking
  Environmental/occupational exposures
  Drugs
  Previous and concurrent illnesses
  Familial disorders

Physical examination
  Lung auscultation
  Digital clubbing
  Extrapulmonary signs

Laboratory tests
  Complete blood count
  Chemistry panel
  Urinalysis
  Hypersensitivity pneumonitis serologic tests[a]
  Connective tissue disease serologic tests[a]
  Antineutrophil cytoplasmic antibodies[a]
  B-type natriuretic peptide[a]

Imaging studies
  Chest radiography
  High-resolution CT scan of the chest
  Previous chest radiographs and CT scans
  Echocardiography[a]

Pulmonary function tests
  Spirometry, lung volumes, D$_{LCO}$, and oximetry
  Arterial blood gases[a]
  Cardiopulmonary exercise testing[a]

Bronchoscopy[a]

Surgical lung biopsy[a]

[a]These tests are used in selected patients according to the clinical context.

Reproduced with permission from Ryu JH, Daniels CE, Hartman TE, Yi ES. Diagnosis of interstitial lung diseases. Mayo Clin Proc. 2007;82(8):976-986. [PMID: 17673067]

fibrosis (the most common idiopathic interstitial pneumonia) increases with age; the incidence is estimated to be between 10 and 25 per 100,000 population, but it may be higher than 175 per 100,000 in patients older than 75 years. Sarcoidosis, lymphangioleiomyomatosis (which occurs exclusively in women), and familial idiopathic pulmonary fibrosis are more common in middle-aged and younger patients.

Exposure to drugs, environmental and occupational inhalants, radiation, and tobacco smoke are also key diagnostic considerations. Radiation pneumonitis occurs in patients weeks to months after radiation therapy, most often of the head and neck or chest. Pulmonary Langerhans cell histiocytosis, respiratory bronchiolitis interstitial lung disease, and desquamative interstitial pneumonitis occur almost exclusively in current smokers. Occupational exposure of farmers to moldy hay, silage, or other inhaled antigens may indicate farmer's lung, a form of hypersensitivity pneumonitis. Drugs known to cause diffuse pneumonitis include bleomycin and methotrexate.

Rheumatoid arthritis–associated DPLD is one of the multisystem components of rheumatoid arthritis and occurs in as many as 50% of affected patients, more commonly in men. DPLD occurs in approximately 75% of patients with systemic sclerosis and is the most frequent cause of morbidity and mortality in such patients.

Physical examination should focus on pulmonary abnormalities and identification of related systemic processes (**Table 10**). Diminished inspiratory volumes combined with "dry" crackles ("Velcro" crackles) suggest fibrotic lung disease. Prolonged expiration with wheezes or mid-expiratory "squeaks" may indicate small airway involvement. Digital clubbing occurs in 30% of patients with idiopathic pulmonary fibrosis but is rarely present in those with emphysema, organizing pneumonia, or respiratory bronchiolitis interstitial lung disease. Extrapulmonary examination should focus on skin, joint, and other findings suggestive of connective tissue disease or findings that are known to be associated with certain DPLDs.

**TABLE 10 Physical Examination Findings in Interstitial Lung Disease**

| Finding | Relevance |
|---|---|
| Crackles | Common in fibrosing interstitial lung disease; >80% in idiopathic pulmonary fibrosis; less common in sarcoidosis. |
| Mid-inspiratory "squeaks" | Suggestive of small airways disease (bronchiolitis) |
| Increased intensity $P_2$, right ventricular lift, tricuspid regurgitation murmur | Pulmonary hypertension secondary to interstitial lung disease or as a specific feature (scleroderma, pulmonary Langerhans cell histiocytosis); occurs with severe restrictive disease |
| Clubbing | Common in idiopathic pulmonary fibrosis (30%); uncommon/rare in respiratory bronchiolitis interstitial lung disease, cryptogenic organizing pneumonia, and collagen vascular disease |
| Erythema nodosum | Sarcoidosis, inflammatory bowel disease, Behçet syndrome |
| Maculopapular exanthem | Sarcoidosis, amyloidosis, Behçet syndrome |
| Uveitis/conjunctivitis | Sarcoidosis, Behçet syndrome, inflammatory bowel disease, ankylosing spondylitis |
| Lacrimal/salivary gland enlargement | Sarcoidosis, systemic sclerosis |
| Lymphadenopathy, hepatosplenomegaly | Sarcoidosis, amyloidosis |
| Arthritis | Collagen vascular disease, inflammatory bowel disease, sarcoidosis, Behçet syndrome, ankylosing spondylitis |
| Muscle weakness or tenderness | Polymyositis |
| Neurologic abnormalities | Sarcoidosis (cranial nerve deficits), tuberous sclerosis (mental retardation), lymphomatoid granulomatosis |

## Temporal Pattern of Disease Progression

The temporal pattern of DPLD progression varies from acute respiratory failure to insidious progression over years, although most DPLDs develop slowly over weeks to months, and many patients may not recall exactly when they first noted onset of subtle symptoms, such as cough and exercise intolerance. In some patients, radiographic abnormalities are evident before the onset of symptoms. Previous chest radiographs should be reviewed to help establish a pattern of slowly progressive DPLD.

Acute respiratory worsening (over less than 4 weeks) in patients with diffuse pulmonary infiltrates is most often the result of infection or edema. Initial evaluation typically includes testing to exclude cardiogenic pulmonary edema and infection. Exclusion of common causes of diffuse pulmonary infiltrates is an important part of the initial evaluation in any patient with acute respiratory worsening. Failure to respond to appropriate antibiotic therapy should prompt the clinician to consider DPLD as a potential diagnosis. DPLDs that may present with acute worsening leading to fulminant respiratory failure due to diffuse alveolar hemorrhage include vasculitides, such as Wegener granulomatosis, Churg-Strauss syndrome, and microscopic polyangiitis. Eosinophilic pneumonia may present with clinical, physiologic, and radiographic features similar to those that occur in the acute respiratory distress syndrome (ARDS) and should always be considered in the differential diagnosis of patients with idiopathic ARDS. Acute interstitial pneumonia can present as ARDS without known cause (Hamman-Rich syndrome). An acute exacerbation of known idiopathic pulmonary fibrosis has recently been identified as a cause of morbidity and mortality. Patients with these acute exacerbations appear to develop an acute lung injury pattern that correlates with pathologic changes of diffuse alveolar damage; the prognosis in such patients is extremely poor. An acute exacerbation can rarely be the first manifestation of previously undiagnosed idiopathic pulmonary fibrosis or of connective tissue disease–associated interstitial lung disease.

## Radiologic Findings

High-resolution CT (HRCT) chest imaging should be part of the diagnostic evaluation of patients in whom a chest radiograph suggests a diffuse interstitial process. Chest radiography alone rarely provides enough information for a diagnosis. In addition, up to 20% of patients with DPLD have subtle interstitial abnormalities not detectable on a chest radiograph. In symptomatic patients with environmental exposure or connective tissue disease, HRCT imaging should be considered even if the chest radiograph is interpreted as normal. HRCT imaging can narrow the diagnostic possibilities so that directed diagnostic tests, such as serologic tests, pulmonary function tests, and open lung biopsy, can be done.

HRCT findings should be considered in the context of radiographic imaging to establish the rate of change and distinguish chronic from acute processes. HRCT findings are interpreted according to their pattern (for example, consolidative, reticular, cystic) and their distribution (for example, upper lung, lower lung, subpleural, central). Differentiation of HRCT patterns by distinguishing interstitial from alveolar processes is useful, but it is somewhat arbitrary because most DPLDs have both interstitial and alveolar abnormalities. The combination of HRCT pattern and distribution with other associated CT findings, such as pleural effusion, lymphadenopathy, or dilated esophagus, can occasionally confirm the diagnosis of a specific DPLD or at least narrow the diagnostic possibilities.

### Pattern

HRCT shows interstitial involvement as linear and reticular abnormalities that appear as lines forming a lattice. When the reticular lines begin to coalesce, they can form a nodular appearance at their intersection (reticulonodular). When bordering cystic areas, they can stack to form a honeycombed appearance. So-called pseudoreticulation has a similar appearance to interstitial changes, but the abnormalities are caused by atelectasis in gravity-dependent lung zones and improve on prone imaging at full inspiration. Linear and reticular changes should also be distinguished from interlobular septal thickening, which represents lymphatic enlargement of the secondary pulmonary lobules, is centered on a pulmonary artery, and is most often associated with pulmonary edema or lymphangiitic involvement of cancer.

Filling of the alveolar space with water, pus, blood, cells, or other material results in radiologic patterns of either consolidation (complete alveolar filling) or ground-glass opacification (partial alveolar filling). Consolidation and ground-glass opacifications are caused by similar processes and likely represent a spectrum of alveolar filling with or without interstitial thickening. Consolidation is characterized by airspace consolidation with indistinct margins, the presence of air bronchograms, and the silhouette sign when bordering adjacent soft tissue. Ground-glass opacification is characterized by increased alveolar attenuation through which lung architecture can still be identified. Cystic airspaces are enlarged airspaces surrounded by a wall of variable thickness. DPLDs associated with cystic disease include pulmonary Langerhans cell histiocytosis and lymphangioleiomyomatosis, although idiopathic pulmonary fibrosis can also cause cystic changes in areas of honeycombing. A nodular pattern is a nonspecific HRCT pattern consisting of round and discrete parenchymal opacities. The size and distribution of the nodules vary widely. Sarcoidosis is the DPLD most commonly associated with a small nodular pattern distributed centrally along the pulmonary vascular bundles.

### Distribution

After the dominant pattern of involvement has been identified, the distribution of the pattern is the next important consideration. HRCT patterns consist of those that involve the upper lung as opposed to the lower lung and the central lung as opposed to the peripheral lung.

Hypersensitivity pneumonitis and sarcoidosis have an upper lobe involvement, whereas such diseases as idiopathic pulmonary fibrosis and asbestosis have lower lobe distribution. Involvement of the central portion of the lung suggests diseases such as sarcoidosis and pulmonary alveolar proteinosis, whereas a peripheral distribution occurs in idiopathic pulmonary fibrosis, chronic eosinophilic pneumonia, and cryptogenic organizing pneumonia. Mosaic distribution refers to a nonspecific pattern of ground-glass infiltration that variably involves neighboring pulmonary lobules. This pattern can be seen in pulmonary vascular disease and airways disease. Air trapping is demonstrated on expiratory views and suggests diseases that have small-airway (bronchiolar) involvement. Air trapping can be diffuse and uniform in obliterative bronchiolitis or variable and patchy, causing a geographic appearance in respiratory bronchiolitis–associated interstitial lung disease or hypersensitivity pneumonitis. The geographic appearance consists of patchy areas of ground-glass opacification with sharp edges providing contrast between abnormal and more normal adjacent areas of lung and creating a map-like appearance.

### Associated Findings

In addition to the pulmonary findings on HRCT, several associated findings are helpful in the diagnosis of DPLD. Mediastinal and hilar lymphadenopathy can indicate underlying lymph node involvement when associated with the centrally distributed nodular pattern that occurs in sarcoidosis. Mild lymphatic enlargement unrelated to infection or malignancy is often associated with DPLD and may indicate reactive lymphadenopathy not necessarily associated with active disease involvement. Pleural disease is associated with several DPLDs, including the pleural plaques that are common in patients with asbestosis. Pleural effusions are uncommon in most DPLDs, and therefore their presence may help distinguish DPLD from other diseases. Pleural effusions are commonly associated with pulmonary edema or with lymphangiitic spread of malignancy but are rarely associated with interstitial lung disease and should prompt consideration of heart failure or lymphangiitic involvement of tumor. The pattern of interlobular septal thickening caused by pulmonary edema occasionally can be difficult to distinguish from reticular changes in the interstitium.

---

**KEY POINTS**

- Acute respiratory worsening (over less than 4 weeks) in patients with diffuse pulmonary infiltrates is most often the result of infection or edema.

- Diffuse parenchymal lung diseases that can present with acute respiratory worsening include the vasculitides, eosinophilic pneumonia, and acute interstitial pneumonia.

- High-resolution CT of the chest is more sensitive and specific than chest radiography for diagnosis of diffuse parenchymal lung disease.
- Interpretation of high-resolution CT of the chest in the context of pattern, distribution, and associated findings can narrow the diagnostic possibilities and occasionally is diagnostic of specific diffuse parenchymal lung diseases.
- Pseudoreticulation is a false-positive high-resolution CT finding for diffuse parenchymal lung disease due to atelectasis in gravity-dependent lung zones.

## Histopathologic Diagnosis

If the clinical context, temporal pattern of disease, and HRCT findings do not yield a diagnosis, it may be reasonable to obtain a bronchoscopic or surgical lung biopsy. Physicians and patients must decide how the additional knowledge from lung biopsy would affect the management plan. Patient preferences regarding surgery and immunosuppressive therapy ideally should be discussed in conjunction with the decision about whether to obtain lung biopsy. A thorough understanding of the likely clinical diagnoses and potential management options is important for patients who may benefit from immunosuppressive therapy. If a patient prefers to avoid surgical lung biopsy, empiric therapy or observation without therapy may be appropriate.

The diagnostic yield of surgical lung biopsy is approximately 90%. However, there are a limited number of histopathologic patterns recognized for a large number of DPLDs, and the specificity of lung biopsy depends on the pattern. For example, organizing pneumonia may be found as a nonspecific reparative process in association with histopathologic evidence of infection, infarction, carcinoma, or vasculitis. The organizing pneumonia pattern may also be a primary pathologic finding of cryptogenic organizing pneumonia or associated with a drug reaction, radiation therapy, hematopoietic stem cell transplantation, and other clinical conditions. The key to correlating this and many other pulmonary histopathologic findings with a clinical diagnosis is the interpretation within the clinical-radiographic context.

Lung biopsy specimens may be obtained by transbronchoscopic biopsy or open lung biopsy, which is commonly performed by video-assisted thoracoscopic surgery (VATS). VATS lung biopsy has a reported mortality rate of 2% and a complication rate of between 5% and 10%. High-risk patients with little potential benefit from surgical lung biopsy include those with suspected idiopathic pulmonary fibrosis who have a D$_{LCO}$ less than 20% of predicted or an accelerated clinical decline. Surgical lung biopsy is most informative when HRCT findings are used to direct surgical sampling of two or more lobes. Surgical lung biopsy specimens can provide sufficient tissue to assess the histopathologic architecture, which may be required to establish a diagnosis of usual interstitial pneumonia and nonspecific interstitial pneumonitis.

Bronchoscopic lung biopsy provides only small tissue samples that are generally insufficient to establish the underlying histopathologic architecture but nonetheless can provide enough tissue to demonstrate specific histopathologic features diagnostic of several specific disease processes, including carcinoma, sarcoidosis, and eosinophilic pneumonia. Bronchoalveolar lavage can provide additional diagnostic information, including culture, cytology, and cell differential. Bronchoalveolar lavage is safe and simple to perform and may be helpful to diagnose infections and carcinoma, as well as eosinophilic pneumonia.

### KEY POINTS

- Bronchoscopic lung biopsy may provide a specific histopathologic diagnosis in select diffuse parenchymal lung diseases but is insufficient to diagnose histopathologic patterns that require establishment of an architectural pattern.
- Histopathologic patterns must be interpreted in the context of the individual patient's clinical and radiologic findings to make the diagnosis of a specific diffuse parenchymal lung disease.

# Diffuse Parenchymal Lung Diseases with Known Cause

## Drug-induced and Radiation-induced Interstitial Lung Disease

Many drugs are known to cause a pattern of DPLD (**Table 11**). A high index of suspicion for drug-induced lung disease is essential because early identification and drug withdrawal can prevent morbidity and mortality. All current and recent past medications as well as herbal remedies and over-the-counter medications should be considered. Updated and referenced information for individual drugs is available and searchable at www.pneumotox.com. Establishment of a definitive diagnosis of drug-induced lung disease requires exclusion of other known causes and symptom improvement with drug withdrawal.

Most offending drugs cause a hypersensitivity-type reaction, with presenting symptoms of fatigue, low-grade fever, and cough. Laboratory results are nonspecific, but peripheral blood eosinophilia may be present. Physical examination may reveal crackles and occasionally wheezes or a pleural friction rub. Hypoxemia may be present. Radiographic findings most often include a pattern of reticular lines with scattered ground-glass opacification progressing to consolidation. Hypersensitivity reactions to drugs are often acute in onset and may resolve quickly after the offending agent is removed. Corticosteroids may be beneficial in selected patients with severe disease.

| TABLE 11 Drug-Induced Lung Diseases: Hypersensitivity vs. Fibrotic Interstitial | |
| --- | --- |
| **Temporal/Radiographic Pattern** | |
| **Acute/Cellular Infiltrate +/- Eosinophilia** | **Chronic/Interstitial Infiltrate** |
| Amiodarone | Amphotericin B |
| Azathioprine | Amiodarone |
| Bleomycin | Bleomycin |
| Busulfan | Cyclophosphamide |
| Carbamazapine | Methadone |
| Ethambutol | Methotrexate |
| Fluoxetine | Mitomycin (vinca alkaloids) |
| Granulocyte-macrophage colony-stimulating factor (GM-CSF) | Nitrofurantoin |
| Imatinib mesylate | Nitrosoureas |
| Isoniazid | |
| Sulfonamides | |
| Trazodone | |

In contrast to the acute onset and radiographic presentation of hypersensitivity reactions, chronic interstitial changes can be caused by cellular drug injury over time with a threshold or cumulative dose-effect. Chronic interstitial changes may result in dyspnea due to physiologic impairment of gas exchange but typically cause few systemic symptoms. Withdrawal of the offending drug and treatment with corticosteroids may lead to clinical improvement, stability, or continued disease progression.

Radiation pneumonitis, which occurs in approximately 7% to 20% of patients undergoing radiation therapy (especially of the chest, head and neck, and whole body), is a form of radiation-induced lung injury with the histopathologic findings of alveolar and capillary injury and repair. Patients with a high total dose of radiation, preexisting lung disease (especially chronic obstructive pulmonary disease), and concomitant chemotherapy and radiation therapy are at increased risk. Nonspecific symptoms begin 1 to 6 months after radiation therapy has been completed and include fever, weight loss, dry cough, and dyspnea. Physical examination of the chest usually shows only skin changes from radiation exposure and the occasional presence of a pleural rub. The disease can be severe, with progression over days to weeks leading to acute respiratory failure. The clinical and radiographic worsening over days to weeks is a helpful clue to distinguish radiation pneumonitis from recurrent local or metastatic cancer. The radiographic features typically consist of alveolar opacification of the irradiated portion of the lung with occasional air bronchograms. As confluence progresses, a nonanatomic "edge" may be seen on the chest radiograph, which reflects the border of the radiation port. Radiation pneumonitis can occur even outside the radiation field and rarely affects the contralateral lung. Radiation damage may also lead to pericardial and pleural disease. HRCT imaging is often not needed in patients with the appropriate clinical context and radiographic features. There are no clinical trial data to support treatment recommendations for radiation pneumonitis, but long-term corticosteroid therapy is supported by response rates estimated at 80%. Therapy with prednisone, at an initial dose of 1.0 to 1.5 mg/kg of body weight for several weeks with prolonged taper over weeks to months, is reasonable.

Radiation fibrosis is clinically distinct from radiation pneumonitis, although the diseases may have overlapping clinical presentations. Radiation fibrosis can occur in patients with or without a history of radiation pneumonitis. Radiation fibrosis occurs 6 to 24 months after radiation therapy and represents a long-term fibrotic sequela of lung damage, most often within the radiation field. Symptoms are uncommon, but patients with previous marginal lung function may have worsening dyspnea. The fibrotic process is irreversible.

### KEY POINTS

- Most causes of drug-induced pulmonary disease are the result of a hypersensitivity-type reaction with presenting symptoms of fatigue, low-grade fever, and cough.
- Radiation pneumonitis occurs 1 to 6 months after radiation therapy has been completed.
- Systemic corticosteroids have an estimated response rate of 80% in treating radiation pneumonitis and can result in rapid clinical improvement.

## Connective Tissue Diseases

Connective tissue diseases, along with drugs and environmental causes, are the most common known causes of DPLD. Pulmonary complications in patients with connective tissue diseases may involve the airways, pleura, musculoskeletal structures, and pulmonary vasculature in addition to the lung parenchyma. For example, up to 90% of patients with systemic lupus erythematosus have lung involvement, but interstitial disease is rare in these patients. Interstitial disease usually occurs in patients with a known connective tissue disease; however, the interstitial disease may be the initial finding in patients with an undiagnosed connective tissue disease, especially dermatomyositis, polymyositis, and rheumatoid arthritis. Diagnosis of connective tissue disease in a patient with DPLD affects the evaluation, treatment, and prognosis. Screening serologic testing for connective tissue disease in patients with DPLD is controversial. Serologic testing is most useful when clinical suspicion or physical examination findings suggest the presence of a connective tissue disease.

Treatment of connective tissue disease–related interstitial lung disease is disease-specific, with corticosteroids and/or cytotoxic therapies directed at the patient's connective tissue disease. The presence and extent of pulmonary involvement are often the major prognostic factor. Monitoring progression of lung disease or response to therapy by serial radiographic imaging and pulmonary function studies is a key determinant in modulating therapy for the systemic disease. Infection and drug-induced lung disease should always be considered in patients treated with cytotoxic or immunomodulating therapies who present with acute respiratory worsening.

Approximately 75% of patients with systemic sclerosis have DPLD evident on HRCT accompanied by abnormal gas exchange and restrictive changes on pulmonary function testing. Common symptoms in these patients are worsening dyspnea and dry cough; pulmonary hypertension is a common finding. Pulmonary histopathologic findings usually demonstrate nonspecific interstitial pneumonitis. Oral corticosteroid therapy has not consistently proved to be beneficial. A recent randomized, placebo-controlled trial demonstrated less decline of lung volume in patients with systemic sclerosis treated with cyclophosphamide compared with placebo.

Patients with rheumatoid arthritis may develop multiple pulmonary complications, including pleural disease, bronchitis and bronchiectasis, lung nodules, and acute lung injury. Rheumatoid arthritis–associated interstitial lung disease occurs in as many as 50% of patients with rheumatoid arthritis, may precede musculoskeletal joint disease, and is more common in men than in women. Affected patients have gradually progressive restrictive lung disease with impaired gas exchange. Acute respiratory worsening with acute interstitial pneumonia can be the initial presentation. Treatment of rheumatoid arthritis–associated interstitial lung disease is similar to treatment of systemic rheumatoid arthritis. Treatment of rheumatoid arthritis with methotrexate can lead to drug-induced lung disease, which is clinically difficult to distinguish from new-onset or worsening rheumatoid arthritis–associated interstitial lung disease. In addition, atypical pulmonary infections in patients treated with immunosuppressive therapy may mimic interstitial lung disease.

## Hypersensitivity Pneumonitis

Hypersensitivity pneumonitis is an allergic, inflammatory lung disease also called extrinsic allergic alveolitis. It results from exposure to airborne allergens, which cause a cell-mediated immunologic sensitization. Recurrent exposure then leads to inflammatory cytokine recruitment of CD8 lymphocytes, which results in granuloma formation and, over time, may produce parenchymal lung fibrosis. Typical antigens that trigger an allergic response are derived from bacterial and fungal elements in decaying organic matter, including moldy hay, grain dust, lumber, and stagnant water. Mycobacteria are also known antigens that contaminate hot tubs and lead to acute hypersensitivity pneumonitis following recurrent exposure. Animal proteins can be antigenic; implicated sources include bird feces and dander from feathers. Finally, inorganic low-molecular-weight chemicals, including diisocyanates, certain pesticides, and machine lubricants, are also known antigens. The source of antigen exposure is often given credit in the naming of the occupational disease associated with hypersensitivity pneumonitis (**Table 12**).

Hypersensitivity pneumonitis most often occurs in non-smokers whose occupation, hobbies, or lifestyle repeatedly exposes them to a known inhalational antigen. Dyspnea and dry cough are the most common respiratory manifestations; they may be accompanied by fever, weight loss, fatigue, and body aches. Physical examination often reveals mid-lung crackles and occasional "squeaks." Most patients exposed to an inhalational antigen develop symptoms within 4 to 12 hours, and symptoms are alleviated by prolonged abstinence from the offending antigen. Repeat exposure after abstinence often causes the symptom pattern to return.

The disease presentation, severity, and latency are affected by the concentration of antigen, duration of exposure, exposure frequency, and interval between exposures. Generally, hypersensitivity pneumonitis consists of an acute form and a subacute or chronic form. Patients with acute disease usually present with several weeks of symptoms temporally related to antigenic exposure. The chest radiograph usually shows diffuse alveolar infiltrates with an associated reticular pattern.

Patients with chronic hypersensitivity pneumonitis may not recall acute episodes of respiratory worsening that can be linked to antigen exposure. The patient may have chronic fatigue and weight loss with cough and a gradual worsening of exertional dyspnea. In such patients, review of previous chest radiographs may show a gradual progression resulting in mid- and upper-lung–dominant fibrosis and volume loss.

HRCT should be considered in the diagnostic evaluation for all patients with possible hypersensitivity pneumonitis except those whose chest radiograph, symptoms, and exposure to a known antigen source make the diagnosis highly likely. Classic HRCT findings include a pattern of ground-glass opacification and centrilobular nodules in an upper- and mid-lung distribution. The centrilobular nodules are thought

**TABLE 12** Hypersensitivity Pneumonitis: Antigen Source and Associated Disease

| Antigen Source | Associated Disease |
| --- | --- |
| **Organic Antigens: Bacteria, Fungi, Mycobacteria** | |
| Moldy hay, silage, or grain | Farmer's lung |
| Potatoes packed in moldy hay | Potato worker's lung |
| Moldy typesetting water | Bible printer's lung |
| Moldy cheese | Cheese washer's lung |
| Aerosolized hot tub water | Hot tub lung |
| Stagnant humidifier water | Humidifier lung |
| Moldy cork | Suberosis |
| Moldy wood dust | Wood dust or wood trimmer's lung |
| **Organic Antigens: Animal Protein** | |
| Bird feathers and droppings | Bird fancier's lung |
| Processed turkey or chicken serum | Turkey or chicken handler's lung |
| Animal pelts | Furrier's lung |
| Laboratory animal dander, serum, excrement | Laboratory worker's lung |
| **Inorganic Antigens** | |
| Diisocyanate(s) | Chemical lung |
| Aerosolized machine lubricants | Machine operator's lung |
| Pyrethrum | Pesticide lung |

to represent cellular bronchiolitis, and therefore HRCT expiratory imaging often demonstrates air-trapping. Subacute or chronic disease often has a similar pattern of centrilobular nodules and ground-glass opacification, but these findings are associated with reticular lines, honeycomb changes, and traction bronchiectasis. The distribution of findings is most often upper- and mid-lung, but when the disease is severe, it can involve the entire lung. Associated findings include volume loss as the fibrotic disease becomes advanced.

Pulmonary function tests in patients with hypersensitivity pneumonitis may show an obstructive or a restrictive pattern with a low D$_{LCO}$. Laboratory tests may reveal leukocytosis and elevated inflammatory markers. Identification of specific IgG serum precipitins may be clinically useful in select patients. However, false-negative results are common, and false-positive results frequently occur in patients with known exposure but without clinical disease. The key histopathologic features of acute hypersensitivity pneumonitis include poorly formed granulomas with bronchiolitis and lymphoplasmacytic interstitial infiltration. Chronic hypersensitivity pneumonitis can be difficult to distinguish from idiopathic pulmonary fibrosis in the absence of a known exposure. Surgical lung biopsy specimens of multiple lobes show specific histopathologic features of chronic hypersensitivity pneumonitis in two thirds of patients. In the other patients, nonspecific histopathologic findings of usual interstitial pneumonia alone or with nonspecific interstitial pneumonitis are identified. In these patients, the clinical–radiographic correlation is the key to diagnosis and treatment.

Treatment always includes eliminating exposure to the offending antigen coupled with notification of other persons at risk for exposure. In patients with an acute cases with modest symptoms, antigen avoidance may be the only needed treatment. Oral corticosteroids should be considered for patients with hypoxemia or failure to improve after elimination of exposure. In patients with fibrotic changes and chronic hypersensitivity pneumonitis, treatment may initially include prednisone. When necessary, long-term therapy with cytotoxic agents and referral of appropriate patients for lung transplantation should be considered.

## Smoking-related Interstitial Lung Disease

Interstitial lung diseases associated with smoking include pulmonary Langerhans cell histiocytosis, respiratory bronchiolitis–associated interstitial lung disease, and desquamative interstitial pneumonia. Smoking may also be a risk factor for the development of idiopathic pulmonary fibrosis.

Pulmonary Langerhans cell histiocytosis (formerly called histiocytosis X or eosinophilic granuloma) typically presents in a young (less than 40 years of age) current smoker. Pneumothorax occurs in 25% of patients with the disorder. The temporal pattern of the disease tends to be subacute, with gradual worsening of cough and dyspnea. Pulmonary function studies typically reveal an obstructive pattern with low D$_{LCO}$ in those with more severe parenchymal involvement, and those with mild disease may have obstructive, restrictive, or normal lung function. HRCT showing a pattern of nodules accompanied by thin-walled cysts in an upper and middle lung-field distribution is virtually pathognomonic. The initial treatment is smoking cessation. The disease may stabilize in patients who stop smoking, but most patients show evidence of gradual progression. In patients with the related systemic disease of Langerhans cell histiocytosis, chemotherapy with novel agents such as cladribine (2-chlorodeoxyadenosine [2-CdA]) appears to be effective, but such therapy has not been evaluated for treatment of smoking-related pulmonary Langerhans cell histiocytosis without systemic disease.

Respiratory bronchiolitis–associated interstitial lung disease (RB-ILD) and desquamative interstitial pneumonia (DIP) are overlapping disorders that have a similar spectrum of clinical, radiologic, and pathologic features in current or former smokers. RB-ILD is a form of bronchiolitis that occurs in most smokers and is occasionally severe enough to cause clinical symptoms and characteristic radiographic abnormalities. Affected patients present with the gradual onset of persistent cough and dyspnea with impaired gas exchange; pulmonary function tests show an obstructive or mixed obstructive/restrictive pattern. Chest radiograph may be normal but usually shows a pattern of bronchial wall thickening and alveolar infiltrates in a central and basilar distribution. HRCT shows a pattern of centrilobular nodules with air-trapping and scattered ground-glass attenuation. These HRCT findings are also seen, although less extensively, in asymptomatic smokers. DIP is a rare disorder that shares causal and clinical features and treatment with RB-ILD. Treatment of RB-ILD and DIP includes smoking cessation and avoidance of all passive exposure to smoke; most patients who avoid smoke improve. Corticosteroids are commonly used in severe disease but are of uncertain efficacy. The disorders progress in a small subset of patients despite smoking cessation and corticosteroid therapy.

## Idiopathic Interstitial Pneumonias

The idiopathic interstitial pneumonias are functionally grouped together because the definitive diagnosis commonly requires a diagnostic surgical lung biopsy that reveals a distinct histopathologic pattern. Making a specific diagnosis is essential to manage patients with these diseases. The key step in diagnosis is correlation of the histopathologic findings with the patient's clinical and radiographic findings. Diagnostic criteria for these diseases have been refined in the past decade, complicating clinical evaluation but leading to scientific advancement through clinical trials. Combined input from the radiologist, pathologist, and clinician is the current standard for diagnosis of atypical cases of idiopathic pulmonary fibrosis and other idiopathic interstitial pneumonias.

### Idiopathic Pulmonary Fibrosis

Idiopathic pulmonary fibrosis constitutes 25% to 35% of clinically encountered interstitial lung diseases. Current diagnostic criteria classify the diagnosis as "definite" when a surgical lung biopsy specimen shows usual interstitial pneumonia in the appropriate clinical–radiographic context. However, the pattern of usual interstitial pneumonia is not specific for idiopathic pulmonary fibrosis.

The diagnosis of idiopathic pulmonary fibrosis is "probable" in the absence of surgical lung biopsy when typical HRCT features are present in the appropriate clinical context. The clinical context is typically a middle-aged or older person with interstitial lung disease in whom no cause can be identified. Presenting manifestations generally include dry cough and dyspnea without systemic symptoms. Physical examination characteristically shows bibasilar dry inspiratory crackles. Digital clubbing is present in 30% of patients. Laboratory tests are not helpful unless there is clinical suspicion for underlying connective tissue disease. Pulmonary function tests show physiologic impairment of oxygen uptake and restriction of lung volumes. The disease is characteristically slowly progressive. HRCT findings are important in the diagnostic evaluation and may obviate the need for surgical lung biopsy. HRCT features that suggest usual interstitial pneumonia include reticular opacities and honeycombing with a peripheral and basilar predominance and minimal or no ground-glass opacifications. If these HRCT features are not present, the diagnosis of idiopathic pulmonary fibrosis requires surgical lung biopsy. Bronchoscopic lung biopsy is not helpful because recognition of usual interstitial pneumonia requires a larger sample than can be obtained by this procedure.

Because of the poor prognosis of idiopathic pulmonary fibrosis (2- to 3-year mortality rate 50%) and the lack of effective treatment, management of newly diagnosed disease is challenging. Traditional treatment with corticosteroids and cytotoxic therapies is not known to affect survival, and the risk of these therapies may outweigh their benefit. When appropriate, patients should be referred for lung transplantation or considered for enrollment in clinical trials.

Several complications are common in patients with idiopathic pulmonary fibrosis. Recent studies suggest pulmonary arterial hypertension is relatively common in patients with idiopathic pulmonary fibrosis and is associated with a poorer prognosis. Diagnosis of pulmonary arterial hypertension should prompt treatment with oxygen when resting, exercise-induced, or nocturnal hypoxemia is present. Treatment of pulmonary hypertension with vasodilators has been shown to improve dyspnea scores and distance walked in 6 minutes. The efficacy of vasodilator therapy in idiopathic pulmonary fibrosis is being investigated, and recommendations for treatment of patients whose disease is complicated by pulmonary arterial hypertension remain uncertain. Gastroesophageal reflux disease (GERD) is a risk factor for idiopathic pulmonary fibrosis, but the relationship of GERD to the pathogenesis, progression, or treatment of the idiopathic pulmonary fibrosis remains uncertain. Screening of patients with idiopathic pulmonary fibrosis for GERD is controversial, but patients who have symptomatic GERD should be treated with lifestyle modifications and a proton pump inhibitor; if these measures fail, surgical treatment should be considered.

Idiopathic pulmonary fibrosis has long been thought of as a slowly progressive disorder that worsens gas exchange, leading to respiratory distress, hypoxemia, and eventually death. Recently, a clinical syndrome of accelerated worsening of previously stable disease has been described and termed acute exacerbation of idiopathic pulmonary fibrosis. Although previously thought to be uncommon, acute exacerbation of disease may be a relatively common cause of death in affected patients. The clinical context is acute worsening (less than 1 month) of respiratory symptoms and gas exchange, along with new lung infiltrates occurring in the absence of identifiable infection, pulmonary embolism, or cardiac dysfunction (**Table 13**).

Surgical lung biopsy specimens from these patients have consistently shown superimposed diffuse alveolar damage on a background of usual interstitial pneumonia. Short-term prognosis is poor, and therapy is not effective. Limited data suggest that systemic anticoagulation may improve outcome, but recommendations for routine use are uncertain.

## Nonspecific Interstitial Pneumonitis

Nonspecific interstitial pneumonitis is a rare idiopathic disorder that shares many clinical and radiologic features with idiopathic pulmonary fibrosis. HRCT features of nonspecific interstitial pneumonitis include basilar or mid-lung reticular changes, rarely with honeycombing, and a dominant pattern of ground-glass opacification in the mid- and lower-lung zones. A diagnosis of nonspecific interstitial pneumonitis requires open lung biopsy. The histopathologic pattern of the disorder includes lymphoplasmacytic interstitial infiltration in a uniform pattern that disrupts the normal lung architecture and may be accompanied by chronic fibrosis. The prognosis and response to treatment are better when the pattern involves cellular inflammation rather than fibrosis. The diagnosis depends on excluding histopathologic features of organizing pneumonia, usual interstitial pneumonia, and diffuse alveolar damage.

The histopathologic pattern of nonspecific interstitial pneumonitis is most frequently the manifestation of connective tissue disease–associated interstitial lung disease, hypersensitivity pneumonitis, drug-induced lung disease, or HIV infection. A patient with a new diagnosis of nonspecific interstitial pneumonitis requires evaluation for diseases known to cause that pattern, especially connective tissue disease. Treatment consists of corticosteroids with or without cytotoxic agents. Prognosis is better than for idiopathic pulmonary fibrosis but remains poor for patients with a dominant fibrotic pattern on lung biopsy specimen.

## Cryptogenic Organizing Pneumonia

Cryptogenic organizing pneumonia (formerly called idiopathic bronchiolitis obliterans organizing pneumonia) is an idiopathic lung disease with the relatively nonspecific histopathologic correlate of organizing pneumonia. In some patients, organizing pneumonia is a reparative process that can occur as a secondary finding in association with pulmonary infection, infarction, carcinoma, and Wegener granulomatosis. In other patients, organizing pneumonia represents a histopathologic process that can accompany radiation therapy, connective tissue disease, and drug-related injury. When organizing pneumonia occurs as a primary histopathologic process without any associated cause, it is called cryptogenic organizing pneumonia.

Cryptogenic organizing pneumonia typically affects middle-aged nonsmokers, with both sexes being equally affected. The temporal pattern of disease onset and progression of symptoms are subacute. Symptoms usually consist of cough with fatigue, low-grade fever, anorexia, and weight loss. Most patients are initially diagnosed with viral pneumonitis or bacterial pneumonia after 1 to 2 weeks of symptoms. Cryptogenic organizing pneumonia is often considered 6 to 8 weeks later, usually after one or more courses of ineffective antimicrobial therapy. The chest radiograph most commonly shows a pattern of multiple patchy alveolar opacities with or without air bronchograms. Their distribution is peripheral and bilateral; the infiltrates may be migratory with resolution of established opacities as new areas appear on serial imaging. Imaging may also be nonspecific, showing interstitial infiltrates and alveolar opacification or showing one or more rounded nodules that may be interpreted as malignancy.

---

**TABLE 13** Diagnostic Criteria for Acute Exacerbation of Idiopathic Pulmonary Fibrosis

Previous or concurrent diagnosis of idiopathic pulmonary fibrosis

Unexplained worsening or development of dyspnea within 30 days

High-resolution CT scan with new bilateral ground-glass opacification and/or consolidation superimposed on a background reticular or honeycomb pattern consistent with usual interstitial pneumonia

No evidence of pulmonary infection by endotracheal aspiration or bronchoalveolar lavage

Exclusion of alternative causes, including the following:

    Left heart failure

    Pulmonary embolism

    Identifiable cause of acute lung injury

Adapted with permission from Collard HR, Moore BB, Flaherty KR, et al; Idiopathic Pulmonary Fibrosis Clinical Research Network Investigators. Acute exacerbations of idiopathic pulmonary fibrosis. Am J Respir Crit Care Med. 2007;176(7):636–643. [PMID: 17585107] Copyright 2007, American Thoracic Society.

Pulmonary function tests may show an obstructive or restrictive pattern. Diagnosis requires organizing pneumonia as the primary histopathologic finding in conjunction with clinical exclusion of known associated conditions. Surgical lung biopsy is the preferred technique, although bronchoscopic lung biopsy occasionally provides sufficient tissue for diagnosis.

Although some patients with mild disease improve without treatment, systemic corticosteroids result in rapid symptomatic improvement and gradual resolution of radiologic findings. Corticosteroid therapy should be continued at a dose of 1.0 to 1.5 mg/kg of prednisone for 1 to 3 months, with a prolonged taper over 6 to 12 months. The disorder commonly recurs during corticosteroid tapering. The prognosis is generally good and only occasionally requires long-term treatment with corticosteroid-sparing cytotoxic therapy.

### Acute Interstitial Pneumonia

Acute interstitial pneumonia (also known as Hamman-Rich syndrome and idiopathic diffuse alveolar damage) is clinically distinct from most DPLDs in that it presents with acute respiratory worsening resulting in fulminant respiratory failure and usually requiring mechanical ventilation within days or weeks after the onset of symptoms. Acute interstitial pneumonia is a distinct disease entity, but its clinical, radiologic, and pathologic features are indistinguishable from those of diffuse alveolar damage secondary to known causes of lung injury. The diagnosis requires exclusion of known causes of diffuse alveolar damage, such as an acute exacerbation of idiopathic pulmonary fibrosis, connective tissue disease, pneumonia, sepsis, or inhalational injury. Pulmonary infections and acute eosinophilic pneumonia may present with similar clinical and radiographic features. Prognosis is poor, with an estimated 50% short-term mortality rate and no known effective therapy. Patients who recover from the initial illness may relapse or have progression of an underlying interstitial lung disease.

### KEY POINTS

- Connective tissue diseases, along with drugs and environmental causes, are the most common known causes of diffuse parenchymal lung disease.

- Typical antigens that trigger hypersensitivity pneumonitis are derived from bacterial and fungal elements in decaying organic matter, including moldy hay, grain dust, lumber, and stagnant water.

- Diffuse parenchymal lung diseases associated with smoking include pulmonary Langerhans cell histiocytosis, respiratory bronchiolitis–associated interstitial lung disease, and desquamative interstitial pneumonia.

- Histopathologic findings in the idiopathic interstitial pneumonias are nonspecific, and diagnosis of specific diseases requires clinical and radiographic correlation with histopathologic findings.

- Accelerated worsening of previously stable idiopathic pulmonary fibrosis is a specific diagnosis called acute exacerbation of idiopathic pulmonary fibrosis, which is frequently the cause of death in patients with the disorder.

- Cryptogenic organizing pneumonia is typically initially misdiagnosed as viral pneumonitis or bacterial pneumonia but does not respond to antimicrobial therapy and demonstrates migratory infiltrates on chest imaging.

## Miscellaneous Diffuse Parenchymal Lung Diseases

### Sarcoidosis

Sarcoidosis is a multisystem, granulomatous, inflammatory condition of unknown cause that occurs in young adults of both sexes. The temporal pattern of disease progression ranges from asymptomatic to acute systemic presentations with fever, erythema nodosum, polyarthralgia, and hilar lymphadenopathy (Löfgren syndrome). An estimated 90% of patients have pulmonary involvement at the time of presentation. Sarcoidosis commonly involves the eyes and skin; the central nervous system, heart, and gastrointestinal tract are less commonly involved. A traditional staging system for sarcoidosis is based on chest radiographic findings at presentation and is useful for prognosis (**Table 14**). HRCT is not required in most patients, but findings can be characteristic when demonstrating a pattern of reticulonodular abnormalities in a central distribution along the bronchovascular lymphatic vessels associated with bilateral hilar and mediastinal lymphadenopathy.

The diagnosis of sarcoidosis requires histopathologic demonstration of organ involvement with noncaseating granulomatous inflammation in conjunction with the appropriate clinical and radiographic findings and the exclusion of other diseases. Diagnostic tissue can be obtained from any involved organ. Bronchoscopy has a diagnostic yield of up to 90% when multiple transbronchial lung biopsies are combined with endobronchial biopsies. Approximately 20% of patients present with mediastinal and hilar lymphadenopathy without parenchymal abnormalities. In these patients, mediastinoscopy is usually obtained but is more invasive than bronchoscopic needle aspiration of lymph nodes. A recent study reports that bronchoscopic needle aspiration of mediastinal and hilar lymph nodes using endobronchial endoscopic ultrasonography has a sensitivity of 85% for diagnosing sarcoidosis. Gastrointestinal endoscopic ultrasonography also offers easy access to enlarged mediastinal lymph nodes and is safe and well tolerated, with similar high sensitivity as transbronchial biopsy and endobronchial endoscopic ultrasonography.

**TABLE 14** Radiographic Classification of Sarcoidosis

| Stage | Radiographic Pattern | Frequency of Presentation (%) | Frequency of Spontaneous and Radiographic Remission (%) |
|-------|---------------------|-------------------------------|---------------------------------------------------------|
| 0 | Normal | 10 | |
| I | Hilar lymphadenopathy | 20 | 50-90 |
| II | Hilar lymphadenopathy; abnormal lung parenchyma | 50 | 40-70 |
| III | No lymphadenopathy; abnormal lung parenchyma | 20 | 10-20 |
| IV | Parenchymal fibrotic change with architectural distortion | <5 | 0 |

Sarcoidosis resolves spontaneously in up to two thirds of patients. Treatment may not be indicated in patients with asymptomatic radiographic abnormalities. When treatment is indicated, corticosteroids alleviate symptoms and improve lung function and radiographic findings, but they have not been shown to alter the course of the disease. The dose and duration of therapy have not been well studied. Prednisone, 0.5 mg/kg for 1 to 3 months and gradual tapering with alternate-day dosing of 10 to 20 mg to complete 9 to 12 months of therapy, is a reasonable recommendation. Patients who do not tolerate corticosteroids or who have resistant disease may be treated with methotrexate, hydroxychloroquine, or azathioprine. A recent study of infliximab versus placebo in patients with chronic sarcoidosis showed minimal improvement in lung function in the treated patients. No significant differences in symptoms were noted, and the use of infliximab and other tumor necrosis factor α inhibitors does not have a clearly defined role in treatment of sarcoidosis.

## Lymphangioleiomyomatosis

Lymphangioleiomyomatosis is a rare progressive cystic lung disease accounting for less than 1% of all interstitial lung disease and occurring almost exclusively in women in their third or fourth decade. The disorder occurs as either a sporadic isolated pulmonary disease or, in approximately 15% of patients, in conjunction with tuberous sclerosis. In a recent study of 243 women with pulmonary disease and tuberous sclerosis–associated disease, the most common symptom at presentation was breathlessness. Nearly 90% of all patients diagnosed with lymphangioleiomyomatosis (with or without tuberous sclerosis) presented with respiratory complications; 36% presented for medical evaluation because of spontaneous pneumothorax, with an overall incidence of spontaneous pneumothorax of 55% in all patients. Pulmonary function tests usually show obstructive disease, but the findings may be normal in early disease.

The diagnosis is based on imaging studies in the appropriate clinical context. Many young women are initially diagnosed with emphysema. Spontaneous pneumothoraces, chylothorax, and young age indicate that lymphangioleiomyomatosis should be considered. Chest radiographic findings paradoxically show diffuse reticulonodular infiltrates associated with hyperinflation. HRCT findings may be diagnostic when demonstrating a pattern of diffuse, thin-walled, small cysts that are distributed diffusely throughout the lung. Surgical lung biopsy is not required, but when obtained, shows proliferation of smooth-muscle cells and cysts. The disease has been causally associated with estrogen, but treatment with hormonal manipulation and progestins is not effective. The disease is slowly progressive and results in severe lung disease and need for lung transplantation.

**KEY POINTS**

- Löfgren syndrome is a form of sarcoidosis that presents with fever, erythema nodosum, polyarthralgias, and hilar lymphadenopathy.

- In patients with sarcoidosis and interstitial lung disease, bronchoscopy has a diagnostic yield of up to 90% when multiple transbronchial lung biopsies are combined with endobronchial biopsies.

- Bronchoscopic needle aspiration of mediastinal and hilar lymph nodes using endobronchial ultrasonography has a sensitivity of 85% for diagnosing sarcoidosis.

- Lymphangioleiomyomatosis is a rare progressive cystic lung disease occurring almost exclusively in women in their third or fourth decade as a sporadic disorder or in conjunction with tuberous sclerosis.

## Bibliography

Aziz ZA, Wells AU, Bateman ED, et al. Interstitial lung disease: effects of thin-section CT on clinical decision making. Radiology. 2006;238(2):725-733. [PMID: 16344334]

Collard HR, Moore BB, Flaherty KR, et al; Idiopathic Pulmonary Fibrosis Clinical Research Network Investigators. Acute exacerbations of idiopathic pulmonary fibrosis. Am J Respir Crit Care Med. 2007;176(7):636-643. [PMID: 17585107]

Garwood S, Judson MA, Silvestri G, et al. Endobronchial ultrasound for the diagnosis of pulmonary sarcoidosis. Chest. 2007;132(4):1298-104. [PMID: 17890467]

Ryu JH, Daniels CE, Hartman TE, Yi ES. Diagnosis of interstitial lung diseases. Mayo Clin Proc. 2007;82(8):976-96. [PMID: 17673067]

Ryu JH, Moss J, Beck GJ, et al; NHLBI LAM Registry Group. The NHLBI lymphangioleiomyomatosis registry: characteristics of 230 patients at enrollment. Am J Respir Crit Care Med. 2006;173(1):105-111. [PMID: 16210669]

Tashkin DP, Elashoff R, Clements PJ, et al; Scleroderma Lung Study Research Group. Cyclophosphamide versus placebo in scleroderma lung disease. N Engl J Med. 2006;354(25):2655-2666. [PMID: 16790698]

Trahan S, Hanak V, Ryu JH, Myers JL. Role of surgical lung biopsy in separating chronic hypersensitivity pneumonia from usual interstitial pneumonia/idiopathic pulmonary fibrosis: analysis of 31 biopsies from 15 patients. Chest. 2008;134(1):126-132. [PMID: 18339775]

# Occupational and Environmental Lung Disease

## Approach to Occupational and Environmental Lung Disease

Many lung diseases can be caused by an occupational or environmental exposure; however, identifying an exposure-related case is often difficult because the clinical and pathologic expressions of occupational and environmental lung diseases are indistinguishable from those of nonoccupational lung diseases. Rarely is a presentation pathognomonic of a specific exposure-related disorder, such as an elderly pipefitter who presents with a dry cough and dyspnea on exertion associated with a chest CT scan showing bilateral, partially calcified pleural plaques and lower lobe–predominant interstitial lung disease. This patient has the classic presentation of asbestos-related lung disease with pleural plaques and asbestosis. It is more common that important occupational or environmental factors contributing to a lung ailment are difficult to ascertain and in some cases have unrecognized biologic significance. The first cases of "popcorn lung" (bronchiolitis obliterans in microwave popcorn workers) were described in 2002, a result of the shrewd observation by one clinician who noted severe fixed airflow obstruction in patients without typical risk factors for this disease and noted that all had in common employment in one particular industry. Additional cases were subsequently identified in the flavoring industry worldwide. Work exposure to diacetyl, a butter flavoring chemical, is now thought to be the potential link to this newly recognized lung disease.

More than 20,000 chemicals are used in industry. Many more are introduced each year, and toxicologic data for most of them are limited. The clinician in practice plays an important role in recognizing sentinel cases due to well-established and novel exposures. Maintaining a high index of suspicion for exposure-related illness and consulting experts in occupational medicine and local public health resources when concern for an index case arises help to identify and to prevent cases of occupational and environmental lung disease.

## When to Suspect Occupational and Environmental Lung Disease

In the evaluation of a lung disease suspected of being caused or aggravated by occupational or environmental exposures, it can be helpful to consider clinical scenarios in which the suspicion for exposure-related lung disease should be heightened and an exposure history expanded. These include the following:

1. Patient concern that symptoms, signs, or diagnostic abnormalities may be due to an occupational or environmental factor.
2. Patient report of a temporal pattern of signs and symptoms, with improvement over the weekend or during vacation.
3. Patient report that several coworkers are affected with a similar illness.
4. Patient report of known hazardous substances at work.
5. Lack of a therapeutic response to aggressive appropriate treatment.
6. Diagnosis of a lung disease in a patient without established risk factors or outside recognized epidemiologic parameters for the specific disease.
7. Identification of multiple cases of a rare disease in one practice or one geographic area (clustering).

Not meeting labor force age of 18 to 65 years does not rule out a work-related illness. Many minors and retirees work, often in relatively dangerous trades. Their employment may be casual, poorly supervised, uninsured, and difficult to monitor.

## Taking an Exposure History

Systematically collecting comprehensive information about a patient's past employment, hobbies, and household and neighborhood exposures is impractical. Taking a focused exposure history aimed at identifying occupational or environmental risk factors for the specific disease under evaluation is more feasible. This history inevitably varies from patient to patient. Evaluation for a disease with long latency, such as a pneumoconiosis, will go back many years and focus on fibrogenic dusts. Assessment of a patient with possible occupational asthma can usually start with the job where the patient first developed symptoms and focus on substances that can induce occupational asthma.

There are several key components to an occupational and environmental history:

1. The job title is much less relevant than the job process, the job tasks, and the nature of substances with which the patient has contact; consulting Material Safety Data Sheets (MSDSs) is helpful in determining the nature of various substances. MSDSs are designed to provide both workers and emergency personnel with the proper procedures for handling or working with a particular substance. MSDSs include information such as physical data, storage, disposal, protective equipment, and spill/leak procedures.

2. The level of exposure is important to ascertain. Frequency, duration, intensity of exposure, and distance from the exposure source are important, as is the presence of visible dust in the air or on surrounding equipment and the presence of strong odors.

3. Temporal relationship of symptoms to work exposure is relevant. Are symptoms better at home, on days off, or during vacation? Before the onset of symptoms, was there a change in job process or exposure?

4. Non–work-related environmental exposure from hobbies, home products, pets, and travel also has to be considered.

If a focused exposure history is unrevealing but the presentation and pattern of the disease in question continue to raise concern for an occupational or environmental cause, referral to an occupational/environmental medicine specialist should be considered. Clinical management of an exposure-related illness often requires removal from exposure in addition to pharmacologic and supportive therapy. Occupational attribution of a patient's illness also affects case management, including compensation and cost reimbursement. Additionally, a workplace or public health response may be needed to identify other persons who may be at risk for the disease and to ensure that the relevant exposure is mitigated or eliminated.

**KEY POINT**

- The occupational/environmental history should include information about the work process; materials to which a person is exposed; the frequency, duration, and intensity of exposure; and non–work-related exposures.

# Asbestos-associated Lung Disease

## Pathophysiology

Asbestos fibers are naturally occurring fibrous, hydrated silicate minerals that are ubiquitous in the soil. Both serpentine or curly fibers (chrysotile, most common in commercial use) and straight and needle-like fibers (amphibole, including amosite, crocidolite, tremolite) cause the various asbestos-related lung diseases (**Table 15**).

Inhaled asbestos fibers are deposited at the bifurcations of the respiratory bronchioles with some reaching the alveoli. Alveolar epithelial cells transport some fibers into the pulmonary interstitium, whereas others migrate to the pleura by way of the lymphatic channels. The mechanisms by which asbestos fibers produce pleural disorders are poorly understood. Promotion of asbestosis involves macrophages accumulating around asbestos fibers. These macrophages become activated and trigger an inflammatory cascade that leads to alveolitis and peribronchiolitis. This inflammatory response is perpetuated with the help of various growth factors, such as

| **TABLE 15** Respiratory Diseases Associated with Asbestos Exposure |
|---|
| Pleural disease |
|   Pleural plaques (localized, often partially calcified) |
|   Diffuse pleural thickening |
|   Rounded atelectasis |
|   Benign pleural effusion |
|   Mesothelioma |
| Parenchymal lung disease |
|   Asbestosis |
|   Lung cancer |

interleukin 8, interferon-$\gamma$, platelet-derived growth factor, insulin-like growth factor, fibroblast growth factor, and tumor necrosis factor $\alpha$. The process results in the proliferation of fibroblasts and formation of scar tissue leading to the characteristic interstitial findings of asbestosis.

## Epidemiology

Asbestos-related lung disease was first described in the early 1900s. The use of asbestos increased rapidly during the 20th century and with it the incidence of asbestos-related health effects. Introduction of strict asbestos regulations in many industrialized countries in the 1970s has led to a decline in rates of asbestosis since the 1990s and to rates of mesothelioma leveling off in many countries, including the United States, with an anticipated downward trend in another 5 to 10 years. Asbestos continues to be used in less industrialized countries, placing many workers at risk for preventable asbestos-related disease.

## Risk Factors

The most important risk factor for development of asbestos-related lung disease is the cumulative exposure to the asbestos fiber. Variability in prevalence of disease in populations with comparable cumulative exposure is likely due to difference in fiber size, type, and distribution. What renders one person potentially more susceptible at a lower cumulative dose than another is not fully understood but is thought to relate to factors such as genetics, sex, ethnic origin, immune function, and fiber clearance. Between 1940 and 1979, an estimated 19 million workers had significant occupational asbestos exposure. The largest number of exposed workers was in the construction industry, the automotive servicing industry, and the shipbuilding and repair industry.

## Diagnosis, Evaluation, and Management

### Pleural Plaques

Pleural plaques are focal, often partially calcified, fibrous tissue collections on the parietal pleura and are considered a marker of asbestos exposure (**Figure 6**).

Pleural plaques are the most common sequelae of asbestos exposure and typically develop bilaterally, with a

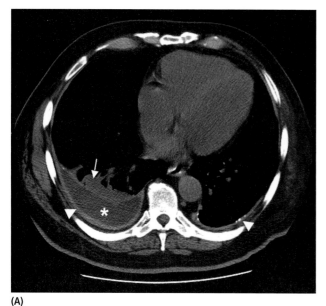

(A)

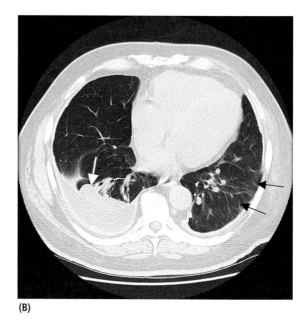

(B)

**FIGURE 6.**
**Chest CT-image showing complex asbestos-related lung disease in a navy engineer.**
Mediastinal *(A)* and lung *(B)* windows show bilateral partially calcified pleural thickening *(arrowheads)*, asbestosis *(black arrows)*, rounded atelectasis on the right with a classic "comet tail" *(white arrows)*, and a loculated right sided benign pleural effusion *(star)*.

latency of 10 to 20 years. Pleural plaques alone rarely, if ever, lead to symptoms. Often, they are noticed incidentally on a chest radiograph. A standard chest radiograph detects 50% to 80% of pleural plaques identified by chest CT scan. Other causes of pleural plaques (especially a unilateral pleural plaque) are previous hemothorax or empyema, mesothelioma, lymphoma, multiple myeloma, and pleural metastases. The callus formed after a rib fracture may also mimic pleural thickening. Talc, mica, tin, barite, and silica may also cause pleural plaques, although some of these materials may simply be contaminated with asbestos. Patients with pleural plaques should be monitored for the development of additional asbestos-related intrathoracic disease.

### Diffuse Pleural Thickening

Diffuse pleural thickening consists of more extensive fibrosis of the pleura than occurs with circumscribed pleural plaques. Thickening extends into the visceral pleura and obliterates the costophrenic angles. The prevalence of diffuse pleural thickening is much lower than that of localized pleural plaques. It is more likely to be associated with pulmonary impairment, including breathlessness and restrictive pulmonary physiology. Patients with diffuse pleural thickening may develop hypercapnic respiratory failure as their lungs become encased by a thick pleural rind that prevents the lungs from expanding. Surgical decortication has shown mixed results and is not routinely recommended.

### Rounded Atelectasis

Rounded atelectasis (also known as shrinking pleuritis, Blesovsky syndrome, and folded-lung syndrome) is the result of infolding of thickened visceral pleura with collapse of the adjacent peripheral lung. It can present clinically as single or multiple masses, which must be distinguished from a malignancy. The classic radiographic finding is a "comet tail" on chest CT scan extending from the hilum toward the base of the lung and then sweeping into the inferior pole of the lesion (see Figure 6B).

Rounded atelectasis can be progressive and associated with pulmonary impairment consisting of dyspnea and restrictive pulmonary physiology. As in diffuse pleural thickening, decortication has shown mixed results and is not routinely recommended. Other conditions that have been associated with rounded atelectasis include parapneumonic effusions, heart failure, Dressler syndrome, pulmonary infarcts, and chest trauma with hemothorax.

### Benign Pleural Effusion

Benign asbestos-related pleural effusion is a diagnosis of exclusion. It may occur early or late after asbestos exposure (see Figure 6A). Most patients with such effusions are asymptomatic; however, significant pleuritic pain and sometimes fever can be present. The effusion is typically exudative and may be hemorrhagic. Other causes, such as infection, malignancy (especially mesothelioma in presentations with long latency), and pulmonary embolism, must be excluded. Most benign effusions resolve spontaneously without permanent clinical sequelae.

### Asbestosis

The term *asbestosis* is sometimes used to refer to any thoracic manifestation resulting from asbestos exposure. Strictly speaking, the term refers only to bilateral interstitial fibrosis of the lung parenchyma caused by inhalation of asbestos fibers. The diagnosis can usually be based on clinical findings without histopathologic confirmation. The presence of an exposure history of appropriate duration, latency (typically 20 to 30 years), and intensity and radiographic evidence of interstitial fibrosis on chest radiograph or chest CT scan (**Table 16**) (see also Figure 6*A*) are usually sufficient for diagnosis.

Additional helpful clinical findings are breathlessness, bibasilar inspiratory crackles, and/or digital clubbing on physical examination and pulmonary function testing showing a restrictive pattern and decreased DLCO. Other pneumoconioses and other causes of pulmonary fibrosis, such as metal or organic dust, drugs, infectious agents, connective tissue diseases, and idiopathic pulmonary fibrosis, must be excluded. If a diagnosis of asbestosis cannot be established on clinical grounds, thoracoscopic biopsy should be obtained (transbronchial biopsy specimens are inadequate for diagnosis). The histopathologic pattern of asbestosis is usual interstitial pneumonia with the presence of at least one asbestos body on iron stain. There is no effective pharmacologic therapy for asbestosis. Immunosuppressive therapy has been tried without success. Management includes supplemental oxygen if necessary based on resting and 6-minute oxygen walk values, influenza and pneumococcal vaccinations, smoking cessation if applicable, and aggressive therapy for intercurrent infections.

### Asbestos-related Lung Cancer

An association between occupational exposure to asbestos and lung cancer is well established. Most cases occur in patients with asbestosis, but a diagnosis of asbestosis is not necessary to attribute lung cancer to asbestos exposure. Cigarette smoke and asbestos have a synergistic (multiplicative) effect on the risk for lung cancer. The clinical presentation, diagnostic evaluation, histopathologic findings, treatment, and prognosis of asbestos-related lung cancer do not differ from those in lung cancer caused by tobacco use alone. However, such a diagnosis may have legal implications, and patients should be counseled to obtain further information to this effect.

### Chronic Obstructive Pulmonary Disease

Chronic obstructive pulmonary disease (COPD) results in airflow limitation that is not fully reversible and is usually progressive (see Chronic Obstructive Pulmonary Disease). Smoking is the most common risk factor for COPD. Over the last two decades, increasing evidence has shown that various occupational and environmental exposures can cause or contribute to the development of COPD. The most extensively studied occupational exposures with epidemiologic and pathologic data to support a causative link to COPD are coal, silica, and cadmium exposure. Quantitative pathologic assessment of emphysema in coal and hard-rock miners confirms a relationship between dust exposure and the degree of emphysema independent of tobacco use. Several population- and community-based studies have shown a significant association between COPD and occupational exposure to gases, fumes, vapors, and dust. These studies also support that work in certain industries, such as the textile industry or agriculture, is associated with a greater risk for COPD (**Table 17**).

In 2003, the American Thoracic Society published a statement on the occupational contribution to the overall burden of airways disease, which concluded that 15% of cases of both asthma and COPD are likely to be work related. Another study based on U.S. National Health and Nutrition Examination Survey (NHANES) III data estimates the percentage of COPD attributable to work at 19% overall and 31% in never-smokers.

### Diagnosis and Management

Unlike occupational asthma, occupational COPD has no distinct definition. The clinical and pathologic presentation of most occupational COPD is indistinguishable from

---

**TABLE 16 Chest CT Findings Typical for Asbestosis**

| |
|---|
| Pleural plaques or thickening (90% of patients) |
| Thickened intralobular and interlobular lines (must be confirmed on prone imaging) |
| Parenchymal bands, often contiguous with the pleura |
| Honeycombing (in patients with advanced disease) |
| Curvilinear subpleural lines of varying length, often parallel to the pleura (must also be confirmed on prone imaging) |

---

**TABLE 17 Agents Associated with Increased Risk for Chronic Obstructive Pulmonary Disease**

| **Minerals** |
|---|
| Coal (mining) |
| Silica |
| Man-made mineral fibers |
| Cement (construction) |
| **Metals** |
| Vanadium |
| Cadmium |
| **Organic Dusts** |
| Cotton, hemp, jute (textile industry) |
| Grain dust (agricultural and farm workers, flour mill workers, and bakery workers) |
| Wood (paper milling) |
| **Mixed Dusts – Gases, Fumes, Particles** |
| Welding fumes |
| Fire smoke (biomass) |

nonoccupational COPD, and there are no laboratory tests or pulmonary physiology tests that aid in establishing the diagnosis as work-related. The diagnosis of occupational COPD is currently mostly based on inference from results of population studies to causation in the individual patient.

Patients present with cough, sputum production, and dyspnea on exertion. Pulmonary function tests show variable degrees of airflow obstruction and sometimes a decreased DLCO, depending on the degree of emphysema. Pharmacologic management is similar to that of other forms of COPD, except that removal from exposure must also be considered. Control of exposure at the workplace is key to preventing additional cases. Interventions to reduce or prevent continued inhalational exposures include substitution of the inciting agent with less or nonhazardous agents, engineering controls (enclosing a process), improved ventilation, and personal protective equipment.

### KEY POINTS

- Pleural plaques are the most common sequelae of asbestos exposure and typically develop bilaterally, with a latency of 10 to 20 years.

- Asbestosis is characterized by bilateral interstitial fibrosis of the lung parenchyma caused by inhalation of asbestos fibers, with a latency of 20 to 30 years.

- Cigarette smoke and asbestos have a synergistic (multiplicative) effect on the risk of lung cancer.

- The most extensively studied occupational exposures with epidemiologic and pathologic data to support a causative link to chronic obstructive pulmonary disease are coal, silica, and cadmium exposure.

### Bibliography

American Thoracic Society. Diagnosis and initial management of nonmalignant diseases related to asbestos. Am J Respir Crit Care Med. 2004;170(6):691-715. [PMID: 15355871]

Balmes J, Becklake M, Blanc P, et al; Environmental and Occupational Health Assembly, American Thoracic Society. American Thoracic Society Statement: Occupational contribution to the burden of airway disease. Am J Respir Crit Care Med. 2003;167(5):787-797. [PMID: 12598220]

Hessel PA, Gamble JF, McDonald JC. Asbestos, asbestosis, and lung cancer: a critical assessment of the epidemiological evidence. Thorax. 2005;60(5):433-436. [PMID: 15860721]

Hnizdo E, Vallyathan V. Chronic obstructive pulmonary disease due to occupational exposure to silica dust: a review of epidemiological and pathological evidence. Occup Environ Med. 2003;60(4):237-243. [PMID: 12660371]

Kreiss K, Gomaa A, Kullman G, et al. Clinical bronchiolitis obliterans in workers at a microwave-popcorn plant. N Engl J Med. 2002;347(5):330-338. [PMID: 12151470]

Peipins LA, Lewin M, Campolucci S, et al. Radiographic abnormalities and exposure to asbestos-contaminated vermiculite in the community of Libby, Montana, USA. Environ Health Perspect. 2003;111(14):1753-1759. [PMID: 14594627]

Rushton L. Occupational causes of chronic obstructive pulmonary disease. Rev Environ Health. 2007;22(3):195-212. [PMID: 18078004]

# Pleural Disease

Pleural effusions are a consequence of five different pathophysiologic processes: (1) transpleural pressure imbalance (for example, the transudative effusion of heart failure); (2) increased capillary permeability (the exudative effusion of pneumonia); (3) impaired lymphatic drainage (the exudative effusion of malignancy); (4) transdiaphragmatic movement of fluid from the peritoneal cavity (the transudative effusion of hepatic hydrothorax); and (5) pleural effusions of extravascular origin (the exudative effusion of chylothorax).

The incidence of pleural effusions in the United States is estimated to be 1.5 million annually. The most common cause of all pleural effusions is the transudate from heart failure. The exudates from parapneumonic effusion and malignancy are the next most common causes.

## Evaluation and Diagnosis

The evaluation of pleural effusion should begin with a medical history focusing on previous coronary artery bypass graft surgery, occupational exposure (particularly to asbestos), pneumonia or pleurisy, recent or remote malignancy and its treatment, chest or upper abdominal trauma, the duration of the effusion, and whether the effusion has recurred if a previous therapeutic thoracentesis had been done. On physical examination, digital clubbing may suggest lung cancer as the most likely cause of the effusion and cirrhosis of the liver as an uncommon cause.

Asymptomatic patients with a pleural effusion may have transudative fluid (hypoalbuminemia, nephrotic syndrome, or atelectasis) or exudative fluid (benign asbestos pleural effusion, rheumatoid pleural effusion, or yellow nail syndrome, which is a rare disorder that consists of pleural effusion, lymphedema, and yellow dystrophic nails). Symptomatic patients with a pleural effusion may present with a transudate, as from heart failure, or an exudate from parapneumonic effusion, malignancy, pulmonary embolism, or tuberculous pleural effusion (with pleuritic pain).

If the chest radiograph shows only a solitary pleural effusion, diagnoses associated with subdiaphragmatic diseases should be considered; these include transudates from hepatic hydrothorax and peritoneal dialysis and exudates from pancreatic disease, abscesses (hepatic, splenic, and subdiaphragmatic), chylous ascites, metastatic cancer, Meigs syndrome (consisting of the triad of ascites, pleural effusion, and benign ovarian tumor), and retroperitoneal lymphoma. However, solitary effusions can also originate in the thorax; these include heart failure effusion, tuberculous effusion, rheumatoid effusion, chylous effusion, and effusions associated with viral pleurisy, lupus pleuritis, lymphoma, pulmonary embolism, closed chest trauma, drugs, hypothyroidism, and uremic pleuritis. With bilateral effusions and a normal heart size, the differential diagnosis should include exudates from malignancy, esophageal perforation (usually left greater than right), and lupus pleuritis, as well as transudates from constrictive pericarditis and nephrotic syndrome. In a patient with signs of heart failure, treatment and a repeat chest radiograph may be most appropriate, whereas in a patient with acute pleuritic chest pain, immediate evaluation for thromboembolic disease may be indicated.

The resolution time of specific effusions, whether spontaneous resolution or with treatment, also helps to narrow the differential diagnosis. Pleural effusions tending to resolve within 2 weeks after onset (with appropriate treatment in some patients) include those from acute pancreatitis, heart failure, pulmonary embolism, traumatic chylothorax, and lung, heart, or liver transplantation. Effusions typically resolving in less than 2 months include parapneumonic effusion and effusions from post–cardiac injury syndrome and tuberculous pleurisy. Effusions resolving after 2 to 6 months include some cases of benign asbestos pleural effusion and effusions from rheumatoid pleurisy and tuberculous pleurisy. Pleural effusions that do not resolve until 6 months to 1 year after onset include benign asbestos pleural effusion and effusions from post–coronary artery bypass graft surgery, malignant disease, and rheumatoid pleurisy. Benign persistent effusions have a limited differential diagnosis that includes lymphatic abnormalities (chylothorax, lymphangiectasia, and yellow nail syndrome) and an unexpandable lung (trapped lung).

After therapeutic thoracentesis, some pleural effusions reaccumulate over several days to 1 week. Such rapidly reaccumulating effusions include transudates (as from hepatic hydrothorax, peritoneal dialysis, trapped lung, and extravascular pleural migration of a central venous catheter with saline or glucose infusion) and exudates (as from chylothorax, lung entrapment, malignant ascites, Meigs syndrome, and secondary iatrogenic hemothorax complicating a diagnostic tap).

A prethoracentesis differential diagnosis should be generated because pleural fluid analysis in isolation is usually nondiagnostic. Routine laboratory tests should be obtained, as should, in selected patients, echocardiography, chest CT scan, tuberculin skin test, and measurement of brain natriuretic peptide, rheumatoid factor, antinuclear antibody, erythrocyte sedimentation rate, amylase, and lipase.

**KEY POINTS**

- The most common cause of all pleural effusions is a transudate from heart failure; parapneumonic and malignant effusions are the most common exudates.
- A prethoracentesis differential diagnosis of possible pleural effusion should be generated based on the clinical presentation, physical examination, laboratory studies, and chest imaging because pleural fluid analysis in isolation may often be nondiagnostic.

## Pleural Fluid Analysis

In a patient with a new pleural effusion, a diagnostic thoracentesis is often required; however, in the patient with classic symptoms of heart failure without atypical features, such as fever or chest pain, observation with treatment is warranted. In other circumstances, such as suspected pulmonary embolism, a contrast-enhanced CT scan may be the initial step. Depending on the size of the effusion in patients with pneumonia, empiric therapy along with observation may be preferable. Effusions occur commonly after coronary artery bypass graft surgery and may be treated by observation if the effusion is well tolerated or modest in size.

As fluid is aspirated from the pleural space, the color, character, and odor should be noted, as these characteristics may narrow the differential diagnosis (**Table 18** and **Table 19**).

The next deductive step is to determine whether the fluid is a transudate or an exudate. According to Light's modified criteria, an effusion is likely an exudate if:

- the pleural fluid total protein/serum total protein ratio is greater than 0.50, and/or
- the pleural fluid lactate dehydrogenase (LDH) concentration is greater than 0.67 of the upper limits of normal of the serum LDH concentration.

| **TABLE 18** Color of Pleural Fluid and Associated Diagnoses | |
|---|---|
| **Color** | **Diagnosis** |
| Pale yellow | Transudate; some exudates |
| Red | Malignancy, benign asbestos pleural effusion, post–cardiac injury syndrome, pulmonary infarction, trauma |
| White | Chylothorax; cholesterol effusion |
| Brown | Chronic bloody fluid; amebic liver abscess rupture |
| Black | *Aspergillus niger* infection |
| Yellow-green | Rheumatoid pleurisy |
| Totally clear or color of infusate | Extravascular migration of central venous catheter |
| Green | Biliopleural fistula |

**TABLE 19** Character of Pleural Fluid and Associated Diagnoses

| Character | Diagnosis |
|---|---|
| Water-like | Duropleural fistula |
| Pus | Empyema |
| Milky | Chylothorax; cholesterol effusion |
| Viscous | Mesothelioma, empyema |
| Debris | Rheumatoid pleurisy |
| Turbid | Inflammatory exudates or lipids |
| "Anchovy" paste | Amebic liver abscess rupture |
| Satin-like sheen | Cholesterol effusion |

If the conditions of both tests are not met, the fluid is almost always a transudate. However, treatment (for example, diuretics for heart failure), a dual diagnosis (heart failure and a concomitant parapneumonic effusion), or some specific diagnoses (chylothorax) can result in discordant exudates (an exudate by either the protein or LDH criterion but a transudate by the other criterion). The differential diagnosis of a transudative effusion is usually discernible from the clinical presentation (**Table 20**).

Exudative effusions are associated with many conditions, including infections, connective tissue disease, other inflammatory conditions, malignancy, lymphatic abnormalities, and iatrogenic causes. The results of the pleural fluid analysis may increase or decrease the posttest probability that the effusion is exudative; however, a high or low clinical suspicion should not be affected by borderline test results. For example, pleuritic pain suggests an exudate even if tests are borderline.

Almost all exudates have a total nucleated cell count greater than $1000/\mu L$ $(1 \times 10^9/L)$; cell counts greater than $10,000/\mu L$ $(10 \times 10^9/L)$ with a predominance of neutrophils occur most commonly in parapneumonic effusions, acute pancreatitis, and subdiaphragmatic abscesses. When the total nucleated cell count is greater than $50,000/\mu L$ $(50 \times 10^9/L)$, the effusion is usually a complicated parapneumonic effusion or caused by empyema and rarely by acute pancreatitis and pulmonary infarction. Chronic exudates with a mononuclear cell predominance and total nucleated cell counts less than $5000/\mu L$ $(5 \times 10^9/L)$ are typical of tuberculous pleural effusion and malignancy. Effusions containing at least 80% lymphocytes of the total nucleated cells are caused by a limited number of exudative effusions (**Table 21**).

Finding more than 10% eosinophils in the pleural fluid also narrows the differential diagnosis (**Table 22**).

A pleural fluid pH less than 7.30 occurs consistently with exudates from complicated parapneumonic effusions, esophageal rupture, and chronic rheumatoid pleurisy and less frequently from malignant effusions, lupus pleuritis, and tuberculous effusions. Pleural fluid acidosis may occur with hemothorax, pancreaticopleural fistula, and pulmonary infarction. The pathophysiologic mechanisms resulting in low pleural fluid pH and pleural fluid glucose are interrelated. Therefore, if pleural fluid pH measurement is not available in

**TABLE 20** Causes of Transudative Effusions

| Diagnosis | Comment |
|---|---|
| Atelectasis | Small effusion caused by increased intrapleural negative pressure; common in patients in the intensive care unit |
| Constrictive pericarditis | Bilateral effusions with normal heart size; 95% with jugular venous distention |
| Duropleural fistula | Cerebrospinal fluid in pleural space; caused by trauma and surgery |
| Extravascular migration of central venous catheter | With saline or dextrose infusion |
| Glycinothorax | High pleural fluid to serum glycine ratio following bladder irrigation with rupture |
| Heart failure | Most common cause of transudates; diuresis can increase pleural fluid protein and lactate dehydrogenase, resulting in discordant exudate |
| Hepatic hydrothorax | Occurs in 6% of patients with cirrhosis and clinical ascites; up to 20% do not have clinical ascites |
| Hypoalbuminemia | Edema fluid rarely isolated to pleural space; small bilateral effusions |
| Nephrotic syndrome | Typically small and bilateral; unilateral effusion with chest pain suggests pulmonary embolism |
| Peritoneal dialysis | Small bilateral effusions common; rarely large right effusion develops within 72 hours of initiating dialysis |
| Superior vena cava obstruction | Due to acute systemic venous hypertension |
| Trapped lung | Unexpandable lung; unilateral effusion as a result of imbalance in hydrostatic pressures from remote inflammation |
| Urinothorax | Unilateral effusion caused by ipsilateral obstructive uropathy |

**TABLE 21 Exudative Pleural Effusions with at Least 80% Lymphocytes**

| Diagnosis | Comment |
| --- | --- |
| Acute posttransplant lung rejection | New or increased effusion 2 to 6 weeks after transplantation |
| Chylothorax | Lymphoma a common cause; a protein-discordant exudate[a] |
| Lymphoma | Often 100% of nucleated cells are lymphocytes; diagnostic yield on cytology and pleural biopsy high with non-Hodgkin lymphoma |
| Post–coronary artery bypass graft surgery | Occurs more than 2 months after surgery; not associated with trapped lung |
| Rheumatoid pleurisy (chronic) | May be associated with unexpandable lung |
| Sarcoidosis | May be protein-discordant[a] |
| Tuberculosis | Most common cause of lymphocyte-predominant exudate world-wide; typically 90% to 95% lymphocytes |
| Fungal infections, mainly histoplasmosis; less commonly cryptococcosis | Uncommon presentations |
| Yellow nail syndrome | Typically a protein-discordant exudate[a]; occurs in 36% of patients during course of disease |

[a]Protein-discordant exudates: an exudate by pleural fluid protein to serum protein ratio only.

**TABLE 22 Exudative Pleural Effusions with Greater Than 10% Eosinophils**

| Disease | Comment |
| --- | --- |
| Benign asbestos pleural effusion | 30% incidence of pleural fluid eosinophilia; up to 50% eosinophils/total nucleated cells |
| Carcinoma | Prevalence of pleural fluid eosinophilia similar in malignant and nonmalignant effusions |
| Churg-Strauss syndrome | High pleural fluid eosinophilia; associated with peripheral blood eosinophilia |
| Drug-induced | Dantrolene, bromocriptine, nitrofurantoin, valproic acid |
| Fungal disease | Most commonly coccidioidomycosis |
| Hemothorax | Pleural fluid eosinophilia develops 1 to 2 weeks after hemothorax |
| Lymphoma | Hodgkin lymphoma |
| Parasitic disease | Paragonimiasis, hydatid disease, amebiasis, ascariasis |
| Pneumothorax | Effusion in 10% to 20% of patients; tissue eosinophilia and pleural fluid eosinophilia occur within hours |
| Pulmonary embolism | Associated with pulmonary infarction and hemorrhagic effusion |
| Sarcoidosis | Rare |
| Tuberculosis | Rare |

an institution, the same information can be gained by identifying a pleural fluid glucose concentration less than 60 mg/dL (3.33 mmol/L) with normal plasma glucose or a pleural fluid/plasma glucose ratio less than 0.50.

Pleural fluid amylase should be measured when the clinical presentation suggests acute pancreatitis, pancreaticopleural fistula, or esophageal perforation, which is most commonly iatrogenic, especially from esophageal dilatation or malignancy. The isoamylase in acute pancreatitis and a pancreaticopleural fistula is pancreatic in origin. An elevated pleural fluid salivary-like isoamylase occurs almost always with esophageal perforation and malignancy, usually adenocarcinoma of the lung followed by adenocarcinoma of the ovary.

Triglycerides should be measured in the pleural fluid if a lymphatic leak is a consideration; serum triglyceride concentration greater than 110 mg/dL (1.24 mmol/L) suggests a chylothorax, whereas a concentration less than 50 mg/dL (0.56 mmol/L) makes chylothorax highly unlikely. A diagnosis of chylothorax can be confirmed by detecting chylomicrons in the pleural fluid.

The sensitivity of cytologic analysis of pleural fluid ranges from 40% to 90% in patients with known malignancy. The reasons for the variation include the following: the effusion may be associated with the malignancy, but malignant cells are not detected in the pleural fluid (these are termed paramalignant effusions, the causes of which include impaired lymphatic drainage, postobstructive pneumonia, and pulmonary embolism); the type of tumor (high positivity with adenocarcinoma and low positivity in Hodgkin lymphoma); the number of specimens submitted; the stage of pleural involvement (the more advanced stage, the higher the sensitivity); and the expertise of the cytopathologist.

# Management

Most pleural effusions resolve with treatment of the underlying disease. The only effusions that usually require invasive treatment of the pleural space are complicated parapneumonic effusions, empyema, and malignancy.

## Parapneumonic Effusions

If the parapneumonic effusion persists untreated for 1 to 2 weeks, loculations may develop that usually require drainage of the pleural space with a small-bore catheter. In pleural effusions associated with pneumonia, the presence of loculated pleural fluid, pleural fluid pH less than 7.20, pleural fluid glucose less than 60 mg/dL (3.33 mmol/L), positive pleural fluid Gram stain or culture, or the presence of gross pus in the pleural space predicts a poor response to antibiotics alone; such pleural effusions are treated with drainage of the fluid through a catheter or chest tube. Thoracic empyema (pus in the pleural space) develops when antibiotics are not given and the pleural space is not drained in a timely manner. In this case, video-assisted thorascopic surgery (VATS) is indicated to break down loculations and drain pus from the pleural cavity.

Early antibiotics directed at the pneumonia and timely small-bore chest tube drainage (with or without fibrinolytic agents) for complicated parapneumonic effusions (defined as a pleural fluid pH less than 7.30, glucose less than 60 mg/dL [3.33 mmol/L], LDH greater than 1000 U/L, fluid loculation, or positive Gram stain or culture) typically can preclude the need for VATS or thoracotomy.

## Malignant Pleural Effusions

Patients with recurrent, symptomatic malignant pleural effusions not responsive to chemotherapy require drainage for relief of dyspnea. Drainage can be accomplished either by placing an indwelling catheter as an outpatient or performing pleurodesis (typically an inpatient procedure) using a chemical agent, such as large-particle talc, as a slurry through a chest tube or by poudrage (the surgical application of powder) at VATS. A large, multicenter trial using large-particle talc showed the procedure to be safe with no episodes of respiratory failure.

## Tuberculous Pleural Effusions

Tuberculous pleural effusions, whether or not treated with antituberculosis drugs, resolve in 4 to 16 weeks. However, a patient with a tuberculous effusion who does not receive drug therapy has a 65% chance of developing pulmonary or extrapulmonary tuberculosis within the next 5 years. Therefore, a patient with a positive tuberculin skin test and a lymphocyte-predominant, exudative pleural effusion, without an alternative diagnosis, should be treated with the same 6-month multidrug regimen used for treatment of pulmonary tuberculosis. There are insufficient data to support the use of adjunctive corticosteroids in the treatment of tuberculous effusions.

## Trapped Lung

Trapped lung is characterized by visceral pleural restriction from a remote inflammatory process that results in transpleural pressure imbalance and a transudative pleural effusion (**Figure 7**). However, the effusion often presents as a protein-discordant exudate that is diagnostically problematic. The protein concentration in pleural fluid of vascular origin depends on the protein reflection coefficient, solvent filtration into the pleural space, and the bulk flow of fluid by way of the pleural lymphatic vessels. In trapped lung, solvent filtration may not be increased and lymphatic bulk flow may be impaired, resulting in an increased total protein concentration. Therefore, finding a pleural effusion with protein in the exudative range makes the diagnosis of trapped lung likely. If the patient has no significant symptoms from a small trapped lung, observation is appropriate. However, with significant visceral pleural restriction and a large pleural effusion, decortication should be recommended if the underlying lung on CT scan is relatively normal.

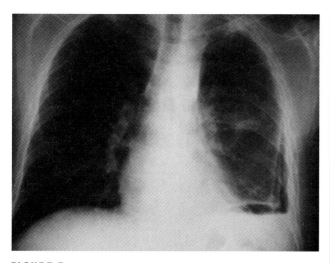

**FIGURE 7.**
**Trapped lung.**
Note a small left-sided pneumothorax with an air-fluid level with evidence of visceral pleural thickening.

- Patients with recurrent, symptomatic malignant pleural effusions not responsive to chemotherapy require drainage for relief of dyspnea.
- Patients with a positive tuberculin skin test and a lymphocyte-predominant, exudative pleural effusion without an alternative diagnosis should be treated for pulmonary tuberculosis.

## Pneumothorax

Pneumothorax consists of air within the pleural space. Primary spontaneous pneumothorax occurs without a precipitating event in patients with no known lung disease. Risk factors include cigarette smoking, family history, Marfan syndrome, homocysteinuria, and thoracic endometriosis. Subpleural blebs and bullae are commonly detected by CT scan and predispose to primary pneumothorax. There is no relationship to physical activity. In smokers, recurrence exceeds 50% unless the patient stops smoking. Secondary pneumothorax is associated with overt lung disease, most commonly chronic obstructive pulmonary disease (**Table 23**). Underlying lymphangioleiomyomatosis and thoracic endometriosis should be considered in a young, nonsmoking woman with pneumothorax. Chest CT scan may confirm the diagnosis of lymphangioleiomyomatosis. Iatrogenic pneumothorax is common and may complicate transthoracic needle aspiration, central intravascular line placement, thoracentesis, pleural biopsy, or mechanical ventilation. Tension pneumothorax (**Table 24**) requires immediate treatment.

Treatment of spontaneous pneumothorax depends on its size and whether underlying lung disease is present. An approach to management stratifies small (less than 2 cm) and large (2 cm or more) pneumothoraces between the lung and chest wall. A 2-cm pneumothorax approximates half the volume of the hemithorax. Simple aspiration is less likely to succeed in secondary spontaneous pneumothorax and is only recommended as an initial treatment of pneumothoraces less than 2 cm in minimally breathless patients younger than 50 years. Patients with primary spontaneous pneumothoraces that resolve with aspiration may be discharged, but hospitalization is recommended for patients with secondary spontaneous pneumothoraces. Small chest tubes are as effective as large ones, and small tubes should initially be used. Suction is not initially indicated because of the risk of re-expansion pulmonary edema and can be added after 48 hours if the pneumothorax persists. Initial tube thoracostomy, preferably with a small-bore catheter, is appropriate for secondary pneumothoraces more than 2 cm, particularly in patients older than 50 years. Patients with either primary or secondary pneumothorax treated with tube thoracostomy should, after re-expansion, undergo induction of pleurodesis, preferably by intrapleural talc administration. VATS induces effective pleurodesis and should be considered for refractory or recurrent pneumothoraces or to minimize the risk of recurrence for patients with special occupations, such as airline pilots. Pleurodesis via tube thoracostomy reduces the risk of recurrence to about 25%, whereas thoracoscopy reduces the risk to about 5%.

### Bibliography

Gopi A, Madhvan SM, Sharma SK, Sahn SA. Diagnosis and treatment of tuberculous pleural effusion in 2006. Chest. 2007;131(3):880-889. [PMID: 17356108]

| **TABLE 23** Causes of Secondary Pneumothorax |
| --- |
| Airways disease, including chronic obstructive pulmonary disease (the most common cause) and status asthmaticus |
| Interstitial lung diseases, including Langerhans cell histiocytosis, lymphangioleiomyomatosis, sarcoidosis, and idiopathic pulmonary fibrosis |
| Necrotizing pneumonia and *Pneumocystis jirovecii* pneumonia |
| Connective tissue diseases with pulmonary involvement, lung cancer, and thoracic endometriosis (catamenial pneumothorax) |
| Cystic fibrosis |

**TABLE 24** Treatment of Pneumothorax

**Primary Spontaneous Pneumothorax**

If the pneumothorax has a more than 2-cm rim of air between the lung margin and chest wall or if dyspnea is present, aspiration followed by repeat aspiration as needed should be done initially. Mildly symptomatic, small (less than 2-cm) primary spontaneous pneumothoraces may be observed.

If simple aspiration is unsuccessful, small-bore intercostal catheter drainage should be used.[a]

If intercostal tube drainage is unsuccessful after 48 hours, refer to a chest physician with referral to a chest surgeon if unsuccessful by 3 to 5 days.

**Secondary Spontaneous Pneumothorax**

Aspiration can initially be done in a patient without dyspnea with a more than 2-cm rim of air on chest radiograph.

Intercostal tube drainage should be tried next and managed as above. Referral to a chest physician should occur by 48 hours, with early referral to a chest surgeon for consultation by 3 to 5 days in case of persistent air leak or failure of the lung to re-expand.

**Tension Pneumothorax[b]**

Administer high concentrations of oxygen.

Relieve excessive intrapleural pressure by insertion of a cannula into the pleural space in the second intercostal space, midclavicular line, and remove air until the patient is clinically stabilized.

Immediately place a chest tube into the pleural space.

[a]The chest tube can be removed 24 hours after full lung expansion and cessation of the air leak through an unclamped tube.

[b]Tension pneumothorax occurs when intrapleural pressure exceeds atmospheric pressure throughout the respiratory cycle and may occur with a pneumothorax of any size. It is associated with rapid onset of respiratory distress and cardiovascular compromise and requires rapid intervention.

Heffner, JE. Diagnosis and management of malignant pleural effusions. Respirology. 2008;13(1):5-20. [PMID: 18197908]

Huggins JT, Sahn SA, Heidecker J, et al. Characteristics of trapped lung: pleural fluid analysis, manometry, and air-contrast chest CT. Chest 2007;131(1):206-213. [PMID: 17218577]

Janssen JP, Collier G, Astoul P, et al. Safety of pleurodesis with talc poudrage in malignant pleural effusion: a prospective cohort study. Lancet. 2007;369(9572):1535-1539. [PMID: 17482984]

Porcel JM, Madronero AB, Pardina M, et al. Analysis of pleural effusions in acute pulmonary embolism: radiological and pleural fluid data from 230 patients. Respirology. 2007;12(2):234-239. [PMID: 17298456]

Sahn SA. Pleural effusions of extravascular origin. Clin Chest Med. 2006;27(2):285-308. [PMID: 16716819]

Sahn SA. The value of pleural fluid analysis. Am J Med Sci. 2008;335(1):7-15. [PMID: 18195577]

Sahn SA. Diagnosis and management of parapneumonic effusions and empyema. Clin Infect Dis. 2007;45(11):1480-1486. [PMID: 17990232]

Warren WH, Kalimi R, Khodadadian LM, Kim AW. Management of malignant pleural effusions using the Pleur(x) catheter. Ann Thorac Surg. 2008;85(3):1049-1055. [PMID: 18291195]

# Pulmonary Vascular Disease

## Acute Pulmonary Thromboembolism

Venous thromboembolism (VTE) includes both deep venous thrombosis (DVT) and pulmonary embolism (PE). The pathophysiology of PE includes the formation of a DVT, embolization through the right heart chambers, and the effects of the thrombotic material within the pulmonary arteries. The obstruction of blood flow through the pulmonary arteries has several physiologic consequences, including ventilation/perfusion mismatching and ischemia of the lung parenchyma. The most important clinical effects, however, are the acute obstruction of blood flow and increase in pulmonary vascular resistance, which increase the demand on the right ventricle and may lower cardiac output. These effects can cause right ventricular strain, cardiogenic shock, cardiac arrest, and death.

PE is the third most common cardiovascular disease, after ischemic heart disease and stroke. The age-adjusted rate of death in the United States with a diagnosis of PE is about 1:10,000 per year. Autopsy studies show that fatal PE is frequently undiagnosed ante mortem, and therefore the true incidence may be three to ten times the number diagnosed clinically. The disorder is common in the general population, accounting for as many as 10% of unsuccessful prehospital resuscitation attempts. It is especially common in hospitalized patients and may constitute the greatest mortality risk to some inpatient populations.

### Risk Factors

The risk factors for PE and DVT can be categorized according to the triad of pathogenic conditions first identified by Rudolf Virchow in 1860: venous stasis, vascular (endothelial) damage, and hypercoagulability (**Figure 8**). Most clinical situations associated with those conditions can be identified by a careful history and physical examination.

Hypercoagulability may be associated with clinical conditions (for example, cancer or trauma) or with medications (for example, estrogen in doses used for birth control or even those used for hormone replacement therapy). Other

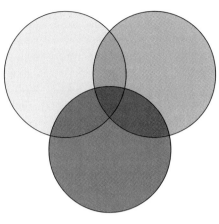

**Venous Stasis**
- Bed rest
- Immobility
- Surgery > 30 min
- CHF
- Previous DVT
- Venous obstruction
- Morbid obesity

**Hypercoagulability**

Drugs
    - Estrogen
    - Tamoxifen
Acquired
    - Lupus "anticoagulant"
    - Cancer associated mediators
Genetic deficiencies
    - Protein C
    - Protein S
    - Antithrombin III
Genetic variants - weakly prothrombotic
    - Factor V $_{Leiden}$
    - Prothrombin 20210A

**Endothelial damage**
- Previous DVT
- Leg trauma
- Hip or knee replacement

**FIGURE 8.**
**Risk factors for pulmonary thromboembolism: Virchow triad.**

CHF = heart failure; DVT = deep venous thrombosis.

hypercoagulable states may only be confirmed by laboratory testing. For example, thrombi can be induced by circulating procoagulant substances (the lupus anticoagulant or mediators released by adenocarcinoma of the lung, breast, and viscera) or from genetic deficiencies in such anticoagulant enzymes as protein C, its cofactor protein S, and antithrombin III. These conditions usually require high-dose anticoagulation. There are, however, some genetic variants that have relatively weak prothrombotic influences, such as mutations of factor V Leiden and prothrombin 20210A, which, at least in their heterozygous forms, only mildly increase the risk for thrombosis in the absence of other conditions. Similarly, elevated levels of factor VIII and even non-O blood groups have been associated with the occurrence of VTE, although the absolute increase in risk for persons in the general population with these findings is very low.

## Primary Prevention

A relatively risk-free method to prevent DVT in immobilized patients is to reduce venous stasis by mechanical compression of the calves. Elastic stockings are useful if they are tailored to provide a gradient of pressures. Intermittent pneumatic compression devices are effective for this purpose by inflating a cuff placed around the lower extremities for several seconds of each minute. Both methods are safe, effective, and well tolerated. They should be applied promptly and maintained during the risk period. This approach has particular value in patients for whom antithrombotic drugs are contraindicated.

Significant clinical data have shown the safety and efficacy of pharmacologic prophylaxis with heparin, low-molecular-weight heparins (LMWHs), or fondaparinux, given subcutaneously (**Table 25**). These medications reduce the incidence of DVT and PE by inhibiting clotting early in the coagulation cascade. Substantial experience has indicated a low bleeding risk associated with these regimens, even in surgical patients. Warfarin, adjusted to an INR of 2.0 to 3.0, is an alternative method of prophylaxis in high-risk patients but is less commonly used.

## Diagnosis and Evaluation

### Clinical Presentation

Although patients with PE may present with the classic symptoms of dyspnea, chest pain, hemoptysis, or syncope, the

| **TABLE 25** Prophylaxis for Deep Venous Thrombosis and Pulmonary Embolism | | |
|---|---|---|
| **Drug** | **Dosage** | **Frequency** |
| Heparin (unfractionated) | 5000 units<br>7500 units | Every 8 or 12 hours |
| Dalteparin | 5000 units | Every 24 hours |
| Enoxaparin | 40 mg | Every 24 hours |
| Fondaparinux | 2.5 mg | Every 24 hours |
| Warfarin | Adjusted to INR 2.0–3.0 | Every 24 hours |

presentation is often more subtle. At times, only nonspecific respiratory or hemodynamic manifestations may occur. Perhaps for this reason, most patients who die of PE have not had a diagnostic evaluation for PE despite the presence of at least one documented symptom or sign of the disorder (**Table 26**). Although a classic pattern of gas exchange disturbance has been described (hypoxemia with increased alveolar–arterial oxygen gradient, respiratory alkalosis), the pattern is not universal and cannot be used to diagnose or exclude PE. The clinical pretest probability of PE can be estimated based on the initial assessment before further diagnostic imaging. Clinical rules have been developed and verified to help establish the diagnosis of DVT or PE; the best-known predictive model is the Wells criteria (**Table 27**).

## Measurement of D-Dimer

D-dimers, which are fragments of cross-linked fibrin (already formed into a mesh by action of factor XIII), are degraded from clot matrix by plasmin and released from thrombi soon after formation. Each fragment has two D units and one E unit in a linkage that cannot be further broken down by plasmin. The plasma concentration of D-dimers is usually elevated in patients with DVT or PE. The levels of D-dimer reflect the rate of fibrinolytic activity on preexisting thrombi but not necessarily the rate of thrombus formation. Although D-dimer levels are more specific than fibrin degradation products, D-dimer levels can still be elevated in various inflammatory conditions and other diseases; therefore, they are not specific enough to confirm the presence of VTE. However, highly precise D-dimer assays (such as those based on immunoassays) are sensitive for thrombosis and can be useful clinically to rule out VTE in some situations. In clinically stable patients (for example, outpatients without hemodynamic compromise) with a low clinical likelihood of VTE, a normal D-dimer value is correlated with an excellent outcome without further workup or treatment for

### TABLE 26 Symptoms and Signs of Pulmonary Embolism

| Finding | Sensitivity (%) | Specificity (%) |
| --- | --- | --- |
| Dyspnea | 73-84 | 28-51 |
| Pleuritic chest pain | 44-66 | 41-70 |
| Cough | 11-37 | 64-85 |
| Leg swelling and pain | 17-28 | 76-91 |
| Hemoptysis | 9-13 | 92-95 |
| Wheezing | 9 | 89 |
| Tachypnea (respiration rate ≥20/min) | 70 | 32 |
| Tachycardia (heart rate ≥100/min) | 24-30 | 77 |
| Crackles | 18-51 | 60-74 |
| Fever (temperature >38.5 °C [101.3 °F]) | 7 | 79-88 |
| Lower extremity edema | 11 | 89-92 |
| Cyanosis | 1-16 | 85-98 |
| $S_4$ | 24 | 86 |
| Loud $P_2$ | 23 | 87 |

### TABLE 27 The Simplified Wells Scoring System for Pulmonary Embolism

| Findings | Score[a] |
| --- | --- |
| Clinical signs/symptoms of deep venous thrombosis (minimum of leg swelling and pain with palpation of the deep veins of the leg) | 3.0 |
| No alternative diagnosis likely or more likely than pulmonary emboli | 3.0 |
| Heart rate >100/min | 1.5 |
| Immobilization or surgery in the past 4 weeks | 1.5 |
| Previous history of deep venous thrombosis or pulmonary emboli | 1.5 |
| Hemoptysis | 1.0 |
| Cancer actively treated within the last 6 months | 1.0 |

[a]Summed probability scores are as follows: low, <2; moderate, 2-6; high, >6.

PE. Whether these findings reflect the absence or the tolerance of thromboembolic disease in this stable population is unknown. However, in patients with a higher clinical likelihood of VTE or clinical instability, D-dimer results should not be used to confirm or exclude the diagnosis.

### Noninvasive Chest Imaging

PE is commonly diagnosed with either contrast-enhanced chest CT scan with specific protocols to detect PE (CT angiography) or with a ventilation/perfusion (V/Q) scintigraphic scan. Either test can confirm the diagnosis of PE, but the CT scan is becoming more widely used. CT findings of filling defects within the segmental or larger pulmonary arteries are specific for PE. Likewise, V/Q scans that show two or more large subsegmental or larger perfusion defects that are not matched by corresponding ventilation defects on a chest radiograph (high probability findings) are highly specific for PE (although this finding can rarely be mimicked by other unusual defects of the pulmonary arteries). A V/Q scan showing normal perfusion reliably rules out PE. Neither minimally abnormal V/Q scans nor normal CT scans can reliably detect smaller defects when compared with conventional pulmonary angiography. However, follow-up studies have shown that it is safe to withhold treatment and further PE workup in clinically stable patients in whom DVT has been ruled out by either method. It is not known whether the good outcome observed in these otherwise stable patients reflects the absence or the tolerance of small emboli. In patients who are unstable or in whom there is a high clinical suspicion for PE, clinical judgment should be used to determine the necessity of pursuing the diagnosis further.

Contrast-enhanced helical CT scanning requires the infusion of radiocontrast media of the same type and dose as used for pulmonary angiography; the most common serious complications of both procedures (radiocontrast medium–induced nephropathy and allergic reactions) are caused by the use of intravenous radiocontrast agents. In addition, for the CT scan to be optimally accurate, the peripherally infused radiocontrast medium must fill the lumen of the pulmonary arteries as the chest is being imaged, which allows the emboli to be visualized as an intra-arterial defect. Certain areas, such as the hila, are prone to false-positive results, and diagnosing emboli in these areas should be done with special care. CT scans are inaccurate in imaging emboli in subsegmental pulmonary arteries, the very situation in which V/Q scans are also the most limited. Advanced helical CT scanning techniques, such as multihead CT detectors, increase sensitivity but also may entail significant doses of radiation.

As an initial test for PE, either contrast-enhanced CT scanning or V/Q scanning is appropriate. Either one can be used reliably to diagnose large PE. However, only a totally normal perfusion scan virtually excludes PE (the only exception is a nonoccluding central saddle embolism that allows reduced but substantially equal flow to all the distal areas of both lungs). CT scans that do not disclose intraluminal filling defects or V/Q scans with matched or small defects should be considered nondiagnostic, and the decision about whether to pursue further workup should be based on a consideration of the individual test results, in combination with the clinical assessment and additional diagnostic information. Because a V/Q scan detects alterations in pulmonary blood flow rather than providing a direct image of a clot, there are many more indeterminate studies because many cardiopulmonary diseases affect pulmonary blood flow. However, V/Q scans have several favorable characteristics. There is no radiocontrast agent load; therefore, renal failure and low perfusion states are not a contraindication. Also, V/Q scans are less affected by obesity than contrast-enhanced CT.

### Pulmonary Angiography

In high-risk patients in whom there is a very high clinical suspicion for PE, negative CT scan results or low- or indeterminate-probability V/Q scans may not provide sufficient data to allow therapy to be withheld. Even segmental or smaller defects that may be missed on scanning have been associated with a significant PE mortality rate in patients with poor cardiopulmonary reserve. Therefore, if the clinical suspicion for PE remains strong or the patient is unstable, a negative CT scan and nondiagnostic V/Q scan should be followed up with pulmonary angiography.

Pulmonary angiography is a sensitive and safe method for diagnosing PE. However, it is uncomfortable for the patient, is expensive, requires highly skilled personnel, and exposes the patient to radiocontrast media. However, it is a valuable test for PE when clinical circumstances require a high degree of accuracy. As contrast-enhanced CT improves and its resolution approaches that of pulmonary angiography, it is likely that fewer angiographic studies will be done for diagnosis of PE. In addition, if the contrast-enhanced CT is done as the first diagnostic study, the decision to follow the CT scan with pulmonary angiography rapidly exposes the patient to a second load of radiocontrast media.

## Treatment

### Treatment of the Hemodynamically Stable Patient with Pulmonary Embolism

If the hemodynamic and gas-exchange effects of PE are not severe, it can be treated with the same regimens used for proximal vein DVT; unfractionated heparin, LMWH, and fondaparinux are all safe and effective (**Table 28**).

All of these drugs, including heparin, are effective and safe for VTE treatment when given subcutaneously in a weight-adjusted dose without adjustment by laboratory monitoring. However, unfractionated heparin is commonly administered by a continuous intravenous infusion, which generally requires hospitalization and dose adjustment based on activated partial thromboplastin time values. Therefore, intravenous heparin therapy is more complicated and costly

**TABLE 28** Treatment of Acute Deep Venous Thrombosis and Pulmonary Embolism

| Drug | Dose | Route | Frequency |
|---|---|---|---|
| Heparin (unfractionated) | 80 units/kg bolus, then 18 units/kg/hour | Intravenous | Continuous |
| Heparin (unfractionated) | 250 units/kg | Subcutaneous | Every 12 hours |
| Dalteparin | 200 units/kg | Subcutaneous | Every 24 hours |
| Enoxaparin | 1.0 mg/kg or 1.5 mg/kg | Subcutaneous Subcutaneous | Every 12 hours Every 24 hours |
| Tinzaparin | 175 units/kg | Subcutaneous | Every 24 hours |
| Fondaparinux | 5.0 mg (BW <50 kg [110 lb]) 7.5 mg (BW 50-100 kg [110-220 lb]) 10.0 mg (BW >100 kg [220 lb]) | Subcutaneous | Every 24 hours |

BW = patient body weight.

than subcutaneous treatment with heparin, LMWH, or fondaparinux. LMWH and fondaparinux are metabolized in the kidney, and if they are used in patients with renal impairment, therapy must be monitored and dosage adjusted by measuring plasma anti-Xa levels, thereby increasing the cost of therapy.

Warfarin does not provide sufficient acute antithrombotic effects to be useful in the immediate treatment of acute DVT or PE, but is useful in maintenance therapy. Direct thrombin inhibitors, such as lepirudin and argatroban, have been used to treat DVT and PE, but because of their uncertain safety and efficacy, they are generally used only in patients with heparin-induced thrombocytopenia and thrombosis or other contraindications to the use of heparin and LMWH.

### Treatment of Unstable Pulmonary Embolism
Hemodynamic instability from PE is a result of the acutely elevated pulmonary arterial resistance, which may lead to right ventricular strain, ischemia, and catastrophic cardiac dysfunction. The high mortality rate in these patients justifies a more intensive approach to anticoagulation. However, because unstable PE is generally a rapidly developing event that does not lend itself to randomized clinical trials, treatment recommendations for unstable PE are based on expert judgment and extrapolation from other clinical situations.

The initial heparin dosage for unstable PE is controversial. Some clinicians prefer high-dose heparin infusions during the first 24 hours after a massive embolic event because of the accelerated generation of thrombin platelet factor IV, which opposes the antithrombin effect of unfractionated heparin and LMWH. However, no clinical studies have compared standard-dose to higher-dose unfractionated heparin or to LMWH in unstable patients with PE.

Cardiopulmonary support may be indicated in patients with PE, including administration of oxygen in those with arterial hypoxemia. Careful fluid loading may increase right atrial and right ventricular end-diastolic pressure and improve function. However, overloading the right ventricle may

decrease right coronary perfusion pressure, thereby worsening right ventricular function. Systemic vasoconstrictive agents, such as norepinephrine, may raise the mean arterial pressure (a determinant of right coronary flow) during PE-associated shock.

Most deaths from PE are sudden deaths, and, therefore, the prognosis is generally good if the diagnosis is made and treatment is started. However, many patients die of PE in the first 2 weeks after presentation. During this time, almost 5% of DVTs re-embolize, even when treated. Stable patients usually tolerate these incidental emboli, but hemodynamically compromised patients may not. In patients with unstable PE, insertion of an inferior vena cava filter decreases the short-term re-embolization rate by nearly 80%. Although some filters may increase the long-term risk of symptomatic DVT recurrence, they may be lifesaving during unstable PE. Newer filters are removable and may offer the same short-term protection with fewer long-term complications.

The role of thrombolytic therapy in PE is unclear. There are no clinical trials comparing thrombolytic agents with other forms of therapy for massive PE, and, therefore, management decisions must be made by inference from studies in stable patients. The Urokinase in Pulmonary Embolism Trial reported a short-term improvement in cardiac output and pulmonary pressure with thrombolytic therapy but no improvement in morbidity or mortality, as well as increased bleeding. Furthermore, after 1 week, the perfusion recovery and hemodynamics in the patients given heparin without thrombolytic therapy were identical to those of the patients given thrombolytic therapy.

Although rapid (but not necessarily more complete) clot resolution may not affect the outcome of stable patients with PE, those with hemodynamically unstable PE might benefit from rapid relief of right ventricular strain. The mortality rate from PE increases greatly in patients who develop hypotension and shock and require cardiopulmonary resuscitation; the acute beneficial hemodynamic benefits of thrombolytic therapy may have a much greater benefit for these patients. In general, patients with persistent shock and those requiring ongoing norepinephrine therapy should be considered for treatment with thrombolytic agents unless the patient is at high risk for bleeding.

Whether patients with submassive pulmonary embolism (that is, with evidence of right ventricular strain on echocardiography but no hemodynamic instability) benefit from thrombolytic therapy in addition to heparin is controversial. Thrombolytic therapy has not been shown to improve survival rates or to reduce rates of respiratory failure or shock in those patients. In general, thrombolytic therapy is not used for these patients. One approach is to assess the legs and to place a removable inferior vena cava filter if residual clot is found, because even a small recurrent clot can cause death if there is little reserve. Thrombolytic agents have been used for treating combined submassive PE and substantial residual clot, but there is no good evidence to support such therapy.

Thrombolytic therapy is costly and is associated with significant risks. A review of clinical trials disclosed a 2.1% rate of intracranial hemorrhage and 1.6% rate of fatal intracranial hemorrhage when thrombolytic agents were used for thromboembolic disease. Therefore, thrombolytic therapy should likely be reserved for management of patients with persistent hypotension due to PE who have no contraindications. However, patient selection is difficult, and these agents should be administered only by physicians experienced in their use.

Acute pulmonary embolectomy is rarely warranted because medical therapy is so successful, patient selection is so difficult, and the results of acute embolectomy are so variable. However, if experienced surgeons are available, embolectomy can be lifesaving in patients with confirmed massive embolism who fail to respond to medical therapy.

The use of echocardiography in pulmonary embolism is controversial. Although echocardiographic findings consistent with right heart strain are associated with worse outcomes, there are no clinical data to determine how echocardiographic findings would alter the risk/benefit ratios of any of the interventions mentioned above. Some experts recommend echocardiography in all patients with PE to help identify those in whom additional interventions may become necessary. Others recommend that additional interventions be limited to those with more clinical evidence of cardiopulmonary deterioration. Therefore, the decision to perform echocardiography and the use of the results in management decisions must be based on individualized clinical judgment.

## Prognosis and Follow-up

During the first 5 or so days of therapy for PE, heparin, LMWH, or fondaparinux is necessary because these drugs prevent propagation of thromboemboli; warfarin is used to prevent recurrence. Warfarin is initiated simultaneously with heparin, and both therapies are overlapped for a minimum of 4 to 5 days and until the INR has reached the therapeutic range for two measurements taken 24 hours apart.

The duration of long-term therapy should be tailored to the clinical situation. In most patients with acute PE, much of their perfusion defects and right ventricular dysfunction resolves after a few weeks of anticoagulant therapy. However, therapy should usually be continued for at least 3 months; substantially shorter regimens increase the recurrence rate. There is some evidence to suggest that patients who had DVT or PE postoperatively may do just as well with 4 weeks of therapy, but that finding has not been proved directly in clinical trials. The duration of follow-up anticoagulation necessary for patients with transient risk factors is controversial, but anticoagulation should probably continue at least until the causative risk factors have resolved.

Patients with unresolved risk factors for thromboembolism and who are therefore at high risk of recurrence may require prolonged (possibly lifelong) anticoagulation. Persistent risk factors may reflect such chronic conditions as immobility, heart failure, persistent venous obstruction, or even an unrecognized hypercoagulable state. Perhaps for this reason, patients with "unprovoked" VTE have high rates of recurrence and may require longer-term anticoagulation. Some studies suggest that patients with unprovoked PE who have elevated serum D-dimer levels several weeks after anticoagulation has been stopped (whatever the duration of therapy) have a higher risk of recurrence. Those patients may benefit from prolonged anticoagulation.

**KEY POINTS**

- The risk factors for venous thromboembolism consist of disorders associated with three basic pathogenetic conditions: venous stasis, vascular (endothelial) damage, and hypercoagulability.

- In clinically stable patients with a low clinical likelihood of venous thromboembolism, a normal serum D-dimer can exclude pulmonary embolism; in patients with a higher clinical likelihood of venous thromboembolism or clinical instability, D-dimer results cannot confirm or exclude the diagnosis.

- Heparin, low-molecular-weight heparin, and fondaparinux are safe and effective for treatment of stable venous thromboembolism when given subcutaneously in a weight-adjusted dose without adjustment by laboratory monitoring.

- Thrombolytic therapy should probably be limited to unstable patients with pulmonary embolism who have persistent shock and patients requiring ongoing norepinephrine therapy unless the patient is at high risk for bleeding.

- Patients who have had a pulmonary embolism and have unresolved risk factors for thromboembolism are at high risk of recurrence and may require prolonged (possibly lifelong) anticoagulation.

# Pulmonary Hypertension

Pulmonary hypertension comprises a broad range of disorders in which the resistance to blood flow through the pulmonary vasculature increases. The increased pulmonary vascular resistance causes a rise in pulmonary arterial pressures, but the more important pathophysiologic effect is hemodynamic deterioration due to right ventricular overload. At first, mild increases in pulmonary vascular resistance may be asymptomatic or cause only mild dyspnea on exertion. As the disease progresses, resistance increases further, and the right ventricle cannot maintain normal flow through the pulmonary arteries. Exercise tolerance decreases and may be accompanied by hemodynamic symptoms such as dizziness during exercise. In patients with advanced disease, the right ventricle is in a state of constant overload and dysfunction. Affected patients are dyspneic at rest and may have syncopal episodes during exercise or with peripheral vasodilation as cardiac output becomes unstable.

Pulmonary hypertension is categorized by possible causes, including their associated conditions (**Table 29** and **Table 30**). This method of categorization may also help determine the prognosis and appropriate therapies.

The diagnostic approach often begins with determining whether the obstruction occurs within specific macroscopic pulmonary arteries (for example, chronic thromboembolic pulmonary hypertension), diffusely within smaller branches of the pulmonary artery (for example, idiopathic pulmonary arterial hypertension [PAH]), or as a result of pulmonary venous congestion (for example, left ventricular failure). In addition, patients with extensive parenchymal lung disease often have pulmonary hypertension in the advanced stages of

their disease as the capillary bed is obliterated, dissolved, or aggravated by hypoxic vasoconstriction of remaining vessels.

## Chronic Thromboembolic Pulmonary Hypertension

After an acute PE, many patients continue to have some persistent, but clinically unimportant, perfusion defects. In about 1% to 2% of patients, however, the thromboemboli within the pulmonary arteries become remodeled into large occlusive scars, causing chronic thromboembolic pulmonary hypertension (CTEPH). The vessel wall becomes massively thickened and the lumen progressively narrowed or obliterated.

| TABLE 29 Classification of Pulmonary Arterial Hypertension |
|---|
| Idiopathic pulmonary arterial hypertension |
| Familial pulmonary arterial hypertension |
| Pulmonary arterial hypertension associated with: |
|    Collagen vascular disease |
|    Congenital systemic-to-pulmonary shunts (large, small, repaired, unrepaired) |
|    Portal hypertension |
|    HIV infection |
|    Drugs and toxins |
|    Other (glycogen storage disease, Gaucher disease, hereditary hemorrhagic telangiectasia, hemoglobinopathies, myeloproliferative disorders, splenectomy) |
| Associated with significant venous or capillary involvement: |
|    Pulmonary veno-occlusive disease |
|    Pulmonary capillary hemangiomatosis |

| TABLE 30 Classification of Pulmonary Hypertension from Other Causes |
|---|
| **Pulmonary Venous Hypertension** |
| Left-sided atrial or ventricular heart disease |
| Left-sided valvular heart disease |
| **Pulmonary Hypertension Associated with Other Lung Disease or Hypoxia** |
| Chronic obstructive pulmonary disease |
| Interstitial lung disease |
| Sleep-disordered breathing |
| Alveolar hypoventilation disorders |
| Chronic exposure to high altitude |
| **Pulmonary Hypertension Due to Thrombotic and/or Embolic Disease** |
| Thromboembolic obstruction of proximal pulmonary arteries |
| Thromboembolic obstruction of distal pulmonary arteries |
| Pulmonary embolism (tumor, parasites, foreign material) |
| **Miscellaneous** |
| Sarcoidosis, pulmonary Langerhans cell histiocytosis, lymphangioleiomyomatosis, compression of pulmonary vessels (lymphadenopathy, tumor, fibrosing mediastinitis) |

Occlusion of the proximal pulmonary vascular bed may cause elevation of the pulmonary vascular resistance, cor pulmonale, and right ventricular dysfunction. Untreated, the disorder may be progressive and fatal.

The reason why some patients with PE develop CTEPH is unclear. Most patients who develop CTEPH were previously diagnosed with acute PE or DVT, but their initial presentations appear, in retrospect, indistinguishable from those of patients whose acute clots resolve.

No modality of treatment of the initial acute PE has been shown to protect against CTEPH. However, posttreatment V/Q scans may detect patients prone to develop chronic disease, especially if performed in patients whose cardiopulmonary function does not return to normal. In patients with abnormal scans, echocardiography can clarify the condition of the right ventricle and, by inference, of the pulmonary vasculature.

### Diagnosis and Treatment

Patients with CTEPH often present with unexplained progressively worsening dyspnea in the absence of (or out of proportion to) airway or pulmonary parenchymal disease. The predisposing acute PE may have been asymptomatic or undiagnosed, and therefore only about 50% of patients have a history of clinically detected PE.

A V/Q scan invariably shows perfusion defects, although the size of the defects frequently underestimates the extent of disease. This finding can help distinguish CTEPH from small-vessel PAH, in which perfusion defects on V/Q scan are minimal. Echocardiography often shows right ventricular hypertrophy, a sign of advanced disease. Although measurement of the pulmonary artery pressure may be imprecise, some indication of right ventricular dysfunction usually can be observed.

Pulmonary angiography can confirm the diagnosis and determine whether the large-vessel obstruction is amenable to surgical endarterectomy. In CTEPH, the embolic material is organized into the arterial wall, and angiography shows gradual tapering of the lumen, with webs and luminal irregularities being evidence of ineffectual attempts at recanalization.

The definitive treatment of CTEPH is pulmonary thromboendarterectomy. The procedure is best done in specialized centers with extensive experience managing this disease and can result in significant improvement in functional status and quality of life.

## Pulmonary Arterial Hypertension

PAH refers to diseases that cause elevated resistance in the small pulmonary arteries or arterioles. The mortality rate of untreated PAH is very high, and timely diagnosis is a critical part of the management. The classic form of the disease is called idiopathic PAH to distinguish it from familial PAH and PAH linked to other disorders. These disorders have in common the presence of varying degrees of vasoconstriction of the small pulmonary arteries, proliferation of cellular elements within the arterial wall, and eventual obliteration of the vascular lumen. As the cross-sectional area of the pulmonary arteries decreases, normal dilation and recruitment of vessels during exercise is no longer possible. Pulmonary artery pressure rises during exercise but may initially cause few symptoms as the right ventricle enlarges to maintain flow. With further obstruction, the right ventricle cannot maintain output during exercise, causing progressive dyspnea and dizziness during exertion. In its advanced stages, PAH causes right ventricular failure even at rest, manifested as dyspnea, dizziness, and, in severely affected patients, syncope. The right ventricle progressively fails, causing severe debilitation and, if untreated, death.

Familial PAH is transmitted in an autosomal dominant pattern with variable penetrance; many patients with familial PAH have a mutation in the bone morphogenic protein receptor 2 gene (*BMPR2*). The sporadic form is far more common, accounting for about 93% of cases. PAH may also be associated with HIV infection, connective tissue disease, cirrhosis with portal hypertension, congenital systemic-pulmonary-cardiac shunts, and certain drugs (including the appetite suppressant fenfluramine, which was withdrawn from the market in 1997).

### Diagnosis and Evaluation

PAH should be distinguished from secondary forms of pulmonary hypertension, in which the elevated pulmonary vascular resistance is a result of parenchymal damage, chronic or nocturnal hypoxia, or pulmonary venous disease. The clinical presentation of idiopathic PAH is similar to that of other forms of pulmonary hypertension. The symptoms tend to be nonspecific, including progressively worsening dyspnea and dizziness, although these symptoms usually occur in the absence of (or out of proportion to) pulmonary disease or left-sided heart disease. Physical examination may disclose signs of elevated pulmonary artery pressure and right ventricular strain (loud $P_2$, fixed split $S_2$, tricuspid regurgitation, elevated jugular venous distention). Chest radiographs may show enlarged pulmonary arteries, right atrium, and right ventricle. Echocardiography in more advanced stages may show ventricular hypertrophy. Echocardiography may give reasonable estimates of pulmonary artery pressure and cardiac output, although it is not sensitive enough to rule out PAH or quantify its severity. Echocardiography is also useful to rule out left-sided heart disease and congenital heart disease. The V/Q scan in PAH is either normal or shows a scattered, "moth eaten" perfusion pattern in the peripheral lung zones. Additional testing to rule out other causes of pulmonary hypertension includes pulmonary function tests, polysomnography (if sleep-disordered breathing is suspected), liver chemistry tests, and serologic tests for HIV infection or connective tissue disease.

It is often recommended that patients be referred to specialized centers for confirmation of the diagnosis and for further management. Pulmonary artery catheterization is a key diagnostic test that may be combined with pulmonary angiography if the V/Q scan suggests large-vessel obstruction. Although pulmonary artery catheterization is invasive, it is safely and routinely performed in the evaluation of pulmonary hypertension in order to determine pulmonary artery pressure, cardiac output, and right atrial pressure. In addition, it allows an immediate assessment of the pulmonary vascular response to vasodilator medications, such as inhaled nitric oxide, prostacyclin, or adenosine.

### Treatment

The treatment of pulmonary hypertension has improved markedly over the past two decades; however, the treatments are complicated and require a significant amount of logistical support. Therefore, pulmonary hypertension is often treated in specialized referral centers.

*Prostacyclin Analogues*
Prostacyclin is a potent vasodilator of the pulmonary arteries, and prostacyclin analogues (epoprostenol, treprostinil, and iloprost) may provide immediate symptomatic improvement in patients with severe PAH. These agents may have other disease-modifying properties, such as improvement of the vascular remodeling processes and enhancement of right atrial and ventricular function. Epoprostenol, which is given intravenously, has been shown to improve exercise capacity, quality of life, and survival in patients with PAH and is considered first-line therapy for patients with severe (New York Heart Association [NYHA] functional class IV) idiopathic PAH and severe systemic sclerosis–associated PAH. Treprostinil, which is given subcutaneously three or four times daily, and iloprost, which is inhaled six to ten times daily, are more convenient for the patient and may be used in less severe forms of the disease.

*Endothelin-1 Receptor Antagonists*
Endothelin-1 is a potent vasoconstrictor that has been implicated in the development and progression of PAH. The endothelin receptor antagonists bosentan and ambrisentan may reverse some of the hemodynamic effects of PAH. They are used most commonly in moderate PAH and have been shown to improve cardiac index, pulmonary vascular resistance, respiratory comfort, functional class, and survival. The most clinical experience has been with bosentan, which has shown significant survival advantage when compared with historical survival data. Annually, about 10% of patients treated with bosentan develop elevated aminotransferase levels, which are sufficient to require cessation of therapy in 3% of patients. Ambrisentan, a newer agent, has a much lower rate of aminotransferase elevation, but there is not as much clinical experience with this drug in PAH.

*Sildenafil*
Pulmonary vascular smooth muscle dilatation is mediated by cyclic guanosine 3′-5′monophosphate (cGMP), which is induced by nitric oxide and degraded by phosphodiesterases. Sildenafil, a phosphodiesterase inhibitor, has been found to be useful in PAH. In patients with milder PAH, sildenafil can improve exercise performance, symptoms, and hemodynamics.

*Anticoagulants*
Anticoagulation is used as an adjunct to therapy in many forms of pulmonary hypertension. Pathologic specimens of patients with pulmonary hypertension often disclose in situ thrombosis of the pulmonary vascular bed. Although anticoagulation for PAH has not been tested in large randomized clinical trials, retrospective data and a prospective trial referencing historical controls suggest that anticoagulation is associated with improved survival, especially in patients with nonuniform blood flow on perfusion scans.

*Calcium Channel Blockers*
Although early studies of calcium channel blockers suggested that they may be of benefit in many patients with PAH, only about 5% of patients have any long-term response. Because of the availability of safer and more effective medications, calcium channel blockade is no longer recommended as first-line therapy for patients with PAH.

*Adjunctive Medical Treatments*
Supplemental oxygen is helpful for patients with PAH who have even mild degrees of hypoxemia, reversing the hypoxic vasoconstriction. Diuretics may be helpful in patients with right ventricular overload, provided the ventricular overdistention is not reversed too rapidly, thus resulting in hypotension. Digoxin is sometimes used in advanced right ventricular failure, although it is not as validated in clinical trials and its potential adverse effects require close monitoring.

*Adjunctive Surgical Treatments*
Although medical therapy for PAH is improving, patients with severe advanced disease may require lung transplantation. In some patients, right ventricular failure may be so severe that atrial septostomy is required to improve hemodynamics until transplantation is possible. Although randomized controlled trials have not been performed, one small case series showed modest improvement in hemodynamics and clinical performance after percutaneous atrial septostomy in selected patients with severe pulmonary hypertension.

## Prognosis and Follow-up

Despite improvements in therapy for PAH, the mortality rate is still high. Management is often performed in centers with special expertise in the diagnosis and treatment of PAH. Patients must be followed carefully with clinical indicators, such as the maximum distance walked in 6 minutes, which have correlated with survival in clinical studies. Patients who become severely compromised despite medical therapy may require lung transplantation. Factors associated with poor prognosis in idiopathic PAH include severe symptoms (advanced NYHA functional class), poor exercise tolerance, worsened hemodynamics (elevated mean right atrial pressure and pulmonary artery pressure, reduced cardiac index), and the development of a pericardial effusion.

**KEY POINTS**

- In up to 2% of patients who have had a pulmonary embolism, the thromboemboli within the pulmonary arteries become remodeled into large occlusive scars, causing chronic thromboembolic pulmonary hypertension.

- Pulmonary angiography can diagnose chronic thromboembolic pulmonary hypertension and determine whether the large-vessel obstruction is amenable to surgical endarterectomy.

- Pulmonary arterial hypertension is characterized by the presence of vasoconstriction of the small pulmonary arteries, proliferation of cellular elements within the arterial wall, and eventual obliteration of the vascular lumen.

- Pulmonary arterial hypertension should be distinguished from secondary forms of pulmonary hypertension, in which the elevated pulmonary vascular resistance is a result of parenchymal damage, chronic or nocturnal hypoxia, or pulmonary venous disease.

- The prostacyclin analogues epoprostenol, treprostinil, and iloprost may provide immediate symptomatic improvement in patients with severe pulmonary arterial hypertension; the endothelin receptor antagonists bosentan and ambrisentan may reverse some of the hemodynamic effects of moderate pulmonary arterial hypertension.

- Sildenafil can improve exercise performance, symptoms, and hemodynamics in patients with mild pulmonary arterial hypertension.

**Bibliography**

Anderson, D R, Kahn SR, Rodger MA, et al. Computed tomographic pulmonary angiography vs ventilation-perfusion lung scanning in patients with suspected pulmonary embolism: a randomized controlled trial. JAMA. 2007;298(23):2743-2753. [PMID: 18165667]

Badesch DB, Abman SH, Ahearn GS, et al. Medical therapy for pulmonary arterial hypertension: ACCP evidence-based clinical practice guidelines. Chest. 2004;126(1 Suppl):35S-62S. [PMID: 15249494]

Büller HR, Agnelli G, Hull RD, et al. Antithrombotic therapy for venous thromboembolic disease: the Seventh ACCP Conference on Antithrombotic and Thrombolytic Therapy. Chest. 2004;126(3 Suppl):401S-428S. [PMID: 15383479]

Büller HR, Davidson BL, Decousus H, et al. Subcutaneous fondaparinux versus intravenous unfractionated heparin in the initial treatment of pulmonary embolism [erratum in N Engl J Med. 2004;350(4):423]. N Engl J Med. 2003;349(18):1695-1702. [PMID: 14585937]

Fedullo PF, Auger WR, Kerr KM, Rubin LJ. Chronic thromboembolic pulmonary hypertension. N Engl J Med. 2001;345(20):1465-1472. [PMID: 11794196]

Geerts WH, Pineo GF, Heit JA, et al. Prevention of venous thromboembolism: the Seventh ACCP Conference on Antithrombotic and Thrombolytic Therapy. Chest. 2004;126(3 Suppl):338S-400S. [PMID: 15383478]

Kearon C, Ginsberg JS, Julian JA, et al; Fixed-Dose Heparin (FIDO) Investigators. Comparison of fixed-dose weight-adjusted unfractionated heparin and low-molecular-weight heparin for acute treatment of venous thromboembolism. JAMA. 2006;296(8):935-942. [PMID: 16926353]

McLaughlin VV, Presberg KW, Doyle RL, et al; American College of Chest Physicians. Prognosis of pulmonary arterial hypertension: ACCP evidence-based clinical practice guidelines. Chest. 2004;126(1 Suppl):78S-92S. [PMID: 15249497]

Stein, P D, Fowler SE, Goodman LR, et al; PIOPED II Investigators. Multidetector computed tomography for acute pulmonary embolism. N Engl J Med. 2006;354(22):2317-2327. [PMID: 16738268]

# Pulmonary Neoplastic Disease

## Evaluation of a Pulmonary Nodule

Evaluation of a pulmonary nodule must balance the need to detect and treat a malignancy quickly and the desire to avoid invasive procedures for a benign nodule. A solitary pulmonary nodule is defined as a nodular opacity that is up to 3 cm in diameter and surrounded by normal lung and not associated with lymphadenopathy. Lesions larger than 3 cm are considered lung masses. CT screening studies have shown that when a cancer is detected, other smaller benign nodules are usually present. When one predominant 1-cm or larger nodule and one or more tiny nodules are present, the larger nodule should be considered separately. The Fleischner Society for Thoracic Imaging and Diagnosis has published recommendations for the need and frequency of follow-up for nodules of various sizes (**Table 31**). No follow-up is recommended for nodules that are smaller than 4 mm in never-smokers with no other known risk factors for malignancy (history of a first-degree relative with lung cancer or significant radon or asbestos exposure).

The likelihood that a nodule is malignant depends on such factors as its size and surface characteristics and the patient's age, smoking history, and history of previous malignancy. The size of the nodule is perhaps the most important feature. Screening studies have shown that more than 98% of nodules smaller that 8 mm and the majority of nodules smaller than 2 cm are benign, whereas the majority of nodules larger than 2 to 3 cm are malignant. CT series have also shown that 93% to 95% of noncalcified lung masses larger than 3 cm are malignant (excluding those with documented size stability). Nodules with smooth borders are usually benign; nodules with spiculated borders have a high likelihood of being malignant (**Figure 9**). A history of smoking is the greatest single recognized risk for lung cancer. The risk

**TABLE 31** Recommendations for Pulmonary Nodule Evaluation Based on Risk

| Nodule Size (mm) | Low Risk[a] Follow-up | High Risk[b] Follow-up |
|---|---|---|
| <4 | None | 12 months; if unchanged, stop |
| 4-6 | 12 months; if unchanged, stop | 6-12 months; if unchanged, 18-24 months |
| 6-8 | 6-12 months; if unchanged, 18-24 months | 3-6 months; if unchanged, 9-12 and 24 months |
| >8 | Consider contrast CT study, PET scan, or biopsy; if followed, 3, 9, and 24 months | Same as low risk |

PET = positron emission tomography.

[a]Low risk: Never-smoker and no other risk factors.

[b]High risk: Current or former smoker or other risk factors.

Modified from MacMahon H, Austin JH, Gamsu G, et al; Fleischner Society. Guidelines for management of small pulmonary nodules detected on CT scans: a statement from the Fleischner Society. Radiology. 2005;237(2):395-400. [PMID: 16244247] Copyright 2005, Radiological Society of North America.

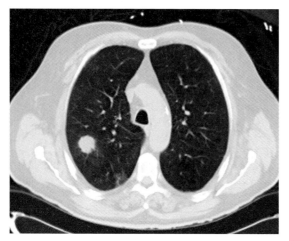

**FIGURE 9.**
**Spiculated pulmonary nodule.**
A 71-year-old former smoker had a nodule on a preoperative chest radiograph. CT scan showed a 24-mm spiculated nodule, which enhanced on PET scan without abnormal uptake elsewhere. The nodule was a non–small cell lung cancer at resection.

increases with the duration of smoking, number of cigarettes smoked per day, tar content of the cigarettes, and onset of smoking at an early age. Only 10% of all lung cancers occur in persons younger than 45 years and only 1% in patients younger than 35 years. The risk gradually increases at age 50 years, and the age-specific lung cancer incidence rates for both women and men are highest after age 70 years.

A history of malignancy is another indicator of possible cancer. The lung is a common site of metastasis from various tumors, the most common being tumors of the breast, head and neck, colon, thyroid gland, and kidney.

Review of previous chest imaging studies is important in the evaluation of nodules to determine whether a nodule is stable, is becoming larger, or is shrinking. In addition to previous chest radiographs and chest CT scans, abdominal imaging, which shows the lower aspect of the chest, and CT scans done to assess the coronary arteries, which show the lungs, should be reviewed.

A solid nodule that is stable on chest radiograph or CT scan for 2 years is considered benign. Growth of a nodule is a strong indicator that it may be malignant. The nodule doubling time for lung cancer varies from 1 month to 1 year, with most cancers doubling in 50 to 100 days. Benign nodules such as granulomas or round pneumonias may grow but usually at a slower or faster pace than a malignant nodule. Ground-glass nodules may represent low-grade adenocarcinomas (bronchioloalveolar cell carcinoma); these tumors may grow slowly or become partly solid, changes that may not be evident for several years of follow-up.

Contrast-enhanced CT scans and positron emission tomography (PET) imaging can help determine whether a nodule is malignant. A multicenter study reported that contrast-enhanced CT scans had a sensitivity of 98% and a specificity of 73% for detecting malignant neoplasms. The test involves administration of conventional, iodinated radiocontrast material at a specific rate, with thin-section CT assessments through the nodule at 1-minute intervals. Malignant neoplasms enhance significantly more (greater than 15 Hounsfield units) than do inactive granulomas and benign neoplasms. The overall negative predictive value is 96%, making contrast-enhanced CT perhaps the most appropriate initial test after an indeterminate nodule has been detected on chest radiograph; if the CT scan is negative (nonenhancing), it is highly likely that the nodule is benign.

PET and integrated CT-PET are becoming more widely available and also provide additional staging information in the setting of malignancy. PET scanning with 18F-fluorodeoxyglucose (18-FDG) has a sensitivity of about 95% and a specificity of 85% for identifying a nodule as malignant. However, PET scanning has a low sensitivity for small nodules and is usually not used for nodules smaller than 1 cm.

**KEY POINTS**

- No follow-up is indicated for pulmonary nodules that are smaller than 4 mm detected on CT scans in patients at low risk for lung cancer.

- Review of previous imaging studies is the first step in the evaluation of a pulmonary nodule.

- A pulmonary nodule that does not show enhancement on CT and/or PET scanning is likely benign.

# Screening for Lung Cancer

Lung cancer is usually diagnosed as a result of an evaluation in a symptomatic patient, and therefore many cancers are diagnosed at an advanced stage. No screening test for lung cancer in patients at risk for the disease, including chest radiography, sputum cytology, or chest CT, has been shown to reduce mortality from lung cancer.

The most sensitive imaging test for detecting pulmonary nodules is the CT scan. Conventional chest CT scanning requires radiation dosages and image-acquisition times that are impractical for screening purposes. The development of low-dose, fast-spiral CT greatly reduced the radiation dose and the scan time, making screening feasible. Prospective single-arm observational studies have shown that screening with spiral CT detects a large percentage of lung cancers at an early stage when the prognosis is favorable, but it is not clear whether the improved survival is true improvement or only apparent because of the inherent biases associated with screening. Using a validated prediction model, a recent evaluation of nonrandomized screening studies showed that CT detected three times as many cancers as predicted and that most of these cancers were early stage, but there was not a corresponding reduction in the expected number of advanced-stage cancers or in lung cancer deaths. Randomized controlled trials of CT screening for lung cancer are under way in the United States and Europe.

**KEY POINT**

- Screening for lung cancer has not been shown to reduce mortality from the disease in at-risk patients and is not currently recommended.

# Bronchogenic Carcinoma

Bronchogenic carcinoma, or lung cancer, is classified primarily into two types: small cell lung cancer (SCLC) and non–small cell lung cancer (NSCLC). This distinction is essential for staging, treatment, and prognosis. Approximately 95% of all cancers originating in the lung fall into these subtypes. NSCLC, which comprises more than 80% of all cases of lung cancer, consists of three histologic subtypes: adenocarcinoma, squamous cell carcinoma, and large cell carcinoma.

## Risk Factors

Approximately 90% of all cases of lung cancer are caused by cigarette smoking. The risk of a current smoker with a 40-pack-year smoking history is approximately 20 times that of someone who has never smoked. The most effective method for reducing one's risk is not to start smoking, or for those who do smoke, to quit. After a patient has quit smoking, the risk for lung cancer falls for about 15 years before it levels off and remains about twice that of a never-smoker. The presence of airway obstruction on pulmonary function testing is associated with about a four- to sixfold increase in the risk for lung cancer. The combination of smoking history and asbestos exposure increases the risk for lung cancer to as high as 50 to 90 times that of a never-smoker. The risk is also increased by passive smoking (second-hand smoke) and exposure to asbestos, radon, metals (arsenic, chromium, and nickel), ionizing radiation, and polycyclic aromatic hydrocarbons. Several studies have shown that the risk for lung cancer is increased by the presence of pulmonary fibrosis.

## Clinical Presentation

Most patients with lung cancer are symptomatic at the time of clinical presentation, which reflects the aggressive nature of the disease, the frequent absence of symptoms until the late stage, and the lack of a proven screening test. Symptoms may result from local effects of the tumor, regional or distant spread, or distant effects not related to metastases (paraneoplastic syndromes). Symptoms that stem from local effects of the tumor include cough, hemoptysis, chest pain, and dyspnea. Lung cancer can spread to essentially any body tissue, and the presenting symptom may be due to metastatic disease. Spread may occur by direct extension, by way of the lymphatic vessels, or hematogenously. The most frequent sites of distant metastasis are the liver, adrenal glands, bones, and brain.

Paraneoplastic syndromes occur in approximately 10% of patients with bronchogenic carcinoma (**Table 32**).

Lung cancer, usually SCLC, is the most common cancer to be associated with a paraneoplastic neurologic syndrome, and the neurologic symptoms typically precede the diagnosis of SCLC (**Figure 10**). Paraneoplastic neurologic syndromes are thought to be immune-mediated based on the identification of

**TABLE 32** Most Common Paraneoplastic Syndromes Associated with Lung Cancer

| System Syndrome | Paraneoplastic |
|---|---|
| Musculoskeletal | Hypertrophic osteoarthropathy<br>Digital clubbing<br>Polymyositis, dermatomyositis |
| Endocrinologic | Cushing syndrome<br>Syndrome of inappropriate antidiuretic hormone secretion<br>Hypercalcemia |
| Neurologic | Lambert-Eaton syndrome<br>Peripheral neuropathy<br>Encephalomyelitis |
| Vascular/hematologic | Thrombophlebitis<br>Nonbacterial thrombotic endocarditis<br>Thrombocytosis<br>Leukemoid reaction |
| Miscellaneous | Cachexia |

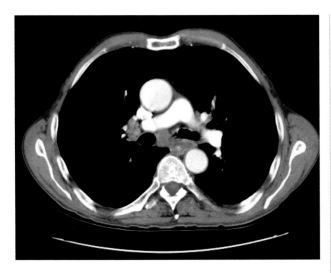

**FIGURE 10.**
**Small cell lung cancer with paraneoplasia.**
A 76-year-old current smoker presented with a 25-kg (55-lb) weight loss and persistent diarrhea. CT scan of the chest showed subcarinal lymphadenopathy, and limited-stage small cell lung cancer was diagnosed by transbronchial needle aspiration. A paraneoplastic antibody panel was positive for antineuronal nuclear antibody type I (ANNA-1) supporting that the gastrointestinal dysmotility was paraneoplastic.

various autoantibodies, most commonly antineuronal nuclear antibodies ANNA-1 (formerly anti-Hu), ANNA-2 (formerly anti-Ri), and ANNA-3. Purkinje cell cytoplasmic antibodies include PCA1 (formerly anti-Yo) and PCA2. The finding of a paraneoplastic autoantibody in a patient presenting with a neurologic syndrome should expedite the evaluation for malignancy (see MKSAP 15 Neurology).

## Diagnosis

The clinical evaluation for suspected lung cancer requires a careful history and physical examination, a complete blood count and serum chemistry panel that includes liver tests and measurement of serum calcium, and a chest CT scan through the adrenal glands. Further testing is directed by the presence of localized pain, lymphadenopathy, or specific laboratory findings. Measuring tumor markers in the serum is not recommended. Pulmonary function testing should be done in patients who are being considered for surgical resection. A quantitative ventilation/perfusion lung scan or cardiopulmonary exercise testing may assist in the selection of surgical candidates among patients who have marginal pulmonary function.

Diagnosis and staging of lung cancer should be done simultaneously. For example, in a patient with a 4-cm lung mass and mediastinal lymphadenopathy on CT, a transthoracic needle aspirate of the mass may provide a histologic diagnosis but not the stage; therefore a second procedure will be needed for staging the tumor.

In early-stage disease, whether a diagnosis is needed before surgery depends on the clinical circumstances. A 2-cm enlarging peripheral nodule in a former smoker with a CT-PET scan showing uptake only in the lesion may not require biopsy before resection; the likelihood of identifying a specific benign lesion in this setting is low, and a nonspecific positive result would still lead to a resection because of the high likelihood of malignancy. In addition, a false-negative result would delay therapy. In advanced disease, diagnosis and staging are best accomplished with a single invasive test or a noninvasive test such as sputum cytology. A cancer presenting as a large mass or central lesion is often easily diagnosed by bronchoscopy. The visual extent of the tumor at bronchoscopy can also guide surgical resection, or biopsy of involved tissue may establish lack of resectability.

## Staging

Staging for NCSLC is critical to determining treatment for patients with resectable disease and avoiding unnecessary surgery in patients with advanced disease. Staging of NSCLC is by the TNM system, and validated changes in this system have been implemented in 2009 (**Table 33**).

Staging of SCLC is by the Veterans Administration Lung Study Group designations of limited disease, which consists of disease confined to one hemithorax and therefore one radiation port, or extensive disease, which extends beyond one hemithorax. Performance status is measured by various methods including the Karnofsky performance status and Eastern Cooperative Oncology Group scale of performance.

### Role of Positron Emission Tomography

PET is based on the principle that cancer cells have a high rate of glycolysis compared with nonneoplastic cells. The PET tracer 18-FDG is taken up into cells, is metabolically trapped, and accumulates. False-positive PET scans have been reported with tuberculosis, fungal diseases, other infections, and sarcoidosis. Inflammatory disorders such as a rheumatoid nodule or cryptogenic organizing pneumonia may also cause false-positive PET scans. False-negative PET scans may occur with low-grade tumors, such as bronchoalveolar cell carcinoma, carcinoid tumor, and tumors less than 1 cm in diameter.

For evaluation of mediastinal lymph node metastasis, PET has a sensitivity and specificity of approximately 90% and 85%, respectively, which is better than CT staging of the mediastinum in which there is an approximately 30% to 40% rate of both false-positive and false-negative results. PET has also been shown to detect distant metastases in 10% to 20% of patients who were otherwise thought to be candidates for surgery. Because of the possibility of false-positive PET scans, a biopsy or other imaging proof of distant metastasis should be obtained before determining that a patient has unresectable disease. CT-PET integrates the CT and PET images and has been shown to have higher sensitivity and specificity

**TABLE 33** Stage Grouping for Non–Small Cell Lung Cancer

| Stage Subset | TNM | Descriptors |
|---|---|---|
| IA | T1a,bN0M0 | T1a: ≤2 cm, T1b: >2 cm ≤3 cm |
| IB | T2aN0M0 | T2a: >3 cm ≤7 cm |
| IIA | T1a,bN1M0<br>T2aN1M0<br>T2bN0M0 | T2b: >5 cm ≤7cm |
| IIB | T2bN1M0<br>T3N0M0 | T3: >7 cm, or invasion of chest wall or diaphragm or <2 cm from carina as before, or a metastatic nodule in the same lobe. |
| IIIA | T1,2N2M0<br>T3N1,2M0<br>T4N0,1M0 | T4: metastatic nodule on the ipsilateral side in a different lobe |
| IIIB | T4N2M0<br>Any TN3M0 | |
| IV | Any T, any N, M1a,b | M1a: metastatic nodule contralateral lobe, pleural effusion, or pleural nodules<br>M1b: distant metastasis |

Modified from Goldstraw P, Crowley J, Chansky K, et al; International Association for the Study of Lung Cancer International Staging Committee; Participating Institutions. The IASLC Lung Cancer Staging Project: proposals for the revision of the TNM stage groupings in the forthcoming (seventh) edition of the TNM Classification of malignant tumours [erratum in J Thorac Oncol. 2007;2(10):985]. J Thorac Oncol. 2007;2(8):706-714. [PMID: 17762336] Copyright 2007, Lippincott, Williams & Wilkins.

for assessing lung cancer stage than CT and PET done separately (**Figure 11**).

### Nonsurgical Mediastinal Staging

Transbronchial needle aspiration through a flexible bronchoscope may be used to sample the paratracheal, subcarinal, and hilar lymph nodes. Several recent series have shown improvement in yields with endobronchial ultrasonography when compared with blind bronchoscopic needle aspiration. Endobronchial ultrasonography is real-time imaging of the mediastinal nodes, which enables the needle to be seen in

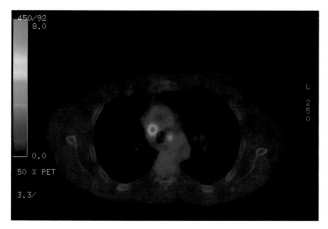

**FIGURE 11.**
**Mediastinal lymphadenopathy on CT-PET.**
A 50-year-old smoker presented with cough and had an obstructing squamous cell carcinoma of the right lower lobe. Staging PET scan showed uptake in both the normal-sized left and right paratracheal nodes. Ultrasound-guided bronchoscopic needle aspiration confirmed involvement of both the ipsilateral and the contralateral mediastinal nodes, thus making the tumor unresectable.

the node at the time of sampling. Yields of 90% for the paratracheal and subcarinal nodes have been reported. The addition of the procedure reduces the need for mediastinoscopy to stage N2 (ipsilateral mediastinal) and N3 (contralateral mediastinal) nodes. Sampling of mediastinal nodes by esophagoscopy with ultrasound-guided fine-needle aspiration is an alternative method for diagnosis and staging.

### Treatment

NSCLC in stages I or II should be treated with surgery whenever possible. If the postoperative predicted $FEV_1$ and DLCO are greater than 40%, surgery is generally well tolerated. Advances in surgical technique, use of limited resection, and postoperative care may provide the opportunity for surgical resection in patients with NSCLC previously thought not to be candidates for resection. A quantitative perfusion scan or an exercise assessment, specifically measuring aerobic capacity, may help determine whether surgery is appropriate in patients who have less than 40% predicted $FEV_1$ and DLCO. Operative mortality has been demonstrated to be lower in centers with the highest volumes of procedures and focused expertise. Patients with stage I disease who are not candidates for surgery or who refuse surgery may be candidates for radiation therapy.

Limited-stage SCLC is treated primarily with combination chemotherapy and radiation therapy, and extensive-stage disease is treated with chemotherapy alone. (For a further discussion of treatment of lung cancer, see MKSAP 15 Hematology and Oncology.)

### Endobronchial Therapy

In addition to its role in the diagnosis and staging of lung cancer, bronchoscopy is used to treat lung cancer by photodynamic therapy, laser therapy, and brachytherapy.

Bronchoscopy may also be used to treat large airway compromise from the cancer with placement of airway stents.

Photodynamic therapy appears to be most appropriate for radiographically occult superficial squamous cell tumors but is also used in other forms of NSCLC; laser therapy and brachytherapy may be used in either NSCLC or SCLC. Photodynamic therapy may also be used for palliation of extensive endobronchial disease.

Laser endobronchial resection should be considered in patients who do not respond to other treatment modalities, have an identifiable bronchial lumen, and show evidence of functioning lung tissue beyond the level of the endobronchial obstruction. Palliation of symptoms is often immediate, although temporary, and median survival after laser resection is approximately 6 months.

Brachytherapy is the intraluminal application of radiation and is generally used in patients who have previously received maximal doses of external-beam radiation. Brachytherapy is appropriate for both intrinsic and extrinsic malignant airway obstruction when functioning lung may be maintained or regained by achieving airway patency. Response rates range from 30% to 80%, with success more likely in patients who had a favorable response to previous external-beam radiation. Hemorrhage or fistula formations are the most frequent complications.

Bronchoscopic placement of prosthetic airway stents can palliate both intrinsic and extrinsic malignant obstruction. Silastic stents (which are removable), metal stents, and combinations of metal and silastic materials have been used. Symptomatic improvement after regaining airway patency may be immediate and impressive. Complications with the silastic stents include migration, mucus obstruction, and granulation tissue formation. Cough may be troublesome, even when dyspnea is improved. The metal stents become incorporated into the bronchial wall and may be irretrievable or removed with great difficulty, and the formation of granulation tissue is more prevalent. Malignant growth may occur through the wall of the uncovered metal stents or proximal or distal to either type of stent.

---

**KEY POINTS**

- After smoking cessation, the risk of lung cancer decreases for about 15 years and then it remains about twice that of a never-smoker.
- The three most important factors in the treatment and prognosis of lung cancer are cell type, cancer stage, and performance status of the patient.
- Diagnosis and staging of lung cancer are best done simultaneously.
- PET scanning (or integrated CT-PET) is cost effective for preoperative staging of patients with known or suspected non–small cell lung cancer.
- Treatment for stages I or II non–small cell lung cancer should be surgical resection whenever possible.
- Endoscopic ultrasound-guided needle aspiration through either the trachea or esophagus is an accurate alternative to mediastinoscopy for staging lung cancer.
- Bronchoscopic treatment of lung cancer includes brachytherapy, photodynamic therapy, and central airway debulking and stent placement.

## Other Pulmonary Neoplasms

### Carcinoid Tumors

Bronchial carcinoid tumors are low-grade malignant neoplasms that consist of neuroendocrine cells and account for 1% to 2% of all tumors of the lung. Patients may present with hemoptysis, have evidence of bronchial obstruction, or be asymptomatic. The association of carcinoid syndrome (flushing and diarrhea) with bronchial carcinoid tumor is rare. Surgical resection is often curative, and in the absence of nodal metastasis, the 10-year survival rate for patients with typical carcinoid tumors is greater than 90%. Prognosis is worse in patients with tumors larger than 3 cm or in the presence of nodal metastasis. The term "atypical carcinoid" is used when there is histologic evidence of increased mitotic activity, nuclear pleomorphism, and/or necrosis. Atypical carcinoids tend to have a higher rate of metastasis and to be larger at diagnosis than typical carcinoid tumors. The 5-year survival rate for patients with atypical carcinoid tumors is approximately 60% to 70%, and, when feasible, surgery is the therapy of choice.

### Metastatic Neoplasms to the Lung

Approximately 10% to 30% of all malignant nodules resected from the lung are metastases. Carcinomas that are frequent sources for pulmonary metastases include those of the head and neck, colon, kidney, breast, and thyroid gland, as well as melanoma. In addition to solitary or multiple nodules, metastases of carcinoma to the lung include lymphangiitic, endobronchial, pleural, and embolic patterns. The finding of multiple or innumerable nodules is the most common clinical situation. Depending on the size and location of the nodules, a diagnosis may be obtained by transthoracic needle aspiration or bronchoscopy. Surgical resection may be appropriate for a solitary pulmonary metastasis when evidence of other sites of metastatic disease have been excluded. Although randomized studies have not been performed, evidence suggests improved survival in some patients who have resection of a solitary pulmonary metastasis from sarcoma, renal cell carcinoma, breast cancer, and colon cancer.

# Mediastinal Masses

The mediastinum is the area between the two pleural surfaces in the center of the chest and is bordered anteriorly by the sternum, posteriorly by the spinal column, superiorly by the thoracic outlet, and inferiorly by the diaphragm. The mediastinum is further divided into the anterior, middle, and posterior compartments. These divisions are helpful clinically because disease processes presenting as masses develop primarily in one compartment based on the contents of that compartment.

## Anterior Mediastinal Masses

Contents of the anterior mediastinum include the upper esophagus, trachea, thymus, aortic arch, and lymphatic vessels. Masses in the anterior mediastinum are usually one of 5 T's: Thyroid (or parathyroid) tumors, Thymoma (or thymic carcinoma), Teratoma (or germ cell tumors), Thomas Hodgkin disease, and T-cell lymphoma. Thyroid and parathyroid tumors tend to occupy the superior-most aspect of the anterior mediastinum and may be palpable on examination or palpable when the patient swallows as the tumor is elevated into the neck.

Thymomas may be malignant or benign. Benign thymomas are generally well encapsulated; malignant thymomas invade the adjacent tissues. Thymoma is associated with various paraneoplastic effects, the most common being myasthenia gravis (**Figure 12**). Approximately 35% to 50% of patients with a thymoma have myasthenia gravis, and approximately 15% of patients with myasthenia gravis have a thymoma. Other paraneoplastic syndromes associated with thymoma include pure red cell aplasia and hypogammaglobulinemia. Teratomas may be evident on plain chest radiograph or CT scan.

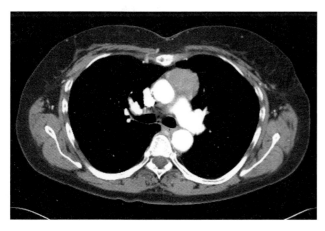

**FIGURE 12.**
**Thymoma with myasthenia gravis.**
A 56-year-old woman presented with a 2-month history of ptosis and progressive difficulty chewing and swallowing. CT scan showed an anterior mediastinal mass that was a stage 1 thymoma at resection. Acetylcholine receptor antibodies were positive at 46.8 nmol/L (normal <0.02 nmol/L), supporting the diagnosis of myasthenia gravis.

## Middle Mediastinal Masses

Contents of the middle mediastinum include the pericardium/heart, distal trachea, main bronchi, and lymph nodes. Masses in the middle mediastinum include enlargement of lymph nodes from metastasis, lymphoma, granulomatous disease (sarcoidosis, fungal infections, pulmonary tuberculosis), and giant lymph node hyperplasia (Castleman disease). Also included are pericardial or bronchogenic cysts, vascular masses and enlargements, and diaphragmatic hernias.

## Posterior Mediastinal Masses

Contents of the posterior mediastinum include the esophagus, descending aorta, sympathetic ganglia, and peripheral nerves. Masses most often originate from the esophagus or from neural tissue. Esophageal lesions include leiomyomas, fibromas, and lipomas. Neural tumors include neurofibroma and neurilemmoma (schwannoma).

Approximately half of all patients with mediastinal tumors present with cough, venous distention, hoarseness, back pain, or chest pain. The radiographic features can be helpful because the compartment containing the mass suggests a differential diagnosis. Routine imaging studies are often otherwise nonspecific and do not usually replace the need for tissue for a diagnosis. Recognition of an indeterminate mediastinal mass is usually an indication for biopsy or removal. If thymoma is suggested, resection is performed. Substernal thyroid glands are observed unless symptomatic. If both MRI and CT give a strong indication that a lesion is a cyst, follow-up is indicated. If lymphoma is suspected, an excisional biopsy is indicated.

**KEY POINTS**

- Carcinoid tumors are histologically described as typical and atypical; both have a good prognosis if surgically removed.

- Single or multiple pulmonary nodules may represent metastases to the lung, and common sources include tumors of the head and neck, kidney, thyroid gland, colon or rectum, and breast.

- Determining in which compartment (anterior, middle and posterior) a mass in the mediastinum resides is a diagnostic clue to the cause of the mass.

## Bibliography

Alberg AJ, Ford JG, Samet JM; American College of Chest Physicians. Epidemiology of lung cancer: ACCP evidence-based clinical practice guidelines (2nd edition). Chest. 2007;132(3 Suppl):29S-55S. [PMID: 17873159]

Bach PB, Silvestri GA, Hanger M, Jett JR; American College of Chest Physicians. Screening for lung cancer: ACCP evidence-based clinical practice guidelines (2nd edition). Chest. 2007;132(3 Suppl):69S-77S. [PMID: 17873161]

Duwe BV, Sterman DH, Musani AI. Tumors of the mediastinum. Chest. 2005;128(4):2893-2909. [PMID: 16236967]

Gould MK, Fletcher J, Iannettoni MD, et al.; American College of Chest Physicians. Evaluation of patients with pulmonary nodules: when is it lung cancer? ACCP evidence-based clinical practice guidelines (2nd edition). Chest. 2007;132(3 Suppl):108S-130S. [PMID: 17873164]

Rea F, Rizzardi G, Zuin A, et al. Outcome and surgical strategy in bronchial carcinoid tumors: single institution experience with 252 patients. Eur J Cardiothorac Surg. 2007;31(2):186-191. [PMID: 17140801]

Rivera MP, Mehta AC; American College of Chest Physicians. Initial diagnosis of lung cancer: ACCP evidence-based clinical practice guidelines (2nd edition). Chest. 2007;132(3 Suppl):131S-148S. [PMID: 17873165]

Silvestri GA, Gould MK, Margolis ML, et al.; American College of Chest Physicians. Noninvasive staging of non-small cell lung cancer: ACCP evidenced-based clinical practice guidelines (2nd edition). Chest. 2007;132(3 Suppl):178S-201S. [PMID: 17873168]

Spiro SG, Gould MK, Colice GL; Initial evaluation of the patient with lung cancer: symptoms, signs, laboratory tests, and paraneoplastic syndromes: ACCP evidenced-based clinical practice guidelines (2nd edition).Chest. 2007;132(3 Suppl):149S-160S. [PMID: 17873166]

# Sleep Disorders and High-Altitude Pulmonary Disease

## Excessive Daytime Sleepiness

Excessive daytime sleepiness is a persistent or recurrent inability to achieve and to sustain the alertness required to accomplish the tasks of daily living. Sleepiness is different from fatigue, and inadequate sleep duration is the most common cause of excessive sleepiness (**Table 34**). Complications include sleep attacks, increased risk of accidents, impaired cognition, performance decrements, and mood disorders.

Evaluation of excessive daytime sleepiness consists of a careful history with inquiries into sleep duration and quality. Subjective measures (for example, the Epworth Sleepiness Scale) or objective measures (for example, the Multiple Sleep Latency Test [MSLT]) can be used to assess the presence and severity of excessive daytime sleepiness. Mean sleep latency on the MSLT is generally less than 8 minutes in patients with clinically significant sleepiness. Polysomnography is not indicated in the routine evaluation unless sleepiness is clearly related to insufficient sleep, or a specific sleep, medical, neurologic, or psychiatric disorder is present. Drug screening for sedative agents may be appropriate.

Therapy for excessive daytime sleepiness includes proper sleep hygiene (including obtaining an adequate amount of sleep) and treatment of disorders that can cause or exacerbate excessive sleepiness. Patients with significant sleepiness, which is associated with functional impairment or may pose a danger to the person and which persists despite treatment of insufficient sleep and known treatable conditions, may benefit from psychostimulant agents, such as amphetamines, methylphenidate, or modafinil. Such patients should be counseled to refrain from driving or engaging in activities that might be potentially dangerous whenever they are drowsy.

| **TABLE 34** Differential Diagnosis of Excessive Sleepiness |
| --- |
| **Insufficient Sleep** |
| **Sleep Fragmentation** |
| Obstructive sleep apnea |
| Periodic limb movement disorder |
| **Central Nervous System Disorders** |
| Narcolepsy |
| Idiopathic hypersomnia |
| Kleine-Levin syndrome (a rare disorder characterized by recurring periods of excessive amounts of sleep and altered behavior) |
| **Disturbances of the Circadian Timing of Sleep and Wakefulness** |
| Shift work sleep disorder |
| Jet lag |
| **Medical, Neurologic, and Psychiatric Disorders** |
| Hypothyroidism |
| Cirrhosis |
| Encephalitis |
| Depression |
| **Medication or Substance Use** |
| Abuse |
| Sedating medications |

**KEY POINTS**

- Excessive daytime sleepiness is a persistent or recurrent inability to achieve and sustain alertness required to accomplish the tasks of daily living.
- Excessive daytime sleepiness is most commonly secondary to insufficient sleep.

## Obstructive Sleep Apnea

An obstructive apnea is defined as a significant reduction in airflow (a decrease in the peak thermal sensor amplitude by at least 90% from baseline) for at least 10 seconds that occurs despite efforts to breathe and that is secondary to upper airway obstruction. An obstructive hypopnea is characterized by a reduction in nasal pressure of at least 30% of baseline for at least 10 seconds that is accompanied by at least 4% oxygen desaturation. The severity of obstructive sleep apnea (OSA) is commonly based on the apnea-hypopnea index (AHI; sum of apneas and hypopneas per hour of sleep): mild sleep apnea consists of an AHI 5 to 15/hour; moderate sleep apnea, AHI 16 to 30/hour; and severe sleep apnea, AHI greater than 30/hour. It is estimated that 24% of men aged 30 to 60 years and 9% of similarly aged women have OSA (AHI at least 5/hour).

## Pathophysiology

The patency of the upper airway is maintained during the waking state by activation of muscles that dilate this region; the dilating activity of these muscles is significantly reduced during sleep and is exceeded by forces that promote closure of the airway. The airway is more vulnerable to closure in patients with OSA than in unaffected persons. In a patient whose airway has closed, airway patency is reestablished during brief arousals that accompany the termination of apnea-hypopneas. Closure recurs with the resumption of sleep. Respiratory events generally occur less frequently during non–rapid eye movement sleep than in rapid eye movement sleep. In some persons, respiratory events occur predominantly or exclusively in the supine sleep position.

Apnea-hypopneas are commonly associated with oxygen desaturation, mild to moderate hypercapnia, and changes in blood pressure and heart rate; there is a relative bradycardia and reduction in blood pressure during respiratory events, and tachycardia and an increase in blood pressure during the termination of apnea-hypopneas. Premature ventricular contractions may also occur.

## Risk Factors and Complications

Risk factors for OSA include excessive body weight, abnormalities of craniofacial anatomy, male sex, underlying medical or neurologic disorders (myxedema, acromegaly, and stroke), alcohol use, certain medications (muscle relaxants, sedatives, opioids, and anesthetics), and aging.

Patients with untreated OSA have a greater likelihood of developing coronary artery disease, acute myocardial infarction during sleep, systemic and pulmonary arterial hypertension, heart failure, recurrent atrial fibrillation, stroke, insulin resistance, mood disorders, and parasomnias. OSA may also negatively affect quality of life and academic and occupational performance, may increase the risk of vehicular and work-related accidents, and may increase the overall mortality rate.

## Clinical Features

Excessive daytime sleepiness is the most common manifestation of OSA (**Table 35**).

Clinical and physical examination features are neither sensitive nor specific enough for the diagnosis of OSA. Polysomnography is required to determine the presence and severity of OSA. Although attended in-laboratory polysomnography remains the standard technique for diagnosing OSA, portable home sleep testing is becoming more common, and its use is expected to increase in the future. An MSLT is indicated if significant sleepiness persists despite optimal therapy.

## Treatment

Therapy is recommended for all patients with an AHI at least 15/hour and for patients with excessive daytime sleepiness, insomnia, impaired cognition, mood disorder,

**TABLE 35** Clinical and Physical Examination Features of Obstructive Sleep Apnea

| Clinical Features |
| --- |
| Habitual snoring |
| Reports of witnessed apneas |
| Awakenings with gasping or choking |
| Insomnia |
| Nighttime diaphoresis |
| Morning headaches |
| Nocturia |
| Erectile dysfunction |
| Daytime fatigue or sleepiness |
| Alterations in mood |
| Neurocognitive decline |

| Physical Examination |
| --- |
| Excessive weight |
| Large neck circumference |
| Nasal obstruction |
| Tonsillar enlargement |
| Low-lying palate |
| Narrow oropharynx |
| Macroglossia |
| Retro- or micrognathia |

hypertension, ischemic heart disease, or stroke and an AHI between 5 and 15/hour. Various treatment modalities are available (**Table 36**).

Positional sleep therapy consists of measures to prevent sleep in a supine position for patients whose OSA occurs exclusively or predominantly during a supine sleep position and whose AHI normalizes during sleep in a lateral or prone sleep position.

Supplemental oxygen is not recommended as a primary therapy for OSA and should not be used to replace positive airway pressure therapy. Oxygen therapy may be beneficial if marked oxygen desaturation related to respiratory events does not respond to positive airway pressure therapy alone. No pharmacologic agent is consistently effective in treating OSA. Patients should be counseled not to drive or engage in other potentially dangerous activities unless their OSA is optimally treated and they are fully alert.

### Positive Airway Pressure

Positive airway pressure is the treatment of choice for most patients with OSA. This therapy involves the generation of air pressure by a turbine or fan, and the air is channeled to the upper airways via a tight-fitting nasal or oronasal mask. This air pressure acts as a pneumatic splint that maintains nasopharyngeal airway patency during sleep. In most patients, a continuous positive airway pressure (CPAP), which provides a

| **TABLE 36** Therapy for Obstructive Sleep Apnea |
| --- |
| **General Measures** |
| Optimal weight management |
| Avoidance of alcohol, sedatives, and muscle relaxants |
| Positional sleep therapy |
| **Positive Airway Pressure Therapy** |
| Continuous positive airway pressure |
| Auto-titrating positive airway pressure |
| Bilevel positive airway pressure |
| Adaptive servoventilation |
| **Oral Devices** |
| Mandibular repositioners |
| Tongue-retaining devices |
| **Upper Airway Surgery** |
| Uvulopalatopharyngoplasty |
| Genioglossal advancement |
| Hyoid myotomy and suspension |
| Mandibular advancement |
| Maxillomandibular advancement |
| Tracheostomy |

single constant fixed-level pressure throughout the respiratory cycle, is applied. Auto-titrating positive airway pressure continuously adjusts the delivered pressure using device-specific diagnostic and therapeutic algorithms to compensate for the degree of upper airway obstruction. In some patients, an additional positive pressure assist during inspiration is added to the basal continuous positive pressure level (analogous to pressure support added to positive end-expiratory pressure in an intubated patient with an endotracheal tube) that helps support minute ventilation whenever this is necessary. Methods providing this inspiratory pressure boost include bilevel positive airway pressure (BPAP) and adaptive servoventilation (ASV). BPAP uses higher pressure level during inspiration and a lower pressure during expiration; the inspiratory boost increases the size of each breath and enhances minute ventilation. ASV provides an adjustable degree of pressure support (difference between inspiratory and expiratory positive airway pressure) superimposed upon a set level of CPAP.

In general, CPAP is used when opening the airway is sufficient and BPAP or ASV when CPAP is needed to open the airway and additional ventilatory support is needed for a component of hypoventilation. Optimal therapy must be determined by polysomnography and titration of therapy to relieve hypoxemia and hypercarbia.

Effective positive airway pressure therapy of the appropriate type has been shown to improve sleep quality, lower the AHI, increase arterial oxygen saturation, and reduce daytime sleepiness in patients with OSA. It improves blood pressure control in patients with OSA and hypertension and enhances cardiac function in those with comorbid heart failure.

Optimal positive airway pressure therapy reduces the mortality rate associated with OSA.

Suboptimal adherence to CPAP and BPAP devices is common in clinical practice, and rates of discontinuation are high. Therefore, objective monitoring of use and periodic follow-up are important to ensure adherence. Education regarding the benefits of therapy and the use of heated humidification have been reported to enhance compliance.

### Upper Airway Surgery

Surgery is indicated for patients with specific underlying surgically correctable craniofacial or upper airway abnormalities that contribute to OSA, including nasal polyps, nasal septal deviation, tonsillar enlargement, or retrognathia. Upper airway surgery may also be considered in selected patients with OSA who desire surgery, reject other therapeutic modalities, and can undergo the procedure. Uvulopalatopharyngoplasty and other surgical procedures for OSA increase the dimensions of the retropalatal airspace, retrolingual airway, or both. Data on long-term effectiveness of upper airway surgery are limited, but it is less effective than CPAP therapy. Polysomnography is routinely indicated after upper airway surgery to determine its therapeutic efficacy, and long-term follow-up is advisable to monitor for disease recurrence. Rarely, tracheostomy may be indicated for severe life-threatening OSA that does not respond to other therapy. Tracheostomy is highly effective treatment for OSA, superior even to CPAP because the patient breathes with the tracheostomy tube or stoma open at night, bypassing the upper airway. However, tracheostomy is invasive and has its own morbidity.

### Oral Devices

Mandibular repositioners and tongue-retaining devices are used to treat patients with primary snoring or mild to moderate OSA. Mandibular repositioners advance the mandible and tongue by realigning the lower teeth forward in relation to the upper teeth, whereas tongue-retaining devices secure the tip of the tongue in a forward position in a soft bulb situated over the teeth.

Both devices enlarge the pharyngeal airway and prevent the posterior displacement of the tongue and mandible during sleep. Oral devices may be considered for patients who cannot tolerate or are unwilling to use positive airway pressure therapy, or who either refuse or have failed to respond to upper airway surgery. Oral devices have reported efficacy rates of 30% or up to 80% in patients with severe or mild-to-moderate OSA, respectively. A follow-up polysomnography is indicated after the device has been adjusted to determine its therapeutic benefit.

### Management of Residual Sleepiness

Excessive daytime sleepiness may persist despite adherence to positive airway pressure therapy in some patients with OSA.

The presence of insufficient sleep, narcolepsy, surreptitious use of sedating medications, or mood disorders should be excluded. Modafinil, a wake-promoting agent, is an adjunct therapy to improve residual daytime sleepiness in patients receiving optimal positive airway pressure therapy. However, modafinil should not be used as sole therapy in patients presenting with excessive daytime sleepiness, and it does not reverse the adverse cardiovascular consequences related to OSA.

**KEY POINTS**

- Using heated humidification and educating the patient about the benefits of positive airway pressure therapy can enhance compliance to therapy for obstructive sleep apnea.

- In-laboratory attended polysomnography remains the gold standard for diagnosing obstructive sleep apnea and titrating positive airway pressure therapy.

- The optimal continuous positive airway pressure for obstructive sleep apnea should eliminate apneas, hypopneas, and snoring in all sleep positions and during all sleep stages; normalize oxygen saturation; and improve sleep quality.

## Central Sleep Apnea

Central sleep apnea (CSA) is characterized by the recurrent cessation or reduction of airflow lasting for at least 10 seconds secondary to an absence of inspiratory effort. Patients with

CSA may present with insomnia, nocturnal dyspnea, or excessive sleepiness secondary to repetitive nighttime awakenings or may be asymptomatic with the central apnea being an incidental finding during polysomnography performed for another indication.

CSA is classified as hypercapnic or nonhypercapnic. Hypercapnic CSA is associated with hypoventilation (high $Pco_2$) and a diminished response to hypercapnia. Nonhypercapnic CSA is characterized by a normal or low waking $Pco_2$ and an increased ventilatory response to hypercapnia. There are various types of CSA (**Table 37**). Of the subtypes, primary central sleep apnea and some cases of central sleep apnea related to medical disorders and medications are hypercapnic. Many of the other types are associated with increased respiratory drive and low waking $Pco_2$, with pauses in breathing when the patient falls asleep and the $Pco_2$ increases toward a higher sleep set point or cyclical breathing when high respiratory drive leads to an overshoot beyond the $Pco_2$ set point, resulting in a pause in breathing followed by deep breathing when that set point is reached.

Risk factors for primary CSA include a high carbon dioxide ventilatory drive (that is, increased response to hypercapnia) and male sex.

CSA can develop acutely after ascent to high altitudes. In patients with heart failure, the likelihood of CSA is increased in persons older than 60 years and those with atrial fibrillation and low awake $Pco_2$.

Polysomnography is necessary for the diagnosis of CSA. Cessation of respiration is associated with absent ventilatory

| **TABLE 37** Types of Central Sleep Apnea |
|---|
| **Primary Central Sleep Apnea** |
| Accounts for an estimated 5% to 10% of sleep-related breathing disorders |
| Prevalence is greater among men and increases with age. |
| More common during the onset of NREM sleep than during stable NREM or REM sleep. |
| **Cheyne-Stokes Respirations** |
| Recurring periods of gradually waxing and waning tidal volume (crescendo-decrescendo ventilation) with repetitive central apnea-hypopneas alternating with prolonged hyperpneas (increased depth of breathing) |
| Can develop in patients with heart failure or neurologic disorders, with a prevalence of about 10% in patients with strokes or renal failure |
| **Sleep-Onset Central Apneas** |
| Central apneas can occur during the transition between wakefulness and sleep as $Pco_2$ fluctuates above and below the apneic threshold and generally disappear once stable sleep, with stable higher levels of $Pco_2$, is attained |
| **Central Apnea Emerging during CPAP Titration** |
| Central apneas develop during CPAP titration in patients with predominantly obstructive or mixed apnea–hypopneas during an earlier diagnostic polysomnography |
| **Central Apnea Related to Medical Disorders or Medication Use** |
| Due to medical disorders (heart failure, brainstem lesions, and renal disorders) or the regular use of long-acting opioids |
| CPAP = continuous positive airway pressure; NREM = non–rapid eye movement; REM = rapid eye movement. |

efforts. Transcutaneous carbon dioxide may be measured and aids in classifying central apneas as hypercapnic or nonhypercapnic for the purpose of individualizing treatment.

## Treatment

Specific treatment is unnecessary for sleep-onset central apneas that are transitory and do not give rise to insomnia. Optimal management of underlying causes of secondary central apneas, such as heart failure, may be beneficial.

### Oxygen Therapy

Low-flow oxygen supplementation may decrease nonhypercapnic CSA in some patients. Oxygen therapy improves hypoxemia, reduces the hypopcapnia induced by reflex hyperventilation, and increases $PCO_2$ above the apneic threshold.

### Positive Airway Pressure Therapy

Positive airway pressure therapy (CPAP, BPAP, or ASV) can reduce respiratory events and improve cardiac function in patients with CSA due to heart failure. Patients with hypercapnic CSA may benefit from the assisted ventilation provided by BPAP, with improvements in both $Po_2$ and $Pco_2$. CPAP alone may improve the CSA in patients without hypercapnia.

### Pharmacologic Therapy

Respiratory stimulants have been used for certain types of central apneas, including acetazolamide for high-altitude periodic breathing, theophylline for CSA related to heart failure, and medroxyprogesterone for patients with obesity-hypoventilation syndrome, which consists of obesity with alveolar hypoventilation (awake $Pco_2$ greater than 45 mm Hg) without other known causes of hypoventilation. Hypnotic agents may help minimize sleep-onset central apneas but should be avoided (as should other respiratory suppressants such as narcotics, benzodiazepines, and muscle relaxants) in patients with hypercapnic forms of CSA.

### KEY POINTS

- Hypercapnic central sleep apnea is associated with hypoventilation (high $Pco_2$) and a diminished response to hypercapnia.
- Nonhypercapnic central sleep apnea is characterized by a normal or low waking $Pco_2$ and an increased ventilatory response to hypercapnia.

# Sleep and Respiratory Diseases

## Chronic Obstructive Pulmonary Disease

COPD may be associated with frequent nighttime awakenings due to nocturnal coughing or dyspnea. Polysomnography may show an increase in sleep latency, reduction in sleep efficiency, and decrease in total sleep time. Changes in arterial blood gases, including hypoxemia and hypercapnia, can occur in patients with advanced COPD. Nocturnal oxygen desaturation from COPD is more severe during rapid eye movement (REM) sleep than non-REM sleep. Mechanisms responsible for nocturnal hypoxemia include episodic hypoventilation, ventilation/perfusion mismatching, and decreased lung volumes. Episodes of hypoventilation may also result in arousals and further aggravate the sleep fragmentation.

The overlap syndrome is characterized by the presence of both OSA and COPD. Patients with the overlap syndrome tend to have lower $Po_2$ and higher $Pco_2$, higher pulmonary arterial pressures, and a worse clinical course than persons with COPD alone. Patients with COPD should be screened for OSA if they have hypercapnia or pulmonary hypertension that is inconsistent with their degree of airflow limitation. In addition to pharmacologic therapy for COPD, patients with the overlap syndrome require positive airway pressure therapy that may include an additional pressure assist during inspiration (BPAP).

## Asthma

Nocturnal dyspnea, coughing, and wheezing secondary to asthma may give rise to significant sleep disturbance, with an increase in the frequency of awakenings and a decrease in sleep efficiency. Nighttime worsening of airway hyperreactivity and bronchoconstriction has been postulated to be due to circadian variability in airflow, greater parasympathetic tone during sleep, and changes in levels of inflammatory mediators, epinephrine, and cortisol.

## Restrictive and Neuromuscular Disorders

Sleep in patients with restrictive lung disease and neuromuscular disorders may be associated with nocturnal hypoventilation, nocturnal oxygen desaturation, frequent arousals, and excessive daytime sleepiness. The clinical course of kyphoscoliosis may be complicated by both obstructive and central apnea-hypopneas. Various neuromuscular disorders are associated with nocturnal ventilatory impairment, such as alveolar hypoventilation, that may precede waking abnormalities in respiration by several months to years; these disorders include muscular dystrophy, myotonic dystrophy, amyotrophic lateral sclerosis, and poliomyelitis. Patients with maximal inspiratory pressures less than 60 cm $H_2O$ or forced expiratory volume less than 50% of predicted are at higher risk for sleep-related hypoventilation and hypoxemia, which occur predominantly during REM sleep. Patients with neuromuscular disorders may also present with either obstructive or central apnea-hypopneas.

Patients with prominent respiratory accessory muscle use while awake caused by either advanced COPD with hyperinflation or restrictive disorders, including pulmonary fibrosis, chest wall abnormalities, and neuromuscular diseases, may have episodic hypoventilation during sleep when function of those muscles is less reliable, especially during REM sleep when accessory muscles are hyperpolarized and unavailable. The repeated arousals and sleep fragmentation lead to daytime sleepiness and also aggravate daytime carbon dioxide retention. Effective nocturnal ventilatory support using BPAP can improve sleep quality, improve gas exchange during sleep (more normal $Pco_2$ and reduced episodes of hypoxemia), and also improve daytime function and gas exchange.

### KEY POINTS

- Muscular dystrophy, myotonic dystrophy, amyotrophic lateral sclerosis, and poliomyelitis are associated with nocturnal ventilatory impairment, such as alveolar hypoventilation, that may precede waking abnormalities in respiration by several months to years.

- Patients with prominent awake respiratory accessory muscle use may have episodic hypoventilation during sleep when function of those muscles is less reliable and especially during rapid eye movement sleep when accessory muscles are hyperpolarized and unavailable.

# High-Altitude Pulmonary Disease

Respiratory disorders related to ascent to high altitude include high-altitude periodic breathing, acute mountain sickness, high-altitude pulmonary edema, and complications of air travel. These disorders are all consequences of the relative hypoxia and hypocarbia associated with high altitude.

## Sleep Disturbances and High-Altitude Periodic Breathing

Recurrent periods of central apneas can occur on ascent to altitude, typically greater than 4000 meters (13,123.36 ft). Central apnea is due to an increase in hyperventilation in response to hypoxia, leading to hypocapnic (low $Pco_2$) alkalosis and cycling respiration. If severe, it can cause sleep fragmentation, sleep-related dyspnea, and daytime sleepiness and fatigue. Both sleep quality and periodic breathing improve with acclimatization to altitude. If severe, symptoms can be alleviated with oxygen therapy or administration of acetazolamide, which is effective in preventing high-altitude periodic breathing (high-altitude insomnia).

## Acute Mountain Sickness

Clinical features of acute mountain sickness consist of lightheadedness, nausea, anorexia, headache, and a tingling sensation of the extremities; these symptoms arise as a result of hypoxia itself or are due to hyperventilation that develops in response to hypoxia. Hyperventilation, in turn, produces respiratory alkalosis. Symptoms generally develop within 6 to 12 hours of ascent to high altitude. Management consists of descent to a lower altitude and treatment with acetazolamide and dexamethasone. Acetazolamide and dexamethasone can also be used as prophylaxis for acute mountain sickness.

## High-Altitude Pulmonary Edema

High-altitude pulmonary edema (HAPE) is a form of noncardiogenic pulmonary edema that results from pulmonary vasoconstriction and elevated pulmonary arterial pressures in response to acute hypoxia, which leads to leakage of fluid and pulmonary hemorrhage into the alveolar spaces. Affected patients often present with significant dyspnea; cough productive of blood-tinged, frothy sputum; and cyanosis. Auscultatory crackles and elevated jugular venous pressure may be present. Persons with underlying pulmonary hypertension or mitral stenosis may be at greater risk of developing HAPE. Severe oxygen desaturation may require prompt descent if portable oxygen sources are unavailable. Hyperbaric chambers may also be beneficial. Nifedipine, which inhibits hypoxic pulmonary arterial vasoconstriction, has been used both to prevent and to treat HAPE.

## Air Travel of Patients with Chronic Respiratory Disorders

Commercial air travel poses challenges to hypoxemic patients, particularly those who require continuous oxygen therapy for chronic respiratory or cardiovascular disorders. Most commercial airplane cabins are pressurized to the equivalent of 5000 to 8000 feet, and patients with chronic hypoxia may not tolerate the lower $Po_2$ and barometric pressure associated with air travel. The hypoxia inhalation test (inhalation of a 15% oxygen–85% nitrogen mixture to simulate 8000 feet) or regression formulas may be used to determine whether a patient needs additional in-flight supplemental oxygen. Oxygen supplementation is indicated if the estimated in-flight $Po_2$ will be less than 55 mm Hg. Air travel is not recommended for patients with a pneumothorax because of the possibility of a tension pneumothorax developing as the volume of gas contained within the pneumothorax increases because of a decreasing barometric pressure associated with progressively higher ascents.

### KEY POINTS

- High-altitude pulmonary edema is a form of noncardiogenic pulmonary edema caused by leakage of fluid and hemorrhage into the alveolar spaces.

- Patients who require continuous oxygen therapy for chronic respiratory or cardiovascular disorders may not tolerate commercial air travel and should be assessed to determine whether they will require additional in-flight supplemental oxygen.

### Bibliography

Allam JS, Olson EJ, Gay PC, Morgenthaler TI. Efficacy of adaptive servoventilation in treatment of complex and central sleep apnea syndromes. Chest. 2007;132(6):1839-1846. [PMID: 18079219]

Bhullar S, Phillips B. Sleep in COPD patients. COPD. 2005;2(3):355-361. [PMID: 17147000]

Bradley TD, Logan AG, Kimoff RJ, et al; CANPAP Investigators. Continuous positive airway pressure for central sleep apnea and heart failure. N Engl J Med. 2005;353(19):2025-2033. [PMID: 16282177]

Eckert DJ, Jordan AS, Merchia P, Malhotra A. Central sleep apnea: Pathophysiology and treatment. Chest. 2007;131(2):595-607. [PMID: 17296668]

Kushida CA, Littner MR, Hirshkowitz M, et al; American Academy of Sleep Medicine. Practice parameters for the use of continuous and bilevel positive airway pressure devices to treat adult patients with sleep-related breathing disorders. Sleep. 2006;29(3):375-380. [PMID: 16553024]

Luks AM, Swenson ER. Medication and dosage considerations in the prophylaxis and treatment of high-altitude illness. Chest. 2008; 133(3):744-755. [PMID: 18321903]

Mermigkis C, Chapman J, Golish J, et al. Sleep-related breathing disorders in patients with idiopathic pulmonary fibrosis. Lung. 2007;185(3):173-178. [PMID: 17436039]

Morgenthaler TI, Kapen S, Lee-Chiong T, et al; Standards of Practice Committee; American Academy of Sleep Medicine. Practice parameters for the medical therapy of obstructive sleep apnea. Sleep. 2006;29(8):1031-1035. [PMID: 16944671]

Philippe C, Stoïca-Herman M, Drouot X, et al. Compliance with and effectiveness of adaptive servoventilation versus continuous positive airway pressure in the treatment of Cheyne-Stokes respiration in heart failure over a six month period. Heart. 2006;92(3):337-342. [PMID: 15964943]

Seccombe LM, Peters MJ. Oxygen supplementation for chronic obstructive pulmonary disease patients during air travel. Curr Opin Pulm Med. 2006;12(2):140-144. [PMID: 16456384]

# Critical Care

## Recognizing the Seriously Ill Patient

Recognizing serious illness can be challenging in patients with little comorbidity whose condition may not seem immediately unstable. Manifestations of instability may be nonspecific but usually reflect organ hypoperfusion, including mental status changes (confusion, agitation, coma), decreased urine output, skin changes (pallor, sweating, cyanosis, or cool extremities), and abnormal vital signs (especially hypotension, tachycardia, tachypnea, and hyper- or hypothermia). Shortness of breath, nausea, vomiting, and chest pain may also be present. The presenting signs and symptoms, although nonspecific, are usually very sensitive and indicate that immediate action needs to be taken. In the initial evaluation of the unstable patient, a brief directed history should be obtained at the bedside. The primary physical examination should immediately assess airway, breathing, circulation, and level of consciousness. Chart review focuses on the patient's history and hospital course, medications, and the vital signs preceding the event. Initial treatment should correct any abnormalities. Often these initial therapies consist of rapid resuscitation with intravenous fluids and administration of oxygen. Adjunct laboratory tests may include a bedside plasma glucose determination and measurement of venous or arterial blood gas levels. Adjunct treatments that also provide diagnostic information include naloxone and dextrose (D50) administration, which is appropriate in some patients with decreased consciousness. After the vital signs have stabilized to an acceptable level with treatment, a more detailed secondary evaluation of the patient should be done to make an accurate diagnosis.

## Respiratory Failure

Patients are admitted to the intensive care unit (ICU) for monitoring and management of respiratory insufficiency for three basic conditions: (1) hypoxemic respiratory failure; (2) ventilatory, or hypercapnic, respiratory failure; and (3) impaired upper airway. However, often more than one of these factors contributes to respiratory failure. Calculation of the alveolar-arterial difference (A-a gradient) can be useful in discerning the primary mechanism of respiratory failure (**Table 38**).

### Hypoxemic Respiratory Failure

Acute hypoxemic respiratory failure is recognized by an acute fall in $PO_2$ or oxyhemoglobin saturation (for example, a $PO_2$ to less than or equal to 60 mm Hg or $PO_2$/fraction of inspired oxygen [$FIO_2$] less than or equal to 200 [$PO_2$ less than 200 on 100% oxygen or less than 100 on 50% oxygen]). In pure hypoxemic respiratory failure, the $PCO_2$ is typically normal or reduced. Conditions causing acute hypoxemic respiratory failure include alveolar collapse and flooding with fluid, pus, or blood. Continued perfusion of these unventilated lung units

| **TABLE 38** Pathophysiology and Correction of Common Causes of Hypoxemia | | | | |
|---|---|---|---|---|
| **Clinical Situation** | **Gas Exchange Derangement** | **A-a Oxygen Difference[a]** | **Corrects with ↑ Ventilation** | **Corrects with Supplemental Oxygen** |
| High altitude | Low inspired arterial $PO_2$ | Normal | Partially | Yes |
| Narcotic overdose | Hypoventilation | Normal | Yes | Yes |
| Asthma, COPD | Low V/Q | Widened | No | Yes |
| ARDS, heart failure | Shunt | Widened | No | No |

A-a = alveolar to arterial; ARDS = acute respiratory distress syndrome; COPD = chronic obstructive pulmonary disease; $PCO_2$ = arterial carbon dioxide tension; $PO_2$ = arterial oxygen tension; V/Q = ventilation/perfusion.

[a]A-a difference is the difference between predicted alveolar oxygen and measured arterial oxygen. At sea level, the A-a gradient is calculated as follows: (150 mm Hg − $PCO_2$/0.8) − $PO_2$ (less than 10 if intrapulmonary gas exchange is normal).

can lead to profound, refractory hypoxemia that does not adequately correct with increased alveolar ventilation or supplemental oxygen. Rather, hypoxemia is reversed by application of positive end-expiratory pressure (PEEP) to the lung, which opens up, or "recruits," flooded or collapsed alveoli.

## Acute Lung Injury and the Acute Respiratory Distress Syndrome

Acute lung injury (ALI) is a noncardiogenic form of pulmonary edema characterized by acute and persistent lung inflammation and increased vascular permeability. Diffuse inflammatory injury of the alveolar epithelial cells and capillary endothelial cells results in leakage of fluid, protein, and inflammatory cells into the interstitium and alveoli. The pathologic correlate is diffuse alveolar damage, but the diagnosis typically is made clinically rather than histologically (**Table 39**).

ALI causes hypoxemic respiratory failure, defined by a $Po_2/Fio_2$ less than or equal to 300. The subset of patients with ALI who have severe hypoxemia ($Po_2/Fio_2$ less than or equal to 200) is considered to have the acute respiratory distress syndrome (ARDS). In addition to a decreased $Po_2/Fio_2$ ratio, the diagnosis of either ALI or ARDS requires the presence of bilateral pulmonary infiltrates on a chest radiograph and the absence of evidence to suggest increased left atrial pressure (for example, left ventricular dysfunction).

There is substantial evidence that the routine use of pulmonary artery catheters for the management of medical ICU patients (including those with ARDS) offers no survival benefit. Therefore, the exclusion of cardiogenic edema increasingly relies on clinical, laboratory, and echocardiographic evaluation to exclude left ventricular dysfunction rather than measurement of the pulmonary capillary wedge pressure. More than 60 disorders can precipitate ALI and ARDS by either direct insult to the lung or by marked systemic inflammation elsewhere in the body that releases mediators that can cause pulmonary capillary leak (and also affect multiple

organs). Sepsis is the most common cause of ARDS and must be considered in any patient who develops ARDS in association with a new fever or hypotension or who is at risk for a serious infection. Pneumonia is the most common cause of ARDS in patients outside of the hospital. About one third of hospitalized patients who aspirate gastric contents develop ARDS. Signs and symptoms typically manifest within 24 to 48 hours of the inciting event.

### Heart Failure

Left ventricular dysfunction can result in acute onset of bilateral pulmonary infiltrates that are radiographically indistinguishable from ALI. Differentiating cardiogenic from noncardiogenic edema has important clinical implications because the hypoxemia associated with cardiogenic edema may rapidly improve with aggressive diuresis combined with temporizing measures such as noninvasive positive pressure ventilation (NPPV).

### KEY POINTS

- Hypoxemic respiratory failure caused by diseases that create shunt physiology correct with positive end-expiratory pressure but not with supplemental oxygen.
- The diagnosis of the acute respiratory distress syndrome (ARDS) is predominantly made on a clinical basis, and pulmonary artery catheters no longer have a major role in the diagnosis and management of ARDS.

## Ventilatory (Hypercarbic) Respiratory Failure

Ventilatory respiratory failure refers to inadequate alveolar ventilation, but the airways and alveoli are not collapsed or flooded as in hypoxemic respiratory failure. The primary manifestation of ventilatory failure is hypercapnia. Hypoxemia may also occur because of V/Q mismatch or hypoventilation and a failure to replenish alveolar oxygen. Elevation of $Pco_2$ arises from increased carbon dioxide production ($Vco_2$), decreased alveolar ventilation ($V_A$), or both according to the following equation:

$$Pco_2 = (Vco_2 \times k)/V_A \text{ (where k is a constant} = 0.863)$$

Fever and increased mechanical work of breathing are important clinical causes of elevated $Vco_2$, whereas decreased respiratory drive, weakness of respiratory muscles, and elevated dead-space ventilation (ventilated but underperfused lung units) contribute to reduced $V_A$.

Hypoxemic and ventilatory failure can be present concomitantly. For example, patients with severe ARDS have hypoxemic failure from shunt (perfused but underventilated lung units) but may also have hypercapnia due to increased $Vco_2$ and markedly elevated dead-space ventilation. Dead-space ventilation, which normally constitutes less than 30% of each breath, can increase to over 60% in such patients,

---

**TABLE 39 Diagnostic Criteria for Acute Lung Injury**

Acute Onset
  Less than 48 hours
Bilateral infiltrates
Absence of heart failure
  No clinical evidence of increased left atrial pressure
  Pulmonary capillary wedge pressure <18 mm Hg if available
Reduced $Po_2/Fio_2$
  201–300 for acute lung injury
  ≤200 for acute respiratory distress syndrome

$Fio_2$ = fraction of inspired oxygen; $Po_2$ = arterial oxygen tension.

thereby exceeding the patient's ability to maintain normal $P_{CO_2}$ by increasing total minute ventilation. Elevation in dead-space ventilation is an independent predictor of mortality in ARDS.

### Neuromuscular Disease

Decreased ventilatory drive, impaired respiratory muscle strength, and chest wall disorders may cause ventilatory failure even in the absence of respiratory disease, an effect referred to as *bellows failure*.

*Evaluation and Management of Respiratory Muscle Weakness*

There are other respiratory complications of neuromuscular weakness besides chronic ventilatory failure (**Table 40**). Cough is often impaired owing to weakness of expiratory muscles (the rectus abdominis being the most important). Upper airway patency, swallowing, and prevention of aspiration all depend on pharyngeal, bulbar, and laryngeal muscles. Management focuses on implementing assisted ventilation, airway clearance regimens, and interventions to minimize aspiration risk. Chest physiotherapy, including incentive spirometry, postural drainage, and manually and mechanically assisted cough, reduce the risk of mucous plugging, atelectasis, and pneumonia. An endotracheal tube more often in acute (and less often in chronic conditions) or a tracheostomy may be required to ensure a patent airway.

In the ICU, serial bedside measurements of vital capacity and maximum negative inspiratory force are used to assess the need for mechanical ventilation in patients with neuromuscular disease. Patients with vital capacity less than 20 mL/kg, patients who cannot generate more than 30 cm $H_2O$ of negative inspiratory force, or patients with declining values are at high risk for ventilatory failure. Serial pulmonary function tests and measurement of arterial blood gas levels may not be sensitive predictors of ventilatory failure in patients with bulbar dysfunction, who are prone to aspiration that can cause rapid deterioration regardless of test results.

*Causes of Ventilatory Failure from Neuromuscular Disease*

**Reduced Ventilatory Drive.** Excessive sedation from a drug overdose is the most common cause of insufficient respiratory drive in the acute care setting. Patients with respiratory failure resulting exclusively from hypoventilation have a normal alveolar-arterial oxygen difference and need only increased alveolar ventilation to normalize gas exchange. Narcotics are potent respiratory depressants, but any sedating medication in sufficient quantity can cause ventilatory failure. The opioid antagonist naloxone reverses narcotic overdose but requires continuous intravenous infusion to achieve a sustained effect. Flumazenil reverses sedation from benzodiazepines and, like naloxone, has a short half-life. Stroke typically does not cause a decrement in ventilatory drive in the absence of elevated intracranial pressure or specific involvement of the brainstem. Severe hypothyroidism is an uncommon cause of hypoventilation.

**Spinal Cord Injury.** The phrenic nerve arises from cervical spinal nerves 3, 4, and 5 (C3-C5). Like patients with other causes of diaphragm weakness, patients with spinal cord injuries require the use of abdominal muscles to move air in and out of the chest. As a result, they often have orthopnea and may have paradoxical abdominal movement during the respiratory cycle (in which the abdomen moves inward as the chest expands and vice versa). Complete injury at level C3 and above results in long-term dependence on mechanical ventilatory support, whereas injuries in the C4 to C5 region cause variable degrees of diaphragmatic dysfunction. Many patients with acute C4-C5 injury initially require mechanical ventilation, but alleviation of cord inflammation, recruitment of accessory muscles, regained muscle strength, and transition from flaccid to rigid paralysis, which increases stability of the chest wall, allow for independent ventilation in most patients.

**Generalized Neuromuscular Weakness.** Acute inflammatory demyelinating polyneuropathy (AIDP, Guillain-Barré syndrome) is the most common cause of respiratory failure from neuromuscular weakness in the acute care setting. AIDP produces respiratory failure in up to one third of affected patients. Myasthenia gravis is a relatively infrequent cause of acute ventilatory failure that occasionally resembles AIDP during initial presentation; usually, the diagnosis is relatively straightforward because most patients have an established diagnosis of myasthenia gravis. Motor neuron disease (for example, amyotrophic lateral sclerosis) may also present with acute ventilatory failure, although again, most patients have well-established disease. Botulism remains an important cause of acute ventilatory failure worldwide but is rare in the United States.

### Restrictive Lung Disease

*Extrapulmonary*

The mechanical work of breathing is markedly increased in some disorders, thereby precipitating ventilatory failure even in the absence of intrinsic lung disease or weakness. Such patients have a restrictive pattern on pulmonary function tests. These disorders include chest wall diseases such as kyphoscoliosis, morbid obesity, large pleural effusions, and elevated intra-abdominal pressure from ascites, bowel edema, or

| **TABLE 40** Respiratory Complications of Neuromuscular Weakness |
| --- |
| Chronic ventilatory failure |
|   Pulmonary hypertension |
| Atelectasis |
| Aspiration |
| Pneumonia |
| Sleep-disordered breathing |

intraoperative gas insufflation. Kyphoscoliosis cannot be surgically corrected in adults, but affected patients are suitable candidates for NPPV, particularly at night when accessory muscle compensation is not as effective. Patients with extrapulmonary causes of restriction who develop infection or other acute illnesses may experience sudden declines in ventilatory function resulting in the need for intensive care.

## Pulmonary

Ventilatory failure due to fibrotic lung disease typically is accompanied by severe hypoxemia and carries a poor prognosis. Exacerbation of idiopathic pulmonary fibrosis, which is characterized by diffuse alveolar damage superimposed on fibrosis, is increasingly recognized as a cause of death in patients with even mild baseline decrements in pulmonary function tests (see also Diffuse Parenchymal Lung Disease).

## Obstructive Lung Disease

### Pathophysiology

The cause of acute ventilatory failure in patients with exacerbations of asthma or chronic obstructive pulmonary disease (COPD) is increased airway resistance and also dynamic hyperinflation that reduces chest-wall compliance. Both contribute to excessive work of breathing. Bronchospasm, airway edema, and secretions, as well as excessive expiratory airway collapse, can severely reduce airway diameter, resulting in markedly prolonged expiration. Increased respiratory drive and high metabolic demands increase minute ventilation, and there is incomplete expiration between breaths. Progressive stacking of breaths leads to an equilibration at a higher lung volume with higher positive end-expiratory alveolar pressure (auto-PEEP or intrinsic PEEP), associated with dynamic air trapping and hyperinflation. The associated flattening of the diaphragm decreases its function and forces greater reliance on accessory muscles, further increasing carbon dioxide production and oxygen consumption as a result of the inefficiency of these muscles compared with a properly functioning diaphragm. Severe air trapping can also cause alveolar rupture and marked reductions in venous return to the right heart, resulting in pneumothorax and hypotension, respectively. The presence of high airway resistance, decreased chest-wall compliance from overinflation, and elevated dead-space ventilation at baseline makes patients with advanced COPD particularly vulnerable to ventilatory failure during exacerbations. The work of increasing minute ventilation is too high, and the respiratory muscles fatigue. Upper airway disease is a less commonly encountered cause of obstructive ventilatory failure. Specific conditions include upper airway infection (for example, Ludwig angina) as well as angioedema associated with trauma, food allergy, angiotensin-converting enzyme inhibitor therapy, or C1 inhibitor deficiency.

### Medical Management of Obstructive Ventilatory Failure

Nearly 25% of COPD exacerbations result in hospitalization, and the mortality rate among patients requiring ICU admission is approximately 25%. Heart failure, pneumonia, pneumothorax, and pulmonary embolism should also be considered during the assessment of patients with COPD and ventilatory failure. Medical management is addressed in the chapter on Chronic Obstructive Pulmonary Disease, and noninvasive and invasive mechanical ventilation for an acute exacerbation are addressed below.

Some patients with life-threatening asthma exacerbations may not appear severely ill and then quickly decompensate. Serial spirometry or measurement of peak expiratory flow can distinguish deceptively severe and rapidly improving exacerbations. Patients with persistent $FEV_1$ or peak expiratory flow less than 40% of predicted after 1 hour of aggressive bronchodilator therapy are candidates for ICU admission. Patients with severe respiratory distress in whom pulmonary function tests cannot be reliably done should receive maximal medical support and possibly mechanical ventilation without delay.

Typically, patients with an asthma exacerbation initially present with respiratory alkalosis. Slightly elevated or even normal $PCO_2$ levels often indicate impending respiratory arrest rather than recovery, and clinical correlation is critical for interpreting arterial blood gas findings in this setting.

Treatment of an asthma exacerbation focuses initially on reversal of hypoxemia and bronchoconstriction with oxygen and bronchodilators (**Table 41**). Severe exacerbations typically cause mild to moderate hypoxemia, and oxygen requirements beyond 3 to 4 L/min by nasal cannula should prompt an evaluation for pneumonia, heart failure, and pulmonary embolism. High-dose inhaled short-acting $\beta_2$-agonists are the first-line treatment for bronchoconstriction. Early use of anticholinergic agents appears to offer a modest degree of bronchodilation beyond that achieved with $\beta_2$-agonists alone. Systemic corticosteroids are recommended for all patients requiring admission.

Although there is little evidence to support routine use of magnesium sulfate or helium-oxygen mixtures (heliox), both treatments are safe and may offer significant benefit to the most severely affected patients. Treatment with methylxanthines, antibiotics, aggressive hydration, mucolytic agents, chest physiotherapy, or sedatives is not recommended unless dictated by atypical clinical factors unique to the patient.

Indications for mechanical ventilation include decreased level of consciousness, agonal respirations, and increasing work of breathing and fatigue despite at least 1 hour of aggressive bronchodilator therapy.

**TABLE 41** Initial Management of Life-threatening Asthma Exacerbations

| Established Interventions[a] | Comment |
|---|---|
| Inhaled bronchodilators | |
| High-dose selective short-acting β-agonist | For example, albuterol, 2.5 mg by nebulizer every 20 min x 3, then 2.5 to 10 mg every 1 to 4 hours as needed |
| Anticholinergic agent | For example, ipratropium bromide, 0.5 mg every 20 min x 3, then as needed |
| Systemic corticosteroids | For example, methylprednisolone, 60 mg intravenously daily |
| Supplemental oxygen | Titrate to keep oxygen saturation >90% |
| **Adjunct Interventions[b]** | |
| Magnesium | For example, magnesium sulfate, 2 g intravenously x 1 |
| Heliox | 60% helium:40% oxygen |
| Noninvasive ventilation | Limited reported clinical experience |

[a]Supported by randomized trials and uniformly included in treatment guidelines.

[b]Less evidence to support use; inconsistently included in treatment guidelines.

## KEY POINTS

- Ventilatory failure refers to inadequate alveolar ventilation resulting in carbon dioxide retention and occurs in the setting of increased carbon dioxide production, decreased respiratory drive, excessive work of breathing, increased dead-space ventilation, and neuromuscular weakness.

- Management of critically ill patients with neuromuscular weakness entails close monitoring for, and treatment of, ventilatory failure; minimizing aspiration risk; and assisting with airway clearance.

- Auto-positive end-expiratory pressure contributes to increased work of breathing during exacerbations of obstructive lung disease.

- Serial objective measurement of airflow obstruction, such as forced expiratory volume in 1 second and peak expiratory flow, are valuable for determining the severity of asthma exacerbations.

- Patients with asthma having an acute exacerbation of asthma who do not respond to aggressive bronchodilator therapy within at least 1 hour are candidates for admission to the intensive care unit.

- A slightly elevated, or even normal, $P_{CO_2}$ in a patient with an asthma exacerbation may indicate impending respiratory failure.

- The need for large amounts of supplemental oxygen in patients with presumed exacerbations of asthma or chronic obstructive pulmonary disease should prompt consideration of alternative diagnoses.

## Noninvasive Mechanical Ventilation

NPPV consists of delivery of mechanically assisted positive airway pressure breaths without the use of an endotracheal tube or tracheostomy. In patients with new-onset respiratory failure, NPPV often entails the use of a ventilator that delivers breaths through a tight-fitting mask placed over the patient's nose and/or mouth. Inspiratory and expiratory pressures are individualized based on patient tolerance and clinical status. The end-expiratory positive airway pressure (EPAP) that is applied splints the upper airway and recruits the lungs to a higher volume. EPAP is analogous to continuous positive airway pressure (CPAP) used for sleep apnea and to positive end-expiratory pressure (PEEP) used in a closed system in intubated patients on mechanical ventilation. EPAP reduces the work of breathing in patients with obstructive disease by counteracting auto-PEEP, thus decreasing the work of inspiration. When NPPV is used, an inspiratory positive airway pressure (IPAP) is also set. The difference between the IPAP and the set EPAP is the driving pressure that increases the size of each breath (or provides similar-sized breaths with less work) and improves overall minute ventilation and is analogous to pressure support used in a closed system in intubated patients on mechanical ventilation.

### Indications

Noninvasive ventilation is being used increasingly in patients with acute respiratory failure to avoid endotracheal intubation as well as to facilitate weaning from invasive ventilation. There is now significant evidence identifying patients who are most likely to benefit from NPPV and/or CPAP.

#### Obstructive Lung Disease

Based on multiple, randomized, controlled studies showing reduced need for intubation, shortened hospital stays, and decreased mortality rates, NPPV is now the standard of care for patients with moderate to severe COPD exacerbations. Although there is a physiologic rationale for using NPPV in patients with asthma exacerbations, there is only limited evidence supporting its use in this setting. Guidelines for asthma management do not consistently recommend a trial of NPPV in patients failing to respond to standard therapy.

### Cardiogenic Pulmonary Edema

CPAP improves gas exchange in heart failure by recruiting flooded alveoli as well as reducing preload and afterload. Various trials have found that CPAP reduces the need for intubation in this setting. Early studies of NPPV found an increased risk for myocardial infarction associated with its use. However, this risk was not substantiated in subsequent studies that indicated NPPV may be particularly beneficial in patients with heart failure and hypercapnia.

### Immunosuppressed Patients

Immunosuppressed patients are especially vulnerable to developing ventilator-associated pneumonia. Use of NPPV in patients with ventilatory failure who have had solid-organ transplantation and in patients with AIDS or hematologic malignancies has been shown to reduce the need for intubation and to reduce the mortality rate. The greatest benefit appears to be achieved with early initiation of treatment and in patients with single-organ failure.

### Postoperative Patients

CPAP reduces the need for intubation in patients with hypoxemic respiratory failure complicating abdominal surgery, presumably by reducing atelectasis. NPPV improves outcomes in patients with hypoxemic respiratory failure after lung resection.

## Patient Selection

Patients who are alert, cooperative, and able to protect their airway and who receive treatment before the onset of severe respiratory acidosis (pH less than 7.10) are the most likely to benefit from NPPV. There are also many contraindications to NPPV (**Table 42**).

## Application

A major challenge to the successful implementation of NPPV in critically ill patients is reaching physiologically beneficial pressures in a timely fashion with good patient tolerance. Generally, nasal masks, which allow the patient to speak, eat, and drink, are considered more comfortable, but oronasal (full face) masks, which are less likely to have air leaks, typically are used initially in unstable patients.

Treatment is initiated with relatively low pressures and gradually titrated upward with close bedside monitoring of patient synchrony with the ventilator, comfort, relief of dyspnea, vital signs, tidal volumes, and gas exchange. Delivery of noninvasive ventilation via a ventilator designed for invasive mechanical ventilation offers the potential for greater oxygen delivery than bilevel devices used for sleep-disordered breathing, but the choice of ventilator is a secondary concern for most patients. Complications include pressure

**TABLE 42** Contraindications to Noninvasive Positive-Pressure Ventilation[a]

**Medical Instability**

Respiratory or cardiac arrest

Severe respiratory acidosis (pH <7.10)

Hemodynamic instability

Cardiogenic shock

Cardiac arrhythmia

Upper gastrointestinal bleeding

**Unable to Protect Airway**

Excessive secretions

Severe bulbar dysfunction

Excessive somnolence/encephalopathy

**Mechanical Issues**

Unable to fit mask/large air leak
   Recent facial trauma or surgery
   Facial deformity
Upper airway obstruction

[a]Timing, severity, and clinical context are used to determine whether a contraindication is absolute or relative for many of the above factors.

ulcers on the nasal bridge, mucosal pain, sinus congestion, and gastric insufflation (which is associated with inspiratory pressures greater than 20 cm $H_2O$). To reduce the risk of respiratory arrest, elective intubation should be considered in patients who do not respond to a 1- to 2-hour trial of noninvasive support.

### KEY POINTS

- Patients with respiratory failure secondary to chronic obstructive pulmonary disease exacerbations, heart failure, immunosuppressed states, and postoperative hypoxemia are the most likely to benefit from noninvasive positive-pressure ventilation.

- Immediate transition to noninvasive positive-pressure ventilation from invasive mechanical ventilation may facilitate weaning in selected patients who successfully tolerated a weaning trial.

- Noninvasive positive-pressure ventilation is not beneficial, and is potentially harmful, when used in patients who deteriorated during a weaning trial.

## Invasive Mechanical Ventilation

The decision to intubate a patient is often based on such clinical factors as the patient's clinical course and physiologic reserve, rather than a single absolute indication (**Table 43**). Patients with marked decrease in level of consciousness have poor control of their airway and often require intubation for support and to facilitate safe further assessment of their condition. Ventilator modes differ based on whether they deliver

**TABLE 43** Findings Suggestive of the Need for Invasive Mechanical Ventilation

| Clinical Parameters |
| --- |
| Lack of improvement after 2 hours of noninvasive positive-pressure ventilation |
| Difficulty maintaining airway |
|    Decreased level of consciousness |
|    Narrowed upper airway |
|    Excessive secretions |
|    Impaired cough |
| Hemodynamic instability |
| Prominent accessory muscle use |

| Laboratory and Ventilatory Parameters |
| --- |
| Severe respiratory acidosis (pH <7.20) |
| Severe hypoxemia ($Po_2$/$Fio_2$ <200) |
| Rise in $Pco_2$ >10 mm Hg |
| Respiration rate >35/min |
| Unable to generate negative inspiratory force >30 cm $H_2O$ |

a preset volume, preset pressure, or a hybrid of volume and pressure. The volume-limited assist/control mode minimizes work of breathing and is routinely employed in patients requiring substantial ventilatory support.

## Acute Respiratory Distress Syndrome

The combination of decreased lung compliance, elevated dead-space ventilation, and profound hypoxemia makes invasive mechanical ventilation necessary in almost all patients with ARDS. Increasing PEEP corrects hypoxemia by recruiting flooded and collapsed alveoli. Positive-pressure breaths support ventilation and reduce the work of breathing. However, large tidal volumes can injure the lung by causing alveolar overdistention.

The ARMA trial established that the use of low (6 mL/kg predicted weight) rather than standard (12 mL/kg predicted weight) tidal volumes reduced the mortality rate from 40% to 30%. The application of this lung protective ventilator strategy, which also targets an end-inspiratory passive recoil (plateau) pressure less than 30 cm $H_2O$, often requires permissive hypercapnia as well as the use of a high $Fio_2$ in patients with severe ARDS. The subsequent ALVEOLI study found that an "open-lung" strategy using higher levels of PEEP does not offer an advantage over lower PEEP levels sufficient to improve oxygenation. Increased vascular permeability is the primary cause of flooded alveoli in early ARDS and is directly related to hydrostatic pressure. Patients with ARDS are more likely to develop flooded alveoli at any level of hydrostatic pressure than normal persons. In an attempt to mitigate the effects of intravascular volume on increasing hydrostatic pressure in patients with ARDS, a recent study compared liberal and conservative fluid management in hemodynamically stable patients with acute lung injury and normal renal function and found no difference in survival, but the conservative strategy shortened the duration of mechanical ventilation and length of ICU stay without increasing nonpulmonary organ failure. The conservative fluid strategy targeted central venous pressure less than 4 mm Hg or pulmonary capillary wedge pressure less than 8 mm Hg.

Whether systemic corticosteroids have a role in the management of ARDS remains controversial. A recent multicenter study found no benefit to corticosteroids in unresolving ARDS and possible harm when treatment was initiated beyond 2 weeks of the onset of ARDS. A subsequent smaller study found systemic corticosteroids initiated early (day 3 after the onset of ARDS) reduced the duration of mechanical ventilation and improved ICU survival.

A minority of patients with ARDS develop life-threatening hypoxemia despite aggressive use of supplemental oxygen and PEEP. Inhaled nitric oxide reduces ventilation/perfusion mismatch in this setting but did not reduce mortality rates in clinical trials. Continuous prostacyclin by nebulization is a less expensive alternative to nitric oxide that also improves ventilation/perfusion mismatch but has not been shown to improve survival.

Oxygenation improves in most patients with severe ARDS when they are placed in a prone position. Studies have found that repositioning patients did not reduce mortality, but it remains unclear whether the lack of efficacy was due to suboptimal patient selection and duration of repositioning.

## Obstructive Lung Disease

Patients with obstructive lung disease frequently require ventilator settings that allow for prolonged expiration. Severe airway obstruction limits expiratory flow rates and may prevent complete exhalation if sufficient time is not allowed before initiation of the subsequent breath. When incomplete exhalation occurs, positive pressure accumulates within the lung to create autologous positive end-expiratory pressure (auto-PEEP) and dynamic hyperinflation. This condition can be uncomfortable for the patient, impede synchronous patient efforts with the mechanical ventilator, increase the risk of barotrauma, and cause hypotension due to impaired venous blood return to the thorax. An examination of the airflow versus time waveform on the mechanical ventilator may help identify expiratory airflow that does not cease prior to the next inhalation (**Figure 13**). Checking end-expiratory pressure during an end-expiratory pause (that is, without airflow) will allow pressure to equalize between the alveoli and the airways and will confirm the presence of auto-PEEP. If hypotensions occur in this setting, it may be necessary to disconnect the endotracheal tube from the mechanical ventilator for several seconds to allow complete exhalation and the return of alveolar pressure to atmospheric pressure. The primary ventilator strategy in patients with obstructive disease who develop auto-PEEP is to accommodate the need for prolonged

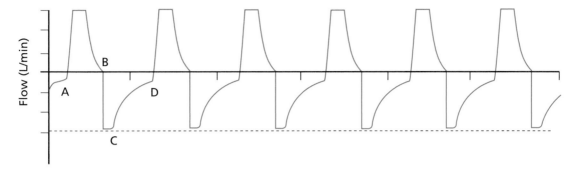

**FIGURE 13.**
**Pressure-time curve of a mechanically ventilated patient.**
Note that positive end-expiratory pressure (PEEP) is being delivered by the mechanical ventilator, evidenced by the persistent pressure throughout expiration. A pause following the second expiration shown demonstrates the presence of intrinsic (auto) PEEP.

A-B = inspiration; B = end of inspiration, beginning of exhalation; B-C-D = expiratory flow.

Reproduced with permission from: Raoof S, Khan FA. Mechanical ventilation manual. Philadelphia. American College of Physicians, 1998.

expiratory time by minimizing minute ventilation. This can be accomplished by lowering the tidal volume and/or respiratory rate. High inspiratory flow rates shorten inspiratory time and, to a modest degree, also allow more time for expiration. Depending on the patient's baseline respiratory status, the need to minimize minute ventilation may require tolerating $PCO_2$ levels above baseline (permissive hypercapnia).

Patients with COPD often present with acute-on-chronic hypercapnia, and minute ventilation is adjusted to achieve the patient's baseline $PCO_2$ levels. Immediate correction of the $PCO_2$ to normal (35-45 mm Hg) can result in unmasking of severe alkalosis due to compensatory bicarbonate retention that has occurred in response to the chronic hypercarbia. Conversely, prolonged normalization of $PCO_2$ levels, with consequent loss of chronic renal compensation, results in acute respiratory acidosis during subsequent weaning trials when the patient's $PCO_2$ rises to baseline level.

Markedly elevated airway pressures, severe dynamic hyperinflation, and ventilator dyssynchrony make the management of intubated patients with asthma particularly challenging. Typical ventilator strategies include a relatively low minute ventilation and permissive hypercapnia to manage the dynamic overinflation. Imposing permissive hypercapnia on patients with baseline normocarbia often requires heavy sedation and, occasionally, short-term use of neuromuscular blocking agents.

## Weaning

NPPV may provide a means of shortening the time to extubation in patients with acute respiratory failure. One randomized study found early extubation directly to NPPV of 50 patients with exacerbations of COPD shortened ICU stays and improved survival. However, these benefits were not duplicated in subsequent studies, and this approach is suitable only for highly selected patients with acute on chronic respiratory failure.

NPPV has also been used with mixed results in the postextubation management of patients initially intubated for respiratory failure who met standard weaning criteria. In a recent randomized controlled trial, patients who tolerated a spontaneous breathing trial but were deemed to be at increased risk for postextubation respiratory failure received either early prophylactic NPPV or standard care. Patients given early NPPV were less likely to develop respiratory failure after extubation and had lower ICU mortality. In contrast, two randomized studies found that NPPV is not efficacious and is possibly even harmful when used in patients who are already clinically deteriorating during a trial of extubation. The larger multicenter study was terminated early after an interim analysis found increased mortality in the NPPV group. Some reports indicate that patients with COPD with acute-on-chronic respiratory failure may benefit from "rescue" NPPV in this setting.

Before a patient's endotracheal tube is removed, it is important to determine whether the patient can maintain adequate gas exchange (ventilation and oxygenation) independent of the ventilator and whether the patient can maintain airway patency independent of the tube. Ventilator weaning protocols, which use systematic daily screening for potential weaning candidates followed by spontaneous breathing trials when appropriate, reduce the overall time on mechanical ventilation. A typical approach is to measure the rapid shallow breathing index (RSBI), which consists of the respiration rate divided by the tidal volume in liters, in all hemodynamically stable, sufficiently alert patients with a baseline oxygen saturation greater than 90% on $FIO_2$ less than or equal to 0.40 and PEEP less than or equal to 5 cm $H_2O$. The RSBI is obtained while the patient is on a T-piece or receiving low levels of CPAP and/or pressure support. Patients with a RSBI less than 105/min/L should undergo a 30- to 90-minute spontaneous breathing trial; if the trial is well tolerated, mechanical ventilation is no longer necessary.

The multicenter Awakening Breathing Controlled (ABC) trial tested the results of linked sedation and ventilator weaning protocols using a "wake up and breathe" approach. In both groups, patients were given a targeted sedation strategy. All patients in the control group received daily spontaneous breathing trials (SBTs, consisting of CPAP ventilator settings) for 2 hours to determine readiness for extubation. Patients on the ABC intervention were given spontaneous awakening trials (SATs as step A consisting of total cessation of sedation long enough to wake to verbal stimulus or tolerate for 4 hours) followed by SBTs as step B. The ABC "wake up and breathe" intervention resulted in a 3-day reduction of mechanical ventilation, 1-day reduction in coma, 4-day reduction in ICU and hospital stay, and 14% lower mortality rate at 1 year (58% mortality rate in control group reduced to 44% in treatment group). This intervention resulted in a 50% reduction in the overall exposure to benzodiazepines. Whether this results in long-term neuropsychologic improvements in addition to the profound outcome improvement is now being investigated.

Before the endotracheal tube is removed, it is also imperative to consider the patient's strength of cough, secretion burden, aspiration risk, and upper airway patency. The use of NPPV to facilitate extubation or to prevent reintubation has produced mixed results. Tracheostomy improves patient comfort and facilitates weaning. Although there is a consensus that tracheostomy should be performed within 21 days of intubation, the optimal timing remains unclear. Increasingly, bedside percutaneous dilational tracheostomy is used in lieu of surgical placement, based on excellent reported outcomes.

## Ventilator-associated Pneumonia

Ventilator-associated pneumonia (VAP), which is defined as pneumonia with onset at least 48 hours after the initiation of invasive mechanical ventilation, affects 10% to 25% of intubated patients and is associated with a 25% to 50% mortality rate. Placing intubated patients in a semirecumbent position (that is, elevation of the head of the bed to greater than 45 degrees) reduces the risk of VAP, as do interventions that shorten the duration of mechanical ventilation, including protocol-based weaning and daily sedation holidays. Avoidance of enteral feeding early in the course of illness and use of postpyloric feeding tubes may offer modest risk reduction. Studies have shown that selective decontamination of the digestive tract with antibiotics and subglottic suction catheters reduce VAP risk. Two randomized controlled trials showed that tracheobronchial colonization causing VAP occurred less often in patients whose mouths had been decontaminated with topical antibiotics.

Although VAP cannot be reliably diagnosed strictly on clinical grounds, the optimal approach to the diagnosis is controversial. Earlier studies indicated that bronchoscopically obtained specimens for quantitative cultures have improved specificity for diagnosing VAP and reduced antibiotic use compared with routine culture of endotracheal aspirates. However, bronchoscopy is more expensive and may not be readily available. A recent randomized, multicenter comparison of treatment based on endotracheal aspirates and bronchoscopically derived samples in 650 patients found equivalent mortality, length of ICU stay, and days requiring mechanical ventilation. This study excluded immunosuppressed patients more apt to harbor resistant organisms. There is evidence that shortened antibiotic courses of approximately 1 week are sufficient, although infections due to resistant gram-negative organisms, such as *Pseudomonas*, may require longer treatment courses.

**KEY POINTS**

- Use of low tidal volume (6 mL/kg predicted weight) reduces mortality in patients with acute respiratory distress syndrome.

- Avoidance of auto–positive end-expiratory pressure (and dynamic hyperinflation) often requires the use of permissive hypercapnia in patients with exacerbations of obstructive lung disease who are receiving invasive mechanical ventilation.

- Ventilation should be targeted to the patient's baseline $P_{CO_2}$ for patients with acute on chronic ventilatory failure.

- Protocol-driven approaches to daily spontaneous breathing trials and to sedation weaning shorten the duration of mechanical ventilation.

- Strength of cough, secretion burden, aspiration risk, and upper airway patency must be assessed in patients passing spontaneous breathing trials before removal of the endotracheal tube.

- Antibiotic courses of approximately 1 week are now recommended in most patients with ventilator-associated pneumonia, although infections due to resistant gram-negative organisms such as *Pseudomonas* may require longer treatment courses.

## Sepsis

The incidence of sepsis rises exponentially after age 65 to 70 years, and age-specific mortality rates are much higher in patients with baseline comorbidities, such as diabetes mellitus or heart disease. Sepsis is most common in men, nonwhites, and the elderly, with gram-positive organisms accounting for over 50% of all cases.

The prognosis for a patient with severe sepsis can be approximated by adding 15% to 20% predicted mortality for each sepsis-induced dysfunctional organ. Another major prognostic indicator reported in recent studies is that patients with refractory septic shock (defined as having received multiple liters of volume replacement and still requiring vasopressor support to maintain a mean arterial blood pressure of

65 to 70 mm Hg or more) have a 28-day mortality rate in recent studies of 40% to 45%, which is improved from the 60% widely reported in previous years.

## Pathophysiology

Sepsis is a complex dysregulation of both inflammation and coagulation. Primary cellular injury may result directly from infection or when a toxic microbial stimulus initiates a deleterious host inflammatory response. A network of inflammatory mediators are generated, including tumor necrosis factor (TNF)-$\alpha$, interleukin-1 (IL-1), and other cytokines and chemokines that activate leukocytes and promote leukocyte-vascular endothelial adhesion and damage. Endothelial damage leads to tissue factor expression and activation of the tissue factor–dependent clotting cascade and subsequent formation of thrombin. The result is the development of microaggregates of fibrin, platelets, neutrophils, and erythrocytes with impairment of capillary blood flow and decreased oxygen and nutrient delivery to tissues. Higher levels of circulating and intracellular TNF-$\alpha$, IL-1, IL-6, and soluble adhesion molecules, which are markers for activated or damaged endothelium, have been detected in older patients with sepsis. Increasing age even in the absence of sepsis is associated with rising circulating levels of IL-6, D-dimers, activated coagulation factor VII, and other coagulation factors, indicating activation of inflammatory and coagulation pathways.

## Diagnosis

The diagnostic criteria for sepsis are the presence of a known or suspected infection (documented positive cultures are not required) and the presence of at least two of the following criteria for the systemic inflammatory response syndrome: temperature greater than 38.0 °C (100.4 °F) or less than 36.0 °C (96.8 °F), leukocyte count greater than 12,000/$\mu$L ($12 \times 10^9$/L) or less than 4000/$\mu$L ($4 \times 10^9$/L), respiration rate greater than 20/min, and heart rate greater than 90/min. The criteria for severe sepsis require evidence of one sepsis-induced organ dysfunction, such as hypoxemia, shock, delirium, thrombocytopenia, or rising serum creatinine or bilirubin level. However, vital signs and leukocyte abnormalities are not always sensitive in older patients or immunosuppressed patients. For example, fever may be blunted or absent in approximately 15% of older patients with bacteremia compared with less than 5% of patients younger than 65 years. The index of suspicion for sepsis must be high (especially in older patients) when any of the following nonspecific clinical signs or symptoms of infection are present: delirium, weakness, anorexia, malaise, urinary incontinence, or falls. Various biologic markers of sepsis have been studied, for example, procalcitonin, C-reactive protein, and IL-6, but none of them has been validated for routine clinical use. Microbiologic findings are also useful, and culture specimens must be obtained from the suspected site of infection. Blood cultures should always be obtained, even though only one in three patients with sepsis has a positive blood culture and only two in three have positive cultures from any site.

## Management of Sepsis

### Source Control and Antibiotic Therapy

The source of a patient's sepsis should be identified and controlled by removing an infected central intravascular line or draining an abscess. Empiric antibiotic therapy should be initiated within 1 hour of recognition of sepsis after cultures have been taken from the blood and other suspected sites of infection. Inadequate initial antibiotic therapy is independently associated with poor outcomes, and initial empiric therapy should include agents with activity against all probable pathogens. Because of increasing antibiotic resistance, broad and early antibiotic therapy must be balanced with de-escalation against identified organisms and/or cessation of antibiotics once the infection has resolved. Recent studies indicate an advantage to shorter antibiotic regimens for some sites of infection (1 week for ventilator-associated pneumonia) over traditionally longer courses (10 to 14 days). In community-acquired pneumonia, as few as 5 days of antimicrobial therapy may be sufficient as long as the patient has been afebrile at least 48 hours before therapy is discontinued.

### Assessment and Management of Septic Shock

Initial resuscitation of a patient with severe sepsis and septic shock should begin early, with a goal of maintaining adequate tissue perfusion. The defining features of inadequate tissue perfusion may include any of the following: low arterial or central venous pressure, tachycardia, tachypnea, central venous oxygen saturation less than 70%, oliguria, acidosis, delirium, cold extremities, and livedo reticularis.

When caring for a patient in shock, causes other than sepsis should be considered, such as cardiogenic, hypovolemic, anaphylactic, and neurogenic shock. When the cause is unclear, bedside echocardiography may help differentiate shock caused by a pulmonary embolism (right ventricular dilation), acute myocardial infarction (focal wall motion abnormalities), hypovolemia (poorly filled hyperdynamic left ventricle), and sepsis (global decrease in contractility). In patients with known or suspected infection, persistent hypotension despite adequate fluid resuscitation mandates the use of vasopressors. Because of volatile changes in blood pressure that may occur in septic shock, arterial cannulation may be used for continual monitoring of blood pressure and titration of vasopressor therapy. In addition, central venous catheters are needed to infuse vasopressors.

Most patients need at least 4 to 6 L of intravascular volume replacement within the first 6 hours, and one of the biggest pitfalls of management is underestimating the intravascular volume deficit. Patients with sepsis typically have an elevated cardiac index and low systemic vascular resistance as well as a low pulmonary artery occlusion pressure. These parameters have traditionally been measured by pulmonary artery catheterization, with titration of fluids to target wedge pressures and delivery of blood or inotropic agents to drive oxygen delivery to supraphysiologic levels; however, at least four international landmark studies have now shown that neither pulmonary artery catheterization nor use of specific protocols that incorporate data from such catheters yields superior outcomes in most patients. Aggressive resuscitation delivered for 6 hours in an emergency department has generated renewed interest in determining the best and most balanced approach. This emergency department protocol involves the insertion of a special type of central venous line used to measure and titrate the central venous oxygen saturation above 70%, a practice that has not been widely adopted but is being subjected to other confirmatory trials.

Whether to use crystalloid or colloid is controversial, with normal saline being the fluid of choice in most patients. Albumin or other colloid infusions are sometimes used in situations of low oncotic pressure and extensive third-spacing. Vasopressor therapy with norepinephrine, vasopressin, or dopamine may be necessary when appropriate fluid challenge fails to restore adequate tissue perfusion or during life-threatening hypotension, but no trials have established a single superior approach to handling initial vasopressor choice. Bicarbonate infusions have not been shown to be helpful in refractory shock, even in the presence of lactic acidosis and are used only in patients with severe shock.

## Activated Protein C

More than 90% of patients with sepsis have acquired thrombophilic and inflammatory derangements. Administration of the body's natural anticoagulants with anti-inflammatory properties has been tested in patients with severe sepsis. Protein C is an endogenous protein that is predominantly "unactivated" in the circulation, becoming "activated" by thrombin-thrombomodulin complexes and the endothelial protein C receptor. Activated protein C inhibits thrombin formation by blocking coagulation factors Va and VIIIa, enhances fibrinolysis of microthrombi by inhibiting plasminogen activator inhibitor-1, reduces release of inflammatory mediators and cellular adhesion molecules, stabilizes endothelial injury, and alters apoptosis. Endogenous activation of protein C is impaired in sepsis.

Drotrecogin alfa (activated protein C) is approved by the U.S. Food and Drug Administration and international regulatory authorities for patients with severe sepsis who are at high risk for death. In a phase III trial in which patients were followed for 2.5 years, severely ill patients treated with activated protein C had a higher survival rate (45.6%) than those treated with placebo (33.8%, $P = 0.001$, absolute risk reduction 12%, number needed to treat 8.5), whereas less severely ill patients treated with activated protein C had a lower survival rate; however, this rate was not significantly lower (59.2% vs. 63.8%, $P = 0.2$). A recent trial in patients at low risk of death was stopped early because of futility; activated

protein C should not be given to septic patients at low risk of death (for example, those with only one dysfunctional sepsis-induced organ system).

Drotrecogin alfa therapy should be considered in patients with all of the following: septic shock requiring vasopressors despite fluid resuscitation **and** sepsis-induced ARDS requiring mechanical ventilation, **and** any two sepsis-induced dysfunctional organs. The therapy is given as a continuous infusion for 96 hours and requires no titration for age or liver or kidney function and no specific laboratory monitoring.

Drotrecogin alfa therapy increases bleeding risk at rates similar to those of heparin. Serious bleeding increases by 1.5% to 2.5% above that expected with placebo, and intracerebral hemorrhage occurs in 0.6% of treated patients. Because the drug has a half-life of less than 15 minutes, it can be stopped when bleeding occurs, and its anticoagulant effect usually remits within 1 hour without any specific antidote. Nonetheless, drotrecogin alfa is contraindicated in the presence of active bleeding, concurrent therapy with other anticoagulant drugs, and platelet counts less than $30,000/\mu L$ ($30 \times 10^9/L$), and in patients with risks of uncontrollable or central nervous system bleeding. Drotrecogin alfa therapy is expensive, but it is cost effective if used in appropriate patients.

## Corticosteroids

Replacement-dose hydrocortisone is no longer recommended routinely for patients with septic shock who achieve a systolic blood pressure of at least 90 mm Hg with fluids and vasopressors, although corticosteroids may be useful for patients with more profound, refractory shock. Although an early study reported improved mortality rates in patients with relative adrenal insufficiency who were treated with hydrocortisone and fludrocortisone, the landmark CORTICUS study failed to demonstrate any survival advantage for patients in septic shock with a systolic blood pressure of at least 90 mm Hg. Most patients with sepsis meet the CORTICUS criteria, and corticosteroid therapy would not be indicated. When such therapy is used, patients should be monitored for hyperglycemia, immunosuppression, poor wound healing, delirium, and ICU-acquired weakness.

## Glucose Control

Hyperglycemia is common in severe sepsis and may impair antimicrobial defense mechanisms and worsen the coagulopathy of sepsis. Intensive insulin therapy with a goal of maintaining plasma blood glucose levels between 80 (4.4 mmol/L) and 110 mg/dL (6.11 mmol/L) resulted in reduced mortality in one large randomized, controlled trial, but this survival advantage was not duplicated by a subsequent study of medical ICU patients. In addition, other multicenter studies have been stopped early because of hypoglycemia and other adverse events occurring more commonly in patients with tight glucose control. The recently reported NICE SUGAR study, a large international randomized trial, found that intensive glucose control increased the mortality rate in adults in the ICU; a glucose target of 180 mg/dL (9.99 mmol/L) resulted in lower mortality than did a target of 81 to 108 mg/dL (4.5 to 6.0 mmol/L). There is now a more modest goal of maintaining glucose levels below 150 mg/dL (8.33 mmol/L).

## Transfusion Strategies
Packed erythrocytes are often transfused into septic patients with tissue hypoperfusion marked by hypotension or lactic acidosis, active bleeding, profound anemia, or coronary artery disease. In the absence of these indications, erythrocyte transfusion strategies should be approached conservatively. A large, randomized trial showed that a target hemoglobin concentration of 7 to 9 g/dL (70 to 90 g/L) resulted in no additional mortality compared with the traditional target of 10 g/dL (100 g/L). Indeed, there was a trend toward improved outcomes in the conservatively transfused patients. However, in a study of 80,000 patients, older patients with myocardial infarction were shown to have higher survival rates when the hemoglobin concentration was maintained at 10 to 11 g/dL (100 to 110 g/L). After stabilization, the transfusion threshold should be a hemoglobin concentration of 7 g/dL (70 g/L) with the exception of older patients with a history of myocardial infarction and uncorrected coronary anatomy.

## Mechanical Ventilation in Sepsis
Many patients with severe sepsis require mechanical ventilation. A lung-protective (low tidal volume) strategy of ventilation is recommended in such patients. Mechanically ventilated patients should have the head of their bed raised to 45 degrees to reduce the risk of ventilator-associated pneumonia. To reduce time on mechanical ventilation and in the ICU and hospital, a protocol-driven "linked" sedation and ventilator weaning strategy should be used.

## Miscellaneous Issues
Other important aspects of the management of sepsis include prophylaxis for deep venous thrombosis with low-dose unfractionated heparin, low-molecular-weight heparin, or mechanical prophylactic devices and prevention of stress ulcers with $H_2$-receptor blockers or proton pump inhibitors.

### KEY POINTS
- The criteria for severe sepsis require evidence of one sepsis-induced organ dysfunction, such as hypoxemia, shock, delirium, thrombocytopenia, or rising serum creatinine or bilirubin level.
- Recent studies indicate an advantage to shorter antibiotic regimens for some sites of infection (1 week for ventilator-associated pneumonia) over traditionally longer courses (10 to 14 days).

- In community-acquired pneumonia, as few as 5 days of antimicrobial therapy may be sufficient as long as the patient has been afebrile at least 48 hours before therapy is discontinued.
- Drotrecogin alfa (activated protein C) therapy should be considered in patients with all of the following: septic shock requiring vasopressors despite fluid resuscitation **and** sepsis-induced ARDS requiring mechanical ventilation **and** any two sepsis-induced dysfunctional organs
- Replacement-dose hydrocortisone is not recommended routinely for patients with septic shock who achieve a systolic blood pressure of at least 90 mm Hg with fluids and vasopressors.
- After stabilization, the transfusion threshold in patients with sepsis should be a hemoglobin concentration of 7 g/dL (70 g/L) with the exception of older patients with a history of myocardial infarction and uncorrected coronary anatomy.

# Emergent Disorders in Critical Care

## Intensive Care Unit–acquired Weakness
More than 50% of patients with sustained critical illness are believed to have weakness due to axonal neuropathy and primary myopathy (independent of neuropathy). Patients typically have generalized, flaccid weakness and difficulty weaning from mechanical ventilation. Distinguishing neuropathy from myopathy is often difficult in critically ill patients; therefore, the term ICU-acquired weakness is used to encompass the previously described entities of critical-illness myopathy and critical-illness neuropathy. There is controversy over the best evaluation for ICU-acquired weakness. One approach is to base the diagnosis on serial examinations and to limit testing for alternative causes of weakness to patients with persistent, fixed, or focal neurologic deficits. Other proposed diagnostic algorithms incorporate nerve conduction studies and electromyography. Although ICU-acquired weakness is thought to result primarily from systemic inflammation, other potential risk factors include immobilization and exposure to systemic corticosteroids and neuromuscular blocking agents. ICU-acquired weakness increases overall mortality and can cause prolonged disability. However, many patients recover rapidly over weeks.

## Acute Inhalational Injuries
About 50% of all deaths in burn injuries are related to inhalation injury. Morbidity and mortality increase when burn injury is associated with smoke inhalation. Early hypoxemia is predictive of poor outcome. Early thermal injuries are most common with steam (usually confined to the upper airway) and findings of rhinitis, pharyngitis, laryngitis, tracheitis, and

bronchitis. Continued exposure to steam can produce distal parenchymal injury and pulmonary edema.

Smoke is extremely complex and can contain various toxins. Many of the less soluble toxins can cause distal bronchiolitis and alveolitis. Clinical features indicating smoke inhalation include any of the following: facial burns, soot marks, singed eyebrows or facial hair, hoarseness, stridor, or carbonaceous sputum. The full extent of airway compromise may not be evident until 12 to 24 hours after the initial injury. Soot deposition of particulate matter from combustion causes immediate airway irritation and reflex bronchoconstriction. Initial symptoms may vary from mild airway irritation with cough and tachypnea to acute respiratory failure. Although most patients recover from the initial insult, many subsequently develop bacterial pneumonia, usually within 4 to 5 days. The degree of recovery depends on the duration of exposure and the type of smoke, which together determine the extent of proximal airway and distal pulmonary parenchymal injury. Residual tracheal stenosis, reactive airways disease, bronchiectasis, bronchiolitis obliterans, and interstitial fibrosis may occur. Hypoxic damage to other organs can result in multiorgan system failure, sepsis, and death. Neurologic impairment may result from hypoxic damage or may reflect carbon monoxide or cyanide toxicity.

Inhalation of asphyxiants, such as carbon monoxide, hydrogen cyanide, nitrogen, and methane, causes impaired oxygen delivery and tissue hypoxia. Carbon monoxide poisoning is responsible for up to 80% of all deaths associated with fires and inhalation injuries (see Carbon Monoxide Poisoning in Poisonings and Overdoses below). Cyanide toxicity results from fires involving incomplete combustion of plastics and acrylics. One third of patients with smoke inhalation from domestic fires have high blood levels of cyanide (see Cyanide Poisoning in Poisonings and Overdoses below). In the initial assessment of patients with suspected inhalational injury, measurement of arterial blood gases is useful to determine the extent of hypoxia, hypercarbia, and acidosis. Cutaneous pulse oximetry readings are falsely elevated if carboxyhemoglobin levels are increased, whereas the percentage of oxyhemoglobin measured by arterial CO-oximetry is an accurate measure of the arterial oxygen saturation. The CO-oximeter measures absorption at several wavelengths to distinguish oxyhemoglobin from carboxyhemoglobin and determine the oxyhemoglobin saturation.

Radiographic evidence of pulmonary injury typically appears 24 to 36 hours after injury. Direct laryngoscopy and fiberoptic bronchoscopy can be used to assess the extent of tracheal and parenchymal edema and burns. Treatment of all patients with inhalational injury includes supportive care with fluids and early enteral feedings, especially if burns are present. Laryngeal edema is treated with aerosolized racemic epinephrine, which is more active topically because of slower absorption. Bronchospasm is treated with inhaled bronchodilators. Management often requires aggressive pulmonary toilet, frequent chest physiotherapy, and repeated bronchoscopy. Antibiotics should be administered if there is coexistent infection; most secondary pneumonias are caused by *Staphylococcus aureus* and *Pseudomonas aeruginosa*. Prophylactic antibiotics and corticosteroids have been shown to increase infections with resistant organisms. If cyanide toxicity is suspected, oxygen and sodium thiosulfate should be given. Although nitrites can be used to treat cyanide toxicity, care must be taken because nitrites convert hemoglobin to methemoglobin. This may worsen carbon monoxide toxicity if there is coexisting carboxyhemoglobinemia.

## Anaphylaxis

Anaphylaxis is a life-threatening allergic reaction associated with cutaneous, respiratory, cardiovascular, or gastrointestinal manifestations resulting from exposure to an offending agent (**Table 44**). Food allergies are the leading cause of anaphylaxis. The frequency of anaphylaxis is increasing, a fact that has been attributed to the increased number of potential allergens to which people are exposed. The true incidence of anaphylaxis is unknown, partly because of the lack of a precise and uniform definition of the disorder. Fatal anaphylaxis is rare. Although it occurs in all age groups, the elderly have the highest mortality rate.

In anaphylaxis, a foreign protein is the antigen that, on initial exposure, activates IgE antibody on mast cells and basophils. Clinical manifestations result from the release of immune mediators from the mast cells and basophils, including histamine, leukotrienes, tryptase, and prostaglandins. Although prior exposure is essential for the development of true anaphylaxis, reactions occur even when prior exposure has not been documented. Factors influencing the severity of a reaction include degree of host sensitivity and dose, route, and rate of administration of the antigen. The faster a reaction develops, the more severe it is likely to be. Parenteral exposures tend to result in faster and more severe reactions. Most reactions occur within minutes to hours after exposure, but symptoms may begin as long as 3 to 4 days after exposure.

The manifestations of anaphylaxis vary in intensity. Patients commonly are restless because of severe pruritus from urticaria. The level of consciousness may be depressed, or the patient may be anxious or agitated. The classic skin manifestation is urticaria. Local erythema at the site of an insect bite or diffuse erythema and edema may also occur. Local reactions, even if severe, are not predictive of systemic anaphylaxis on reexposure. Angioedema may occur with marked edema of the tongue and lips that may obstruct the airway. Upper airway edema may cause hoarseness or stridor. Complete airway obstruction is the most common cause of death in anaphylaxis. Wheezing is common when patients have lower airway compromise from bronchospasm or mucosal edema. Tachycardia usually is present, but bradycardia may occur in very severe reactions. Hypotension, cardiovascular collapse, or

**TABLE 44** Causes, Pathogenesis, Diagnosis, and Prophylaxis of Anaphylaxis

| Cause | Pathogenesis | Diagnostic Test | Prophylaxis |
|-------|--------------|-----------------|-------------|
| Drugs<br>Foods<br>Insect stings<br>Allergenic extracts<br>Hormones<br>Seminal fluid<br>Latex<br>Cold urticaria | IgE antibody | Skin test<br>In vitro IgE antibody assay | Avoidance<br>Desensitization<br>Immunotherapy |
| Radiocontrast media | Complement activation | None | Premedication with antihistamines, corticosteroids, or ephedrine<br>Use of hypo-osmolar contrast |
| Aspirin and NSAIDs | Leukotriene generation | Aspirin challenge | Avoidance, desensitization |
| Food-dependent exercise-induced | Unknown | None (food tests may be contributory) | Avoid food intake |
| Idiopathic | Unknown | None | Antihistamines, corticosteroids |
| Transfusion (blood and blood products) | Anti-IgA (IgG or IgE) | Measurement of IgA | Washed, packed cells; IgA-deficient gamma globulin |

Reproduced with permission from Slavin RG, Reisman RE. Expert Guide to Allergy and Immunology. Philadelphia, PA: American College of Physicians; 1999.

respiratory arrest may occur in severe reactions. Shock may occur without prominent skin manifestations or a history of exposure; therefore, anaphylaxis is part of the differential diagnosis for patients who present with shock and no obvious cause. Although the diagnosis of anaphylaxis is almost always made clinically, elevated urine and serum histamine and plasma tryptase concentrations may help support the diagnosis.

## Treatment

Prompt treatment of anaphylaxis is critical and can be life-saving. Initial treatment includes basic life support measures with high-flow oxygen, cardiac monitoring, and intravenous access. These measures are appropriate for asymptomatic patients with a history of a serious reaction and recent reexposure or for patients with local reactions only. Subcutaneous or intramuscular epinephrine is used to treat acute anaphylaxis, but there are limited data on its appropriate dosing, timing, or repeated administration. Patients taking β-blockers may not respond to standard epinephrine doses. In these patients, larger doses of epinephrine or glucagon may be useful. $H_1$- and $H_2$-antihistamines, corticosteroids, or both, are also often used, but there are few data on their effectiveness. Corticosteroids are used primarily to decrease the incidence and severity of delayed or biphasic reactions but do not influence the acute course of the disease because of their slow onset of action. Inhaled $β_2$-agonists are indicated for patients with bronchospasm. It is imperative to assess airway patency because of the potential for compromise secondary to upper airway obstruction or bronchospasm. Endotracheal intubation may be difficult because of laryngeal or oropharyngeal edema. Bag-valve-mask ventilation should be utilized initially when intubation is not possible. Surgical airway intervention using standard cricothyroidotomy is an option.

Patients with anaphylaxis who present with moderate or severe symptoms should be observed and monitored in the ICU for at least 12 hours for the development of delayed or protracted reactions. Affected patients may develop hypotension from vasodilation and capillary fluid leakage, and large-volume resuscitation with isotonic crystalloids is indicated. Refractory hypotension should be treated with repeated doses of epinephrine or a continuous epinephrine infusion. If ineffective, other vasopressors with α-adrenergic activity, such as norepinephrine or dopamine, may be used. Military antishock trousers have been used to treat refractory hypotension.

## Hypertensive Emergencies

Hypertensive emergencies affect approximately 1% of all adults with hypertension and are more frequent in men, the elderly, and black Americans. The morbidity and mortality associated with a hypertensive crisis are related to the degree of end-organ damage on presentation. Up to 83% of patients presenting with a hypertensive emergency have evidence of single-organ involvement. The 1-year mortality rate for an untreated hypertensive emergency approaches 90%. The presence of end-organ damage defines a hypertensive emergency, not the absolute level of the presenting blood pressure. Hypertensive urgencies usually present with diastolic blood pressures greater than 120 mm Hg and are not associated with end-organ damage. Blood pressure management in these patients can be achieved over several days to weeks. In hypertensive emergencies, immediate treatment of the blood pressure within minutes to hours is necessary to prevent further end-organ damage and complications. The central nervous, cardiovascular, and renal systems are most commonly affected in a hypertensive crisis. Almost 25% of patients present with cerebral infarction.

Most hypertensive crises occur in patients with chronic essential hypertension that is inadequately or poorly controlled or in patients with hypertension who have abruptly discontinued antihypertensive medications.

### Evaluation

The physical examination and laboratory and radiograph evaluation should determine whether there is end-organ damage associated with the elevated blood pressure. Blood pressures should be measured both in the supine and standing positions. A significant difference in blood pressure between the two arms suggests aortic dissection. Hypertensive encephalopathy presents with changes in the level of consciousness, focal neurologic deficits, and visual field defects. The posterior reversible encephalopathy syndrome is one presentation with headache, altered level of consciousness, seizures, and variable visual changes that may extend to cortical blindness. Retinal hemorrhages, exudates, or papilledema may also be present on examination. Measurement of serum electrolytes, blood urea nitrogen, serum creatinine, and cardiac enzymes, along with a complete blood count, urinalysis, toxicology studies (for example, cocaine, amphetamines, phencyclidine), a chest radiograph, and electrocardiogram, should be done routinely in patients who present with a hypertensive crisis. A CT scan of the head or MRI of the brain may be necessary if there is evidence of encephalopathy or other cerebral pathology. If aortic dissection is considered, transesophageal echocardiography, CT scan of the chest, or an aortic angiography must be performed.

### Treatment

Too rapid and aggressive lowering of the blood pressure can result in additional end-organ hypoperfusion compounding the damage to key organs. Patients who present in hypertensive crisis usually have chronic hypertension, and the blood pressure should be treated adequately but never decreased to a normal level. In general, the mean arterial pressure should be lowered by no more than 25% in the first hour of treatment and subsequently decreased to systolic levels of 160 mm Hg and diastolic levels between 100 and 110 mm Hg in the next 2 to 6 hours. More rapid blood pressure lowering may be attempted if there is evidence of myocardial ischemia, left ventricular failure with pulmonary edema, acute aortic dissection, intracranial and subarachnoid hemorrhages, pheochromocytoma, and preeclampsia/eclampsia. Antihypertensive treatment with short-acting, titratable, intravenous bolus doses or intravenous infusion is usually indicated in these instances. These medications include intravenous hydralazine, nitroprusside, nitroglycerin, β-blockers (labetalol, metoprolol, esmolol), calcium channel blockers (nicardipine), and angiotensin-converting enzyme inhibitors (**Table 45**). Oral medications are usually reserved for patients who present with hypertensive urgencies who will be discharged to home with subsequent follow-up. Patients with hypertensive emergencies are treated initially in the emergency department, but subsequent treatment should be performed in the ICU where close monitoring and titration of medications can be done. Many of the presenting signs and symptoms associated with a hypertensive crisis reverse with appropriate therapy. Treatment decreases the risk for further complications. Long-term control of hypertension as an outpatient will be necessary to prevent recurrent hypertensive crises.

## Hyperthermic Emergencies

Hyperthermia is a disorder of thermoregulation that results in elevation of body temperature above the normal range. Body temperatures above 40.0 °C (104.0 °F) are life-threatening, and brain death begins at 41.0 °F (105.8 °F). The most important causes of severe hyperthermia (temperature greater than 40.0 °C [104.0 °F]) are heat stroke, malignant hyperthermia, and neuroleptic malignant syndrome.

Nonexertional heat stroke from impaired thermoregulation occurs in various cardiovascular, neurologic, and psychiatric disorders and in patients taking diuretics and

| TABLE 45 Antihypertensive Agents That Are Useful in Hypertensive Crises | | | |
|---|---|---|---|
| **Drug** | **Best Used for** | **Main Side Effect** | **Contraindications** |
| Diazoxide | — | Profound hypotension | Thiazide allergy |
| Enalapril | Left ventricular failure | — | Angioedema |
| Labetalol | Stroke, intracranial hemorrhage | Nausea | Asthma, overt cardiac failure, >first-degree heart block, severe bradycardia |
| Nicardipine | Vascular surgery | Headache | Severe aortic stenosis |
| Nitroglycerin | Unstable angina, myocardial infarction | Headache | Constrictive pericardial disease |
| Phentolamine | Pheochromocytoma | Tachycardia, headache | Acute coronary ischemia |

Reproduced with permission from Physicians' Information and Education Resource (ACP PIER). Philadelphia, PA: American College of Physicians; 2009.

anticholinergic agents, particularly patients who are exposed to a hot environment. Exertional heat stroke results from strenuous exercise in very hot and humid weather. The first sign of serious heat stroke is the absence of sweating and warm and dry skin. At temperatures above 40.6 °C (105.0 °F), loss of consciousness, muscle rigidity, seizures, rhabdomyolysis with renal failure, disseminated intravascular coagulation, and ARDS can occur. Death is imminent at temperatures above 45.0 °C (113.0 °F). Unlike patients with fever, patients with hyperthermia derive no benefit from centrally active antipyretic agents. Fans, cooling blankets, ice packs, cold intravenous fluids, and oxygen (and for severe hypothermia, cold gastric and peritoneal lavage) are used. Benzodiazepines decrease excessive shivering during treatment.

Malignant hyperthermia is an inherited skeletal muscle disorder characterized by a hypermetabolic state precipitated by exposure to volatile inhalational anesthetics (halothane, isoflurane, enflurane, desflurane, sevoflurane) and the depolarizing muscle relaxants succinylcholine and decamethonium. Malignant hyperthermia usually occurs on exposure to the drug but can occur several hours after the initial exposure and can develop in patients who were previously exposed to the drug without effect. Increased intracellular calcium leads to sustained muscle contractions with skeletal muscle rigidity and masseter spasm, tachycardia, hypercarbia, hypertension, hyperthermia, tachypnea, and cardiac arrhythmias. Rhabdomyolysis and acute renal failure can develop. The disorder should be suspected in patients with a family history of adverse effects of anesthesia. The disorder is life-threatening if not treated immediately, and the mortality rate is estimated at 10%. Supportive treatment includes discontinuing the drug, hydration, oxygen, and cooling measures. Dantrolene sodium, a skeletal muscle relaxant, is given as an intravenous bolus every 5 or 10 minutes until symptoms resolve. The response to dantrolene is not pathognomonic, but the diagnosis is supported if symptoms resolve rapidly and completely. Pretreatment of susceptible patients with dantrolene before administration of necessary anesthetic agents is preventive.

The neuroleptic malignant syndrome is a life-threatening disorder caused by an idiosyncratic reaction to neuroleptic tranquilizers (dopamine $D_2$-receptor antagonists) and some antipsychotic drugs (**Table 46**). The most common offending neuroleptic agents are haloperidol and fluphenazine. The syndrome can occur with all drugs that cause central dopamine receptor blockade and usually occurs soon after starting a new drug or with dose escalation. It has also been reported in patients with Parkinson disease who abruptly discontinue their antiparkinsonian drugs. The syndrome is more common (2:1) in men than in women, and risk factors include physical exertion and dehydration, affective psychiatric disorders and organic brain syndrome, thyrotoxicosis, concomitant use of lithium and anticholinergic agents with a neuroleptic agent, use of high-potency neuroleptic agents, and parenteral administration of these agents.

**TABLE 46** Drugs That May Cause the Neuroleptic Malignant Syndrome

Neuroleptic agents (dopamine $D_2$-receptor antagonists)
 Haloperidol
 Fluphenazine
 Trifluoperazine
 Thioridazine
 Chlorpromazine
 Perphenazine
Antipsychotic agents (serotonin dopamine receptor antagonists)
 Clozapine
 Risperidone
Other agents
 Metoclopramide

Most patients with the syndrome develop muscle rigidity, hyperthermia, cognitive changes, autonomic instability, diaphoresis, sialorrhea, seizures, arrhythmias, and rhabdomyolysis within 2 weeks after initiating the drug. Symptoms can occur any time during drug therapy and may persist for up to 1 month, or longer if parenteral medications were given. Some disorders are mild and resolve without treatment, but drug therapy alleviates symptoms within 2 to 3 days. With early treatment, the prognosis is good, although some patients have persistent ataxia, dementia, or parkinsonism. Death may occur from respiratory or cardiovascular failure, disseminated intravascular coagulation, or myoglobinuric acute renal failure. Recurrences are uncommon. If neuroleptic drug therapy is required in a patient who developed the syndrome, the drug or class of drugs should be changed or the offending drug should be started at a lower dose. If the syndrome occurs when antiparkinsonian drugs are discontinued, the drugs should be restarted immediately. Because of the risk of neuroleptic malignant syndrome, drug "holidays" are no longer routinely advised for patients with Parkinson disease. Drug therapy with dantrolene and/or bromocriptine has been reported to decrease mortality and duration of symptoms. Therapy is started with intravenous dantrolene sodium and oral bromocriptine. When symptoms begin to resolve, dantrolene is discontinued and bromocriptine is continued for 10 days or up to 3 weeks if parenteral neuroleptic agents were used. Benzodiazepines can also be used.

## Hypothermic Emergencies

### Accidental Hypothermia

Hypothermia consists of a core tympanic, esophageal, or rectal body temperature of less than 35.0 °F (95.0 °F). Hypothermia is classified as mild (core temperature 32.2 to 35.0 °C [90.0 to 95.0 °F]), moderate (28.0 to 32.2 °C [82.4 to 90.0 °F]), and severe (less than 28.0 °C [82.4 °F]). Many drugs and conditions can lead to excessive heat loss, decreased heat production, and impaired thermoregulation. Primary accidental exposure to cold temperatures in addition to underlying chronic diseases is often found in patients with severe hypothermia.

The elderly, who regulate their core temperature less effectively than younger persons and who have diminished perception of ambient temperature, are at risk for severe hypothermia. The elderly patient is also more susceptible to intraoperative hypothermia because sedatives and general anesthetic agents impair thermoregulation.

Hypothermia produces various multisystem disturbances. Cardiovascular abnormalities include tachycardia followed by progressive bradycardia, conduction abnormalities including atrial and ventricular fibrillation, and the characteristic J wave (Osborne wave, **Figure 14**).

Respiratory depression and neurologic impairment worsen with moderate to severe hypothermia. Warming is the primary treatment for hypothermia. There are three types of rewarming techniques: passive external rewarming, active external rewarming, and active core rewarming. Complications of rewarming include compartment syndromes, rhabdomyolysis, disseminated intravascular coagulation, pulmonary edema, and acute tubular necrosis.

### Therapeutic Hypothermia

Therapeutic hypothermia has been shown to improve neurologic function in comatose patients following out-of-hospital cardiac arrest. Mild hypothermia is thought to suppress some of the chemical reactions responsible for reperfusion injury after cardiac arrest, thereby preventing or alleviating cerebral injury and promoting neurologic recovery. Two randomized controlled trials evaluating neurologic recovery and survival after out-of-hospital ventricular fibrillation cardiac arrest were performed in 2002 using mild to moderate hypothermia (32.0 to 34.0 °C [89.6 to 93.2 °F]). The Hypothermia after Cardiac Arrest Study Group found that patients cooled to 33.0 °C (91.4 °F) for 12 hours had better neurologic recovery but no improvement in survival than normothermic patients. The European Hypothermia after Cardiac Arrest Study Group found that patients cooled to 32.0 to 34.0 °C (89.6 to 93.2 °F) for 24 hours had better survival and neurologic recovery at 6 months than normothermic patients. As a result, the International Liaison Committee on Resuscitation recommended that patients remaining unconscious after out-of-hospital cardiac arrest from ventricular fibrillation or nonperfusing ventricular tachycardia should be cooled to 32.0 to 34.0 °C (89.6 to 93.2 °F) for at least 12 hours to optimize neurologic recovery and possibly survival. Further studies are necessary to determine whether these findings are applicable to patients who survive cardiac arrest from other causes.

### Poisonings and Overdoses

Analgesic ingestion is the most common form of overdose, although deaths are more common from other agents. The diagnosis is made by clinical findings and toxicology results. Clinical findings may allow for classification into one of the common toxic syndromes (**Table 47**). Patients may not have all of the components of a syndrome, but the pattern

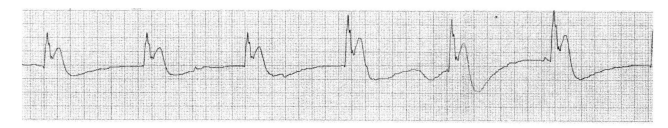

**FIGURE 14.**
**Electrocardiogram showing Osborne waves.**
Hypothermia [body temperature <30.0 °C (86.0 °F)] is associated with bradycardia, either sinus or with atrial fibrillation, and the appearance of the classic Osborne waves at the QT interval. They are best seen in the inferior and lateral chest leads. Osborne waves are defined by the shoulder or "hump" between QRS and ST segments.

| **TABLE 47** Syndromes Resulting from Drug Overdose | |
| --- | --- |
| **Syndrome** | **Manifestations** |
| Cholinergic | "SLUDGE" – Salivation, Lacrimation, increased Urination and Defecation, Gastrointestinal upset, and Emesis. Also bronchorrhea, bradycardia, fasciculations, confusion, miosis |
| Anticholinergic | Dry skin and mucous membranes, hyperthermia, tachycardia, mydriasis, delirium, thirst, urinary retention |
| Sympathomimetic | Hypertension, tachycardia, seizures, central nervous system excitation, mydriasis, diaphoresis |
| Opiates/sedatives | Miosis (usually), respiratory depression, depressed level of consciousness, hypotension, hypothermia, hyporeflexia |

of findings may be sufficient to establish a general diagnosis. Often, treatment of the toxic syndrome is as helpful as identifying the specific agent. Toxicology immunoassays can detect many substances, including opiates, benzodiazepines, cocaine, barbiturates, tricyclic antidepressants, salicylates, acetaminophen, tetrahydrocannabinol (marijuana), and phencyclidine (PCP). Quantitative serum levels of acetaminophen and salicylates should be measured in all patients suspected of a toxic ingestion (even when the ingestion of other agents is suspected or reported). Co-ingestion of multiple toxins occurs frequently. Effective therapies for acetaminophen and salicylate overdoses are available, and their presence may be overlooked by attention to other agents (for example, cocaine or sedatives).

## Alcohols

Alcohol poisoning results most frequently from binge drinking. Alcohol poisoning can also result from drinking products that contain ethylene glycol (antifreeze) or methyl alcohol (methanol), which have toxic acid metabolites, or isopropyl alcohol, which has high potency relative to ethanol but does not have toxic acid metabolites. Ingestion of these alcohols causes neurologic and cardiopulmonary symptoms. Complications include aspiration, severe hypovolemia, and cardiopulmonary arrest. Methanol is metabolized to formic acid, which may cause ocular toxicity. Ethylene glycol is metabolized to oxalic acid, which may cause renal failure; calcium oxalate crystals are found in the urine. Both cause an anion gap metabolic acidosis and an osmolar gap. Treatment for methanol and ethylene glycol overdose must be initiated immediately with oral or intravenous ethanol or intravenous fomepizole. Definitive treatment is hemodialysis. Isopropyl alcohol produces ketones and causes an osmolar gap but no metabolic acidosis, retinal toxicity, or renal failure. Mechanical ventilation may be needed for decreased level of consciousness.

## Amphetamines

All amphetamines cause an adrenergic syndrome from release of catecholamines, thus producing tachycardia, hyperthermia, agitation, hypertension, mydriasis, and acute psychosis. Myocardial ischemia, seizures, intracranial hemorrhage, stroke, and renal failure can result. Overdose of the recreational drug "ecstasy" (3, 4-methylenedioxy-methamphetamine) is associated with bruxism, jaw clenching, and hyponatremia due to elevated antidiuretic hormone concentration, which may result in seizures, cerebral edema, and death in some users. Fulminant hepatic failure has been reported. Treatment is supportive, and benzodiazepines are given for extreme agitation.

## Carbon Monoxide Poisoning

Carbon monoxide is a gas produced from incomplete combustion of carbonaceous material. Common sources include vehicle exhaust fumes, poorly functioning natural gas heating or cooking systems, inhaled smoke, and propane-powered equipment. Carbon monoxide causes a left shift of the oxyhemoglobin dissociation curve, resulting in impaired offloading of oxygen to tissue. Common initial symptoms are headache, dizziness, and nausea. More severe exposures cause chest pain, difficulty thinking, disorientation, dyspnea, weakness, or palpitations. The traditional classic finding of cherry red lips rarely occurs. A delayed neuropsychiatric syndrome with cognitive deficits, personality changes, headache, parkinsonism, dementia, psychosis, and peripheral neuropathy can occur 3 to 40 days after recovery.

The diagnosis of carbon monoxide poisoning requires a high index of suspicion. Pulse oximetry is not useful because it may overestimate arterial oxygenation. Venous or arterial carboxyhemoglobin should be measured, although the concentration may not correlate with symptom severity. The normal carboxyhemoglobin level is 2% to 3% in nonsmokers and up to 10% in smokers. The initial level may not reflect severity of exposure if the patient was treated with 100% oxygen before arrival at the hospital or has a delayed presentation. There are nomograms that can extrapolate the carboxyhemoglobin level to the time of rescue. In general, anyone who was unconscious at the scene has a very high level and a near-fatal exposure. Patients are given 100% oxygen until the level is normal. Hyperbaric oxygen reduces the half-life of carbon monoxide to 20 to 25 minutes and may decrease the incidence of postexposure cognitive deficits (**Table 48**).

## Cyanide Poisoning

Cyanide poisoning results from inhalation of gaseous hydrogen cyanide or the ingestion of potassium or sodium cyanide. Hydrogen cyanide poisoning is also common as a result of smoke inhalation from fires. Ingestion of cyanide is most often associated with suicides and homicides. Inhalation results in seizures, coma, and cardiopulmonary arrest. Chronic exposure to low levels results in weakness

| **TABLE 48** Potential Indications for Hyperbaric Oxygen in Acute Carbon Monoxide Exposure |
|---|
| Poisoning |
| Coma |
| Loss of consciousness (at the scene or persisting at time of hospital arrival) |
| Neurologic findings other than headache |
| Carboxyhemoglobin level >25% to 40% |
| Pregnancy and carboxyhemoglobin level >15% |
| Myocardial ischemia |
| Arrhythmias |
| Ischemic heart disease and carboxyhemoglobin level >20% |
| Persistent symptoms after normobaric oxygen treatment for 4 to 6 hours |

and paralysis. Traditional therapy for cyanide poisoning includes inhalation of amyl nitrite, followed by the administration of intravenous sodium nitrite or sodium thiosulfate. Other antidotes include hydroxycobalamin, 4-dimethylaminophenol (4-DMAP), cobalt salts, solutions A and B (a solution of ferrous sulfate in aqueous citric acid and sodium carbonate), and glucose.

Cocaine Toxicity

Cocaine can be used orally, intravenously, by intranasal insufflation, or by smoking. Crack or rock cocaine, the alkaloid form, is commonly smoked. Signs of clinical toxicity are shown in **Table 49**. Management of cocaine toxicity includes benzodiazepines for agitation, combativeness, and seizures. The neuroleptic agent haloperidol is used only for overt psychosis because of its potential for lowering the seizure threshold. Based on concerns of unopposed α-vasoconstriction, β-blockers are avoided. For myocardial ischemia, aspirin and nitroglycerin are administered. A diagnostic evaluation should be done for acute myocardial infarction, including cardiac catheterization for new focal wall motion abnormalities. Many times there is spasm, but occasionally there is plaque rupture and thrombus requiring intervention. Surgery is often needed after gastrointestinal ingestion of cocaine packets. Endoscopy with retrieval should not be performed because of the risk of rupture with extraction of the packets.

Therapeutic Drug Overdoses

Many therapeutic agents may be deleterious in excess (**Table 50**).

**TABLE 49 Signs of Cocaine Toxicity**

**Sympathomimetic**

Tachycardia
Hypertension
Mydriasis
Hyperthermia
Agitation

**Cardiovascular**

Arrhythmias
Myocardial ischemia
Aortic dissection

**Neurologic**

Seizures
Cerebral infarction
Intracerebral, intraventricular, or subarachnoid hemorrhage

**Respiratory**

Barotrauma
Bronchospasm
Noncardiogenic pulmonary edema
Hemorrhage

**Rhabdomyolysis**

Acetaminophen overdose may result in significant hepatotoxicity and mortality. Toxicity in adults occurs with ingestion of more than 7.5 to 10.0 g in 8 hours or less. A 4-hour serum acetaminophen level should be obtained and compared with the Rumack-Matthew Nomogram for single acute ingestions. The nomogram is not applicable for chronic ingestions or ingestion of extended-release forms. For extended-release acetaminophen, the drug levels should be measured at 4 and 8 hours. Charcoal is given up to 4 hours after ingestion or longer with extended-release ingestions. N-Acetylcysteine (NAC) is the antidote and is most effective when given within 8 hours of ingestion. NAC can still be administered after 24 hours if the acetaminophen levels remain elevated. Concurrent aggressive antiemetic therapy is often needed because the formulation has a disagreeable smell and taste, and many patients are already nauseated. Therefore, the intravenous regimen is better tolerated and is usual therapy in many ICUs. A course of NAC may be considered even in patients who present late or chronically ingest acetaminophen if their serum aminotransferase levels are elevated.

β-Blocker and calcium channel blocker toxicity may result in bradycardia, conduction abnormalities, and hypotension. Glucagon and calcium chloride are given for refractory

**TABLE 50 Antidotes and Interventions for Specific Therapeutic Agents**

| Agent | Antidote/Intervention |
|---|---|
| Acetaminophen | N-Acetylcysteine |
| Amphetamines | Benzodiazepines |
| Benzodiazepines | Flumazenil |
| β-Adrenergic blockers | Glucagon, calcium chloride, ventricular pacing |
| Calcium channel blockers | Calcium chloride, glucagon, pacing |
| Warfarin derivatives | Vitamin K, fresh frozen plasma |
| Nitroprusside (cyanide) | Nitrites, sodium thiosulfate, hydroxycobalamin |
| Digoxin | Digoxin specific antibody Fab fragments |
| γ-Hydroxybutyrate | Respiratory support |
| Heparin | Protamine sulfate |
| Hypoglycemic agents | 50% glucose, somatostatin |
| Iron | Deferoxamine |
| Isoniazid | Pyridoxine |
| Lithium | Hemodialysis |
| Nitrites (methemoglobin) | Methylene blue |
| Narcotics | Naloxone, nalmefene |
| Salicylates | Urine alkalinization, hemodialysis |
| Theophylline | Multiple-dose charcoal, hemoperfusion |
| Tricyclic antidepressants | Blood alkalinization, α-agonist |

hypotension. Isoproterenol can be titrated to try to maintain heart rate. Ventricular pacing may be required.

Lithium has a narrow therapeutic range, and serum lithium levels do not necessarily correlate with symptoms. Toxicity occurs at lower serum levels in patients on long-term therapy. Major manifestations of toxicity include tremor, hyperreflexia, agitation, clonus, seizures, and altered mental status. Charcoal should be given. Intravascular volume should be optimized, but forced diuresis is not effective. Hemodialysis is very effective in removing lithium and should be done whenever there is significant alteration in consciousness.

Salicylate toxicity may result in metabolic acidosis, tachypnea, respiratory alkalosis, and hyperthermia. Coagulopathy, hepatotoxicity, hypoglycemia, depressed level of consciousness, and seizures may develop. Patients on long-term therapy develop toxicity at lower levels than one-time ingestors. Serum salicylate levels greater than 35 mg/dL are treated with alkalinization of the urine to pH of 7.0 to 8.0 to enhance renal clearance. Hemodialysis effectively eliminates the toxin and should be used for patients with altered mental status and for acute renal failure.

Tricyclic antidepressant toxicity causes arrhythmias, depressed level of consciousness, seizures, and hypotension. Evidence of cardiotoxicity (wide QRS interval, wide-complex arrhythmias) requires immediate treatment with boluses of sodium bicarbonate. Seizures are treated with benzodiazepines. Refractory hypotension should be managed with an α-agonist such as norepinephrine or phenylephrine. The use of an intra-aortic balloon pump is a temporizing measure in refractory cases. Tricyclic antidepressants are tightly protein-bound and cannot be dialyzed. If the ingestion is not lethal and the patient can be supported during the first few hours, the patient often stabilizes as the drug is distributed widely into tissue.

Some herbal or alternative medicines and nutritional supplements have inherent toxicity, but poisoning may also result from misuse, contamination, or interaction with other medications. Cardiac glycosides or digoxin-like substances have been detected in herbal teas and laxatives. Products containing ephedrine and pseudoephedrine can result in a sympathomimetic syndrome. Ginkgo biloba and garlic are associated with bleeding. Ginseng has been associated with hypoglycemia. Contaminants identified in Asian patent medicines include arsenic, lead, and mercury.

## Rhabdomyolysis

Rhabdomyolysis results from skeletal muscle injury that releases cellular contents, including myoglobin, potassium, phosphorus, and muscle enzymes, into the circulation. Rhabdomyolysis can cause myoglobinuria and renal failure, depending on the amount of myoglobin released into the circulation and the urine. Risk factors include alcohol use, strenuous exercise, and seizures. Rhabdomyolysis can be caused by any condition that results in extensive skeletal muscle damage,

especially trauma from crush injuries; prolonged immobility, especially on hard surfaces when deeply unconscious from sedative drug overdose or other condition; electrical injuries; burns; drugs and toxins (statins, cocaine, amphetamines, heroin, and phencyclidine [PCP]), and infections. Malignant hyperthermia and the neuroleptic malignant syndrome are associated with rhabdomyolysis. Prolonged exercise may precipiate rhabdomyolysis, especially in patients with inherited myopathy or type V glycogen storage disease (McArdle disease). Not all patients have obvious symptoms, but the predominant symptoms include dark, red, or cola-colored urine; myalgias; and muscle stiffness, tenderness, and weakness, usually of the large muscles of the legs and lower back. Muscle swelling and edema are rare.

The diagnosis is confirmed by laboratory findings (**Table 51**). Elevation of the total serum creatine kinase level is a sensitive but not a specific marker for rhabdomyolysis. Serum levels two to three times normal in a patient with symptoms and/or risk factors is highly suggestive of the diagnosis. After the initial insult, serum creatine kinase levels peak within 24 hours; persistent elevation suggests ongoing muscle injury or development of a compartment syndrome. A positive urine orthotolidine dipstick for blood in the absence of erythrocytes suggests myoglobinuria. A normal urine dipstick test result does not rule out the diagnosis because myoglobinuria may be absent or resolve early in the course of rhabdomyolysis.

Treatment should be aimed at early and aggressive fluid resuscitation to increase oxygen delivery and the glomerular filtration rate. Isotonic crystalloid solutions are administered to maintain a urine output of 200 to 300 mL/h. Central venous pressure monitoring may be helpful in guiding fluid therapy in patients with underlying cardiac or renal disease. Hyperkalemia is treated with glucose and insulin, oral or rectal sodium polystyrene sulfonate, intravenous bicarbonate, or hemodialysis. Other electrolyte disturbances rarely

| TABLE 51 Laboratory Abnormalities in Rhabdomyolysis |
|---|
| Elevated total serum creatine kinase level |
| Hyperkalemia |
| Positive serum myoglobin |
| Myoglobinuria |
| Hyperphosphatemia |
| Hypocalcemia |
| Elevated lactate dehydrogenase, aminotransferases, aldolase, carbonic anhydrase III, and hydroxybutyric acid |
| Hyperuricemia |
| Anion gap metabolic acidosis |
| Elevated serum creatinine and a decreased blood urea nitrogen/serum creatinine ratio |
| Prolonged prothrombin time and activated partial thromboplastin time and thrombocytopenia |

require therapy. Rhabdomyolysis may result in severe hypovolemia from fluid shifts and extravasation into the damaged muscle and interstitium, compartment syndromes, and acute tubular necrosis. Disseminated intravascular coagulation occurs frequently but is not usually associated with bleeding or thromboses. Compartment syndrome should be suspected in a patient with severe focal muscle tenderness and a firm muscle compartment. A decompressive fasciotomy needs to be performed when the measured intracompartment pressures are in excess of 25 to 30 mm Hg. Urine alkalinization (if the serum creatine kinase level is greater than 6000 U/L) and administration of mannitol and loop diuretics to prevent acute kidney injury are commonly used. Alkalinization should be considered earlier in patients with acidemia, dehydration, or underlying renal disease. Bicarbonate administration titrated to a urine pH of 6.5 or higher prevents the breakdown of myoglobin into more toxic compounds. The plasma pH should be carefully monitored to prevent metabolic alkalosis that can worsen preexisting hypocalcemia.

## Acute Abdominal Surgical Emergencies

The term acute abdomen refers to sudden and severe abdominal pain that is less than 24 hours in duration. In almost all patients, acute medical treatment is necessary, and emergent surgery is frequently needed. Rapid assessment and diagnosis are essential because morbidity and mortality are higher in acute surgical emergencies, such as ruptured abdominal aortic aneurysms, intestinal perforation, and intestinal mesenteric ischemia.

The type of pain and its onset and duration may aid in determining the cause. Guarding and rebound tenderness and severe diffuse abdominal pain suggest an acute abdomen with peritonitis. Abdominal pain associated with severe back pain suggests a ruptured abdominal aortic aneurysm or pancreatitis. Intermittent, cramping pain may result from biliary or renal colic. Rupture of the intestine or an abdominal viscus usually has a dramatic sudden onset of symptoms. For example, a history of abdominal surgery could indicate obstruction from adhesions. Serum amylase levels should be measured and abdominal radiographs with supine and upright films should be done to evaluate for air-fluid levels or free peritoneal air suggestive of a intestinal obstruction or perforated viscus. Women of childbearing age should have a pregnancy test because ectopic pregnancy with tubal rupture can present as an acute abdomen. Patients with a history of alcohol use or gallstones may present with acute pancreatitis or cholecystitis. Abdominal ultrasonography may be helpful when the presentation is highly consistent with biliary disease. Abdominal CT scans are more sensitive than plain films for perforation and for many other intra-abdominal conditions and are preferred over abdominal ultrasonography when the presentation is nonspecific or poorly localized.

Abdominal aortic aneurysms occur in 1% of all men over 65 years. The pain is often of acute onset radiating to the back. A pulsatile mass may be palpated in the abdomen. The mortality rate is greater than 50% with free rupture of an aneurysm, and affected patients frequently present with severe hemodynamic instability and cardiovascular collapse. Immediate treatment of patients with moderate hemodynamic compromise should include judicious fluid replacement because overaggressive fluid resuscitation can worsen hemorrhage. Patients presenting with a perforated viscus frequently have generalized peritonitis with board-like rigidity on palpation of the abdomen. The most common organs to perforate are the appendix, stomach, duodenum, and colon. The organ that is responsible may be indicated by the original site of the pain and the age of the patient. The management consists of resuscitation followed by laparotomy.

Intestinal obstruction is significant mechanical impairment or complete cessation of intestinal passage of contents. Mechanical obstruction can occur in either the small bowel or the colon and may be partial or complete. The diagnosis is based on clinical findings and is confirmed by supine and upright abdominal radiographs. Obstruction of the small bowel causes symptoms shortly after onset: cramping abdominal pain around the umbilicus or in the epigastrium, vomiting, and obstipation in patients with complete obstruction. Patients with partial obstruction may develop diarrhea. Severe, steady pain suggests that strangulation has occurred. Hyperactive, high-pitched peristalsis coinciding with cramps is typical. Dilated loops of bowel may be palpable. With infarction, the abdomen becomes tender, and auscultation reveals a silent abdomen or minimal peristalsis. Shock and oliguria indicate either late simple obstruction or strangulation. Obstruction of the colon usually causes milder symptoms that develop more gradually, with increasing constipation leading to obstipation and abdominal distention. Treatment is fluid resuscitation, nasogastric suction, and, in most patients with complete obstruction, surgery. About 85% of partial small-bowel obstructions resolve with medical treatment, whereas about 85% of complete small-bowel obstructions require surgery.

Vascular disorders, usually affecting the small bowel, can result in an acute abdomen. Up to 10% of cases of severe abdominal pain in the elderly have a vascular cause, including mesenteric ischemia, ruptured abdominal aortic aneurysm, and thrombosis. Acute mesenteric ischemia is often the result of cardiac thromboemboli; primary mesenteric vein thromboses may also cause an ischemic acute abdomen. Affected patients present with diffuse abdominal pain—often out of proportion to physical examination findings, intestinal distention, and bloody diarrhea with absent bowel sounds. Laboratory tests reveal a neutrophilic leukocytosis, sometimes with a left shift, and an increased serum amylase level. Abdominal radiography shows many air-fluid levels and widespread edema. Acute ischemic abdomen is a surgical emergency. If bowel ischemia or infarction is suspected, antibiotics should be given.

Some causes of gastrointestinal tract perforation include trauma, the presence of foreign bodies, peptic ulcers, severe vomiting, and intestinal obstruction. Symptoms usually develop suddenly with severe abdominal pain and peritoneal signs followed by shock. Free air under the diaphragm is seen in abdominal radiographs in 50% to 75% of patients. Treatment includes aggressive fluid resuscitation, antibiotics, and surgery.

**KEY POINTS**

- Intensive care unit–acquired weakness is common, is typically diagnosed based on serial physical examinations, and is associated with systemic inflammation, prolonged immobilization, and use of systemic corticosteroids and neuromuscular blockers.

- In the initial assessment of patients with suspected inhalation injury, measurement of arterial blood gases is useful to determine the extent of hypoxia, hypercarbia, and acidosis.

- Patients with anaphylaxis who present with moderate or severe symptoms should be observed and monitored in the intensive care unit for at least 12 hours for the development of delayed or protracted reactions.

- In patients who present with hypertensive crisis, the mean arterial pressure should be lowered by no more than 25% in the first hour of treatment and subsequently decreased to systolic levels of 160 mm Hg and diastolic levels between 100 and 110 mm Hg in the next 2 to 6 hours.

- The neuroleptic malignant syndrome is a life-threatening disorder caused by an idiosyncratic reaction to neuroleptic tranquilizers (dopamine $D_2$-receptor antagonists) and some antipsychotic drugs, especially haloperidol and fluphenazine.

- Patients remaining unconscious after out-of-hospital cardiac arrest from ventricular fibrillation or nonperfusing ventricular tachycardia should be cooled to 32.0 to 34.0 °C (89.6 to 93.2 °F) for at least 12 hours to optimize neurologic recovery and possibly survival.

## Supportive Care in Critical Illness

### Pain, Anxiety, and Delirium

Unrelieved pain, anxiety, and delirium contribute to patient distress, evoke a stress response, complicate the management of life-saving devices, and often negatively affect outcomes. The comfort and safety of patients is a universal goal, and it is, therefore, important to standardize the assessment and management of analgesia, sedation, and delirium in critically ill patients. Delirium occurs in 20% to 40% of non–critically ill hospitalized patients and up to 80% of critically ill surgical

and medical ICU patients. Most ICU patients with delirium have multiple risk factors, and although determining the underlying cause is always the goal, some of the most common causes are iatrogenic.

In non–critically ill hospitalized older patients, delirium has been linked to increased complications, poor functional recovery, and increased mortality both in the hospital and for up to 2 years after discharge. Delirium is classified according to psychomotor behavior as hyperactive, hypoactive, and mixed. Pure hyperactive delirium, which accounts for less than 5% of cases of ICU delirium, is characterized by increased psychomotor activity with agitated behavior. Hypoactive or quiet delirium, which accounts for approximately 45% of cases, is characterized by reduced psychomotor behavior and lethargy. Mixed delirium, which accounts for approximately 50% of cases, alternates unpredictably between a hyperactive and a hypoactive manifestation.

The foundations of current guidelines for the management of pain, anxiety, and delirium are as follows:

1. Pain, anxiety, and delirium should be routinely and objectively assessed.

2. Pain should always be assessed first, preferably using a validated scale such as a visual analogue scale or numeric rating scale.

3. Anxiety should be assessed and sedation levels chosen by goal-directed, nurse-driven protocols. The ICU should adopt a validated sedation scale such as the Sedation Agitation Scale or the Richmond Agitation Sedation Scale (RASS) (**Table 52**). Incorporation of such tools allows titration of sedative medication to the specific target optimal for each patient at the specific point within his/her clinical course, thus maximizing safety and comfort while minimizing oversedation.

4. Delirium should be monitored routinely in all patients. ICU delirium is independently associated with longer lengths of stay and rehospitalization, higher mortality rates, higher costs of care, and a nearly 10-fold higher rate of cognitive impairment at hospital discharge. Current guidelines support the use of the Confusion Assessment Method for the ICU (CAM-ICU) (**Table 53**), a bedside tool that takes less than 1 minute to administer and is 95% sensitive for the diagnosis of delirium.

5. Nonpharmacologic means of relief of pain, anxiety, and delirium should be used whenever possible.

6. For both analgesics and sedatives, intermittent bolus dosing along with daily interruption of continuous infusions is recommended. Some of the many risk factors for delirium may be modifiable. After attention to remediable factors (**Table 54**), the guidelines support haloperidol as the pharmacologic agent of choice for hypoactive and hyperactive delirium; however, there is little evidence on

## TABLE 52 The Richmond Agitation Sedation Scale (RASS)

| | | |
|---|---|---|
| +4 | Combative | Combative, violent, immediate danger to staff |
| +3 | Very agitated | Pulls or removes tube(s) or catheter(s); aggressive |
| +2 | Agitated | Frequent, nonpurposeful movement, fights ventilator |
| +1 | Restless | Anxious, apprehensive but movements not aggressive or vigorous |
| 0 | Alert and calm | |
| −1 | Drowsy | Not fully alert, but has sustained (>10 sec) awakening (eye opening/contact) to voice |
| −2 | Light sedation | Drowsy, brief (<10 sec) awakening to voice or physical stimulation |
| −3 | Moderate sedation | Movement or eye opening (but no eye contact) to voice |
| −4 | Deep sedation | No response to voice, but movement or eye opening to physical stimulation |
| −5 | Unarousable | No response to voice or physical stimulation |

### Procedure for RASS Assessment

**Observe the patient**

If the patient is alert and calm, **score 0.**

If the patient has behavior consistent with restlessness or agitation, **score +1 to +4** using the criteria listed above.

**If the patient is not alert, state the patient's name and ask the patient to open his or her eyes and look at the speaker.**

If the patient awakens and has sustained eye opening and contact, **score −1.**

If the patient awakens but does not have sustained eye opening and eye contact, **score −2.**

If the patient does not awaken but has eye opening or movement in response to voice, **score −3**

**Physically stimulate the patient by shaking shoulder and/or rubbing sternum.**

If the patient does not respond to voice, but responds to physical stimulation, **score −4.**

If the patient does not respond to voice or physical stimulation, **score −5.**

## TABLE 53 The Confusion Assessment Method for the ICU (CAM-ICU)[a]

### Feature 1 - Acute Onset or Fluctuation of Mental Status

Is there an acute change from patient's baseline mental status or a fluctuation in the course of mental status over the past 24 hours? The RASS or other validated sedation scales are typically used for this evaluation.

### Feature 2 - Inattention

Does the patient have inattention? This can be determined using a validated test called the attention screening examination (see reference) which either asks the patient to squeeze only on hearing the letter "A" or nod "yes" when he/she sees certain pictures. Inattention is very simple to assess, even in most intubated patients, and this is the pivotal feature of delirium.

### Feature 3 - Disorganized Thinking

Does the patient have disorganized thinking? This feature is assessed by asking questions included in the CAM training manual and by asking the patient to follow some simple commands like holding up two fingers on each hand that require a minimum of organizational thinking. This assessment is not needed if features 1, 2, and 4 are positive.

### Feature 4 - Altered Level of Consciousness

Does the patient have an altered level of consciousness (at the time of the examination)? This feature is positive if the patient's level of consciousness is currently anything other than alert.

[a]Patients are delirious if they are positive ("YES") for features 1 and 2 and either 3 or 4. A patient video and other training/educational materials are available at www.icudelirium.org.

**TABLE 54 Risk Factors for Delirium**

| Host Factors | Acute Illness | Iatrogenic or Environmental |
|---|---|---|
| Old age | Severe sepsis[a] | Sedative and analgesic use[a] |
| Comorbidities (heart, liver, or renal failure; diabetes; hypertension) | Acute respiratory distress syndrome[a] | Immobilization (restraints or catheters)[a] |
| Preexisting cognitive impairment or dementia | Multiple organ dysfunction syndrome | Total parenteral nutrition[a] |
| Hearing or vision impairment[a] | Drug overdose or illicit drugs | Sleep deprivation[a] |
| Neurologic disease (stroke or seizure) | Health-care–associated infections[a] | Malnutrition[a] |
| Alcoholism and smoking[a] | Metabolic disturbances[a] | Anemia (phlebotomy)[a] |

[a]Potentially modifiable factors.

which to base this decision, and there are no FDA-approved drugs for delirium.

## Delirium Tremens

The term delirium tremens is nearly universally used to refer to delirium due to alcohol withdrawal syndrome. The syndrome usually presents 48 to 96 hours after cessation of drinking, can last up to 2 weeks, and is usually exacerbated at night; the syndrome is characterized by impaired level of consciousness and disorientation, which may fluctuate significantly; reduced attention and global amnesia; impaired cognition and speech; and often hallucinations (usually tactile and/or visual) and delusions (persecutory). Management of the syndrome is similar to that for hyperactive delirium in general, except rather than haloperidol (which lowers the seizure threshold), many patients are given γ-aminobutyric acid (GABA) agonists to approximate the neurologic effects of alcohol at the GABA receptor and to control the extreme agitation and excessive adrenergic autonomic activation. Use of as-needed medications is superior to continuous infusions or standing bolus doses. The $\alpha_2$-adrenergic agonists clonidine and dexmedetomidine are also used to treat the syndrome.

## Other Neuropsychiatric Disorders

The post-ICU syndrome includes significant impairments in patients' ability to think, walk, return to work, organize personal lives, and contribute fully to their families. Up to 75% of ICU survivors develop moderate and sometimes severe cognitive impairment, and 90% have some combination of debilitating neuromyopathy and/or deconditioning. Unlike delirium, which usually resolves in days, neuropsychologic dysfunction may persist for months and is functionally similar to an acquired dementia. The disorder is present in 50% of ICU survivors even up to 2 years after discharge. The risk factors and possible preventive strategies for the post-ICU syndrome are under investigation. Other mental health effects in survivors include severe depression and posttraumatic stress disorder. Comprehensive neuropsychologic and

physical/occupational rehabilitation approaches to these components of recovery are under investigation.

## Prevention

Deep venous thrombosis is a common perioperative complication. The Seventh (2004) ACCP Consensus Conference on Antithrombotic and Thrombolytic Therapy classified patients as a low, moderate, and high risk for developing venous thromboembolism perioperatively. Prophylactic and treatment regimens based on risk are discussed above under Pulmonary Vascular Disease.

Significant gastrointestinal bleeding from stress gastritis and ulceration has decreased with the use of prophylactic agents in high-risk patients. There is a strong relationship between gastrointestinal bleeding and underlying severity of illness. Stress ulcers form soon after critical illness develops and range from superficial injuries to deep ulcerating lesions. Stress ulcers are caused by mucosal ischemia with loss of cytoprotective prostaglandins. Prolonged mechanical ventilation and coagulopathy are the two most important risk factors for developing stress ulcers (**Table 55**). Prophylactic agents, which include antacids, $H_2$-antihistamines, sucralfate, and proton pump inhibitors, decrease

**TABLE 55** Risk Factors for Development of Stress Ulcers in the Intensive Care Unit

| |
|---|
| Mechanical ventilation >48 hours |
| Coagulopathy |
| Extended intensive care unit length of stay |
| Sepsis |
| Shock |
| Trauma (especially head trauma) |
| Hepatic failure |
| Renal failure |
| Burns |

**TABLE 56** Factors Predisposing to the Development of Pressure Ulcers

| |
|---|
| Infection and fever |
| Flaccid paralysis and prolonged immobilization |
| Hypotension |
| Hypovolemia |
| Malnutrition and reduced lean body mass |
| Overnutrition with morbid obesity |
| Spinal cord injuries and neurologic disease |
| Anemia |
| Increased metabolic demands |
| Advanced age |
| Immunosuppression |

significant bleeding from stress ulcers but have not been shown to decrease mortality rates.

Antacids are effective prophylactic agents but require frequent oral dosing. $H_2$-antihistamines are administered by intravenous bolus or by continuous infusion, which more effectively controls gastric pH but does not add further protection against gastrointestinal bleeding. Studies have not shown any increase in health-care–associated pneumonias in patients treated with $H_2$ antagonists. Sucralfate is an oral cytoprotective agent that creates a foam lining in the stomach protecting against acid damage. Proton pump inhibitors, which can be given orally, by intravenous bolus, or by continuous infusion, are more effective in maintaining a gastric alkaline environment than $H_2$-antihistamines. Some ICU clinicians advocate the use of oral proton pump inhibitors as first-line therapy because of their efficacy, cost-effectiveness, and lower risk for acute bleeding than intravenous $H_2$-antihistamines. Caution should be used in patients taking drugs such as itraconazole that require gastric acidity for adequate absorption. Enteral nutrition may provide some protection against stress ulcers.

Pressure ulcers are a major cause of increased morbidity and length of ICU stay in one third of critically ill patients (see also MKSAP 15 General Internal Medicine). They result from prolonged tissue ischemia causing cell death and necrosis. They occur in areas of unrelieved pressure, such as over a bony prominence seen in the ischium, sacrum, trochanter, and the heel. The causes of pressure ulcers are multifactorial (**Table 56**).

Infection is the most common complication of pressure ulcers. Wound-related bacteremia and sepsis secondary to osteomyelitis occur in 26% of patients with nonhealing pressure ulcers and lead to death in 50% of affected patients. The Agency for Healthcare Research and Quality has published guidelines for the prevention and treatment of pressure ulcers (**Table 57**).

## Nutrition

Many studies have documented the importance of early (less than 24 hours after admission) nutritional support in critically ill patients, although nutrition in the early phase of resuscitation may not be effective because the nutrients may not be utilized efficiently. Critically ill patients have increased energy expenditures and often have underlying nutritional deficits. Malnutrition impairs wound healing and immunologic function and increases risk for infection and death. Although enteral nutrition is now preferred for most ICU patients, the specific conditions in which nutrition improves outcome are not clear, nor is the best route for nutritional support in different conditions clearly defined. In several randomized, controlled trials comparing gastric feeding with postpyloric feeding, no significant differences were found in the incidence of aspiration, pneumonia, ICU length of stay, or mortality rates. Prokinetic drugs, such as erythromycin, cisapride, and metoclopramide, may be useful in critically ill patients who have impaired gastric emptying. A balance must be achieved between underfeeding and overfeeding the critically ill patient. Underfeeding may be preferable in patients with very high energy requirements, such as in sepsis or trauma. In one study, patients who received between 33% and 65% of calculated requirements had a lower mortality rate and a shorter duration of mechanical ventilation. However, failure to deliver at least 25% of calculated requirements increased infection and mortality rates. ICU patients generally require 25 to 30 nonprotein kcal/kg/d and 1.0 to 1.5 protein kcal/kg/d to meet the energy expenditures associated with critical illness (**Table 58**).

Studies comparing enteral and parenteral nutrition have reported fewer infections using enteral solutions but no change in sepsis rates, mortality rates, length of stay, or ventilator-free days. Underfeeding using parenteral nutrition with lipid-free or hypocaloric solutions does not prevent hyperglycemia or infections. Recent recommendations by the National Institute for Clinical Excellence state that parenteral nutrition should be limited to a maximum of 50% of the calculated requirements for the first 48 hours. Moderate glycemic control to a plasma glucose level below 150 mg/dL

(8.3 mmol/L) with insulin is now an accepted practice in the ICU, particularly when parenteral nutrition is administered. Enteral and parenteral formulas enriched in arginine, omega-3 fatty acids, glutamine, and nucleotides are thought to enhance the immune response. Studies suggest that immunonutrition in specific subgroups of patients (for example, patients with trauma or after gastrointestinal surgery) may decrease infections but does not ultimately decrease mortality rates.

Traditionally, the Harris-Benedict equation has been the standard for determining energy requirements of critically ill patients, although its use is limited in ventilator-dependent patients, patients who are either morbidly obese or severely malnourished and underweight, transplant recipients, and patients with marked fluid overload, ascites, extensive limb amputations, or paraplegia. Indirect calorimetry to measure energy expenditure from exhaled gas measurements is an alternative method of estimating nutritional requirements that is more accurate than the Harris-Benedict equation in critically ill patients. However, technical limitations and cost limit its usefulness. Serum prealbumin levels can be used to monitor the adequacy of nutrition; a level less than 5 mg/dL (50 mg/L) indicates severe protein and caloric malnutrition.

| TABLE 57 Strategies and Techniques to Prevent Pressure Ulcers |
| --- |
| **Pressure Relief Maneuvers** |
| Scheduled turning and body repositioning every 2 hours |
| Not positioning the patient directly on the trochanter; placing the patient at a 30-degree angle when the patient is lying on the side |
| Using pillows and foam wedges to prevent direct contact between bony prominences; avoiding donut-type devices, which may cause venous congestion and edema |
| Using special protective devices for the heels or placing pillows under the lower extremities |
| Limiting elevation of the bed to minimize shearing forces |
| **Pressure Relief Devices** |
| Mattresses that distribute local pressure over a wide area, such as overlay, foam, and fluid-filled mattresses |
| Electric or battery-powered air-current mattresses and air-fluidized mattresses that redistribute pressure across the body |
| Lifting devices to prevent the patient dragging across the bed sheets |
| **General Measures** |
| Vigilance for early signs of skin inflammation with hyperemia |
| Avoiding hot water baths, using mild cleansing agents with moisturizers, and removing excess skin secretions and excretions |
| Using topical agents such as mucus barriers in moist areas |
| Adequate protein and caloric nutrition |
| Early mobilization and physical therapy |

Data from: Pressure Ulcers in Adults: Prediction and Prevention. Clinical Practice Guideline Number 3. AHCPR Pub. No. 92-0047:May 1992

| TABLE 58 Special Nutritional Requirements in Critical Illness | |
| --- | --- |
| **Disorder** | **Special Nutrition Requirements** |
| Hepatic failure | Decrease protein intake to <1g/kg/d only if encephalopathy is present. Give amino acid formulations high in branched-chain amino acids and low in aromatic amino acids if encephalopathy refractory to lactulose therapy is present. |
| Renal failure | In chronic renal insufficiency, restrict protein intake to 0.6-1.0 g/kg/d if not on hemodialysis. If on dialysis, increase protein to 1.2-1.3 g/kg/d. Do not restrict proteins in acute renal failure. |
| Respiratory failure | Decrease carbohydrate calories and increase fat calories if severe hypercapnia is refractory to mechanical ventilation. |
| Burns | Require total calories of 30 kcal/kg/d. Increase protein intake to >2.5 g/kg/d. Supplemental glutamine and arginine may decrease infections. |
| Pancreatitis | Give elemental or peptide-based jejunal enteral feedings (preferred) for severe pancreatitis or use total parenteral nutrition and monitor lipid intake, maintaining triglyceride levels <400 mg/dL (4.52 mmol/L). |

## End-of-Life Care

The transition from aggressive, life-sustaining interventions to comfort care occurs routinely in the ICU. The right of patients with the capacity for decision-making to refuse all treatments is well established, and all interventions, including artificial nutrition and hydration, can be terminated by the choice of a fully competent patient. However, critically ill patients often cannot make their own medical decisions. Advanced directives can be useful in that they typically designate a proxy for medical decision-making and articulate preferences for care in various clinical situations. However, patients often lack directives, or the information contained in an existing directive does not apply to the patient's condition. As a result, the decision whether to transition to comfort care is frequently determined by surrogates in consultation with the medical team.

Research over the past 20 years indicates that family members of patients dying in the ICU are often dissatisfied with their communication with health care providers and commonly experience anxiety, depression, and posttraumatic stress disorder in the aftermath of the hospitalization. Accessibility, continuity, attentive listening, emotional support, recognition of the patient's values, and encouraging questions on the part of ICU staff improve satisfaction. A recent study found that a structured family conference that combined communication with a brochure on bereavement reduced anxiety, depression, and posttraumatic stress disorder symptoms among family members. Achieving consensus on prognosis and treatment course among providers is also important, as receipt of conflicting information is burdensome to families.

Early and frequent interactions with family members, as well as early involvement of specialists in palliative care, also help address the end-of-life needs of patients and families. It is important to assure family members that their loved one will not suffer during the process of withdrawing life-sustaining therapies. A standardized approach to terminal ventilator weaning that includes a step-wise reduction in ventilator support with close monitoring for distress and appropriate dosage of sedatives can facilitate a comfortable transition for the patient.

**KEY POINTS**

- Prolonged mechanical ventilation and coagulopathy are the two most important risk factors for developing stress ulcers.

- Prophylactic agents, which include antacids, $H_2$-antihistamines, sucralfate, and proton pump inhibitors, decrease significant bleeding from stress ulcerations but have not been shown to decrease mortality rates.

- Patients in the intensive care unit generally require 25 to 30 nonprotein kcal/kg/d and 1.0 to 1.5 protein kcal/kg/d to meet the energy expenditures associated with critical illness.

- It has been shown that a structured family conference that combines communication with a brochure on bereavement reduces anxiety, depression, and posttraumatic stress disorder symptoms among family members of patients in the intensive care unit.

## Bibliography

Dellinger RP, Levy MM, Carlet JM, et al. Surviving Sepsis Campaign: International Guidelines for Management of Severe Sepsis and Septic Shock 2008 [erratum in Intensive Care Med. 2008;34(4):783-785]. Intensive Care Medicine. 2008;34(1):17-60. [PMID: 18058085]

Finfer S, Chittock DR, Su SY, et al; NICE-SUGAR Study Investigators. Intensive versus conventional glucose control in critically ill patients. N Engl J Med. 2009;360(13):1283-1297. [PMID: 19318384]

Girard TD, Kress JP, Fuchs BD, et al. Efficacy and safety of a paired sedation and ventilator weaning protocol for mechanically ventilated patients in intensive care (Awakening and Breathing Controlled trial): a randomised controlled trial. Lancet. 2008;371(9607):126-134. [PMID: 18191684]

Hill NS, Brennan J, Garpestad E, Nava S. Noninvasive ventilation in acute respiratory failure. Crit Care Med. 2007;35:2402-2407.

Keast DH, Parslow N, Houghton PE, Lorton L, Fraser C. Best practice recommendations for the prevention and treatment of pressure ulcers: Update 2006. Adv Skin Wound Care. 2007;20(8):447-460. [PMID: 17762312]

Koh Y. Ventilatory management in patients with chronic airflow obstruction. Crit Care Clinics. 2007;23(2):169-181. [PMID: 17368164]

Schweickert WD, Hall J. ICU-acquired weakness. Chest 2007;131(5): 1541-1549. [PMID: 17494803]

Sprung CL, Annane D, Keh D, et al. Hydrocortisone therapy for patients with septic shock. N Engl J Med. 2008;358(2):111-124. [PMID: 18184957]

# Self-Assessment Test

This self-assessment test contains one-best-answer multiple-choice questions. Please read these directions carefully before answering the questions. Answers, critiques, and bibliographies immediately follow these multiple-choice questions. The American College of Physicians is accredited by the Accreditation Council for Continuing Medical Education (ACCME) to provide continuing medical education for physicians.

The American College of Physicians designates MKSAP 15 Pulmonary and Critical Care Medicine for a maximum of 18 *AMA PRA Category 1 Credits*™. Physicians should only claim credit commensurate with the extent of their participation in the activity. Separate answer sheets are provided for each book of the MKSAP program. Please use one of these answer sheets to complete the Pulmonary and Critical Care Medicine self-assessment test. Indicate in Section H on the answer sheet the actual number of credits you earned, up to the maximum of 18, in ¼-credit increments. (One credit equals one hour of time spent on this educational activity.)

Use the self-addressed envelope provided with your program to mail your completed answer sheet(s) to the MKSAP Processing Center for scoring. Remember to provide your MKSAP 15 order and ACP ID numbers in the appropriate spaces on the answer sheet. The order and ACP ID numbers are printed on your mailing label. If you have *not* received these numbers with your MKSAP 15 purchase, you will need to acquire them to earn CME credits. E-mail ACP's customer service center at custserv@acponline.org. In the subject line, write "MKSAP 15 order/ACP ID numbers." In the body of the e-mail, make sure you include your e-mail address as well as your full name, address, city, state, ZIP code, country, and telephone number. Also identify where you have made your MKSAP 15 purchase. You will receive your MKSAP 15 order and ACP ID numbers by e-mail within 72 business hours.

CME credit is available from the publication date of July 31, 2009, until July 31, 2012. You may submit your answer sheets at any time during this period.

# Self-Scoring Instructions:
# Pulmonary and Critical Care Medicine

**Compute your percent correct score as follows:**

**Step 1**: Give yourself 1 point for each correct response to a question.

**Step 2**: Divide your total points by the total number of questions: 116.

The result, expressed as a percentage, is your percent correct score.

|  | Example | Your Calculations |
|---|---|---|
| **Step 1** | 97 | |
| **Step 2** | 97 ÷ 116 | ÷ 116 |
| **% Correct** | 84% | % |

*Each of the numbered items is followed by lettered answers. Select the ONE lettered answer that is BEST in each case.*

## Item 1

A 28-year-old man is evaluated for a 6-month history of episodic dyspnea, cough, and wheezing. As a child, he had asthma and allergies, but he has been asymptomatic since his early teenage years. His recent symptoms started after an upper respiratory tract infection, and they are often triggered by exercise or exposure to cold air. He is also awakened with asthma symptoms 5 or 6 nights a month. He is otherwise healthy and takes no medications.

On physical examination, vital signs are normal. There is scattered wheezing in both lung fields. Chest radiograph is normal. Spirometry shows an $FEV_1$ of 70% of predicted with a 15% improvement after inhaled albuterol.

**Which of the following is the most appropriate therapy for this patient?**

(A) Azithromycin
(B) Inhaled albuterol as needed
(C) Inhaled low-dose corticosteroids plus inhaled albuterol as needed
(D) Long-acting β-agonist
(E) Long-acting β-agonist plus inhaled albuterol as needed

## Item 2

A 73-year-old woman is evaluated in the emergency department for a 2-week history of worsening dyspnea and a dry cough. She has not had fever or any recent travel. Idiopathic pulmonary fibrosis was diagnosed 2 years ago by open lung biopsy. She also has a history of hypertension and gastroesophageal reflux disease. Her medications are prednisone, diltiazem, hydrochlorothiazide, and omeprazole.

On physical examination, she is afebrile; the blood pressure is 142/86 mm Hg, the pulse rate is 97/min, the respiration rate is 28/min, and the BMI is 27. Oxygen saturation with the patient breathing oxygen, 10 L/min by face mask, is 90%. There are dry crackles at the lung bases extending half way up the chest bilaterally. Cardiac and abdominal examinations are normal. Gram stain of sputum is negative; culture is pending. CT scan of the chest is negative for pulmonary embolism but shows new areas of alveolar infiltrates and consolidation superimposed on previous basilar, reticular, and honeycomb changes.

**Which of the following is the most appropriate next test in the evaluation of this patient?**

(A) Bronchoscopy with bronchoalveolar lavage
(B) Fungal serologies
(C) Right-heart catheterization
(D) Swallowing evaluation

## Item 3

A 65-year-old woman is evaluated in a follow-up examination for dyspnea, chronic cough, and mucoid sputum; she was diagnosed with chronic obstructive pulmonary disease 3 years ago. The patient has a 40-pack-year history of cigarette smoking, but quit smoking 1 year ago. She is otherwise healthy, and her only medication is inhaled albuterol as needed.

On physical examination, vital signs are normal. Breath sounds are decreased, but there is no edema or jugular venous distention. Spirometry shows an $FEV_1$ of 62% of predicted and an $FEV_1/FVC$ ratio of 65%. Chest radiograph shows mild hyperinflation.

**Which of the following is the most appropriate therapy for this patient?**

(A) Add a long-acting $\beta_2$-agonist
(B) Add an inhaled corticosteroid
(C) Add an oral corticosteroid
(D) Add theophylline and montelukast
(E) Continue current albuterol therapy

## Item 4

A 52-year-old woman is evaluated after a screening CT colonography detected a 3-mm nodule in the right lower lobe of the lung. A tortuous colon prevented complete screening colonoscopy. CT scan of the chest showed no additional nodules and was otherwise normal. The patient has never smoked; she works in the home and has not been exposed to potential carcinogens. She has not had a chest radiograph or other imaging procedure, except mammography. Her medical history includes only hyperlipidemia, and her only medication is simvastatin. Her family history is unremarkable.

On physical examination, vital signs are normal. Examination of the skin is normal; there is no lymphadenopathy, and the lungs are clear.

**Which of the following is the most appropriate next step in the management of this patient?**

(A) Chest radiograph in 3 months
(B) CT scan of the chest in 3 months
(C) CT scan of the chest in 6 months
(D) CT scan of the chest in 12 months
(E) No follow-up

## Item 5

A 30-year-old man is evaluated for difficulty weaning from the ventilator. The patient was intubated 7 days ago for a severe exacerbation of asthma. Despite receiving a high-dose inhaled β-agonist; methylprednisolone, 60 mg/d; and aggressive sedation, he had persistent severe auto-positive end-expiratory pressure with elevated ventilator pressures. Therefore, a continuous infusion of vecuronium, a paralytic agent, was started and continued for 24 hours until his respiratory mechanics improved. Today, he underwent a ventilator weaning trial but became tachycardic and diaphoretic with a rapid shallow breathing index of 120.

On physical examination, the patient is alert and responsive; vital signs are normal. There is minimal expiratory wheezing and otherwise normal vesicular breath sounds. He has flaccid weakness involving all extremities, including decreased bilateral hand grip strength. There is no rash. Routine laboratory studies reveal normal liver enzyme tests and renal function.

**Which of the following is the most likely cause for the patient's difficulty weaning from the ventilator?**

(A) Acute inflammatory demyelinating polyneuropathy (Guillain-Barré syndrome)

(B) Churg-Strauss syndrome

(C) Intensive care unit–acquired weakness

(D) Prolonged neuromuscular blockade

## Item 6

A 54-year-old man is evaluated in the emergency department for a 1-hour history of chest pain with mild dyspnea. The patient had been hospitalized 1 week ago for a colectomy for colon cancer. His medical history also includes hypertension and nephrotic syndrome secondary to membranous glomerulonephritis, and his medications are furosemide, ramipril, and pravastatin.

On physical examination the temperature is 37.5 °C (100 °F), the pulse rate is 120/min, the respiration rate is 24/min, the blood pressure is 110/60 mm Hg, and the BMI is 30. Oxygen saturation is 89% with the patient breathing ambient air and 97% on oxygen, 4 L/min. Cardiac examination shows tachycardia and an $S_4$. Breath sounds are normal. Chest radiograph is negative for infiltrates, widened mediastinum, and pneumothorax. Serum creatinine concentration is 2.1 mg/dL (185.6 µmol/L). Empiric unfractionated heparin therapy is begun.

**Which of the following is the best test to confirm the diagnosis in this patient?**

(A) Assay for plasma D-dimer

(B) CT angiography

(C) Lower extremity ultrasonography

(D) Measurement of antithrombin III

(E) Ventilation/perfusion scan

## Item 7

An 18-year-old man is evaluated in the emergency department after his mother found him unconscious in his bed at home. She reported that her son had gone to a party two nights ago, but she was not sure when he returned home. When she checked on him, he was unarousable. He has no significant medical history and takes no medications.

In the emergency department, he is afebrile, blood pressure is 110/70 mm Hg, the pulse rate is 50/min, and respiration rate is 6/min; he is intubated for airway protection.

**Laboratory studies:**

| | |
|---|---|
| Hemoglobin | 12.2 g/dL (122 g/L) |

| | |
|---|---|
| Leukocyte count | 3400/µL ($3.4 \times 10^9$/L) |
| Platelet count | 110,000/µL ($110 \times 10^9$/L) |
| Creatinine | 3.2 mg/dL (282.9 µmol/L) |
| Aspartate aminotransferase | 80 U/L |
| Alanine aminotransferase | 46 U/L |
| Creatine kinase | 18,400 U/L |
| INR | 1.2 |

Alkaline phosphatase, bilirubin, and albumin are normal. Urine dipstick is 4+ positive for occult blood. Blood alcohol level is 0.8 g/dL (174 mmol/L). Toxicology testing is positive for opiates and cocaine. Bladder catheterization reveals only 30 mL of brown urine.

**Which of the following is the most likely cause of the patient's renal failure?**

(A) Hemolytic anemia

(B) Hemolytic-uremic syndrome

(C) Hepatorenal syndrome

(D) Rhabdomyolysis

(E) Sepsis

## Item 8

A 70-year-old man is evaluated in the emergency department for a 2-day history of dyspnea with exertion, orthopnea, and paroxysmal nocturnal dyspnea. He has ischemic heart disease with left ventricular dysfunction and had coronary artery bypass graft surgery 6 weeks ago. His medications include aspirin, nitroglycerin, metoprolol, lisinopril, and furosemide.

On physical examination, the patient is sitting upright and breathing with difficulty; the temperature is 37 °C (98.6 °F), the blood pressure is 150/85 mm Hg, the pulse rate is 105/min and regular, and the respiration rate is 28/min. Oxygen saturation is 89% on ambient air. There are fine crackles at the lung bases bilaterally, and breath sounds are diminished at the right base. There is a regular tachycardia and an $S_3$ at the apex. There is no jugular venous distention or peripheral edema. Hemoglobin is 12.5 g/dL (125 g/L), and the leukocyte count is 10,500/µL ($10.5 \times 10^9$/L). Chest radiograph shows cardiomegaly and small bilateral pleural effusions, greater on the right than the left. Thoracentesis is performed, and pleural fluid analysis shows:

| | |
|---|---|
| Nucleated cell count | 450/µL with 3% neutrophils, 70% lymphocytes, 10% macrophages, 15% mesothelial cells, and 2% eosinophils. |
| Pleural fluid to serum total protein ratio | 0.54 |
| Lactate dehydrogenase (LDH) | 125 U/L |
| Pleural fluid to upper limits of normal serum LDH ratio | 0.52 |
| Glucose | 80 mg/dL (4.44 mmol/L) |
| Total protein | 3.7 g/dL (37 g/L) |
| pH | 7.45 |

| Albumin | 1.5 g/dL (15 g/L) |
|---|---|
| Cholesterol | 35 mg/dL (0.9 mmol/L) |

The serum–pleural fluid albumin gradient is 1.7.

**Which of the following is the most likely diagnosis?**

(A) Heart failure
(B) Parapneumonic effusion
(C) Post–cardiac injury syndrome
(D) Pulmonary embolism

## Item 9

A 20-year-old woman is evaluated in the emergency department for an acute episode of wheezing and dyspnea without cough or sputum production. She has had previous frequent evaluations in emergency departments and urgent care centers for similar episodes. In between these episodes, findings on physical examination and pulmonary function testing, including methacholine challenge, have been normal. She is otherwise healthy and takes no medications.

On physical examination, the patient has inspiratory and expiratory wheezing and is in moderate discomfort. The temperature is 37.1 °C (98.8 °F), pulse rate is 100/min, and the respiration rate is 24/min; oxygen saturation on ambient air is 96%. After receiving albuterol and intravenous corticosteroids, she continues to wheeze and is in moderate respiratory distress. Oxygen saturation on ambient air remains at 96%. Chest radiograph shows decreased lung volumes.

**Which of the following is the most appropriate management for this patient?**

(A) Chest CT scan
(B) Intravenous aminophylline
(C) Intravenous azithromycin
(D) Intravenous terbutaline
(E) Laryngoscopy

## Item 10

A 72-year-old woman is evaluated for fatigue and decreased exercise capacity. The patient has severe chronic obstructive pulmonary disease, which was first diagnosed 10 years ago, and was hospitalized for her second exacerbation 1 month ago. She is a former smoker, having stopped smoking 5 years ago. She has no other significant medical problems, and her medications are albuterol as needed, an inhaled corticosteroid, a long-acting bronchodilator, and oxygen, 2 L/min by nasal cannula.

On physical examination, vital signs are normal. Breath sounds are decreased, and there is 1+ bilateral pitting edema. Spirometry done 1 month ago showed an $FEV_1$ of 28% of predicted, and blood gases measured at that time (on supplemental oxygen) showed pH 7.41, $PCO_2$ 43 mm Hg, and $PO_2$ 64 mm Hg; $DLCO$ is 30% of predicted. There is no nocturnal oxygen desaturation. Chest radiograph at this time shows hyperinflation. CT scan of the chest shows homogeneous distribution of emphysema.

**Which of the following would be the most appropriate management for this patient?**

(A) Lung transplantation
(B) Lung volume reduction surgery
(C) Nocturnal assisted ventilation
(D) Pulmonary rehabilitation

## Item 11

A 71-year-old woman is evaluated for a 3-week history of mild pain in the shoulders and thighs and weakness when rising from a seated position and getting out of bed. She also has a new rash on her hands. Eight months ago she was evaluated for dyspnea and new interstitial infiltrates that resulted in a lung biopsy and a diagnosis of idiopathic nonspecific interstitial pneumonia. She was treated with prednisone, 60 mg/d, for 1 month; the dose was then tapered to 10 mg/d. Her symptoms had been stable on that dose until her new complaints.

On physical examination, there are swelling and discoloration of the eyelids and an erythematous scaly rash over the extensor surfaces of interphalangeal joints of both hands. There is symmetric weakness of the proximal hip flexors and shoulder girdle muscles; hand strength is normal. Laboratory studies show antinuclear antibodies positive at a titer of 1:1280 (previously negative), serum creatine kinase 1270 U/L, and erythrocyte sedimentation rate 60 mm/h; serum electrolytes and complete blood count are normal. Chest radiograph shows bilateral reticular and alveolar abnormalities in the lower- and mid-lung zones.

**Which of the following is the most appropriate management for this patient?**

(A) Electromyography and muscle biopsy
(B) Repeat lung biopsy
(C) Skin biopsy
(D) Taper prednisone dosage

## Item 12

A 74-year-old man is evaluated for a 5-year history of gradually progressive dyspnea and dry cough without wheezing or hemoptysis. For the past 2 years he has had pain and occasional swelling in both knees. He has not had fever or lost weight. He smoked one pack of cigarettes a day from the age of 18 to 60 years. He worked as an insulator for 40 years.

Physical examination shows no digital clubbing or cyanosis. Auscultation of the lungs reveals bilateral end-inspiratory crackles. Pulmonary function testing shows:

| | |
|---|---|
| Total lung capacity | 67% of predicted |
| Residual volume | 72% of predicted |
| FVC | 65% of predicted |
| $FEV_1$ | 75% of predicted |
| $FEV_1$/FVC ratio | 89% |
| $DLCO$ | 52% of predicted |

His chest radiograph is shown on the next page.

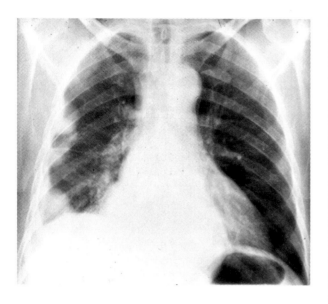

**Which of the following is the most likely diagnosis?**

(A) Asbestosis

(B) Idiopathic pulmonary fibrosis

(C) Rheumatoid interstitial lung disease

(D) Pulmonary sarcoidosis

## Item 13

A 75-year-old woman with a history of chronic obstructive pulmonary disease is evaluated in the intensive care unit for delirium. She had a median sternotomy and repair of an aortic dissection and was extubated uneventfully on post-operative day 4. Two days later she developed fluctuations in her mental status and inattention. While still in the intensive care unit, she became agitated, pulling at her lines, attempting to climb out of bed, and asking to leave the hospital. Her arterial blood gas values are normal. The patient has no history of alcohol abuse. The use of frequent orientation cues, calm reassurance, and presence of family members has done little to reduce the patient's agitated behavior.

**Which of the following is the most appropriate therapy for this patient's delirium?**

(A) Diphenhydramine

(B) Haloperidol

(C) Lorazepam

(D) Propofol

## Item 14

A 60-year-old woman is evaluated 3 weeks after starting continuous positive airway pressure (CPAP) therapy for obstructive sleep apnea. The patient was initially evaluated for excessive sleepiness, and obstructive sleep apnea was diagnosed based on results of polysomnography. It was determined that CPAP at a pressure of 14 cm $H_2O$ normalized respiration and oxygen saturation during sleep. She was prescribed CPAP at this pressure along with heated humidification administered via a nasal mask. She has been using CPAP, but she is still often sleepy during the day. She has a history of hypertension and osteoarthritis, and her medications are hydrochlorothiazide and ibuprofen. She does not smoke or drink alcohol.

On physical examination, she is afebrile; the blood pressure is 145/85 mm Hg, and the BMI is 36.5. She has a slightly receding jaw; otherwise, physical features are unremarkable.

**Which of the following is the most appropriate next step in the management of this patient?**

(A) Order a multiple sleep latency test

(B) Prescribe hormone replacement therapy

(C) Prescribe modafinil

(D) Review CPAP compliance

## Item 15

A 28-year-old man is evaluated for a 9-month history of daily cough productive of yellow sputum and intermittent low-grade fever. He has had three episodes of pneumonia during that time; the symptoms improve with antibiotic therapy but return when therapy is discontinued. The patient does not have a history of aspiration, asthma, or sinusitis, and he takes no medications. He has never smoked.

On physical examination, the temperature is 37.4 °C (99.3 °F), the pulse rate is 88/min, the respiration rate is 18/min, the blood pressure is 116/58 mm Hg, and the BMI is 24. Breath sounds are reduced in the right base; the lungs are otherwise clear. Laboratory tests are normal. Two chest radiographs 3 months apart have shown an infiltrate in the right lower lobe. Contrast-enhanced CT scan of the chest shows right lower lobe bronchiectasis and partial volume loss of this lobe; endobronchial obstruction is suggested. There is no lymphadenopathy.

**Which of the following is the most likely diagnosis?**

(A) Adenocarcinoma

(B) Carcinoid tumor

(C) Small cell carcinoma

(D) Squamous cell carcinoma

## Item 16

A 30-year-old medical resident is evaluated for cough, right-sided chest pain, and fever of 21 days' duration. He has no significant medical history or family history, and he takes no medications.

Hemoglobin is 14 g/dL (140 g/L), and the leukocyte count is 8000/μL ($8 \times 10^9$/L). Chest radiograph shows a right pleural effusion occupying approximately 50% of the hemithorax without other abnormalities. Thoracentesis yields turbid, yellow fluid, and analysis shows:

| Erythrocyte count | 500/µL |
| Nucleated cell count | 3500/µL ($3.5 \times 10^9$/L) with 20% neutrophils, 60% lymphocytes, 10% macrophages, 4% mesothelial cells, and 6% eosinophils |
| Total protein | 4.2 g/dL (42 g/L) |
| Lactate dehydrogenase | 240 U/L |
| pH | 7.35 |
| Glucose | 68 mg/dL (3.8 mmol/L) |

Serum total protein is 7.0 g/dL (70 g/L) and serum lactate dehydrogenase is 100 U/L. Gram stain shows no organisms and culture is pending.

**Which of the following is the most appropriate next step in management?**

(A) Chest CT scan
(B) Flexible bronchoscopy
(C) Pleural biopsy
(D) Repeat chest radiograph after a 5-day course of azithromycin

## Item 17

A 28-year-old man is evaluated in the emergency department for a 2-day history of worsening dyspnea and wheezing in conjunction with an upper respiratory tract infection. The patient has a history of asthma, and his medications are inhaled mometasone and albuterol. In the emergency department, the patient is anxious and is using accessory muscles to breathe; he cannot speak in full sentences. The oxygen saturation is 90% while he is breathing ambient air. Breath sounds are reduced bilaterally, with faint diffuse expiratory wheezes. He is given albuterol by nebulizer, and use of accessory muscles is reduced. Bedside spirometry shows an $FEV_1$ of 35% of predicted; he is given two more treatments of nebulized albuterol.

After treatment, the patient is alert with slight use of accessory muscles; he can speak in short full sentences. Vital signs are stable; oxygen saturation is 98% with the patient receiving oxygen, 2 L/min. Breath sounds are louder than on initial examination, and wheezing is more intense. Spirometry shows an $FEV_1$ of 50% of predicted.

**Which of the following is the most appropriate next step in the management of this patient?**

(A) Admit the patient to a regular medicine ward
(B) Discharge the patient on his baseline asthma treatment regimen
(C) Intubate and admit the patient to the intensive care unit
(D) Monitor the patient in the intensive care unit

## Item 18

A 65-year-old man is admitted to the intensive care unit for gram-negative sepsis. The patient's medical history is significant only for hyperthyroidism for which he takes methimazole. On day 2 in the intensive care unit, he undergoes rapid sequence intubation with propofol and succinylcholine for worsening hypoxemic respiratory failure resulting from the acute respiratory distress syndrome. The patient receives intermittent lorazepam and fentanyl boluses intravenously for sedation. Several hours later, the patient becomes febrile (temperature 40 °C [104 °F]), hypertensive, and tachycardic. On examination, he is diaphoretic and has muscular rigidity. Arterial blood gas analysis shows a metabolic and respiratory acidosis, and laboratory results are significant for an elevated serum creatine kinase level.

**Which of the following is the most likely cause of the patient's clinical deterioration?**

(A) Malignant hyperthermia
(B) Neuroleptic malignant syndrome
(C) Serotonin syndrome
(D) Thyroid storm

## Item 19

A 24-year-old woman with persistent asthma, which is well controlled on low-dose fluticasone and albuterol as needed, became pregnant 2 months ago and asks for advice about asthma therapy during her pregnancy. Before she started fluticasone therapy, she had frequent asthma symptoms and occasional exacerbations requiring emergency department treatment. Since she became pregnant, her asthma has remained under good control. The physical examination is unremarkable, and spirometry is normal.

**Which of the following is the most appropriate management for this patient?**

(A) Continue the current regimen
(B) Stop fluticasone; add theophylline
(C) Stop fluticasone; add salmeterol
(D) Stop fluticasone; add inhaled cromolyn

## Item 20

A 64-year-old woman is evaluated for a 6-week history of dyspnea, dry cough, fever, chills, night sweats, and fatigue, which have not responded to treatment with azithromycin and levofloxacin; she has lost 2.2 kg (5 lb) during that time. The patient had a thorough examination 6 months ago while she was asymptomatic that included routine laboratory studies, age- and sex-appropriate cancer screening, and a chest radiograph; all results were normal. The patient has never smoked, has had no known environmental exposures, and has not traveled recently or been exposed to anyone with a similar illness. Her only medications are aspirin and a multivitamin.

On physical examination, temperature is 37.8 °C (100.0 °F); other vital signs are normal. Cardiac examination is normal. There are scattered crackles in the mid-lung zones with associated rare expiratory wheezes. There is no digital clubbing. Musculoskeletal and skin examinations are normal. Chest radiograph is shown on the next page.

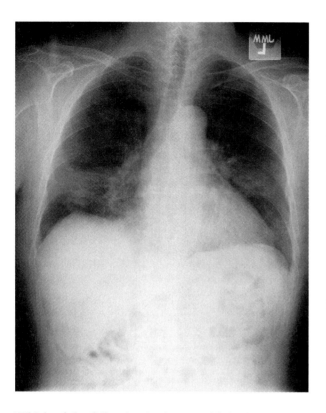

**Which of the following is the most likely diagnosis?**

(A) Cryptogenic organizing pneumonia
(B) Idiopathic pulmonary fibrosis
(C) Lymphocytic interstitial pneumonia
(D) Nonspecific interstitial pneumonia

## Item 21

A 35-year-old woman is evaluated in the hospital for chest pain and dyspnea 1 day after vaginal delivery of her second child. She had an uncomplicated pregnancy but a prolonged labor.

On physical examination, the temperature is 37.0 °C (98.6 °F), the blood pressure is 100/60 mm Hg, the pulse rate is 115/min, and the respiration rate is 22/min. The lungs are clear, heart sounds are normal, and there is no evidence of bleeding on pelvic examination. Complete blood count on admission revealed a hematocrit of 34% and a platelet count of $150,000/\mu L$ ($150 \times 10^9$/L). Chest radiograph is normal. Ventilation/perfusion scan shows mismatched perfusion defects in 20% of her lung volume.

**Which of the following would be an acceptable therapy for this patient?**

(A) Inferior vena cava filter
(B) Intravenous argatroban
(C) Intravenous low-molecular-weight heparin
(D) Subcutaneous unfractionated heparin

## Item 22

A 60-year-old man is evaluated during routine follow-up in November. The patient has severe chronic obstructive pulmonary disease, with dyspnea on minimal exertion and a chronic cough. He has a 40-pack-year history of cigarette smoking, but he quit smoking 3 years ago. His medications are albuterol as needed, inhaled corticosteroids, and tiotropium.

On physical examination, the patient is afebrile, blood pressure is 140/88 mm Hg, pulse rate is 90/min, and respiration rate is 20/min. Oxygen saturation with the patient at rest and breathing ambient air is 86%. Jugular venous distention and a loud $P_2$ are present. The chest is hyperinflated and breath sounds are diminished. There is 1+ pedal edema.

Hemoglobin concentration is 16.5 g/dL (165 g/L). Arterial blood gases show pH 7.35, $P_{CO_2}$ 55 mm Hg, and $P_{O_2}$ 55 mm Hg on ambient air. Spirometry shows an $FEV_1$ of 25% of predicted. Chest radiograph shows hyperinflation but no infiltrates.

**Which of the following is the most appropriate therapy for this patient?**

(A) Continuous oxygen
(B) Nocturnal oxygen
(C) Oxygen as needed
(D) Oxygen during exercise

## Item 23

A 23-year-old man seeks medical advice for an upcoming mountain expedition. A year earlier, a planned 45-day trek to Lhotse in Nepal (elevation 8516 m [27,940 ft]) was cut short when he developed severe dyspnea and cough productive of blood-tinged, frothy sputum shortly after leaving the base camp (elevation 4930 m [16,174 ft]). When his symptoms persisted despite oxygen therapy, he was aided down the mountain. He plans to return to the high Himalayas for another attempt to climb the Lhotse summit.

**Which of the following would be appropriate prophylaxis for this patient?**

(A) Acetazolamide
(B) Dexamethasone
(C) Hydrochlorothiazide
(D) Metoprolol
(E) Nifedipine

## Item 24

A 40-year-old man is evaluated for shortness of breath and left-sided chest discomfort without cough, fever, or hemoptysis. He had a contusion to the left side of his chest and back 1 week ago in an automobile accident. Chest radiograph immediately after the accident showed no fracture of the spine or ribs, but he had severe contusions on his back and on the left side of the chest. The patient has a history of lymphoma.

Examination of the chest shows dullness to percussion and decreased breath sounds on the left side. Chest radiograph shows a moderate-sized, left-sided pleural effusion without a pneumothorax. Serum protein is 5.8 g/dL (58 g/L), cholesterol 200 mg/dL (5.2 mmol/L), and triglycerides 100 mg/dL (1.13 mmol/L). Thoracentesis yields 500 mL of pleural fluid, and analysis shows:

| Cell count | Erythrocytes 300/µL; leukocytes 890/µL (0.89 × 10⁹/L) with 65% lymphocytes, 22% neutrophils, 8% mesothelial cells, and 4% eosinophils |
|---|---|
| Total protein | 3.5 g/dL (35 g/L) |
| Lactate dehydrogenase | 250 U/L |
| pH | 7.50 |
| Amylase | 25 U/L |
| Triglycerides | 145 mg/dL (1.6 mmol/L) |
| Cholesterol | 38 mg/dL (0.98 mmol/L) |

Cytology, Gram stain, acid-fast bacilli stain, and bacterial culture are negative.

**Which of the following is the most likely diagnosis?**

(A) Chylothorax
(B) Lymphomatous pleural effusion
(C) Parapneumonic effusion
(D) Tuberculous pleural effusion

## Item 25

A 56-year-old woman is evaluated for a 2-month history of a drooping eyelid, difficulty chewing food and swallowing, and slurred speech. The symptoms are worse when she is tired. The patient has a 15-pack-year history of cigarette smoking but quit smoking 10 years ago. She is otherwise healthy and takes no medications.

On physical examination, the temperature is 37.0 °C (98.6 °F), the blood pressure is 118/60 mm Hg, the pulse rate is 72/min, the respiration rate is 16/min, and the BMI is 24.5. There is right-sided ptosis; pupils are equal in size and reactive, and eye movements are normal. Brief neurologic examination is normal, and there is no lymphadenopathy. Routine laboratory studies are normal; acetylcholine receptor binding antibody level is 46.8 nmol/L (normal range, less than 0.2 nmol/L). Chest radiograph shows a 3-cm anterior-superior mediastinal mass. CT scan of the chest is shown.

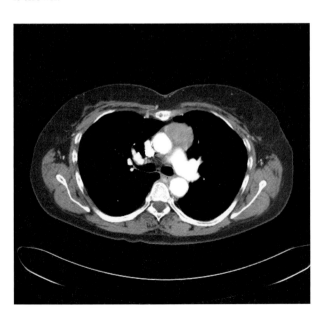

**Which of the following is the most likely diagnosis?**

(A) Esophageal leiomyoma
(B) Neurolemmoma
(C) Sarcoidosis
(D) Small cell lung cancer
(E) Thymoma

## Item 26

A 59-year-old man is evaluated for tachycardia and hypertension 6 hours after undergoing an uncomplicated open cholecystectomy under general anesthesia. The patient had intraoperative high blood pressure and was treated postoperatively with metoprolol, 5 mg every 4 hours by intravenous bolus. The patient underwent repair of a laceration of the liver 5 years ago and had an uncomplicated intraoperative and postoperative course. He has a history of essential hypertension, and his medications are hydrochlorothiazide and metoprolol.

On physical examination, the temperature is 39.2 °C (102.5 °F), the blood pressure is 190/110 mm Hg, and the pulse rate is 115/min. There is significant rigidity of all his extremities.

**Which of the following is the most appropriate therapy for this patient?**

(A) Alcohol sponge baths
(B) Ampicillin-sulbactam
(C) Corticosteroids
(D) Dantrolene
(E) Sodium nitroprusside

## Item 27

A 56-year-old woman is evaluated for a 2-year history of episodic cough and chest tightness. Her symptoms began after a severe respiratory tract infection. Since then, she has had cough and chest discomfort after similar infections, typically lasting several weeks before resolving. She feels well between episodes. She is otherwise healthy and takes no medications. Physical examination reveals no abnormalities, and spirometry is normal.

**Which of the following is the most appropriate next step in the evaluation of this patient?**

(A) Bronchoscopy
(B) CT scan of the sinuses
(C) Exercise echocardiography
(D) Methacholine challenge testing

## Item 28

A 55-year-old man with a 7-year history of severe chronic obstructive pulmonary disease is evaluated after being discharged from the hospital following an acute exacerbation; he has had three exacerbations over the previous 18 months. He is a long-term smoker who stopped smoking 1 year ago. He adheres to therapy with albuterol as needed and inhaled salmeterol and tiotropium and has demonstrated proper inhaler technique.

On physical examination, vital signs are normal. Breath sounds are decreased bilaterally; there is no edema or cyanosis. Oxygen saturation after exertion is 92% on ambient air. Spirometry shows an $FEV_1$ of 32% of predicted and an $FEV_1/FVC$ ratio of 40%. Chest radiograph done in the hospital 3 weeks ago showed no active disease.

**Which of the following should be added to this patient's therapeutic regimen?**

(A) An inhaled corticosteroid
(B) Ipratropium
(C) *N*-acetylcysteine
(D) Oral prednisone

## Item 29

A 54-year-old woman is evaluated after a 1.5-cm nodule was detected in the right lower lobe of the lung on a chest radiograph done to evaluate new-onset dyspnea on exertion. The nodule was not present on a chest radiograph done 8 years ago. The patient lives in Missouri and has not traveled recently. She has a 30-pack-year history of cigarette smoking but quit smoking 3 years ago. Her medical history includes hypertension and hyperlipidemia, and her medications are hydrochlorothiazide and atorvastatin. There is no family history of lung cancer.

On physical examination, the temperature is 36.8 °C (98.0 °F), the blood pressure is 124/72 mm Hg, the pulse rate is 64/min, and the respiration rate is 14/min. The lungs are clear, the skin is normal, and there is no lymphadenopathy. Pulmonary function testing shows mild airway obstruction and no acute response to a bronchodilator. Contrast-enhanced CT scan of the chest shows the nodule to be uncalcified on thin-section images, and there was no significant enhancement (10 Hounsfield units) on dynamic contrast study. *Histoplasma* serology is negative.

**Which of the following is the most appropriate management for this patient?**

(A) Bronchoscopy and biopsy of the lesion
(B) CT-guided transthoracic biopsy of the lesion
(C) Repeat CT scan in 3 months
(D) Video-assisted thoracoscopic surgery to remove the nodule
(E) No further evaluation

## Item 30

A previously healthy 62-year-old man was intubated 3 days ago for the acute respiratory distress syndrome complicating community-acquired pneumonia. His condition improved with antibiotic therapy and supportive care. He was extubated 2 hours ago after tolerating a trial of spontaneous breathing, but he has subsequently developed respiratory distress.

The patient is alert, cooperative, and speaking in short sentences. The temperature is 36.9 °C (98.4 °F), blood pressure is 150/90 mm Hg, pulse rate is 110/min, and respiration rate is 34/min. Oxygen saturation is 86% on $FiO_2$ 0.7 by face mask. There are inspiratory crackles bilaterally, and the patient is using neck and abdominal muscles to breathe.

Cardiac examination reveals regular tachycardia without extra sounds or murmurs; the jugular venous pressure could not be assessed because of the patient's respiratory effort.

Arterial blood gases at the end of the breathing trial on $FiO_2$ 0.4 included pH 7.38, $PCO_2$ 35 mm Hg, and $PO_2$ 68 mm Hg. His current blood gases following extubation on $FiO_2$ 0.7 are pH 7.30, $PCO_2$ 45 mm Hg, and $PO_2$ 56 mm Hg.

Chest radiograph after extubation shows reduced lung volumes but otherwise no change in bilateral alveolar infiltrates from his previous radiograph.

**Which of the following is the most appropriate management for this patient?**

(A) Administer intravenous furosemide
(B) Administer intravenous naloxone
(C) Increase $FiO_2$ to 1.0
(D) Reintubate and resume mechanical ventilation
(E) Start noninvasive positive-pressure ventilation

## Item 31

A 52-year-old man is evaluated for a 7-month history of progressive dyspnea, initially with vigorous exertion; now, even walking slowly causes immediate severe dyspnea and dizziness. The symptoms subside when he is at rest. He has had two syncopal episodes, both while he was walking at a brisk pace. He does not have cough, chest pain, or wheezing. He has no other significant medical history and takes no medications.

On physical examination, the temperature is 37.0 °C (98.6 °F), the blood pressure is 105/60 mm Hg, the pulse rate is 102/min at rest and 120/min after the patient walks across the room, the respiration rate is 20/min, and the BMI is 32. Lung expansion is normal during deep breathing. Jugular venous distention is present. Lungs are clear to auscultation with no wheezes or crackles. There is fixed splitting of $S_2$ with an increased pulmonic component. There is a grade 1-2/6 holosystolic murmur at the left sternal border near the fourth rib that increases with inspiration. The lower extremities are edematous. There is no cyanosis or clubbing.

Complete blood count and resting arterial blood gases are normal. Electrocardiography shows a rightward QRS axis and large R waves in $V_1$. Spirometry and plethysmography are normal. The chest radiograph shows no infiltrates or masses.

**Which of the following is the best next step in the evaluation of this patient?**

(A) Bronchoscopy and transbronchial lung biopsy
(B) Methacholine challenge test
(C) Right-heart catheterization and pulmonary angiography
(D) Transthoracic echocardiography

## Item 32

A 20-year-old male college student is evaluated for a 3-year history of persistent daytime sleepiness. He snores loudly but has had no witnessed apneas or cataplexy. He has occasional episodes of sleep paralysis in which he cannot move for about a minute after awakening from sleep. He typically goes to bed at 11:30 PM on weekdays and at 1:00 AM on weekends. He falls asleep easily, sleeps uneventfully, and awakens at about 6:00 AM on weekdays and 11:00 AM on weekends. His medical history includes depression diagnosed 1 year ago for which he takes a selective serotonin reuptake inhibitor. He drinks three or four caffeinated drinks a day.

**Which of the following is the most appropriate management for this patient?**

(A) Order thyroid function tests
(B) Perform a multiple sleep latency test
(C) Prescribe modafinil
(D) Recommend longer nighttime sleep
(E) Refer for polysomnography

## Item 33

A 37-year-old man with asthma is evaluated for frequent episodes of wheezing and dyspnea unrelieved by short-acting β-agonist therapy. He uses his controller medications regularly, including an inhaled long-acting β-agonist and inhaled high-dose corticosteroids. He has symptoms daily and frequent nocturnal symptoms.

On physical examination, the patient is in mild respiratory distress. The temperature is 37.0 °C (98.6 °F), blood pressure is 140/85 mm Hg, pulse rate is 90/min, and respiration rate is 18/min. He has bilateral wheezing. Spirometry shows an $FEV_1$ of 65% of predicted. After the supervised use of a bronchodilator in the office, there was some relief of symptoms, and repeat spirometry 10 minutes after the administration of the bronchodilator showed that the $FEV_1$ increased to 85% of predicted.

**Which of the following is the appropriate next step in this patient's management?**

(A) Add a leukotriene modifying drug
(B) Have the patient demonstrate his inhaler technique
(C) Have the patient keep a symptom and treatment log
(D) Start oral prednisone therapy

## Item 34

A 19-year-old woman is evaluated in the emergency department for low-grade fever, muscle aches, cough, and progressively severe shortness of breath of 1 week's duration. She requires intubation and mechanical ventilation. The patient recently moved to the United States from Japan. She started smoking cigarettes 3 weeks ago and smokes a pack a day.

On physical examination, the temperature is 37.2 °C (99.0 °F), the blood pressure is 128/60 mm Hg, the pulse rate is 110/min, and the respiration rate is 22/min on mechanical ventilation. Cardiac examination is normal. There are bilateral crackles posteriorly. The rest of the general physical examination is normal. The hemoglobin is 14.3 g/dL (143 g/L); the leukocyte count is 16,888/μL (16.9 × 10⁹/L) with 52% neutrophils, 4% monocytes, 20% lymphocytes, and 24% eosinophils; and the platelet count is 345,000/μL (345 × 10⁹/L). Chest CT scan with intravenous contrast shows bilateral focal areas of consolidation with scattered ground-glass opacification, small bilateral pleural effusions, and no evidence of pulmonary embolism. Bronchoscopy with bronchoalveolar lavage shows no organisms on Gram stain or fungal stain; cell count is elevated, and the differential shows 30% neutrophils, 6% macrophages, 4% lymphocytes, and 60% eosinophils. Blood and sputum cultures are negative after 2 days.

**Which of the following is the most likely diagnosis?**

(A) Acute eosinophilic pneumonia
(B) Churg-Strauss syndrome
(C) Idiopathic acute interstitial pneumonia
(D) *Mycoplasma* pneumonia

## Item 35

A 42-year-old man is evaluated in the hospital for dyspnea and pleuritic chest pain. The patient had a fracture of the right femur 3 weeks ago. He has hypertension, and his only medication is hydrochlorothiazide.

On physical examination, the temperature is 38.1 °C (100.6 °F), the pulse rate is 110/min, the respiration rate is 22/min, the blood pressure is 130/78 mm Hg, and the BMI is 24. Routine laboratory studies are normal; serum troponins are undetectable. Electrocardiography shows increased height of R waves in leads $V_4$-$V_6$; the QRS complex has a leftward axis. Contrast-enhanced CT scan shows pulmonary emboli in the arteries perfusing the lingula and the posterior basal segment of the left lower lobe.

**Which of the following is the most appropriate treatment for this patient?**

(A) Inferior vena cava filter
(B) Intravenous unfractionated heparin
(C) Intravenous tissue plasminogen activator
(D) Mechanical clot dissolution
(E) Surgical embolectomy

## Item 36

A 59-year-old man with chronic obstructive pulmonary disease is evaluated before planned air travel from Denver, Colorado, to Beijing, China. He is physically active but has episodic wheezing and a "racing" heartbeat with exertion. His current therapy consists of inhaled bronchodilators and supplemental continuous oxygen at 2 L/min.

On examination, the pulse rate is 68/min, respiration rate is 18/min, and oxygen saturation is 90% with the patient breathing oxygen, 2 L/min. Cardiac examination is normal. Breath sounds are distant without wheezes or crackles. Chest radiograph shows hyperexpanded lungs but no infiltrates or bullae.

**Which of the following is the most appropriate next step in this patient's management?**

(A) Calculate oxygen needs using a prediction algorithm
(B) Order a hypoxia inhalation test

(C) Prescribe in-flight supplemental oxygen level at 3 L/min

(D) Recommend that the patient not fly

## Item 37

A 36-year-old man is evaluated for a 1-year history of progressive shortness of breath; his wife has noticed that he has a dry cough and wheezing when he returns from work. The patient has worked as an automobile painter for the past 4 years. He has a 5-pack-year history of cigarette smoking, but quit smoking 8 years ago. He has no history of allergic disease.

On physical examination, vital signs and review of systems are normal. Chest radiograph is normal. Pulmonary function testing shows:

| | |
|---|---|
| $FEV_1$ | 52% of predicted |
| FVC | 83% of predicted |
| $FEV_1$/FVC ratio | 47% |
| $D_{LCO}$ | 85% of predicted |

Spirometry after a bronchodilator shows:

| | |
|---|---|
| $FEV_1$ | 83% of predicted |
| FVC | 100% of predicted |
| $FEV_1$/FVC ratio | 62% |

**Which of the following would be an appropriate next step in the evaluation of this patient?**

(A) Chest CT scan

(B) Methacholine challenge test

(C) Obtaining a detailed description of his current job tasks

(D) Skin testing to common aeroallergens

## Item 38

A 20-year-old man with a history of severe asthma is brought to the emergency department obtunded and in severe respiratory acidosis from an acute exacerbation of his asthma. He is intubated in the emergency department, and 30 minutes later he is evaluated in the intensive care unit.

On physical examination, the patient is sedated and unresponsive; he is afebrile, and the blood pressure is 80/40 mm Hg, pulse rate is 140/min, and respiration rate is 24/min. Oxygen saturation is 98%. There are diffusely decreased breath sounds with faint bilateral expiratory wheezes. Cardiac examination reveals distant regular tachycardic rhythm but is otherwise normal. Ventilator settings include volume control mode with a set rate of 24, tidal volume 800 mL (12 mL/kg ideal body weight), positive end-expiratory pressure 5 cm $H_2O$, and $FiO_2$ 0.6. Arterial blood gases are pH 7.30, $PCO_2$ 40 mm Hg, and $PO_2$ 180 mm Hg. Chest radiograph shows hyperinflation and a properly placed endotracheal tube.

**Which of the following would most rapidly improve the patient's hypotension?**

(A) Administer thrombolytic therapy

(B) Disconnect the patient from the ventilator for 30 seconds

(C) Perform pericardiocentesis

(D) Place chest tubes bilaterally

## Item 39

A 57-year-old man is evaluated after a chest radiograph taken in a preoperative assessment for a knee replacement showed a 1.0-cm nodule in the right lower lobe of the lung. The patient lives in Montana and has not traveled recently. He does not recall ever having been exposed to tuberculosis or having been tested for the disease. His most recent chest radiograph was 10 years ago; the result was normal, and the radiograph is no longer available. About 6 months ago he had abdominal pain that was evaluated with an abdominal CT scan, and the pain has since resolved. The patient has a 20-pack-year history of cigarette smoking but quit 10 years ago. He is otherwise healthy.

On physical examination, vital signs are normal, lungs are clear, and there is no lymphadenopathy.

**Which of the following is the most appropriate next step in the management of this patient?**

(A) 18F-fluorodeoxyglucose and positron emission tomography scan (FDG-PET)

(B) MRI of the chest

(C) Repeat CT scan in 3 months

(D) Review of lung images from CT scan of the abdomen

(E) Thin-section CT scan of the chest

## Item 40

A 70-year-old man is evaluated for the insidious onset of dyspnea. He does not have chest pain, cough, hemoptysis, or fever. The patient has advanced adenocarcinoma of the lung, and 1 month ago a left-sided malignant pleural effusion was diagnosed. The effusion was small, and observation was recommended.

On physical examination, the patient is thin and shows minimal increased work of breathing at rest on ambient air. The temperature is 36.9 °C (98.5 °F), the blood pressure is 140/75 mm Hg, the pulse rate is 96/min and regular, and the respiration rate is 22/min; oxygen saturation is 91% on ambient air. There is dullness to percussion in the left base with decreased fremitus and egophony above the level of dullness. There is digital clubbing. Chest radiograph shows left hilar and mediastinal lymphadenopathy and a moderate-sized pleural effusion occupying 50% of the hemithorax with minimal contralateral mediastinal shift. Thoracentesis was terminated because of the patient's coughing and severe anterior chest pain. The lung did not expand after thoracentesis. Analysis of the pleural fluid shows:

| | |
|---|---|
| Erythrocyte count | $10,000/\mu L$ ($10 \times 10^9$/L) |
| Nucleated cell count | $2800/\mu L$ ($2.8 \times 10^9$/L) with 7% neutrophils, 61% lymphocytes, 15% macrophages, 10% mesothelial cells, and 7% eosinophils |
| Total protein | 3.8 g/dL (38 g/L) |
| Lactate dehydrogenase | 250 U/L |
| pH | 7.18 |
| Glucose | 38 mg/dL (2.1 mmol/L) |

Pleural fluid cytology is positive for adenocarcinoma.

Which of the following is the most appropriate management for this patient?

(A) Placement of an indwelling pleural catheter
(B) Radiation therapy
(C) Talc pleurodesis through a small-bore catheter
(D) Video-assisted thoracoscopic surgery with pleural abrasion

## Item 41

A 67-year-old man is evaluated in the emergency department for confusion and agitation secondary to malignant hypertension. Initial blood pressure is 230/130 mm Hg, and funduscopic examination reveals papilledema.

He is admitted to the intensive care unit, and therapy with nitroprusside by continuous infusion is begun; the therapy is titrated over the next 3 days. The encephalopathy and papilledema resolve with control of the blood pressure. However, he becomes more confused and lethargic. The physical examination is normal. He is afebrile, with a blood pressure of 100/70 mm Hg and a pulse rate of 60/min. He is oriented only to person. There are no focal findings on the neurologic examination and no evidence of nuchal rigidity.

Arterial blood gases reveal: pH 7.2; $P_{CO_2}$ 20 mm Hg; $P_{O_2}$ 90 mm Hg (on ambient air). Venous $P_{O_2}$ is 72 mm Hg. Serum electrolyte panel shows: sodium 140 meq/L (140 mmol/L); potassium 3.8 meq/L (3.8 mmol/L); chloride 90 meq/L (90 mmol/L), and bicarbonate 9 meq/L (9 mmol/L).

Which of the following is the most likely cause of the patient's findings?

(A) Cyanide toxicity
(B) Delirium tremens
(C) Hepatic encephalopathy
(D) Hypoxic-ischemic encephalopathy
(E) Wernicke encephalopathy

## Item 42

A 38-year-old man is evaluated for a 1-year history of shortness of breath with exertion and wheezing. He has smoked intermittently since the age of 18 years.

On physical examination, vital signs are normal; BMI is 25. Breath sounds are diminished bilaterally, and there is wheezing posteriorly. Spirometry shows an $FEV_1$ of 55% of predicted and an $FEV_1/FVC$ ratio of 61% of predicted. Chest radiograph shows bilateral basilar lucency. Plasma $\alpha_1$-antitrypsin concentration is 25 mg/dL (4.6 μmol/L).

The patient is counseled to stop smoking and referred to a smoking cessation program. Standard supportive inhaled bronchodilator and long-acting $\beta_2$-agonist therapy is started.

Which of the following therapies is most reasonable to consider for this patient at this time?

(A) Danazol
(B) Intravenous infusion of human $\alpha_1$-antitrypsin
(C) Lung transplantation
(D) Lung volume reduction surgery

## Item 43

A 45-year-old woman is evaluated in the emergency department for an exacerbation of asthma that started 2 days after the onset of an upper respiratory tract infection. Her symptoms include wheezing, a productive cough, and chest tightness that have not responded to frequent use of an albuterol inhaler. Her medical history is unremarkable except for long-standing asthma. She has been hospitalized for asthma five or six times, one of which required treatment in the intensive care unit. Her current medications include a high-dose inhaled corticosteroid, inhaled long-acting β-agonist, and albuterol as needed.

On physical examination, she is alert but anxious; the temperature is 37.0 °C (98.6 °F), the blood pressure is 140/85 mm Hg, the pulse rate is 115/min, and the respiration rate is 32/min. Oxygen saturation is 95% on low-flow supplemental oxygen. Chest examination shows reduced breath sounds over both lung fields with prolonged expiration and minimal wheezing. Spirometry reveals an $FEV_1$ of 1.08 L (35% of predicted) and an FVC of 2.9 L (70% of predicted). After nebulized albuterol/ipratropium bromide, the patient's condition improves minimally. Repeat physical examination shows a temperature of 37.1 °C (99.0 °F), pulse rate of 130/min, and respiration rate of 24/min. Examination of the lungs shows very decreased air entry and minimal wheezing; spirometry shows an $FEV_1$ of 0.96 L (31% of predicted) and FVC of 2.8 L (67% of predicted).

Which of the following is the most important next step in the evaluation of this patient?

(A) Complete blood count
(B) Electrocardiography
(C) Measurement of arterial blood gases
(D) Measurement of peak expiratory flow

## Item 44

A 67-year-old man is evaluated in the surgical intensive care unit. He underwent laparotomy and diverting colostomy for a ruptured diverticulum 72 hours ago, and now has a temperature of 40.0 °C (104.0 °F) and a heart rate of 135/min. In the past 3 hours his mean arterial blood pressure has dropped to 58 mm Hg despite three 1-L boluses of normal saline; urine output was only 15 mL in the past hour. The patient's oxygen saturation is 85% on 100% oxygen by nonrebreather mask. Platelet count is 42,000/μL ($42 \times 10^9$/L).

A portable chest radiograph shows bilateral alveolar infiltrates. A central venous catheter is placed; invasive mechanical ventilation and broad-spectrum antibiotic therapy are begun.

Which of the following is most appropriate next step in the management of this patient?

(A) Activated protein C
(B) Colloid fluid infusion
(C) Insulin drip to maintain plasma glucose less than 110 mg/dL (6.1 mmol/L)
(D) Low-dose dopamine

## Item 45

An 18-year-old woman with a 4-month history of type 1 diabetes mellitus is evaluated in the emergency department for mild diabetic ketoacidosis. She developed flu-like symptoms 48 hours ago, and she did not administer her usual insulin therapy. She takes no other medications, has no known allergies, and has never been hospitalized before.

The patient is examined, and therapy with insulin and fluids is started; an intravenous line and an indwelling urinary catheter are inserted. Shortly thereafter, the patient develops shortness of breath and chest tightness. On repeat examination, she now has facial flushing and bilateral wheezing. Her blood pressure has decreased from 120/90 mm Hg to 90/60 mm Hg, and her pulse rate has increased from 96/min to 120/min with a respiration rate of 30/min. There is no evidence of perioral or oral swelling or upper airway compromise.

**Which of the following is the most appropriate next step in the management of the patient?**

(A) Emergent cricothyroidotomy
(B) Endotracheal intubation
(C) Intramuscular epinephrine
(D) Intravenous glucagon

## Item 46

A 36-year-old woman is evaluated in the office after having had a small (less than 2 cm) spontaneous pneumothorax treated conservatively in the emergency department. The patient had a 6-month history of worsening dyspnea accompanied by a dry cough before the pneumothorax. She has never smoked and has a history of bilateral breast augmentation.

On physical examination, there is no digital clubbing or crackles. High-resolution chest CT scan is shown.

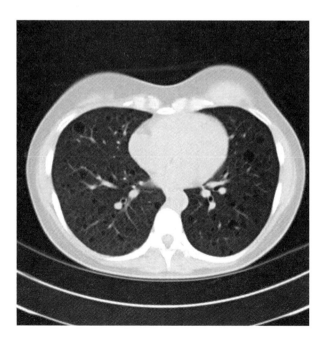

**Which of the following is the most likely diagnosis?**

(A) Emphysema
(B) Idiopathic pulmonary fibrosis
(C) Lymphangioleiomyomatosis
(D) Pulmonary Langerhans cell histiocytosis

## Item 47

A 70-year-old woman is hospitalized for pneumococcal pneumonia. She was ambulatory until the day of admission but is now unable to leave her bed. She has a permanent venous catheter through her left subclavian vein. The patient has a history of stage IIIB non–small cell lung cancer.

On physical examination, the temperature is 37.8 °C (100.0 °F), the blood pressure is 110/70 mm Hg, the pulse rate is 110/min, and the respiration rate is 22/min. On admission, the patient's serum creatinine level was 3.0 mg/dL (265.2 μmol/L); it was 0.7 mg/dL (61.9 μmol/L) 1 month ago.

**Which of the following is the best management to prevent venous thromboembolism in this patient?**

(A) Aspirin
(B) Low-dose unfractionated heparin, subcutaneously
(C) Low-molecular-weight heparin, subcutaneously
(D) Periodic lower extremity ultrasonography
(E) Warfarin to maintain the INR at 2.0 to 3.0

## Item 48

A 65-year-old man is evaluated for a 6-month history of fatigue and decreased exercise capacity. The patient has severe chronic obstructive pulmonary disease with frequent exacerbations and has been hospitalized three times within the past 2 years for exacerbations of his disease. He recently stopped his participation in a pulmonary rehabilitation program. He also has hypertension, and his medications are albuterol as needed; salmeterol; tiotropium; theophylline; an inhaled corticosteroid; oxygen, 2 L/min by nasal cannula; and hydrochlorothiazide.

On physical examination, he is afebrile; the blood pressure is 130/70 mm Hg, the pulse rate is 84/min, the respiration rate is 16/min, and the BMI is 24. Heart and breath sounds are diminished; there is no jugular venous distention, hepatomegaly, or edema. Spirometry shows an $FEV_1$ of 35% of predicted and an $FEV_1/FVC$ ratio of 45%. Oxygen saturation is 92% ($PO_2$ is 65 mm Hg) on supplemental oxygen.

**Laboratory studies:**

| | |
|---|---|
| Hematocrit | 40% |
| Albumin | 3.6 g/dL (36 g/L) |
| Creatinine | 1.0 mg/dL (88.4 μmol/L) |
| Thyroid-stimulating hormone | 3.0 μU/mL (3.0 mU/L) |

Chest radiograph shows hyperinflation but no infiltrates.

**Which of the following would be the most appropriate management for this patient?**

(A) Increase nasal oxygen

(B) Refer for lung transplantation
(C) Refer for lung volume reduction surgery
(D) Screen for depression

## Item 49

A 36-year-old woman with an 18-month history of diffuse cutaneous systemic sclerosis is evaluated for a 6-month history of dry cough and decrease in exercise capacity. She is otherwise healthy and takes no medications.

On physical examination, the blood pressure is 110/68 mm Hg, the pulse rate is 82/min, and the respiration rate is 18/min. Cardiac examination is normal. There are bilateral dry crackles but no other pulmonary abnormalities. The skin over the digits on both hands and parts of the arms and forearms is thickened and tight. Laboratory studies show normal serum electrolytes, creatinine, and complete blood count with leukocyte differential. Anti-Scl-70 antibodies are positive. Pulmonary function tests show an $FEV_1$ of 80% of predicted, an FVC of 76% of predicted, and a $D_{LCO}$ of 83% of predicted. High-resolution chest CT scan shows scant bilateral reticular changes with a basilar and peripheral distribution. There is no evidence of ground-glass opacification. Visual impression of the extent of lung involvement is 10%.

**Which of the following is the most appropriate management for this patient's pulmonary disease?**

(A) Cyclophosphamide and low-dose prednisone
(B) High-dose prednisone
(C) Open lung biopsy
(D) Periodic high-resolution CT scan and lung function testing

## Item 50

A 51-year-old woman is evaluated after a pulmonary nodule was detected in the emergency department where she was evaluated for substernal chest pain. Serial electrocardiograms and measurements of cardiac enzymes were negative for ischemia or infarction. A subsequent exercise stress test showed no ischemia. CT scan of the chest showed a 2.6-cm lobulated right upper lobe lung nodule and no lymphadenopathy. The patient smoked a pack of cigarettes a day for 18 years but stopped smoking 4 years ago. She is otherwise healthy. Her father died of lung cancer at age 63 years.

On physical examination, vital signs are normal and the lungs are clear, there is no palpable lymphadenopathy, and the abdomen is soft and without organomegaly. Positron emission tomography–CT shows that the nodule is metabolically active with significant tracer uptake in the nodule as well as a 1-cm right hilar lymph node and a 9-mm right paratracheal lymph node.

**Which of the following is the most appropriate management for this patient?**

(A) Bronchoscopy with ultrasonography-guided node sampling
(B) Chemotherapy
(C) CT-guided needle biopsy of the lung nodule
(D) Surgical staging with mediastinoscopy

## Item 51

A 22-year-old woman is evaluated in the emergency department for an acute exacerbation of asthma. The patient has a history of multiple hospitalizations for asthma, including one episode requiring invasive mechanical ventilation. Her medications are prednisone, 10 mg/d; inhaled salmeterol; montelukast; and nebulized albuterol every 4 hours as needed. She has used four doses of albuterol in the past 24 hours.

On physical examination, she is alert, diaphoretic, using accessory muscles to breathe, and speaking in short sentences. The respiration rate is 32/min, and oxygen saturation on ambient air is 89%. Breath sounds are decreased bilaterally with a few end-expiratory wheezes. Arterial blood gases are pH 7.48, $P_{CO_2}$ 30 mm Hg, and $P_{O_2}$ 59 mm Hg. Chest radiograph shows hyperinflation but is otherwise normal. Therapy with supplemental oxygen and continuous nebulized albuterol is started.

One hour after her presentation, the patient's examination findings and symptoms are unchanged. Repeat arterial blood gases are pH 7.39, $P_{CO_2}$ 40 mm Hg, and $P_{O_2}$ 95 mm Hg with the patient on an unspecified amount of supplemental oxygen.

**Which of the following is the most appropriate next step in the management of this patient?**

(A) Administer lorazepam
(B) Admit the patient to the intensive care unit
(C) Admit the patient to a regular medicine ward
(D) Discharge the patient on her current medications
(E) Perform laryngoscopy

## Item 52

A 65-year-old man is evaluated for daytime sleepiness. His wife says that he snores nightly and in all sleep positions and that she has witnessed the patient having an apnea episode. The patient has repeated episodes of nighttime awakenings when he feels short of breath and has headaches and dry mouth on awakening in the morning. He typically sleeps for about 8 hours each night but awakens unrefreshed. He often takes a 1-hour nap in mid-afternoon. He does not smoke or drink alcohol, coffee, tea, or cola beverages.

On physical examination, vital signs are normal; BMI is 37. His neck circumference is 45.72 cm (18 in). Oxygen saturation is 90% with the patient breathing ambient air. The patient is edentulous, and examination of his oropharynx reveals a low-lying palate, narrow pharyngeal wall, and a posteriorly displaced tongue. The rest of the physical examination is normal.

**Which of the following is the most appropriate management at this time?**

(A) Continuous positive airway pressure (CPAP) therapy
(B) Instructions on avoiding a supine sleep position
(C) Oxygen therapy
(D) Polysomnography
(E) Referral for a mandibular repositioner

## Item 53

A 60-year-old woman is evaluated in a scheduled follow-up visit in the office. The patient has a long-standing history of asthma, which has been stable for the past 6 months on therapy with a high-dose inhaled corticosteroid and a long-acting β-agonist. She rarely uses her albuterol inhaler except for prophylaxis of exercise-induced bronchospasm. The patient is pleased with the control of the disease, has not been waking up at night with asthma, and has not missed work due to asthma for almost a year. She has no side effects from her current medical regimen.

On physical examination, vital signs are normal; spirometry shows an $FEV_1$ of 3.60 L (85% of predicted) and $FEV_1/FVC$ of 75%.

**Which of the following is the most appropriate management for this patient?**

(A) Continue the inhaled corticosteroid and long-acting β-agonist at current doses
(B) Continue the long-acting β-agonist at the current dose and reduce the dose of the inhaled corticosteroid
(C) Discontinue the inhaled corticosteroid and the long-acting β-agonist
(D) Discontinue the inhaled corticosteroid and start a leukotriene modifying agent
(E) Discontinue the long-acting β-agonist and reduce the dose of the inhaled corticosteroid

## Item 54

A 69-year-old man is evaluated in the hospital for fever, progressive cough productive of purulent sputum, and increasing dyspnea. The patient was diagnosed with severe (GOLD stage III) chronic obstructive pulmonary disease 3 years ago. He smokes a pack of cigarettes a day. His medical history also includes hypertension and hypercholesterolemia, and his medications are albuterol as needed, tiotropium, simvastatin, hydrochlorothiazide, and aspirin.

On physical examination, the patient is in mild respiratory distress and is sitting up in bed. The temperature is 38.2 °C (101.0 °F), the blood pressure is 110/70 mm Hg, the pulse rate is 104/min, and the respiration rate is 20/min; BMI is 25. The oxygen saturation is 88% with the patient breathing ambient air and 93% on oxygen, 2 L/min by nasal cannula. There are bilateral expiratory wheezes but no digital clubbing or peripheral edema.

Chest radiograph shows hyperinflation without infiltrates. Arterial blood gases while the patient was breathing ambient air are pH 7.40, $P_{CO_2}$ 41 mm Hg, and $P_{O_2}$ 53 mm Hg. Spirometry done 2 months ago showed an $FEV_1$ of 45% of predicted and an $FEV_1/FVC$ ratio of 52%. Therapy with nebulized albuterol and ipratropium is begun.

**Which of the following additional therapy would be most appropriate for this patient?**

(A) Inhaled corticosteroids
(B) Inhaled salmeterol
(C) Intravenous theophylline and antibiotics
(D) Intravenous corticosteroids and antibiotics
(E) Noninvasive positive-pressure ventilation

## Item 55

A 60-year-old man is evaluated in the emergency department for a 3-hour history of shaking chills and cough productive of purulent sputum. He has a 35-pack-year history of cigarette smoking but has no other significant medical history.

On physical examination, the temperature is 38.5 °C (101.4 °F), the blood pressure is 150/90 mm Hg, the pulse rate is 115/min and regular, and the respiration rate is 28/min. There is increased dullness to percussion at the right base, crackles in the right mid-lung field, and anterior wheezes. Chest radiograph shows a right lower lobe posterior infiltrate and a moderate-sized pleural effusion; diagnostic thoracentesis reveals a turbid pleural fluid. Analysis of the fluid shows:

| | |
|---|---|
| Erythrocyte count | 750/μL |
| Nucleated cell count | 18,000/μL (18 × 10⁹/L) with 87% neutrophils, 5% lymphocytes, 4% macrophages, and 4% mesothelial cells |
| Total protein | 4.5 g/dL (45 g/L) |
| Lactate dehydrogenase | 1000 U/L |
| pH | 7.20 |
| Glucose | 50 mg/dL (2.8 mmol/L) |

Ultrasonography at the time of thoracentesis showed complex septations in the pleural fluid. Cytology is pending. Therapy with ceftriaxone, azithromycin, and inhaled bronchodilators is started.

**Which of the following is the most appropriate management for this patient?**

(A) Admit to the hospital and perform pleural cavity drainage
(B) Admit to the hospital and repeat chest radiograph in 2 days
(C) Admit to the hospital for video-assisted thoracoscopic surgery
(D) Treat as an outpatient

## Item 56

A 53-year-old woman is evaluated in the emergency department after 1 day of severe right flank pain, fever, and mild nausea. Urinalysis reveals many leukocytes and leukocyte casts. Gram stain of her urine shows gram-positive cocci, and therapy with vancomycin and gentamicin is started. Despite therapy, the patient develops progressive hypoxemia and requires mechanical ventilation.

On examination, she appears very anxious but is not trying to remove the endotracheal tube or any other support devices. The temperature is 37.5 °C (99.5 °F), blood pressure is 120/60 mm Hg, and pulse rate is 130/min. Electrocardiogram shows sinus tachycardia. Blood and urine cultures grow *Enterococcus faecalis*.

**While the patient is on mechanical ventilation, which of the following is the most appropriate sedation strategy?**

(A) Deep continuous sedation

(B) Intermittent bolus dosing of sedatives with daily awakening

(C) No sedation

(D) Sedation with intermittent paralytic agents as tolerated

## Item 57

An 84-year-old woman is transferred to the intensive care unit for severe dehydration and malnutrition. She had an episode of acute gastroenteritis 2 weeks ago, and since then she has had little to eat or drink because of persistent nausea.

On physical examination, she appears cachectic and malnourished; the blood pressure is 80/40 mm Hg, pulse rate is 130/min, and respiration rate is 15/min. She has diffuse abdominal tenderness but no rebound tenderness. Her serum prealbumin level on admission is 10 mg/dL (100 mg/L) (less than 30 mg/dL [300 mg/L] is indicative of malnutrition). The patient weighs 50 kg (110 lb) and is 157 cm (62 in) tall. BMI is 20.3.

**Which of the following is the most appropriate daily nutritional support for this patient?**

(A) 500 kcal and 75 g protein

(B) 1250 kcal and 100 g protein

(C) 1500 kcal and 75 g protein

(D) 3000 kcal and 120 g protein

## Item 58

A 77-year-old woman is evaluated for a 1-year history of progressive dyspnea and dry cough. She has had previous evaluations for these symptoms and has had abnormal chest radiographs and high-resolution CT scans. She also has a history of heart failure, systolic hypertension, Sjögren syndrome, and monoclonal gammopathy of unknown significance; her medications are metoprolol, lisinopril, furosemide, hypromellose artificial tears, potassium chloride, and a multivitamin.

Three weeks ago, the patient had an open lung biopsy that showed polyclonal plasma-cell infiltration of the pulmonary interstitium within the alveolar septa with fibrotic changes, including rare honeycombing consistent with lymphocytic interstitial pneumonia. High-resolution CT scan before the biopsy showed bilateral mid- and lower-lung abnormalities, including scattered ground-glass opacification, rare subpleural reticular changes, and scattered tiny pulmonary nodules with rare cystic air spaces.

On physical examination, she is afebrile, the pulse rate is 78/min, the respiration rate is 16/min, and the blood pressure is 130/78 mm Hg. On cardiac examination, there is no evidence of jugular venous distention and an $S_4$ is present, but there are no murmurs. There are bilateral lower-lung crackles and rare squeaks. There is 1+ edema at the ankles but no digital clubbing. Lung function studies show a mild restrictive pattern.

**Which of the following is the most likely diagnosis?**

(A) Connective tissue disease–related lymphocytic interstitial pneumonia

(B) Idiopathic lymphocytic interstitial pneumonia

(C) Idiopathic pulmonary fibrosis

(D) Primary pulmonary lymphoma

## Item 59

A 54-year-old woman is evaluated for a 1-year history of progressive exertional dyspnea. She does not smoke cigarettes or use illicit drugs. The patient has a history of obesity and has used various appetite suppressants but takes no other medications. She has no significant family or personal or medical history.

On physical examination, she is afebrile; the blood pressure is 100/60 mm Hg, the pulse rate is 98/min, the respiration rate is 20/min, and the BMI is 38. The lungs are clear on auscultation and percussion. There is a loud pulmonic component to $S_2$, which is also split during inhalation and exhalation. Spirometry and plethysmography are normal. Arterial blood gases are normal. Ventilation/perfusion scan shows diffusely nonhomogeneous perfusion but no segmental or subsegmental regions of perfusion defect. Chest radiograph shows enlarged pulmonary arteries and enlarged right-sided heart chambers but no parenchymal abnormalities. Transthoracic echocardiography shows decreased cardiac output, right ventricular hypertrophy and dilation, and right atrial enlargement. The left ventricle is somewhat compressed by the intraventricular septum.

**Which of the following is the most appropriate next step in the management of this patient?**

(A) High-resolution CT scan of the chest

(B) Myocardial perfusion imaging

(C) Right-heart catheterization

(D) Therapeutic trial of enalapril

(E) Transbronchial lung biopsy

## Item 60

A 66-year-old man is evaluated during a routine examination. The patient has smoked a pack of cigarettes a day for 25 years. He has tried to quit smoking with nicotine gum and varenicline but has been unsuccessful. He has mild airway obstruction but good exercise tolerance and no cough, sputum production, or hemoptysis. The importance of smoking cessation is reviewed with the patient.

**Which of the following is the recommended screening strategy for lung cancer in this patient?**

(A) 18F-fluorodeoxyglucose and positron emission tomography scan (FDG-PET)

(B) Chest radiography

(C) Spiral CT scan of the chest

(D) Sputum cytology

(E) No screening

## Item 61

A 30-year-old woman develops bilateral pulmonary infiltrates and hypoxemia 48 hours after undergoing repair of multiple long-bone fractures. Her initial arterial blood gases are pH 7.48, $P_{CO_2}$ 30 mm Hg, and $P_{O_2}$ 45 mm Hg on 100% oxygen by nonrebreather mask. The patient is intubated and placed on mechanical ventilation.

The temperature is 38.3 °C (101.0 °F), the pulse rate is 100/min, the respiration rate is 28/min, and the blood pressure is 120/60 mm Hg. The patient weighs 60 kg (132.3 lb). Oxygen saturation is 83%. She is sedated, hemodynamically normal, and not using accessory muscles to breathe. There are bilateral inspiratory crackles. The ventilator settings are as follows: volume control mode, respiration rate 26/min, tidal volume 360 mL, positive end-expiratory pressure (PEEP) 5 cm $H_2O$, $F_{IO_2}$ 0.8. Arterial blood gases are pH 7.45, $P_{CO_2}$ 33 mm Hg, and $P_{O_2}$ 50 mm Hg.

**Which of the following is the most appropriate next step in the management of this patient?**

(A) Increase $F_{IO_2}$ to 1.0
(B) Increase PEEP to 10 cm $H_2O$
(C) Increase respiration rate to 32/min
(D) Increase tidal volume to 700 mL
(E) Start vecuronium infusion

## Item 62

A 75-year-old woman with long-standing asthma is evaluated for palpitations, nausea, and vomiting of 3 days' duration. Her asthma treatment regimen includes low-dose inhaled corticosteroids, albuterol as needed, and theophylline; her most recent serum theophylline level was 9 μg/mL (49.9 μmol/L). A week ago, she was evaluated at a walk-in clinic for productive cough and sore throat, and therapy with ciprofloxacin was started. The cough improved, but soon afterward her current symptoms developed.

**Which of the following is the most appropriate initial step in the management of this patient?**

(A) Stop the inhaled corticosteroid
(B) Stop albuterol
(C) Stop theophylline
(D) Measure serum amylase and lipase

## Item 63

A 42-year-old man who is a new patient is evaluated for a 6-month history of mild shortness of breath, which occurs primarily with exertion, and also occasional wheezing. He has smoked a half pack of cigarettes daily since the age of 18 years. He is otherwise healthy and takes no medications. He works in an automobile repair shop. His father, a cigarette smoker, died of emphysema at the age of 55 years.

On physical examination, vital signs are normal; BMI is 25. Breath sounds are diminished bilaterally, and there is occasional wheezing posteriorly. Spirometry shows an $FEV_1$ of 58% of predicted and an $FEV_1$/FVC ratio of 65%. Chest radiograph shows bilateral basilar lucency.

**Which of the following is the most appropriate next step in the management of this patient?**

(A) Measure plasma $\alpha_1$-antitrypsin
(B) Measure sweat chloride
(C) Obtain a flow-volume loop
(D) Order high-resolution CT scan of the chest

## Item 64

A 67-year-old woman is evaluated in the hospital for acute abdominal pain. She was admitted for community-acquired pneumonia, and her condition was improving on therapy with antibiotics and fluids. However, on day 3 she developed acute abdominal pain associated with nausea. Her medical history includes a 7-year history of peripheral arterial disease, type 2 diabetes mellitus, hyperlipidemia, and an episode of diverticulitis 2 years ago. Her medications are pravastatin, aspirin, dipyridamole, and metformin.

On physical examination, she appears anxious and in distress; temperature is 38.3 °C (101.0 °F), the blood pressure is 170/100 mm Hg, the pulse rate is 120/min, and the respiration rate is 25/min. She rates her pain as 10 out of 10. She has diffuse abdominal tenderness, more pronounced in the left lower quadrant with rebound tenderness.

**Which of the following is the most appropriate next diagnostic test in this patient?**

(A) Colonoscopy
(B) CT scan of the abdomen
(C) Left pelvic ultrasonography
(D) Leukocyte count and differential
(E) Supine and upright abdominal radiographs

## Item 65

An 87-year-old man is evaluated in the hospital for idiopathic pulmonary fibrosis. He was diagnosed 3 years ago, and his condition has gradually worsened despite therapy with prednisone, azathioprine, and N-acetylcysteine. All therapy has been discontinued over the past 6 months because of failure to respond and side effects. He has been home-bound on high-flow oxygen and has been hospitalized three times in the past year. The patient also has type 2 diabetes mellitus and hypertension, and his current medications are metformin, hydrochlorothiazide, and levofloxacin. He has indicated that he does not want additional aggressive therapy.

On physical examination, the patient is in moderate respiratory distress; temperature is 37.2 °C (99 °F), the blood pressure is 132/93 mm Hg, the pulse rate is 122/min, and the respiration rate is 32/min. Oxygen saturation is 89% with the patient breathing 100% oxygen by face mask. The patient is using accessory muscles to breathe, and there are bilateral dry crackles. Leukocyte count is 7200/μL ($7.2 \times 10^9$/L) with a normal differential count. Chest radiograph shows bilateral lower- and mid-lung fibrotic infiltrates with enlarged pulmonary arteries.

**Which of the following is the most appropriate recommendation?**

(A) Intravenous methylprednisolone

(B) Mechanical ventilation

(C) Noninvasive positive-pressure ventilation

(D) Palliative care

## Item 66

A 75-year-old woman with long-standing asthma is evaluated for a 1-month history of nocturnal asthma symptoms at least weekly and the need to use an albuterol inhaler daily. Her asthma therapy is a moderate-dose inhaled corticosteroid. The patient is otherwise healthy.

On physical examination, she has occasional wheezing, but the rest of the examination is unremarkable. On office spirometry, the $FEV_1$ is 2.2 L (70% of predicted) and FVC is 3.9 L (85% of predicted).

**Which of the following is the most appropriate management for this patient?**

(A) Adding a leukotriene modifier

(B) Adding a long-acting anticholinergic agent

(C) Adding a long-acting β-agonist

(D) Adding theophylline

(E) Doubling the corticosteroid dose

## Item 67

A 54-year-old man is evaluated in the emergency department for a 1-hour history of chest pain with mild dyspnea. The patient had been hospitalized 1 week ago for a colectomy for colon cancer. His medical history also includes hypertension and nephrotic syndrome secondary to membranous glomerulonephritis, and his medications are furosemide, ramipril, and pravastatin.

On physical examination, the temperature is 37.5 °C (99.5 °F), the blood pressure is 110/60 mm Hg, the pulse rate is 120/min, the respiration rate is 24/min, and the BMI is 30. Oxygen saturation is 89% with the patient breathing ambient air and 97% on oxygen, 4 L/min. Cardiac examination shows tachycardia and an $S_4$. Breath sounds are normal. Serum creatinine concentration is 2.1 mg/dL (185.6 μmol/L). Chest radiograph is negative for infiltrates, widened mediastinum, and pneumothorax. Empiric unfractionated heparin therapy is begun.

**Which of the following is the best test to confirm the diagnosis in this patient?**

(A) Assay for plasma D-dimer

(B) CT pulmonary angiography

(C) Lower extremity ultrasonography

(D) Measurement of antithrombin III

(E) Ventilation/perfusion scan

## Item 68

A 71-year-old man is evaluated for a 3-month history of daily nonproductive cough. He walks regularly and his weight has been stable. He has not had hemoptysis, postnasal drainage, or gastroesophageal reflux. The patient smoked a pack of cigarettes a day for 40 years but quit smoking 6 years ago. He has a history of mild airway obstruction, and his only medication is albuterol as needed.

On physical examination, vital signs are normal; the BMI is 23.5. Breath sounds are mildly reduced without wheezes or crackles. There is no lymphadenopathy. Spirometry shows an $FEV_1$ of 80% of predicted, an FVC of 81% of predicted, and an $FEV_1$/FVC ratio of 75%. The $D_{LCO}$ is 80% of predicted. Complete blood count, liver enzymes, and serum calcium are normal. Chest radiograph shows a 3-cm right hilar mass. CT scan shows a 3.4- × 3.2-cm spiculated mass in the right upper lobe and right hilar lymphadenopathy but no mediastinal lymphadenopathy. Bronchoscopy shows erythema and nodular change in the right upper lobe bronchus, and biopsy specimen shows squamous cell carcinoma.

**Which of the following is the most appropriate next step in the management of this patient?**

(A) Dynamic CT contrast enhancement study

(B) Positron emission tomography–CT (PET-CT)

(C) Quantitative lung perfusion scan

(D) Surgical resection

## Item 69

A 21-year-old man was brought to the emergency department obtunded with a temperature of 38.9 °C (102.0 °F) and a blood alcohol level of 0.3 g/dL (65 mmol/L). He was intubated and placed on mechanical ventilation with a tidal volume of 10 mL/kg ideal body weight. His oxygen saturation was 97% on positive end-expiratory pressure (PEEP) of 5 cm $H_2O$ and $FiO_2$ 0.4. Chest radiograph showed an infiltrate in the right lower lobe, and therapy with ceftriaxone and clindamycin was started.

Now, 48 hours after admission, he develops increased respiratory distress. He is afebrile; blood pressure is 120/60 mm Hg, the pulse rate is 115/min, and the respiration rate is 32/min (14/min 24 hours ago). Oxygen saturation is 90% on $FiO_2$ 0.7 and PEEP of 12 cm $H_2O$. The patient is sedated and has inspiratory crackles bilaterally. Jugular venous pressure is 7 cm $H_2O$. There are minimal endotracheal secretions, and no focal neurologic findings. A new chest radiograph shows a normal cardiac silhouette and no effusions. The right lower lobe infiltrate has improved, but there are new bilateral infiltrates.

**Which of the following is the most appropriate management for this patient?**

(A) Adjust tidal volume to 6 mL/kg ideal body weight

(B) Change current antibiotics to vancomycin, levofloxacin, and meropenem

(C) Extubate the patient and start noninvasive positive-pressure ventilation

(D) Insert a pulmonary artery catheter

## Item 70

An 82-year-old homeless man is brought to the emergency department after being found unconscious in December. On physical examination, the patient appears malnourished;

the rectal temperature is 29.0 °C (84.2 °F), the blood pressure is 110/60 mm Hg, and the pulse rate is 55/min. He is unresponsive to voice but responds to deep painful stimuli. His pupils are sluggishly reactive to light.

**Which of the following is the most appropriate next step in this patient's management?**

(A) Active external rewarming of the extremities
(B) Active external rewarming of the truncal areas
(C) Active internal rewarming techniques
(D) Passive rewarming techniques

## Item 71

A 70-year-old man with a 7-year history of chronic obstructive pulmonary disease is evaluated for increased fatigue. The patient has daily cough and has had two exacerbations in the past 8 months. He has smoked a pack of cigarettes a day for the past 55 years and has recently stopped smoking. His medications are albuterol as needed, salmeterol, and tiotropium.

On physical examination, vital signs are normal. Breath sounds are decreased, and heart sounds are distant. Oxygen saturation is 93% with the patient breathing ambient air. Spirometry shows an $FEV_1$ of 39% of predicted and an $FEV_1/FVC$ ratio of 60%. Chest radiograph shows hyperinflation. The patient is referred for pulmonary rehabilitation.

**Which of the following additional therapies would be indicated for this patient?**

(A) Inhaled corticosteroids
(B) Montelukast
(C) Oral corticosteroids
(D) Theophylline

## Item 72

A 63-year-old woman is evaluated for a 3-week history of gradually increasing dyspnea and a mild productive cough with intermittent fever and severe fatigue. The patient was diagnosed with chronic myeloid leukemia 2 months ago; she has no previous history of lung disease. Her medications include imatinib mesylate and a multivitamin.

On physical examination, the temperature is 37.8 °C (100.0 °F), the blood pressure is 110/78 mm Hg, the pulse rate is 96/min, and the respiration rate is 22/min. Oxygen saturation is 92% with the patient breathing ambient air. Laboratory studies show mild anemia with leukocytosis and eosinophilia. Chest radiograph shows new interstitial and alveolar infiltrates. Chest CT scan shows a pattern of ground-glass attenuation and irregular reticular lines distributed in the middle and upper lung zones bilaterally. Bronchoscopy with bronchoalveolar lavage performed 5 days ago showed no evidence for bacterial, fungal, or viral pathogens on smear and culture. Transbronchial lung biopsy performed during bronchoscopy revealed a pathologic diagnosis of organizing pneumonia.

**Which of the following is the most appropriate management for this patient?**

(A) Discontinue imatinib mesylate
(B) Start broad-spectrum antibiotic
(C) Start ribavirin
(D) Start intravenous heparin

## Item 73

A 68-year-old man with chronic obstructive pulmonary disease, hypertension, and hyperlipidemia is being weaned from mechanical ventilation after an exacerbation. The patient's current medications are ipratropium bromide and albuterol (both by metered-dose inhaler through the ventilator), prednisone, lisinopril, and atorvastatin.

He is started on a spontaneous breathing trial, which he initially tolerates well but later shows evidence of oxygen desaturation and agitation. He is given increasing doses of lorazepam to cause sedation, and assist-control ventilation is resumed. The following day he is calm but is not focused and fails to follow commands consistently.

**Which of the following is the best test to assess the patient's mental status?**

(A) Beck Depression Inventory
(B) Confusion Assessment Method for the Intensive Care Unit (CAM-ICU)
(C) CT scan of the head
(D) Metabolic profile
(E) Mini-Mental State Examination

## Item 74

A 46-year-old man is evaluated after being found unresponsive in his hospital bed on day 3 after a right total knee replacement. The patient has a history of asthma, hypertension, and untreated obstructive sleep apnea. His medications are inhaled combination fluticasone and salmeterol, inhaled albuterol, and lisinopril. In the hospital, he was given fondaparinux for thromboembolism prophylaxis and morphine for pain.

The patient is difficult to arouse. He is morbidly obese. The temperature is 35.5 °C (96.0 °F), the pulse rate is 100/min, the respiration rate is 8/min, and the blood pressure is 130/80 mm Hg. Oxygen saturation with the patient breathing ambient air is less than 80%. He has decreased bibasilar breath sounds; heart sounds are normal. Neurologic examination reveals no focal abnormalities. Arterial blood gases are pH 7.08, $P_{CO_2}$ 80 mm Hg, and $P_{O_2}$ 40 mm Hg; 100% oxygen by face mask is started.

**Which of the following is the most appropriate next step in the management of this patient?**

(A) Albuterol by nebulizer
(B) Continuous positive airway pressure at 10 cm $H_2O$
(C) Intravenous heparin and stat chest CT angiography
(D) Intravenous naloxone

## Item 75

An 18-year-old high school soccer player is evaluated for recurrent episodes of dyspnea, chest tightness, and cough that occur during games and that prevent her from continuing playing. The episodes are more common in cold weather, and they resolve spontaneously over 20 to 30 minutes. The patient's father has allergies but no known lung disease. The patient is otherwise healthy and takes no medications.

On physical examination, vital signs are normal and the lungs are clear. Spirometry reveals an $FEV_1$ of 90% predicted and an $FEV_1/FVC$ ratio of 80%. Chest radiograph is normal.

**Which of the following is the most appropriate next step in the evaluation of this patient?**

(A) Allergy skin testing
(B) Exercise challenge test
(C) Measurement of lung volumes and diffusing capacity for carbon monoxide
(D) Measurement of resting arterial blood gases

## Item 76

A 50-year-old man is evaluated for a 1-year history of cough productive of mucoid sputum. He has not had fever or lost weight during that time. The patient has smoked one pack of cigarettes a day for 20 years. He has no history of allergic disease or gastroesophageal reflux disease.

On physical examination, the temperature is 37.0 °C (98.6 °F), the blood pressure is 124/76 mm Hg, the pulse rate is 78/min and regular, and the respiration rate is 15/min; BMI is 25. The lungs are clear, and the chest radiograph is normal. Spirometry shows an $FEV_1$ of 85% of predicted and an $FEV_1/FVC$ ratio of 75%; there is no change in results after administration of a bronchodilator.

**Which of the following is the most likely diagnosis?**

(A) Asthma
(B) At risk for chronic obstructive pulmonary disease (COPD)
(C) Mild (GOLD stage I) COPD
(D) Moderate (GOLD stage II) COPD

## Item 77

A 41-year-old woman is evaluated for a 1-year history of progressive dyspnea on exertion and leg swelling. She can walk on level ground but becomes dyspneic when walking up stairs. The patient had a pulmonary embolism at age 35 years while she was taking oral contraceptive pills; she was treated acutely with heparin and then with warfarin for 6 months. She has no other significant medical history and takes no medications.

On physical examination, she is afebrile; the blood pressure is 120/78 mm Hg, the pulse rate is 97/min, the respiration rate is 16/min, and the BMI is 27. The lungs are clear and diaphragmatic excursion is normal; the $S_2$ has a fixed split. Chest radiograph shows no parenchymal abnormalities. Spirometry and plethysmography are normal. Transthoracic echocardiography reveals a dilated right atrium and a hypertrophied, enlarged right ventricle. There is moderate tricuspid regurgitation but no other valvular abnormalities.

**Which of the following is the most appropriate next diagnostic test in this patient?**

(A) Coronary angiography
(B) Endocardial biopsy
(C) Pulmonary angiography
(D) Ventilation/perfusion scan

## Item 78

A 78-year-old woman is evaluated for a 6-month history of fatigue and an unintentional 9.0-kg (20-lb) weight loss. She has occasional cough but no significant shortness of breath. She has never smoked and takes no medications.

On physical examination, the temperature is 36.8 °C (98.0 °F), the blood pressure is 116/68 mm Hg, the pulse rate is 72/min, the respiration rate is 14/min, and the BMI is 31. There is a palpable 1.5-cm supraclavicular lymph node on the left. The skin is normal, the lungs are clear, and the abdomen is soft and without organomegaly. Complete blood count, liver enzymes, and serum calcium are normal. Chest radiograph shows a 5-cm left lung mass with left hilar lymphadenopathy. CT scan shows a 5-cm left upper lobe mass with left hilar lymphadenopathy and normal-sized mediastinal lymph nodes.

**Which of the following is the most appropriate management for this patient?**

(A) Bronchoscopy with biopsy of the mass
(B) CT-guided transthoracic needle biopsy of the mass
(C) Positron emission tomography–CT (PET–CT)
(D) Supraclavicular lymph node biopsy
(E) Surgical referral for mediastinoscopy

## Item 79

A 60-year-old man is evaluated for the insidious onset of dyspnea on exertion over the past several weeks. He has also had a productive cough and lost 4.5 kg (10 lb). The patient has a 40-pack-year history of cigarette smoking; his medical history includes hypertension, and his only medication is enalapril.

On physical examination, he appears healthy and relaxed. The temperature is 37.0 °C (98.6 °F), the blood pressure is 138/80 mm Hg, the pulse rate is 85/min and regular, and the respiration rate is 18/min; oxygen saturation is 93% on ambient air. There is no cervical, supraclavicular, or axillary lymphadenopathy. There is dullness to percussion at the left lung base with minimally decreased breath sounds compared with the right. Chest radiograph shows evidence of emphysema and a small left-sided pleural effusion. Thoracentesis is done, and analysis of the pleural fluid shows:

| | |
|---|---|
| Erythrocyte count | 1000/µL |
| Nucleated cell count | 1700/µL ($1.7 \times 10^9$/L) with 7% neutrophils, 63% lymphocytes, 18% macrophages, 8% mesothelial cells, and 4% eosinophils |
| Total protein | 4.0 g/dL (40 g/L) |
| Lactate dehydrogenase | 200 U/L |

| pH | 7.25 |
|---|---|
| Glucose | 65 mg/dL (3.6 mmol/L) |
| Amylase | 160 U/L |

Pleural fluid to serum amylase ratio is 2.1. Isoenzyme analysis reveals that 85% of the amylase is salivary. Cytology report is pending

**Which of the following is the most likely diagnosis?**

(A) Acute pancreatitis
(B) Esophageal rupture
(C) Lung cancer
(D) Pancreatic pseudocyst

## Item 80

A 73-year-old woman is admitted to the hospital in August for mental status changes. No family members are available and the patient lives alone. A friend states that the patient takes medications for Parkinson disease but that she ran out of medication 2 days ago. The emergency medical transport team found an empty bottle of levodopa/carbidopa at the house but no evidence of other medications.

On physical examination, the patient is diaphoretic; the temperature is 39.0 °C (102.0 °F), the blood pressure is 170/120 mm Hg, and the pulse rate is 120/min. She is disoriented to time and place but follows simple commands, although there is neck stiffness as well as generalized muscular rigidity. Laboratory tests reveal an anion gap metabolic acidosis. Serum potassium is 5.8 meq/L (5.8 mmol/L), creatine kinase is 1250 U/L, and lactate dehydrogenase is 310 U/L.

**Which of the following is the most likely diagnosis?**

(A) Heat stroke
(B) Malignant hyperthermia
(C) Neuroleptic malignant syndrome
(D) Serotonin syndrome

## Item 81

A 40-year-old woman is evaluated for worsening asthma symptoms after resolution of an acute respiratory tract infection that was treated with supportive measures. The patient has a 15-year history of asthma that has been well-controlled on moderate-dose inhaled corticosteroids plus as-needed inhaled albuterol. Since her respiratory tract infection 10 days ago, her asthma symptoms have worsened; she has had frequent nighttime episodes of wheezing and has used her albuterol inhaler six to eight times a day.

On physical examination, the patient is afebrile and has no chest pain or significant sputum production. Her peak flow is more than 40% below her baseline value.

**Which of the following is the most appropriate management for this patient?**

(A) 7-day course of a fluoroquinolone
(B) Leukotriene modifying agent
(C) Long-acting β-agonist

(D) Nebulized albuterol at home
(E) Short course of an oral corticosteroid

## Item 82

A 60-year-old woman is evaluated for progressive shortness of breath and a dry cough. She was diagnosed with idiopathic pulmonary fibrosis 3 years ago but has no other medical problems.

On physical examination, she has resting hypoxemia and her other vital signs are normal. Clubbing of the fingers is present. There is no jugular venous distention. The cardiac examination reveals no extra sounds or murmurs. There are late inspiratory crackles on pulmonary examination. The rest of the physical examination is normal.

Chest radiograph shows decreased lung volumes and bilateral basal reticular opacities. High-resolution CT scan shows bilateral, basal-predominant, extensive subpleural reticular opacities associated with patchy honeycombing and traction bronchiectasis.

Pulmonary function testing shows significantly decreased FVC, total lung capacity, and functional residual capacity; $D_{LCO}$ is 35% of predicted. There has been a decrement in the FVC greater than 10% in the last 6 months.

**Which of the following is the best treatment option for this patient?**

(A) Interferon-γ
(B) Lung transplantation
(C) *N*-acetylcysteine
(D) Prednisone and azathioprine

## Item 83

A 65-year-old man is being evaluated for clearance to undergo an elective repair of an abdominal aortic aneurysm. The patient has a 5-year history of moderate chronic obstructive pulmonary disease with chronic cough productive of mucoid sputum. He smokes a half pack of cigarettes a day. His medical history also includes hypertension, and he is adherent to therapy with albuterol as needed, an inhaled corticosteroid, salmeterol, and lisinopril.

On physical examination, vital signs are normal; BMI is 22. The chest is normal with no wheezes or rhonchi; there is no jugular venous distention or edema. Spirometry done 6 months ago showed an $FEV_1$ of 55% of predicted and an $FEV_1/FVC$ ratio of 55%. Spirometry done 1 week ago showed minimal change but no response to a bronchodilator. Surgery is scheduled for next week.

**Which of the following would most effectively reduce the patient's risk for postoperative pulmonary complications?**

(A) Incentive spirometry
(B) Leukocyte-depleted blood transfusions
(C) Preoperative systemic corticosteroids
(D) Right-heart catheterization
(E) Smoking cessation

## Item 84

A 64-year-old man with a history of chronic obstructive pulmonary disease is evaluated in the emergency department for increased dyspnea over the past 48 hours. There is no change in his baseline production of white sputum, but he has increased nasal congestion and sore throat. His medications include inhaled tiotropium, combination fluticasone and salmeterol, and albuterol. Therapy with methylprednisolone, 60 mg intravenously, and inhaled albuterol and ipratropium bromide is started.

The patient is alert but in mild respiratory distress. The temperature is 38.6 °C (101.5 °F), the blood pressure is 150/90 mm Hg, the pulse rate is 108/min, and the respiration rate is 30/min. Oxygen saturation with the patient breathing ambient air is 90%. Breath sounds are diffusely decreased with bilateral expiratory wheezes; he is using accessory muscles to breathe. With the patient breathing oxygen, 2 L/min by nasal cannula, arterial blood gases are pH 7.27, $P_{CO_2}$ 60 mm Hg, and $P_{O_2}$ 62 mm Hg; oxygen saturation is 91%.

**Which of the following is the most appropriate next step in the management of this patient?**

(A) Increase supplemental oxygen to 5 L/min
(B) Intubate and begin mechanical ventilation
(C) Start aminophylline infusion
(D) Start noninvasive positive-pressure ventilation

## Item 85

A 67-year-old man is evaluated in the emergency department for the acute onset of dyspnea associated with severe frontal headaches and diaphoresis. He was diagnosed 5 days ago with a left adrenal pheochromocytoma, and surgery is scheduled in 3 days. He has no other significant medical history. His current medications include phenoxybenzamine and propranolol, but the patient is confused about when to take his medications.

On physical examination, he appears anxious and dyspneic; the blood pressure is 220/120 mm Hg, the pulse rate is 120/min, the respiration rate is 28/min, and the oxygen saturation is 92% with the patient breathing ambient air. Auscultation of the lungs reveals bibasilar inspiratory crackles. He has 2+ pedal edema. Chest radiograph shows cardiomegaly and pulmonary congestion. Electrocardiogram shows no evidence of ischemia or infarction.

**Which of the following is the appropriate initial treatment for this patient's hypertension?**

(A) Captopril, orally
(B) Metyrosine, orally
(C) Metoprolol, intravenously
(D) Nicardipine, orally
(E) Nitroprusside infusion

## Item 86

A 47-year-old woman is evaluated in the intensive care unit for sepsis. She was admitted with severe lower lobe pneumonia and is in septic shock despite receiving 8 L of fluid. She has a history of stage IIA colon cancer treated with resection. She is receiving vasopressors and mechanical ventilation; neurologic examination shows no focal abnormalities. Her oxygen saturation is 88% on an $FiO_2$ of 0.75 with a positive end-expiratory pressure of 12 cm $H_2O$. Her extremities are becoming cold and show signs of livedo reticularis. The nasogastric return reveals more than 250 mL of bright red blood. She receives an additional 2 L of fluid, but her blood pressure remains 72/48 mm Hg on norepinephrine.

**Laboratory studies:**

| | |
|---|---|
| Hemoglobin | 9 g/dL (90 g/L) |
| Leukocyte count | 15,500/µL ($15.5 \times 10^9$/L) |
| Platelet count | 50,000/µL ($50 \times 10^9$/L) |
| INR | 2.1 |

**Which of the following would be a contraindication to therapy with activated protein C in this patient?**

(A) Active gastrointestinal bleeding
(B) INR of 2.1
(C) Platelet count of 50,000/µL ($50 \times 10^9$/L)
(D) Resected colon cancer in remission

## Item 87

A 55-year-old woman with a long-standing history of moderate to severe asthma is evaluated for a worsening productive cough, dyspnea, and wheezing. She has not had fever, chills, or chest pain. Her current medications are low-dose inhaled corticosteroids, a long-acting β-agonist, and albuterol.

On physical examination, the temperature is 36.5 °C (97.8 °F), the blood pressure is 110/70 mm Hg, the pulse rate is 84/min, and the respiration rate is 18/min. The cardiac examination is normal; pulmonary examination reveals bilateral wheezing and scattered rhonchi over the upper lung fields. Oxygen saturation is 93% with the patient breathing ambient air. The leukocyte count is 8500/µL ($8.5 \times 10^9$/L) with 45% neutrophils, 35% lymphocytes, 10% eosinophils, and 10% mononuclear cells.

Chest radiograph shows patchy infiltrates in both upper lobes and prominent bronchial markings consistent with bronchiectasis. High-resolution chest CT scan confirms the presence of central bronchiectasis and some mucous plugging.

**Which of the following is the most appropriate next step in the evaluation of this patient?**

(A) Bronchoscopy with lung biopsy
(B) Methacholine challenge test
(C) Positron-emission tomography
(D) Skin test for *Aspergillus fumigatus*
(E) Sweat chloride test

## Item 88

A 55-year-old woman is evaluated in follow-up for chronic obstructive pulmonary disease. The disorder was diagnosed 1 year ago, and she has had two exacerbations requiring hospitalization. She has a chronic cough with sputum production and mild dyspnea on exertion. She smokes a pack and a half of cigarettes a day. She wants to stop smoking and once tried a nicotine patch but was unable to stop. She also has a history of hypertension, seizure disorder, and major depression with suicidal ideation that is in remission. Her medications are albuterol as needed, an inhaled corticosteroid, salmeterol, enalapril, phenytoin, and sertraline.

On physical examination, vital signs and heart rate and rhythm are normal, and there are no murmurs or crackles. Breath sounds are diminished bilaterally. Spirometry shows an $FEV_1$ of 50% of predicted and an $FEV_1/FVC$ ratio of less than 70%. Oxygen saturation with exertion is 93% on ambient air. Chest radiograph shows hyperinflation with no infiltrates.

**Which of the following is the best option for smoking cessation in this patient?**

(A) Bupropion
(B) Bupropion and a nicotine patch
(C) High-dose nicotine patch with as-needed nicotine replacement with gum or spray
(D) Varenicline

## Item 89

A 28-year-old man is evaluated for an abnormal chest radiograph done for chronic intermittent nonproductive cough of 6 months' duration. The radiograph showed bilateral hilar lymphadenopathy and normal lung parenchyma. The patient has fatigue and intermittent mild central chest discomfort when he coughs. He has not had weight loss, fever, night sweats, or recent respiratory illness.

Vital signs and cardiopulmonary examination are normal. There is no cervical or axillary lymphadenopathy and no skin findings. Laboratory studies show normal electrolytes and normal complete blood count with differential; serum calcium is 10.8 mg/dL (2.63 mmol/L). Chest CT scan with contrast shows bilateral hilar and mediastinal and subcarinal lymphadenopathy, along with bilateral small lung nodules with a perihilar distribution.

**Which of the following is the most appropriate next test in the evaluation of this patient?**

(A) Bone marrow biopsy
(B) Bronchoscopy with mediastinal lymph node and lung biopsy
(C) Mediastinoscopy
(D) Serum *Histoplasma* antibody testing

## Item 90

A 65-year-old man is evaluated for a 9-month history of progressive dyspnea; for the past month the dyspnea has been severe and accompanied by dizziness. The patient had an acute pulmonary embolism 3 years ago, treated acutely with heparin and then warfarin for 6 months. He has no other significant medical history and takes no medication.

On physical examination, he is afebrile; the blood pressure is 105/60 mm Hg, the pulse rate is 105/min at rest

and 115/min with minimal exertion, the respiration rate is 22/min, and the BMI is 32. The $S_2$ is split, there is a right ventricular heave, and there is a holosystolic murmur that increases with inspiration. Echocardiography reveals severe right ventricular dilation and dysfunction and right atrial enlargement. Ventilation/perfusion scan shows decreased perfusion to most of the right lower lobe, right middle lobe, and left lower lobe, with normal ventilation. Warfarin therapy is started.

**Which of the following is the most appropriate management for this patient?**

(A) Intravenous tissue plasminogen activator
(B) Oral bosentan
(C) Pulmonary thromboendarterectomy evaluation
(D) Vasodilator therapy

## Item 91

A 61-year-old woman is evaluated for a 3-month history of progressive loss of sensation in her legs accompanied by intermittent pain and paresthesias; she has not had shortness of breath. She can no longer walk unaided and uses a wheel chair. She has lost 9 kg (20 lb) during this time. The patient has smoked a pack of cigarettes a day for 30 years. She had been previously healthy and takes no medications.

On physical examination, the temperature is 36.5 °C (97.7 °F), the blood pressure is 126/54 mm Hg, the pulse rate is 82/min, the respiration rate is 22/min, and the BMI is 23. There is generalized reduction in touch sensation in the legs, worse below the knees and greater on the right. Motor strength is intact. Gait is broad-based and ataxic. Romberg sign is present. There is no lymphadenopathy. Complete blood count; serum creatinine, glucose, calcium, and liver enzymes; and serum protein electrophoresis are normal. ANNA-1 (anti Hu) antibody is detected on a paraneoplastic antibody panel. Electromyography reveals a sensory neuropathy. Chest radiograph shows a left hilar mass. CT scan shows a 5-cm mass with associated left paratracheal and subcarinal lymphadenopathy.

**What is the most likely cause of the patient's symptoms?**

(A) Adenocarcinoma
(B) Carcinoid tumor
(C) Large cell carcinoma
(D) Small cell carcinoma

## Item 92

A 68-year-old man with a history of severe chronic obstructive pulmonary disease and baseline arterial blood gases of pH 7.35, $PCO_2$ 60 mm Hg, and $PO_2$ 60 mm Hg breathing ambient air was admitted to the intensive care unit and intubated for an exacerbation of his respiratory disease. His condition improved over the next 72 hours on therapy with bronchodilators, systemic corticosteroids, and levofloxacin.

He is now afebrile and hemodynamically stable with a respiration rate of 15/min and an oxygen saturation of 95%. He is alert, oriented, and moving all extremities. He has a strong cough and minimal secretions. Breath sounds are clear aside from faint end-expiratory wheezes. Heart sounds are normal. Arterial blood gases are pH 7.42, $P_{CO_2}$ 35 mm Hg, and $P_{O_2}$ 68 mm Hg on the following ventilator settings: volume control mode, tidal volume 600 mL, set rate 15/min, positive end-expiratory pressure 5 cm $H_2O$, and $F_{IO_2}$ 0.35. He is placed on a spontaneous breathing trial but develops marked respiratory distress with a blood pressure of 180/100 mm Hg, pulse rate of 130/min, respiration rate of 28/min, oxygen saturation of 90%, and diaphoresis. He rapidly returns to baseline with resumption of his prior volume control settings.

**Which of the following is the most likely explanation for the patient's difficulty weaning from the ventilator?**

(A) Anxiety
(B) Excessive ventilation on volume control mode
(C) Inadequate oxygenation
(D) Intensive care unit–acquired weakness

## Item 93

A 27-year-old man is evaluated for a 6-month history of cough, which is worse at night and after exposure to cold air. Often his cough is brought on by taking a deep breath or by laughter. He does not have postnasal drip, wheezing, or heartburn. He has a strong family history of allergies.

Physical examination, chest radiograph, and spirometry are normal. He receives no benefit from a 3-month trial of gastric acid suppression therapy, intranasal corticosteroids, and an antihistamine-decongestant combination.

**Which of the following would likely provide the diagnosis of this patient's chronic cough?**

(A) 24-Hour esophageal pH monitoring
(B) Bronchoscopy
(C) CT scan of the chest
(D) CT scan of the sinuses
(E) Trial of inhaled albuterol

## Item 94

A 60-year-old man with an 8-year history of chronic obstructive pulmonary disease is evaluated for a 3-month history of weight loss of 4.4 kg (10 lb), increased fatigue, and decreased exercise capacity. He has had multiple hospitalizations for exacerbations of his disease, including one 2 months ago. He stopped smoking 1 year ago and recently completed a 6-month pulmonary rehabilitation program without much benefit. The patient also has hypertension, and his medications are inhaled albuterol as needed; salmeterol; tiotropium; an inhaled corticosteroid; theophylline; oxygen, 2 L/min by nasal cannula; and enalapril.

On physical examination, vital signs are normal; BMI is 20. Breath sounds are decreased, and heart sounds are distant. There is 1+ bilateral pitting edema, and the 6-minute walk distance is 90 meters. Spirometry shows an $FEV_1$ of 18% of predicted and an $FEV_1/FVC$ ratio of 34%. $D_{LCO}$ is 16% of predicted, and total lung capacity is 108%

of predicted. Arterial blood gases with the patient breathing oxygen are pH 7.37, $P_{CO_2}$ 47 mm Hg, and $P_{O_2}$ 78 mm Hg. There is no evidence of nocturnal oxygen desaturation. Chest radiograph shows hyperinflation, and chest CT scan shows homogeneous emphysema. Electrocardiography shows right ventricular hypertrophy and right atrial enlargement. Echocardiography shows normal left ventricular function; pulmonary artery pressure is slightly increased.

**Which of the following is the most appropriate management for this patient?**

(A) Lung transplantation
(B) Lung volume reduction surgery
(C) Nocturnal assisted ventilation
(D) Repeat pulmonary rehabilitation

## Item 95

A 49-year-old woman is evaluated for fatigue, fever, and a 5.5-kg (12-lb) weight loss since undergoing video-assisted thoracoscopic surgery for a left lower lobe abnormality 3 months ago. Four months ago, the patient developed fever and left-sided chest pain; CT scan (shown) exhibited a left

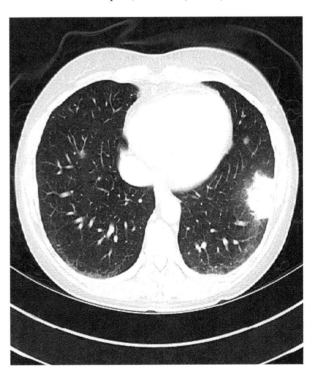

lower lobe abnormality. The abnormality was removed, and the pathologic diagnosis was organizing pneumonia with noncaseating granulomatous features. Fungal stains were negative. She recovered from surgery but remained fatigued and had intermittent fevers. Subsequent evaluation shows a new right upper lobe lesion on CT-positron emission tomographic scan demonstrating marked uptake in the focal lesion and no other abnormalities.

The patient has a history of essential thrombocythemia, which has been treated for the past 18 months with pegylated interferon alfa after the disease failed to respond to hydroxyurea. She takes no other medications and does not smoke.

Bronchoscopy with transbronchoscopic lung biopsy of the lesion in the right upper lobe again demonstrates organizing pneumonia with noncaseating granulomatous inflammation. Cultures are negative.

**Which of the following is the most appropriate management for this patient?**

(A) Follow-up CT in 3 months
(B) Oral voriconazole therapy
(C) Surgical resection of the right upper lobe lesion
(D) Stop pegylated interferon alfa and start prednisone

## Item 96

A 26-year-old woman is evaluated for a 4-month history of progressive dyspnea, initially on exertion only but now also at rest. She was recently evaluated in the intensive care unit for an episode of syncope. Clinical findings were compatible with pulmonary hypertension, which was confirmed with transthoracic echocardiography. Pulmonary function tests and ventilation/perfusion scan were normal. She is sent to the catheterization laboratory. Just before the patient went to the catheterization laboratory, her vital signs were: blood pressure, 95/50 mm Hg; pulse rate, 125/min; and respiration rate, 24/min.

A right-heart catheterization shows a low cardiac index, elevated pulmonary artery pressures, normal pulmonary capillary wedge pressure, and elevated pulmonary vascular resistance.

**Which of the following is the most appropriate management for this patient?**

(A) Emergent pulmonary thromboendarterectomy
(B) Intravenous epoprostenol
(C) Intravenous tissue plasminogen activator
(D) Intubation and mechanical ventilation
(E) Oral diltiazem

## Item 97

A 52-year-old man is evaluated for a 4-week history of nonproductive cough and fatigue without fever. He has lost 2.2 kg (5 lb) over the past several months; he has not traveled recently. The patient underwent resection of a rectal carcinoma 18 months ago followed by chemotherapy and radiation therapy. Chest radiograph at that time was normal. The patient has been otherwise healthy and takes no medications. His father died of colon cancer.

On physical examination, the temperature is 36.6 °C (97.9 °F), the pulse rate is 62/min, the respiration rate is 18/min, the blood pressure is 126/70 mm Hg, and the BMI is 24. The lungs are clear, the abdomen is soft with a well-healed surgical scar, and there is no lymphadenopathy. Laboratory studies, including serum carcinoembryonic antigen (CEA) level, are normal; CEA level was normal at the time of resection. Chest radiograph shows multiple pulmonary nodules. Contrast-enhanced CT scan of the

chest shows five nodules ranging from 1.0 to 1.8 cm in diameter; four are in the right lung (one in the upper lobe, three in the lower lobe) and one is in the left lower lobe. CT scan of the abdomen shows postoperative changes but is otherwise normal.

**Which of the following is the most appropriate next step in the management of this patient?**

(A) Bronchoscopy and biopsy of a nodule
(B) Positron emission tomography–CT (PET–CT)
(C) Transthoracic needle aspiration of a nodule
(D) Video-assisted thoracoscopic resection of the nodules

## Item 98

A 22-year-old woman is evaluated in the intensive care unit 5 days after sustaining multiple long-bone fractures. Her clinical course was complicated by the acute respiratory distress syndrome, and she was intubated and has been receiving mechanical ventilation for the past 3 days. Her medications are hydromorphone and lorazepam.

Over the past 24 hours, the $FiO_2$ and positive end-expiratory pressure have been decreased to 0.4 and 5 cm $H_2O$, respectively, while maintaining an oxygen saturation of 95%. Chest radiograph shows improvement in her bilateral alveolar infiltrates. Sedation is interrupted and she undergoes a spontaneous breathing trial. After 60 minutes, she is diaphoretic, the pulse rate is 120/min, the respiration rate is 30/min, tidal volume is 250 mL, and oxygen saturation is 88%. Full ventilatory support is restarted.

**Which of the following is most likely to expedite this patient's weaning from the ventilator?**

(A) Daily reduction of sedation followed by a spontaneous breathing trial
(B) Extubation and institution of noninvasive positive-pressure ventilation
(C) Increasing $FiO_2$ to 0.6
(D) Repeating spontaneous breathing trial in 48 hours
(E) Tracheostomy

## Item 99

A 71-year-old woman is brought to the emergency department from a nursing home because of confusion, fever, and flank pain. Her temperature is 38.5 °C (101.3 °F), blood pressure is 82/48 mm Hg, pulse rate is 123/min, and respiration rate is 27/min. Mucous membranes are dry, and there is costovertebral angle tenderness, poor skin turgor, and no edema. Hemoglobin concentration is 10.5 g/dL (105 g/L), leukocyte count is 15,600/μL (15.6 × $10^9$/L); urinalysis reveals 50 to 100 leukocytes/hpf and many bacteria/hpf. The patient has an anion gap metabolic acidosis. A central venous catheter is placed, and antibiotic therapy is started.

**Which of the following additional interventions is most likely to improve survival for this patient?**

(A) Aggressive fluid resuscitation

(B) Hemodynamic monitoring with a pulmonary artery catheter

(C) Maintaining hemoglobin concentration above 12 g/dL (120 g/L)

(D) Maintaining $P_{CO_2}$ below 50 mm Hg

## Item 100

A 59-year-old man is evaluated in the emergency department in early June for severe bronchospasm. The patient is a farmer, has no significant medical history, and takes no medications.

On physical examination, he is anxious, agitated, and disoriented to time and place. He is diaphoretic with a large amount of oral and respiratory secretions. The blood pressure is 80/60 mm Hg, the pulse rate is 50/min, and the respiration rate is 26/min. He has diffuse expiratory wheezing. Laboratory studies show normal electrolytes and complete blood count and a respiratory alkalosis.

**Which of the following is the most appropriate management?**

(A) Amyl nitrite

(B) Pralidoxime

(C) Sodium nitrite

(D) Sodium thiosulfate

## Item 101

A 25-year-old woman is evaluated for recurrent episodes of acute dyspnea associated with rapid breathing, tightness in her chest and throat, voice changes, and inspiratory difficulty. When she has these episodes she feels that she "can't get enough air." The symptoms typically start and resolve abruptly, and treatment with albuterol provides only minimal relief.

On physical examination, her vital signs are normal. Lungs are clear. Spirometry shows an $FEV_1$ of 2.8 L (88% of predicted) and $FEV_1/FVC$ ratio of 80%.

**Which of the following is the most appropriate next diagnostic step?**

(A) Chest radiography

(B) CT scan of the neck

(C) Flow volume loops

(D) Thyroid function tests

## Item 102

A 70-year-old woman is evaluated for a 6-month history of fatigue, an unintentional weight loss of 4.4 kg (10 lb), an increase in chronic cough with sputum production, and a decrease in exercise capacity. The patient has a 40-pack-year history of cigarette smoking but stopped smoking 10 years ago when chronic obstructive pulmonary disease was diagnosed. She has no other symptoms and specifically denies abdominal pain, nausea, vomiting, diarrhea, or change in her bowel habits. Her medications are albuterol as needed, an inhaled corticosteroid, and salmeterol. She has been on stable dosages of these drugs for 18 months. Age- and sex-appropriate cancer screening tests done 6 months ago were normal.

On physical examination, the temperature is 37.5 °C (99.5 °F), the blood pressure is 128/76 mm Hg, the pulse rate is 94/min and regular, the respiration rate is 16/min, and the BMI is 20. Heart sounds are distant, and breath sounds are diminished bilaterally. There are no abdominal masses or organomegaly and no peripheral edema.

**Laboratory studies:**

| | |
|---|---|
| Hemoglobin | 15 g/dL (150 g/L) |
| Albumin | 3.0 g/dL (30 g/L) |
| Creatinine | 0.8 mg/dL (70.7 µmol/L) |
| Thyroid-stimulating hormone | 2.0 µU/mL (2.0 mU/L) |

Spirometry shows an $FEV_1$ of 40% of predicted and an $FEV_1/FVC$ ratio of 45%. Chest radiograph shows hyperinflation.

**Which of the following is the most likely reason for this patient's weight loss?**

(A) Breast cancer

(B) Cervical cancer

(C) Colon cancer

(D) Chronic obstructive pulmonary disease

## Item 103

A 44-year-old man is evaluated for a 4-month history of progressive dyspnea and cough. The patient is otherwise healthy and takes no medications. He has smoked 2 packs of cigarettes a day for 20 years.

On physical examination, vital signs are normal. Cardiopulmonary examination is normal. Pulmonary function tests show a mixed obstructive-restrictive defect. High-resolution CT of the chest shows bibasilar reticular or reticulonodular abnormalities in a centrilobular distribution with diffuse areas of ground-glass opacification.

**Which of the following is the most likely diagnosis?**

(A) Cryptogenic organizing pneumonia

(B) Idiopathic pulmonary fibrosis

(C) Nonspecific interstitial pneumonia

(D) Respiratory bronchiolitis interstitial lung disease

## Item 104

A 52-year-old man with a history of amyotrophic lateral sclerosis is admitted to the intensive care unit with hypoxemic respiratory failure as a result of right-sided pneumonia. The patient is intubated, and therapy with ceftriaxone and azithromycin is started. His condition improves after 4 days, but large amounts of thin yellow secretions are being suctioned hourly.

On physical examination, the patient is alert and cooperative. The temperature is 37.0 °C (98.6 °F), pulse rate is 90/min, respiration rate is 14/min, and blood pressure is 120/80 mm Hg; oxygen saturation is 96% on the ventilator. There are diffuse rhonchi and inspiratory crackles over the right hemithorax. One hour into a spontaneous breathing trial, the patient's tidal volume is 500 mL, respiration rate 20/min, and oxygen saturation 95% on $FiO_2$ of 0.4. Arterial blood gases are pH 7.35, $P_{CO_2}$ 55 mm Hg, and $P_{O_2}$

65 mm Hg. Chest radiograph shows slight improvement in the right middle and lower lobe infiltrates.

**When would it be appropriate to extubate this patient?**

(A) Now
(B) When the chest radiograph clears
(C) When the rapid shallow breathing index improves
(D) When supplemental oxygen needs decrease
(E) When the volume of secretions decreases

## Item 105

A 42-year-old man is evaluated in the surgical intensive care unit after surgery for a bowel obstruction. He presented yesterday to the emergency department for a 2-day history of fever, confusion, and abdominal pain. On examination, the patient's temperature was 38.4 °C (101.1 °F). Cardiac examination was normal; examination of the lungs revealed diffuse bilateral crackles. The abdomen was diffusely and markedly tender, with rebound and guarding. Leukocyte count was $18,400/\mu L$ ($18.4 \times 10^9/L$) with 80% segmented neutrophils and 6% band forms. In the emergency department, his plasma glucose concentration was 205 mg/dL (11.4 mmol/L); the patient has no history of diabetes mellitus. Chest radiograph showed pulmonary edema, and the patient was hospitalized; imipenem/cilastatin was started, and he was taken to surgery. The patient was found to have a bowel obstruction with perforation and contamination of the peritoneal cavity. After surgery, the plasma glucose concentration is 300 mg/dL (16.7 mmol/L).

**Which of the following is the most appropriate management of the patient's hyperglycemia?**

(A) Any insulin regimen that follows a sliding scale
(B) Intravenous insulin drip
(C) Subcutaneous intermediate-acting basal insulin
(D) Subcutaneous long-acting basal insulin

## Item 106

A 35-year-old man is evaluated for episodic wheezing, dyspnea, and cough. Two months ago he had an acute episode of cough, dyspnea, wheezing, and chest tightness within minutes of inhaling high concentrations of ammonia solution after an accidental spill at work. In the emergency department, the chest radiograph was normal, and he received inhaled bronchodilators and a brief course of oral corticosteroids. The patient does not have a history of asthma or allergies and is otherwise healthy and takes no medications.

The physical examination is normal. Spirometry shows an $FEV_1$ of 90% of predicted; $FEV_1/FVC$ ratio is 82%.

**Which of the following is the most appropriate next test in this patient's evaluation?**

(A) Bronchoscopy with biopsy
(B) Inhalation challenge with chlorine
(C) Methacholine challenge test
(D) Spirometry before and after work

## Item 107

A 51-year-old man is evaluated during a routine follow-up examination in November. He was diagnosed with GOLD stage I chronic obstructive pulmonary disease 2 years ago. He has a 20-pack-year history of cigarette smoking but stopped smoking 18 months ago. He also has hypertension, and his medications are inhaled albuterol as needed and hydrochlorothiazide. The patient had influenza and pneumococcal vaccinations 1 year ago.

**Which of the following is the most appropriate immunization strategy for this patient at this time?**

(A) Pneumococcal vaccination only
(B) Trivalent intranasal live influenza vaccination only
(C) Trivalent intranasal live influenza and pneumococcal vaccinations
(D) Trivalent killed influenza and pneumococcal vaccinations
(E) Trivalent killed influenza vaccination only

## Item 108

A 57-year-old man with sarcoidosis is evaluated for a 4-week history of progressive dyspnea. He also has fatigue, ankle swelling, lower extremity aching, and lack of appetite. The patient had sarcoidosis diagnosed 7 years ago. The disease has slowly progressed despite therapy. He has no other medical disorders, and his medications are methotrexate, 15 mg weekly; prednisone, 20 mg/d; folic acid; and trimethoprim-sulfamethoxazole.

On physical examination, he is afebrile; blood pressure is 104/96 mm Hg, the pulse rate is 110/min, and the respiration rate is 28/min. Oxygen saturation is 90% with the patient breathing oxygen, 3 L/min by nasal cannula. Cardiac examination reveals a loud $P_2$ and fixed splitting of $S_2$; jugular venous distention is present. The chest is clear to auscultation. There is pitting edema at both ankles to the mid-shin. Chest radiograph, which is unchanged from 3 months ago, shows small lung volumes with fibrosis extending into the mid- and upper lungs bilaterally and bilateral hilar lymph node enlargement. Spirometry, which is also unchanged from 3 months ago, shows a moderate restrictive pattern.

**Which of the following is the most appropriate next diagnostic test for this patient?**

(A) Bronchoscopy with bronchoalveolar lavage
(B) Pulmonary angiography
(C) Transthoracic echocardiography
(D) Ventilation/perfusion scan

## Item 109

A 32-year-old woman developed worsening hypoxemia and respiratory distress 12 days after she underwent myeloablative allogeneic stem cell transplantation for recurrent non-Hodgkin lymphoma. She had been intermittently febrile for the previous 5 days despite broad-spectrum antibiotic therapy. A chest radiograph showed bilateral alveolar infiltrates, which were not present on a radiograph taken 2 days before.

Arterial blood gases were pH 7.48, $P_{CO_2}$ 30 mm Hg, and $P_{O_2}$ 56 mm Hg with the patient breathing 80% oxygen by face mask; oxygen saturation was 86%. Noninvasive positive-pressure ventilation (NPPV) was started.

Now, 2 hours after she began NPPV, the patient is alert, speaks in three-word sentences, and is using accessory respiratory muscles. The temperature is 38.8 °C (101.8 °F), the blood pressure is 120/60 mm Hg, the pulse rate is 116/min, and the respiration rate is 34/min. There are coarse bilateral inspiratory crackles. Arterial blood gases with the patient breathing 100% oxygen by NPPV are pH 7.40, $P_{CO_2}$ 40 mm Hg, and $P_{O_2}$ 62 mm Hg; oxygen saturation is 91%.

**Which of the following is the most appropriate next step in the management of this patient?**

(A) Continue NPPV at current settings
(B) Discontinue NPPV; start 100% oxygen by non-rebreather mask
(C) Intubate and begin mechanical ventilation
(D) Prescribe low-dose sedation

## Item 110

A 28-year-old man is admitted to the intensive care unit after having sustained a large aneurysmal subarachnoid bleed and is intubated for airway protection and ventilatory support. Because of increased intracranial pressure and patient-ventilator dyssynchrony, propofol infusion is started at 100 µg/kg/min. The patient's medical course is complicated by gram-positive sepsis and adrenal insufficiency on day 3 in the intensive care unit, for which he is treated with broad-spectrum antibiotic therapy, volume resuscitation, norepinephrine, and hydrocortisone with the goal of maintaining a mean arterial pressure greater than 65 mm Hg. On day 4, the patient remains sedated on mechanical ventilation, and he appears to be improving.

On day 5, the patient develops acute kidney injury, hyperkalemia, metabolic acidosis, rhabdomyolysis, and jugular venous distention with cardiac failure. Electrocardiogram shows no signs of an acute myocardial infarction or ischemia and no peaked T waves or conduction disturbances.

**Which of the following is the most urgent next step in the management of this patient?**

(A) CT scan of the head without contrast
(B) Discontinuation of propofol
(C) Intravenous heparin
(D) Plasmapheresis

## Item 111

A 21-year-old woman is evaluated for a positive methacholine challenge test that she had as part of a research study. The patient has no history of wheezing or chest tightness. She has seasonal allergies manifesting as hay fever in fall and spring but is now asymptomatic. She is otherwise healthy and takes no medications.

On physical examination, vital signs are normal. Examination of the conjunctivae, nose, posterior pharynx, heart, and lungs is normal. Routine laboratory studies are all normal.

**Which of the following is the most appropriate management for this patient?**

(A) Albuterol inhaler
(B) Inhaled corticosteroids and a long-acting β-agonist
(C) Seasonal use of nasal corticosteroids
(D) Repeat methacholine challenge testing

## Item 112

A 60-year-old woman is evaluated for a 2-year history of fatigue and daytime sleepiness and an 8-month history of dyspnea that occurs only during moderate exercise. She does not smoke cigarettes and works inside the home. She has hypertension, and her only medication is hydrochlorothiazide.

On physical examination, vital signs are normal. The patient is obese (BMI 33); the neck is short and thick (circumference 50.8 cm [20 in]), and the posterior airway is crowded. Jugular venous distention cannot be adequately assessed. There is increased intensity of $P_2$ with fixed splitting of $S_2$ and a grade 1-2/6 holosystolic murmur that increases with inspiration heard best along the left lower sternal border. Chest radiograph is normal. Spirometry, plethysmography, and arterial blood gases with the patient breathing ambient air are normal. Transthoracic echocardiography shows evidence of right ventricular hypertrophy and mild to moderate pulmonary hypertension. A ventilation/perfusion scan is normal.

**Which of the following is the most appropriate management for this patient?**

(A) Lung transplantation
(B) Nocturnal continuous positive airway pressure therapy
(C) Polysomnography
(D) Right-heart catheterization

## Item 113

A 64-year-old woman who resides in a nursing home and has a history of end-stage kidney disease for which she receives hemodialysis presents with fever, copious sputum production, and hypoxemia. Chest radiograph shows a right-sided infiltrate. She is intubated and started on vancomycin, levofloxacin, and piperacillin-tazobactam for treatment of diffuse right-sided pneumonia.

On day 3 in the hospital, she has been afebrile for 48 hours, and her secretions are scant and white. On physical examination, the temperature is 36.9 °C (98.5 °F), pulse rate is 88/min, respiration rate is 14/min, and blood pressure is 140/86 mm Hg; oxygen saturation is 96% on $FiO_2$ 0.4. There are diffuse right-sided inspiratory crackles. Leukocyte count is 9600/µL (9.6 × $10^9$/L) (20,400/µL [20.4 × $10^9$/L] on admission). Admission sputum culture is now growing methicillin-resistant *Staphylococcus aureus*; blood cultures are negative. Chest radiograph shows slight improvement in the right-sided infiltrate compared with admission.

**Which of the following is the most appropriate antibiotic therapy at this time?**

(A) Complete an 8-day course of all three antibiotics
(B) Complete an 8-day course of vancomycin and discontinue the other antibiotics
(C) Complete a 14-day course of all three antibiotics
(D) Complete a 14-day course of vancomycin and discontinue the other antibiotics
(E) Discontinue all antibiotics

## Item 114

A 30-year-old woman with persistent asthma is evaluated for frequent nocturnal awakenings. She has wheezing several nights a week despite treatment with a moderate-dose inhaled corticosteroid and a long-acting β-agonist. She does not have daytime symptoms. She developed oral thrush when she was taking higher doses of the inhaled corticosteroid. The patient is obese and occasionally snores but has had no witnessed apneic episodes. She has no other symptoms and takes no other medications. She has excellent inhaler technique as documented by direct observation.

On physical examination, vital signs are normal; BMI is 30. The cardiovascular examination is normal, and the lungs are clear.

**Which of the following is the most appropriate management for this patient?**

(A) Increase the evening long-acting β-agonist dose
(B) Increase the dose of inhaled corticosteroid
(C) Prescribe a 2-month trial of omeprazole
(D) Recommend an allergen-impermeable bedcover

## Item 115

A 50-year-old woman with myasthenia gravis is hospitalized because of worsening weakness and transferred to the intensive care unit for monitoring. Her only medication is pyridostigmine bromide.

On physical examination, the patient is alert; the temperature is 36.9 °C (98.4 °F), the blood pressure is 150/90 mm Hg, the pulse rate is 100/min, and the respiration rate is 24/min. Oxygen saturation is 100% with the patient breathing oxygen, 4 L/min by nasal cannula. There is no evidence of bulbar dysfunction. Breath sounds are clear bilaterally but diminished at the bases. Arterial blood gases while the patient was breathing ambient air were pH 7.44, $P_{CO_2}$ 35 mm Hg, and $P_{O_2}$ 90 mm Hg.

**Which of the following would be the most appropriate method for monitoring for ventilatory failure in this patient?**

(A) Arterial blood gas measurements
(B) Bedside measurement of vital capacity
(C) Continuous monitoring of oxygen saturation
(D) Rapid shallow breathing index

## Item 116

A 78-year-old woman is evaluated in the intensive care unit for disorientation. The patient recently developed the acute respiratory distress syndrome secondary to community acquired pneumonia, and mechanical ventilation was started 2 days ago. She lives alone and functions well independently.

The patient is on a ventilator; she has received small doses of lorazepam over the past 48 hours and appears comfortable. She has recently become disoriented, is not interacting as well with her family as she had before, and has had fluctuations in mental status over the past 24 hours.

On physical examination, pulse rate is 92/min, but vital signs are otherwise normal. Neurologic examination shows no focal abnormalities, and cranial nerve examination is normal. She is calm and awake but cannot follow directions to do the "random letter A test" by squeezing the examiner's hand only on hearing the letter "A"; she also cannot organize her thinking to answer simple questions. When asked whether she is seeing things or hearing things that are not there, she shakes her head "No." Laboratory studies show hemoglobin of 9.9 g/dL (99 g/L) and a leukocyte count of 11,000/μL ($11 \times 10^9$/L) with a normal differential. Metabolic panel reveals plasma glucose of 180 mg/dL (10.0 mmol/L); serum total thyroxine and thyroid-stimulating hormone levels are normal.

**Which of the following is the most likely diagnosis?**

(A) Delirium
(B) Dementia
(C) Psychosis
(D) Stroke

# Answers and Critiques

## Item 1    Answer: C

**Educational Objective:** Treat persistent asthma.

Asthma symptoms on 2 or more days a week (or 2 or more nights a month) is the defining characteristic of persistent asthma. Inhaled corticosteroids are the cornerstone of therapy for persistent asthma. Regular use of inhaled corticosteroids is associated with improved pulmonary function, reduced airway hyperresponsiveness, decreased asthma exacerbations, and reduced mortality. Side effects of inhaled corticosteroids include oral candidiasis and dysphonia related to laryngeal muscle myopathy. Systemic effects may occur with use of inhaled corticosteroids and are generally related to the dose and duration of use. In adults, these effects include osteopenia, skin thinning, and increased risk for cataracts or glaucoma. Therefore, the lowest dose consistent with disease control should be used. The treatment should be reevaluated every 3 to 6 months in stable patients, and adjustments made to step-up or step-down therapy based on disease control and occurrence of exacerbations. In between visits, patients should use a written asthma management plan, devised by their physician, to guide potential changes to their treatment.

Albuterol should be used as needed in all patients with asthma, but by itself is not adequate therapy because it does not affect the underlying airway inflammation. Long-acting β-agonists (salmeterol and formoterol) provide bronchodilation for up to 12 hours and are effective in preventing exercise-induced asthma. These drugs do not have a clinically significant anti-inflammatory effect; therefore, their use without concomitant administration of corticosteroids may mask worsening of asthma control and lead to increased asthma-related complications, including the possibility of increased asthma-related deaths. Therefore, long-acting β-agonists are not appropriate as monotherapy or in place of inhaled corticosteroids. The use of antibiotics for atypical infections (*Mycoplasma*, *Chlamydia*) in asthma is under investigation. However, antibiotic therapy is not recommended unless there is evidence of an acute bacterial infection.

### KEY POINT

- Inhaled corticosteroids are the cornerstone of therapy for persistent asthma.

### Bibliography

The National Heart, Lung, and Blood Institute. Expert Panel Report 3 (EPR3): Guidelines for the Diagnosis and Management of Asthma. www.nhlbi.nih.gov/guidelines/asthma/asthgdln.htm. Published 2007. Accessed on May 27, 2009.

## Item 2    Answer: A

**Educational Objective:** Evaluate an acute exacerbation of idiopathic pulmonary fibrosis.

The two immediate diagnostic considerations in this patient are respiratory infection and an acute exacerbation of pulmonary fibrosis. Both diagnostic possibilities may be evaluated by bronchoalveolar lavage with studies to detect bacterial organisms, opportunistic pathogens (for example, *Pneumocystis jirovecii*), and viral pathogens. Routine sputum evaluation for Gram stain and culture is not sensitive enough to detect opportunistic infectious organisms. Diagnostic criteria for an acute exacerbation of pulmonary fibrosis include exclusion of opportunistic respiratory infections via endotracheal aspiration or bronchoalveolar lavage as well as exclusion of pulmonary embolism, left ventricular failure, and other causes of acute lung injury. The incidence of an acute exacerbation of idiopathic pulmonary fibrosis is not certain but likely ranges between 5% and 40%. In patients with pulmonary fibrosis admitted to the intensive care unit for respiratory failure, the incidence may be as high as 60% with a reported mortality rate between 80% and 100%. No therapy has been shown to be beneficial.

Fungal serologies may be helpful to diagnose opportunistic infection in this patient. However, bronchoalveolar lavage is more sensitive, and results more readily available for detecting other opportunistic pathogens that need to be excluded in this immunosuppressed patient. Right-heart catheterization is not part of the initial evaluation of patients with a suspected acute exacerbation of idiopathic pulmonary fibrosis. Aspiration may cause acute lung injury and may trigger an acute exacerbation of idiopathic pulmonary fibrosis, but swallowing evaluation is unlikely to be diagnostic in this patient with no history of aspiration.

### KEY POINT

- Bronchoalveolar lavage is the diagnostic procedure to exclude opportunistic infection in an apparent acute exacerbation of idiopathic pulmonary fibrosis.

### Bibliography

Collard HR, Moore BB, Flaherty KR, et al; Idiopathic Pulmonary Fibrosis Clinical Research Network Investigators. Acute exacerbations of idiopathic pulmonary fibrosis. Am J Respir Crit Care Med. 2007;176(7):636-643. [PMID: 17585107]

## Item 3    Answer: A

**Educational Objective:** Manage moderate chronic obstructive pulmonary disease.

This patient has stage II chronic obstructive pulmonary disease (COPD) as defined by the guidelines of the Global

Initiative for Obstructive Lung Disease (GOLD). GOLD stage II disease is defined by a postbronchodilator $FEV_1/FVC$ ratio less than 70% and an $FEV_1$ less than 80% but more than 50% of predicted with or without chronic symptoms. In patients with GOLD stage II disease, maintenance treatment with one or more long-acting bronchodilators such as a long-acting $\beta_2$-agonist (salmeterol or formoterol) is recommended, along with as-needed albuterol. Pulmonary rehabilitation can be considered in addition to medical treatment in symptomatic patients. Starting or adding a long-acting anticholinergic agent would also be appropriate.

Inhaled corticosteroids, oral corticosteroids, theophylline, and montelukast would be inappropriate for this patient. Theophylline's narrow therapeutic window and poor bronchodilator effect make it a poor choice. Oral corticosteroids are not recommended routinely in COPD because of their systemic side effects. Montelukast is used as a third-line agent in asthma but has not been shown to be efficacious in COPD. The GOLD guidelines recommend consideration of inhaled corticosteroids in patients whose lung function is less than 50% and who experience recurrent exacerbations. When inhaled corticosteroids are combined with a long-acting $\beta_2$-agonist in such patients, the rate of decline in quality of life and health status is significantly reduced and the frequency of acute exacerbations is reduced by 25%; lung function is also improved and dyspnea alleviated.

Continuing current therapy with albuterol would not be appropriate because using a short-acting bronchodilator alone does not afford effective therapy for GOLD stage II disease and requires more frequent treatments.

Two recent long-term studies of more than 11,000 patients have evaluated treatment for patients with GOLD stages II to IV. The TORCH study and the UPLIFT study showed that in patients with COPD, therapy with a long-acting $\beta_2$-agonist or a long-acting anticholinergic agent in addition to a short-acting bronchodilator improved quality of life and pulmonary function without significant adverse effects.

**KEY POINT**

- **In patients with moderate chronic obstructive pulmonary disease, therapy with a long-acting $\beta_2$-agonist or a long-acting anticholinergic agent improves quality of life and pulmonary function compared with therapy with short-acting bronchodilators alone.**

**Bibliography**
Celli BR. Update on the Management of COPD [erratum in Chest. 2008;134(4):892]. Chest. 2008;133(6):1451-1462. [PMID: 18574288]

## Item 4      Answer:  E
**Educational Objective:**  Evaluate a low-risk patient with a very small pulmonary nodule.

Studies of chest CT screening have shown that 25% to 50% of patients have one or more pulmonary nodules detected on the initial CT scan. Even in patients at relatively high risk for lung cancer, the likelihood that a small nodule is malignant is low (<1%). For example, the risk of malignancy is about 0.2% for nodules smaller than 3 mm and 0.9% for nodules 4 to 7 mm. The Fleischner Society recommendations include no follow-up for low-risk patients with nodules 4 mm or smaller and follow-up CT at 12 months for patients with such nodules who are at risk for lung cancer. More frequent follow-up is not recommended for nodules of this size. This small nodule is not likely to be visible on chest radiograph, and, therefore, such imaging would not be helpful.

**KEY POINT**

- **In a patient at low risk for malignancy no follow-up is required for an incidentally noted pulmonary nodule 4 mm or smaller.**

**Bibliography**
MacMahon H, Austin JH, Gamsu G, et al; Fleischner Society. Guidelines for management of small pulmonary nodules detected on CT scans: a statement from the Fleischner Society. Radiology. 2005;237(2):395-400. [PMID: 16244247]

## Item 5      Answer:  C
**Educational Objective:**  Diagnose intensive care unit–acquired weakness.

Patients with intensive care unit (ICU)–acquired weakness have diffuse weakness and decreased muscle tone. The disorder may be first recognized in patients with unexplained difficulty weaning from the ventilator. *ICU-acquired weakness* is a term used to encompass critical-illness polyneuropathy and critical-illness myopathy. Treatment with paralytic agents and systemic corticosteroids, as well as sepsis and immobilization, increase the risk of developing ICU-acquired weakness. Treatment is supportive, including discontinuation or reduction of corticosteroids, aggressive management of existing disorders, and physical rehabilitation.

Acute inflammatory demyelinating polyneuropathy (Guillain-Barré syndrome) can also cause diffuse weakness, but in contrast to this patient, weakness is the presenting symptom. Furthermore, weakness associated with acute inflammatory demyelinating polyneuropathy typically develops gradually over a longer time course (1 to 2 weeks) and typically is preceded by an infection.

Prolonged neuromuscular blockade is a condition in which the effect of paralytic agents, such as vecuronium, can persist for days after discontinuing the medication. However, this is rarely encountered and is caused by altered drug metabolism due to liver and/or renal dysfunction, neither of which this patient has.

Churg-Strauss syndrome is associated with asthma and, in the vasculitic stage, can cause weakness. However, the syndrome most often manifests as mononeuritis multiplex rather than generalized weakness. Furthermore, this patient does not have other manifestations of vasculitis such as rash or renal dysfunction.

- Patients with intensive care unit–acquired weakness have diffuse, flaccid weakness and often present with difficulty with ventilator weaning.

**Bibliography**

Schweickert WD, Hall J. ICU-acquired weakness. Chest. 2007;131 (5):1541-1549. [PMID: 17494803]

## Item 6      Answer:  E

**Educational Objective:**  Confirm the clinical diagnosis of acute pulmonary embolism.

This patient is at high risk for pulmonary embolism because of his recent hospitalization, cancer, and nephrotic syndrome. A positive ventilation/perfusion scan would confirm the diagnosis of pulmonary embolism in this patient with a high pretest probability for the condition, especially in the absence of parenchymal lung defects on chest radiograph.

The probability of pulmonary embolism was very high based on this presentation that included chest pain, dyspnea, recent hospitalization and surgery, active cancer, and a protein-losing nephropathy. A negative D-dimer test would not be sufficient evidence to rule out a pulmonary embolism under these circumstances, and a high D-dimer level would add little to the diagnostic work-up. Decreased antithrombin III levels may result from nephrotic syndrome, and levels are lowered during acute thrombosis, especially during treatment with heparin. Therefore, measuring antithrombin III would add little to the accuracy of the diagnosis of pulmonary embolism or have any implication for immediate management decisions. Lower extremity ultrasonography can disclose asymptomatic deep venous thrombosis in a small percentage of patients presenting with symptoms of pulmonary embolism. However, the yield is relatively low and ventilation/perfusion scanning would have a much higher degree of accuracy. CT angiography is an acceptable modality to diagnose acute pulmonary embolism but requires a significant amount of contrast infusion (as much as a pulmonary angiogram) which would be contraindicated in a patient with an elevated serum creatinine level.

- Either ventilation/perfusion scanning or contrast-enhanced CT scanning (if not contraindicated) performed with a specific protocol to detect pulmonary embolism is an appropriate noninvasive test to diagnose acute pulmonary embolism.

**Bibliography**

Anderson DR, Kahn SR, Rodger MA, et al. Computed tomographic pulmonary angiography vs ventilation-perfusion lung scanning in patients with suspected pulmonary embolism: a randomized controlled trial. JAMA. 2007;298(23):2743-2753. [PMID: 18165667]

## Item 7      Answer:  D

**Educational Objective:**  Diagnose rhabdomyolysis secondary to narcotic overdose.

This patient most likely has rhabdomyolysis, which is caused by skeletal muscle damage that leads to release of intracellular components into the circulation, such as creatine kinase and lactate dehydrogenase, the heme pigment myoglobin, purines, and potassium and phosphate. The syndrome was first identified in patients with traumatic crush injuries, but there are nontraumatic causes, such as alcohol (due to hypophosphatemia), drug use, metabolic disorders, and infections. The classic triad of findings includes muscle pain, weakness, and dark urine. The diagnosis is based on clinical findings and a history of predisposing factors (such as prolonged immobilization or drug toxicity) and confirmed by the presence of myoglobinuria, an increased serum creatine kinase level, and, in some cases, hyperkalemia. The disorder usually resolves within days to weeks. Treatment consists of aggressive fluid resuscitation; fluids should be adjusted to maintain the hourly urine output at least 300 mL until the urine is negative for myoglobin. Acute kidney injury resulting from acute tubular necrosis occurs in approximately one third of patients. Dialysis is sometimes necessary.

Although fulminant hepatic failure may result in coma, dark urine, and renal failure, other tests of synthetic liver function in this patient are normal. There are no clinical features to suggest sepsis. The patient has mild anemia, but the proportionate reduction in the leukocyte and platelet counts suggests alcohol-induced bone marrow suppression. Hemolytic anemia would not explain the patient's elevated creatine kinase level and usually does not cause renal failure. Hemolytic uremic syndrome is not consistent with the clinical findings of polysubstance overdose or the laboratory finding of the elevated serum creatine kinase level.

- Nontraumatic causes of rhabdomyolysis include drug use, metabolic disorders, and infections.

**Bibliography**

Talaie H, Pajouhmand A, Abdollahi M, et al. Rhabdomyolysis among acute human poisoning cases. Hum Exp Toxicol. 2007:26(7):557-561. [PMID: 17884958]

## Item 8      Answer:  A

**Educational Objective:**  Recognize the effect of diuretic therapy on the pleural fluid analysis in patients with heart failure.

The patient's pleural fluid analysis shows a protein discordant exudate (an exudate by protein criterion only) with a pleural fluid to serum total protein ratio of 0.54 and a pleural fluid lactate dehydrogenase (LDH) to upper limits of normal serum LDH ratio of 0.52. Pleural fluid findings may have exudative characteristics in patients with heart failure who are receiving diuretics. A serum–pleural fluid albumin gradient greater than 1.2 suggests a transudate in cases where the pleural fluid to serum total protein ratio or pleural fluid to serum LDH ratio and pleural fluid LDH to upper limits of normal serum LDH ratio suggest an exudate, but the clinical findings suggest a transudate. The increased pleural fluid to serum total protein ratio is the result of a diuretic effect, with more efficient clearance of pleural liquid than pleural protein.

Patients with post–cardiac injury syndrome typically present 3 weeks (range 3 days to 1 year) after coronary artery bypass graft surgery; they usually have pleuritic chest pain and typically dyspnea, pleural or pericardial friction rub, fever, left lower lobe infiltrates, leukocytosis, and an increased erythrocyte sedimentation rate. This patient's findings are not compatible with post–cardiac injury syndrome. The absence of chest pain would be highly unlikely with a pulmonary embolism–induced pleural effusion. No consolidation was detected on chest radiograph, making pneumonia unlikely. Furthermore, a parapneumonic effusion is typically a concordant exudate (both protein and LDH in the exudate range) with a neutrophil predominance, and a low pleural fluid LDH is typically not associated with an acute parapneumonic effusion.

### KEY POINT

- **Diuretic therapy for heart failure can result in either a protein- or lactate dehydrogenase–discordant exudative pleural effusion and, rarely, a concordant exudate.**

### Bibliography
Gotsman I, Fridlender Z, Meirovitz A, Dratva D, Muszkat M. The evaluation of pleural effusions in patients with heart failure. Am J Med. 2001;111(5):375-378. [PMID: 11583640]

## Item 9    Answer:  E

**Educational Objective:**  Evaluate vocal cord dysfunction.

This patient likely has vocal cord dysfunction (VCD). Patients with VCD can have throat or neck discomfort, wheezing, stridor, and anxiety. The disorder can be difficult to differentiate from asthma; however, affected patients do not respond to the usual asthma therapy. Diagnosing VCD is made more difficult by the fact that many of these patients also have asthma. The chest radiograph in this patient showed decreased lung volumes, which is in contrast to hyperinflation that would be expected in acute asthma. Oxygen saturation is typically normal in patients with VCD.

Laryngoscopy, especially when done while the patient is symptomatic, can reveal characteristic adduction of the vocal cords during inspiration. Another test that helps make the diagnosis is flow volume loops, in which the inspiratory and expiratory flow rates are recorded while a patient is asked to take a deep breath and then to exhale. In patients with VCD, the inspiratory limb of the flow volume loop is "flattened" owing to narrowing of the extrathoracic airway (at the level of the vocal cords) during inspiration. Recognition of VCD is essential to prevent lengthy courses of corticosteroids and to initiate therapies targeted at VCD, which include speech therapy, relaxation techniques, and treating such underlying causes as anxiety, postnasal drip, and gastroesophageal reflux disease.

Intravenous aminophylline is not recommended for treating either acute asthma or VCD. Therapy with intravenous terbutaline or other β-agonists for asthma exacerbations is associated with an unacceptably high rate of side effects. Azithromycin is a reasonable choice for acute bronchitis, but there is little evidence that this patient has acute bronchitis, which would manifest with cough, sputum production, and fever. The chest CT scan can be used to exclude parenchymal lung disease or evaluate the possibility of a pulmonary embolism; however, these disorders are unlikely in this patient with previous normal pulmonary examinations and radiographs and excellent oxygenation, and chest CT scan is unlikely to yield useful information.

### KEY POINT

- **Laryngoscopy during an exacerbation of vocal cord dysfunction shows adduction of the vocal cords during inspiration.**

### Bibliography
King CS, Moores LK. Clinical asthma syndromes and important asthma mimics. Respir Care. 2008;53(5):568-580. [PMID: 18426611]

## Item 10    Answer:  D

**Educational Objective:**  Prescribe pulmonary rehabilitation for a patient with severe chronic obstructive pulmonary disease.

This patient who is on maximum medical treatment for chronic obstructive pulmonary disease (COPD) and is still symptomatic would benefit from pulmonary rehabilitation. Comprehensive pulmonary rehabilitation includes patient education, exercise training, psychosocial support, and nutritional intervention as well as the evaluation for oxygen supplementation. Referral should be considered for any patient with chronic respiratory disease who remains symptomatic or has decreased functional status despite otherwise optimal medical therapy.

Pulmonary rehabilitation increases exercise capacity, reduces dyspnea, improves quality of life, and decreases health care utilization. Reimbursement for pulmonary rehabilitation treatment remains an impediment to its widespread use.

The effect of lung volume reduction surgery is larger in patients with predominantly nonhomogeneous upper-lobe disease and limited exercise performance after rehabilitation. The ideal candidate should have an $FEV_1$ between 20% and 35% of predicted, the $D_{LCO}$ no lower than 20% of predicted, hyperinflation, and limited comorbidities. There is no indication for nocturnal assisted ventilation because she does not have daytime hypercapnia and worsening oxygen desaturation during sleep. Lung transplantation should be considered in patients hospitalized with COPD exacerbation complicated by hypercapnia ($PCO_2$ greater than 50 mm Hg) and patients with $FEV_1$ not exceeding 20% of predicted and either homogeneous disease on high-resolution CT scan or $DLCO$ less than 20% of predicted who are at high risk of death after lung volume reduction surgery. Lung transplantation is, therefore, not an option for this patient.

**KEY POINT**

- Pulmonary rehabilitation in patients with advanced lung disease can increase exercise capacity, decrease dyspnea, improve quality of life, and decrease health care utilization.

**Bibliography**

ZuWallack R, Hedges H. Primary Care of the Patient with Chronic Obstructive Pulmonary Disease – part 3: Pulmonary Rehabilitation and Comprehensive Care for the Patient with Chronic Obstructive Pulmonary Disease. Am J Med. 2008;121(7 Suppl):S25-32. [PMID: 18558104]

## Item 11    Answer:  A

**Educational Objective:**  Diagnose and manage dermatomyositis presenting as interstitial lung disease.

This patient's symmetric proximal muscle weakness and pain with an erythematous, scaly rash over the interphalangeal joints (Gottron sign), coupled with a positive antinuclear antibody titer and elevated creatine kinase level, suggest dermatomyositis. Electromyography and muscle biopsy will establish the diagnosis of inflammatory myopathy. Inflammatory myopathy must be distinguished from corticosteroid-induced myopathy because treatment of dermatomyositis requires increased corticosteroids, whereas corticosteroid-induced myopathy is treated with withdrawal of prednisone. Corticosteroid-induced myopathy is not associated with elevated antinuclear antibodies, creatine kinase, or erythrocyte sedimentation rate. Up to 30% of patients with dermatomyositis and polymyositis present without muscle, skin, or joint involvement and have single-organ involvement of the lungs indistinguishable from idiopathic interstitial lung disease. Interstitial lung disease associated with inflammatory myopathy often occurs in the context of antisynthetase antibodies (for example, anti-Jo-1) and the antisynthetase syndrome (acute onset, constitutional symptoms, Raynaud phenomenon, "mechanic's hands," arthritis, and interstitial lung disease).

Repeat lung biopsy is unlikely to yield new diagnostic information in this patient with stable chest radiograph and no new respiratory symptoms. A skin biopsy is likely to reveal nonspecific findings that will not help diagnose the muscle symptoms.

**KEY POINT**

- Up to 30% of patients with dermatomyositis and polymyositis present with single-organ involvement of the lungs indistinguishable from idiopathic interstitial lung disease.

**Bibliography**

Tzelepis GE, Toya SP, Moutsopoulos HM. Occult connective tissue diseases mimicking idiopathic interstitial pneumonias. Eur Respir J. 2008;31(1):11-20. [PMID: 18166591]

## Item 12    Answer:  A

**Educational Objective:**  Diagnose asbestosis.

The diagnosis of asbestosis is based on a convincing history of asbestos exposure with an appropriately long latent period (10 to 15 years) and definite evidence of interstitial fibrosis without other likely causes. This patient worked as an insulator when asbestos exposure was still widespread and is at risk for asbestos-related lung disease. The most specific finding on chest radiograph is bilateral partially calcified pleural plaques. Pleural plaques are focal, often partially calcified, fibrous tissue collections on the parietal pleura and are considered a marker of asbestos exposure.

Rheumatoid lung disease has many manifestations, including an interstitial lung disease, which is most common in patients with severe rheumatoid arthritis. This patient's occasional swelling in both knees is not compatible with the diagnosis of rheumatoid arthritis.

Sarcoidosis occurs most commonly in young and middle-aged adults, with a peak incidence in the third decade. More than 90% of patients with sarcoidosis have lung involvement. The chest radiograph may show hilar lymphadenopathy alone, hilar lymphadenopathy and reticular opacities predominantly in the upper lung zone, or reticular opacities without hilar lymphadenopathy. Pulmonary function tests may reveal a restrictive pattern and reduction in $DLCO$, or may be normal. The patient's age, predominantly lower lobe involvement, occupational history, and pleural plaques argue against pulmonary sarcoidosis.

Idiopathic pulmonary fibrosis presents with slowly progressive dyspnea and a chronic, nonproductive cough. The chest radiograph is almost always abnormal at the time of presentation, with decreased lung volumes and basal reticular opacities. Almost all patients have a physiologic restrictive process (decreased forced vital capacity, total lung capacity, functional residual capacity) as well as impaired gas exchange with a decreased $DLCO$. However, asbestosis is a much more likely diagnosis in a patient with a positive exposure history and radiographic evidence of pleural plaques.

**KEY POINT**

- Pleural plaques are focal, often partially calcified, fibrous tissue collections on the parietal pleura and are a marker of asbestos exposure.

**Bibliography**
Aberle DR, Balmes JR. Computed tomography of asbestos-related pulmonary parenchymal and pleural disease. Clin Chest Med. 1991;12(1):115-131. [PMID: 2009740]

## Item 13    Answer:  B
**Educational Objective:**  Treat delirium in the intensive care unit.

When supportive care is insufficient for prevention or treatment of delirium, symptom control with medication is occasionally necessary to prevent harm or to allow evaluation and treatment in the intensive care unit. The appropriate treatment for this patient is haloperidol. The recommended therapy for delirium is antipsychotic agents, although no drugs are U.S. Food and Drug Administration–approved for this indication. Ongoing randomized, placebo-controlled trials are investigating different management strategies for intensive care unit delirium. A recent systematic evidence review found that the existing limited data indicate no superiority for second-generation antipsychotics compared with haloperidol for delirium. Haloperidol does not cause respiratory suppression, which is one reason that it is often used in patients with hypoventilatory respiratory failure who require sedation. All antipsychotic agents, and especially "typical" agents such as haloperidol, pose a risk of torsades de pointes and extrapyramidal side effects as well as the neuroleptic malignant syndrome.

Diphenhydramine and other antihistamines are a major risk factor for delirium, especially in older patients. Lorazepam is actually deliriogenic, and its use in a delirious patient should be carefully re-evaluated, other than perhaps in patients experiencing benzodiazepine withdrawal or delirium tremens. There is no evidence that propofol has any role in treating delirium.

**KEY POINT**
- **No drug is U.S. Food and Drug Administration–approved for the treatment of delirium, but clinical practice guidelines recommend antipsychotic agents, such as haloperidol.**

**Bibliography**
Campbell N, Boustani MA, Ayub A, et al. Pharmacological management of delirium in hospitalized adults - A systematic evidence review. J Gen Intern Med. 2009;24(7):848-853. [PMID: 19424763]

## Item 14    Answer:  D
**Educational Objective:**  Manage obstructive sleep apnea.

Obstructive sleep apnea is associated with significant, even life-threatening complications, and CPAP is effective therapy. CPAP therapy reduces the number of apneas and hypopneas and improves sleep architecture, hypertension, and quality of life. Excessive sleepiness that persists despite CPAP therapy may be due to poor adherence with treatment, insufficient sleep duration, presence of coexisting sleep disorders, surreptitious use of sedating medications, or mood disorders. Adherence to CPAP therapy is often suboptimal, and many patients remain symptomatic and report either not being able to tolerate the device or using it intermittently. Verifying proper use and adherence is important before CPAP therapy is discontinued or additional studies are ordered or therapy prescribed. Many CPAP devices have data cards or meters that monitor use, and they can be evaluated to determine whether CPAP use is suboptimal.

A multiple sleep latency test can be performed if daytime sleepiness persists in a patient who is consistently able to use CPAP set at an optimal pressure; in this patient it will objectively confirm her complaints of sleepiness but will not aid in identifying its cause. Stimulant and wake-promoting agents, such as caffeine or modafinil, may be used as adjunct therapy to improve residual daytime sleepiness in patients receiving optimal CPAP therapy, but should not be used as a substitute for proper CPAP use. Similarly, hormone replacement therapy is not indicated as sole therapy for postmenopausal women with obstructive sleep apnea.

**KEY POINT**
- **Excessive sleepiness that persists despite positive airway pressure therapy may be due to poor adherence with treatment.**

**Bibliography**
Kushida CA, Littner MR, Hirshkowitz M, et al. Practice parameters for the use of continuous and bilevel positive airway pressure devices to treat adult patients with sleep-related breathing disorders. Sleep. 2006;29(3):375-380. [PMID: 16553024]

## Item 15    Answer:  B
**Educational Objective:**  Recognize a typical presentation of a carcinoid tumor.

A carcinoid tumor is the most likely tumor in a young person who has never smoked and who has evidence of endobronchial obstruction. Bronchial carcinoid is a slow growing tumor that originally was classified as an adenoma but has been reclassified as a malignant neoplasm because of its ability to metastasize. Most bronchial carcinoid tumors are located in proximal airways and cause symptoms by either obstructing an airway or bleeding. Common presenting symptoms include cough or wheeze, hemoptysis, and recurrent pneumonia in the same pulmonary lobe. The carcinoid syndrome is caused by systemic release of vasoactive substances such as serotonin, and the most typical features include cutaneous flushing and diarrhea. Bronchial carcinoids are not commonly associated with the carcinoid syndrome because of their relatively small amount of serotonin production.

Although adenocarcinoma is the most common cancer cell type in a never-smoker, it rarely causes endobronchial obstruction. Small cell and squamous cell cancers frequently cause bronchial obstruction but rarely, if ever, occur in a young, never-smoker. Furthermore, the development of bronchiectasis denotes a chronic process of airway obstruction and infection. It occurs most commonly in association with foreign body aspiration, endobronchial obstruction by an indolent tumor such as carcinoid tumor, or secondary to extraluminal compression. Carcinomas, including those causing endobronchial obstruction, tend to grow very quickly, resulting in patient treatment (or death) before they can cause focal bronchiectasis. Treatment of carcinoid tumor is surgical resection when possible, and, for typical carcinoids, 5-year survival is about 90%.

### KEY POINT

- Carcinoid tumors are neuroendocrine tumors with an indolent growth pattern that often present with endobronchial obstruction.

**Bibliography**
Oberg K, Jelic S; ESMO Guidelines Working Group. Neuroendocrine bronchial and thymic tumors: ESMO clinical recommendation for diagnosis, treatment and follow-up. Ann Oncol. 2008;19(Suppl 2):102-103. [PMID: 18456740]

## Item 16    Answer:  C

**Educational Objective:**  Evaluate a tuberculous pleural effusion.

The patient likely has a tuberculous pleural effusion based on the subacute (3-week) duration of symptoms and the characteristics of the pleural effusion. Because of the patient's age and the presentation with an isolated pleural effusion, primary tuberculosis is most likely. A tuberculous effusion is typically exudative by both protein (pleural fluid to serum protein ratio greater than 0.5) and lactate dehydrogenase (LDH) criteria (pleural fluid to serum LDH ratio greater than 0.6 and pleural fluid to serum upper limits of normal LDH ratio greater than 0.67). The cellular response in the pleural fluid is classically lymphocytic (greater than 80% mature lymphocytes). However, it can be neutrophilic within the first 2 weeks, after which it typically evolves into the classic lymphocyte-predominant exudate. Whereas pleural fluid cultures for *Mycobacterium* are positive in less than one third of cases, the combination of pleural biopsy for histologic evaluation and culture is typically positive in more than two thirds of cases.

The 3-week history of symptoms is too long for a typical bacterial pneumonia, no definite infiltrate was present on the chest radiograph, and the cellular response in the pleural fluid was primarily lymphocytic rather than neutrophilic. Therefore, a bacterial pneumonia with a parapneumonic effusion is unlikely, and an empiric course of azithromycin would not be appropriate. Chest CT scan might be helpful to assess whether there is an underlying parenchymal infiltrate that was not visible on plain chest radiograph, but it would not help in determining the underlying cause of the pleural effusion. Flexible bronchoscopy, with collection of samples for histology and culture, is useful for diagnosing pulmonary tuberculosis in the setting of pulmonary parenchymal disease. However, the yield from culture of bronchopulmonary secretions (obtained either as sputum or bronchoscopic samples) is low, especially in the absence of pulmonary parenchymal abnormalities on chest radiograph.

### KEY POINT

- A patient with tuberculous pleural effusion typically presents with a lymphocyte-predominant exudative effusion; however, within the first 1 to 2 weeks, neutrophils can predominate as the cellular response evolves from neutrophils to lymphocytes.

**Bibliography**
Gopi A, Madhavan SM, Sharma SK, Sahn SA. Diagnosis and treatment of tuberculous effusion in 2006. Chest. 2007;131(3):880-889. [PMID: 17356108]

## Item 17    Answer:  A

**Educational Objective:**  Manage a patient with an exacerbation of asthma.

This patient presented with signs of a severe asthma exacerbation. Decreased breath sounds, accessory muscle use, sternocleidomastoid or suprasternal retractions, inability to speak in full sentences, and paradoxical pulse greater than 15 mm Hg are associated with severe airflow obstruction, although the absence of these findings does not necessarily exclude the presence of a high-risk exacerbation. However, the initial physical examination and findings are less predictive of the clinical course in a patient with asthma than the response to bronchodilators. This patient has responded well to bronchodilators, with improved ability to speak and reduced accessory muscle use. Wheezing may become more prominent in the early stages of recovery owing to improved airflow through narrowed airways. According to the newest National Asthma Education and Prevention Program's guidelines, admission to the intensive care unit is recommended for symptomatic patients with even mild carbon dioxide retention ($PCO_2$ greater than 42 mm Hg) or severely decreased lung function despite aggressive bronchodilator treatment (persistent $FEV_1$ or peak expiratory flow less than 40% of predicted). This patient does not meet the criteria for admission to the intensive care unit or intubation and mechanical ventilation at this time. The best disposition for this patient would be admission to the hospital ward; his $FEV_1$ has not improved enough to warrant discharge.

### KEY POINT

- The response to inhaled bronchodilators is more predictive of the clinical course in a patient with asthma than initial physical examination and findings.

Bibliography

National Heart, Lung, and Blood Institute. National Asthma Education and Prevention Program: Expert Panel Report 3: Guidelines for the diagnosis and management of asthma. www.nhlbi.nih.gov/guidelines/asthma/asthgdln.pdf. Published August 27, 2007. Accessed on July 30, 2009.

## Item 18    Answer:  A

**Educational Objective:**  Diagnose malignant hyperthermia.

This patient most likely has malignant hyperthermia, which is an inherited skeletal muscle disorder characterized by a hypermetabolic state precipitated by exposure to volatile inhalational anesthetics (halothane, isoflurane, enflurane, desflurane, sevoflurane) and the depolarizing muscle relaxants succinylcholine and decamethonium. It usually occurs on exposure to the drug but can occur several hours after the initial exposure and can develop in patients who were previously exposed to the drug without effect. Increased intracellular calcium leads to sustained muscle contractions, with skeletal muscle rigidity and masseter muscle spasm, tachycardia, hypercarbia, hypertension, hyperthermia, tachypnea, and cardiac arrhythmias. Rhabdomyolysis and acute renal failure can develop. Malignant hyperthermia should be suspected in patients with a family history of problems during anesthesia.

The neuroleptic malignant syndrome is a life-threatening disorder caused by an idiosyncratic reaction to neuroleptic tranquilizers (dopamine $D_2$-receptor antagonists) and some antipsychotic drugs. The most common offending neuroleptic agents are haloperidol and fluphenazine. The syndrome occurs with all drugs that cause central dopamine receptor blockade, usually soon after starting a new drug or with dose escalation. It has been reported in patients with Parkinson disease who abruptly discontinue levodopa or anticholinergic therapy. Most patients with the syndrome develop muscle rigidity, hyperthermia, cognitive changes, autonomic instability, diaphoresis, sialorrhea, seizures, arrhythmias, and rhabdomyolysis within 2 weeks after initiating the drug. Because this patient did not receive a neuroleptic agent, neuroleptic malignant syndrome is unlikely. In critical care patients receiving both neuroleptic tranquilizers and depolarizing muscle relaxants, malignant hyperthermia can be differentiated from neuroleptic malignant syndrome by the presence of a mixed (metabolic and respiratory) acidosis in the former condition.

Like the neuroleptic malignant syndrome, the serotonin syndrome presents with high fever, muscle rigidity, and cognitive changes. Findings unique to the serotonin syndrome are shivering, hyperreflexia, myoclonus, and ataxia. The serotonin syndrome is caused by the use of selective serotonin reuptake inhibitors, a category of drug that this patient has not been exposed to.

Thyroid storm is a potential cause of hyperthermia in hospitalized patients, but thyroid storm does not cause muscle rigidity or elevations of the creatine kinase level.

**KEY POINT**

- Malignant hyperthermia is an inherited skeletal muscle disorder characterized by a hypermetabolic state precipitated by exposure to volatile inhalational anesthetics and the depolarizing muscle relaxants.

Bibliography

Chamorro C, Romera MA, Balandin B. Fever in critically ill patients. Crit Care Med. 2008;36(11):3129-3130. [PMID: 18941337]

## Item 19    Answer:  A

**Educational Objective:**  Manage asthma during pregnancy.

Asthma during pregnancy follows the rule of thirds: the condition improves in one third of patients, worsens in one third, and remains unchanged in one third. Uncontrolled asthma has significantly worse impact on pregnancy outcome than the potential risk of medications during pregnancy. Short-acting β-agonists are regarded as safe during pregnancy. Budesonide has been studied in pregnancy and been shown to be safe. There are fewer data on other inhaled corticosteroids, such as fluticasone, which is a U.S. Food and Drug Administration pregnancy risk category C drug (studies of safety in pregnancy are lacking but the potential benefit of the drug may justify the potential risk). The inhaled corticosteroids are, however, believed from clinical experience to be safe during pregnancy, and, therefore, it is generally recommended to keep the patient on the regimen that has been effective for control of asthma.

Theophylline and aminophylline are pregnancy risk category C drugs also, but extensive clinical experience suggests that they are safe during pregnancy. However, the metabolism of these agents may be altered in pregnancy, requiring increased drug level monitoring. Also, inhaled corticosteroids are as effective as theophylline with fewer side effects in pregnant patients. Cromolyn is also considered safe in pregnancy but no safer than inhaled corticosteroids and less effective in persistent asthma. The National Asthma Education and Prevention Program (NAEPP) expert panel guidelines in 2007 affirmed the recommendation of adding long-acting β-agonists to patients whose asthma is not controlled with an inhaled corticosteroid but advised against using long-acting β-agonists as a single controller therapy. There is no need to add a long-acting β-agonist to this patient's asthma regimen because her symptoms are well controlled and substituting the long-acting β-agonist for inhaled fluticasone may result in loss of symptom control and possible increased risk of asthma-related death.

**KEY POINT**

- Clinical experience has shown that inhaled corticosteroids are safe and effective in pregnant patients with asthma.

Bibliography
Schatz M, Dombrowski MP. Clinical practice. Asthma in pregnancy. N Engl J Med. 2009;360(18):1862-1869. [PMID: 19403904]

## Item 20    Answer:  A

**Educational Objective:**  Diagnose cryptogenic organizing pneumonia.

This nonsmoker without any exposure history has acute to subacute development of nonspecific systemic and respiratory symptoms with a dominant alveolar (opacification) process on chest radiograph. The tempo of the disease process is the key to differentiating cryptogenic organizing pneumonia (COP) from other interstitial lung diseases. COP (formerly called idiopathic bronchiolitis obliterans organizing pneumonia) is often acute or subacute, with symptom onset occurring within 2 months of presentation in three fourths of patients. The presentation is so suggestive of an acute or subacute lower respiratory tract infection that patients have almost always been treated with and failed to respond to one or more courses of antibiotics before diagnosis.

Idiopathic pulmonary fibrosis (IPF), nonspecific interstitial pneumonia (NSIP), or lymphocytic interstitial pneumonia (LIP) typically follows a prolonged course with evidence of respiratory symptoms and radiographic findings that progress slowly over months or years. Radiographic findings in COP are also distinct from those in IPF, NSIP, and LIP. A dominant alveolar opacification process is typically present in patients with COP. The opacities are almost always bilateral with varied distribution. One of the key radiographic features of COP is the tendency for COP opacities to "migrate" or involve different areas of the lung on serial examinations. Although the radiographic findings of IPF, NSIP, and LIP are varied, they all have a dominant interstitial (reticular) pattern with or without opacities. LIP (which is very rare) is one of the few interstitial lung diseases that can present with cystic changes on high-resolution CT.

**KEY POINT**

- Cryptogenic organizing pneumonia most often presents with subacute disease progression and bilateral opacities on chest radiograph.

Bibliography
Ryu JH, Daniels CE, Hartman TE, et al. Diagnosis of interstitial lung diseases. Mayo Clin Proc. 2007;82(8):976-986. [PMID: 17673067]

## Item 21    Answer:  D

**Educational Objective:**  Treat stable acute pulmonary embolism.

This patient has had an acute pulmonary embolism 1 day post partum. The patient has no evidence of active bleeding, and there is no increased risk for bleeding from anticoagulation. Subcutaneous administration of unfractionated heparin, low-molecular-weight heparins, and fondaparinux are all safe and effective for the treatment of acute pulmonary embolism. A recent clinical trial showed that high-dose subcutaneous unfractionated heparin, administered without dose adjustment guided by the activated partial thromboplastin time, was as safe and effective as low-molecular-weight heparin administered in the same fashion.

Intravenous argatroban, a direct thrombin inhibitor, might be useful in the setting of heparin-induced thrombocytopenia. However, the patient's platelet count is normal. Monitoring of the platelet count would be appropriate after initiating either unfractionated or low-molecular-weight heparin, but the patient's current platelet count is not a contraindication for either drug; therefore, there is no indication to begin treatment with argatroban. Neither low-molecular-weight heparins nor fondaparinux has been evaluated in large clinical trials for intravenous use. Therefore, although it may be theoretically possible to use these agents intravenously, appropriate dosing and monitoring guidelines have not been validated. There are four generally accepted indications for placement of an inferior vena cava filter: (1) absolute contraindication to anticoagulation (for example, active bleeding); (2) recurrent pulmonary embolism despite adequate anticoagulation therapy; (3) bleeding complication of anticoagulation therapy; and (4) hemodynamic or respiratory compromise severe enough that a subsequent pulmonary embolism might be lethal. This patient has no indication for an inferior vena cava filter.

**KEY POINT**

- Acute pulmonary embolism can be treated initially with subcutaneous unfractionated heparin, low-molecular-weight heparins, or fondaparinux without the need for dosage adjustment.

Bibliography
Kearon C, Kahn SR, Agnelli G, Goldhaber S, Raskob GE, Comerota AJ; American College of Chest Physicians. Antithrombotic therapy for venous thrombolic disease: American College of Chest Physicians evidence-based clinical practice guidelines (8th Edition). Chest. 2008;133(6 Suppl):454S-545S. [PMID: 18574272]

## Item 22    Answer:  A

**Educational Objective:**  Recognize indications for continuous oxygen therapy in patients with chronic obstructive pulmonary disease.

The long-term administration of oxygen for more than 15 hours per day to patients with chronic obstructive pulmonary disease (COPD) increases survival, and may also improve hemodynamics, hematologic characteristics, exercise capacity, lung mechanics, and mental status. Indications for continuous long-term oxygen therapy for patients with COPD include:

- $PO_2$ less than or equal to 55 mm Hg or oxygen saturation less than or equal to 88%

• PO$_2$ less than or equal to 59 mm Hg or oxygen saturation less than or equal to 89% if there is evidence of cor pulmonale, right heart failure, or erythrocytosis (hematocrit greater than 55%).

This patient's resting oxygen saturation is 86% and his PO$_2$ is 55 mm Hg, and, therefore, continuous long-term oxygen therapy is indicated.

Chronic hypoxemia leading to the development of cor pulmonale portends a poor prognosis. Nocturnal oxygen therapy is better than no oxygen therapy at all, but continuous therapy is better than nocturnal therapy in severely hypoxemic patients with erythrocytosis, elevated pulmonary artery pressures, and respiratory acidosis. No study has shown a survival benefit when oxygen is prescribed for exercise-induced oxygen desaturation or when used as needed for symptoms of breathlessness.

**KEY POINT**

• In a patient with severe chronic obstructive pulmonary disease, at-rest oxygen saturation less than or equal to 88% is an indication for long-term continuous oxygen therapy.

**Bibliography**
Kim V, Benndill JO, Wise, RA, Sharajkhaneh A. Oxygen therapy in chronic obstructive pulmonary diseases. Proc Am Thoracic Soc. 2008;5(4):513-518. [PMID: 18453364]

## Item 23      Answer:   E

**Educational Objective:**  Recognize prophylaxis for high-altitude pulmonary edema.

Both the occurrence and severity of respiratory symptoms at high altitude are affected by the degree of elevation, rapidity of ascent, altitude during sleep, comorbid cardiovascular and respiratory disorders, physical exertion at altitude, and individual variations in tolerance to altitude (for example, altitude illness is more common in those with inadequate hypoxic ventilatory drive, prior history of altitude illness, and residence below an altitude of 915 m [3000 ft]).

High-altitude pulmonary edema (HAPE) is a form of noncardiogenic pulmonary edema due to leakage of fluid and hemorrhage into the alveolar spaces. The most effective preventive measure for HAPE is an appropriately gradual ascent to altitude (not greater than 300 to 500 m [984 to 1640 ft] daily above an altitude of 2000 m [6562 ft], with scheduled rest days every 3 or 4 days). Nifedipine is used to prevent and to treat HAPE.

Acetazolamide is used as prophylaxis for periodic breathing related to high altitude and acute mountain sickness (AMS) but is not indicated for HAPE. Dexamethasone is used for the prevention and treatment of AMS; it is not generally considered as a prophylactic agent for HAPE. Diuretics have been used for HAPE, but their role is not clearly established and there is no compelling evidence for their use. β-Blockers are not indicated for either the prevention or treatment of HAPE. Other agents that might be potentially useful for preventing HAPE include the phosphodiesterase inhibitors tadalafil and sildenafil, as well as salmeterol, but additional studies are required to ascertain their precise role for this indication.

**KEY POINT**

• Nifedipine is used both to prevent and to treat high-altitude pulmonary edema.

**Bibliography**
Luks AM, Swenson ER. Medication and dosage considerations in the prophylaxis and treatment of high-altitude illness. Chest. 2008;133 (3):744-755. [PMID: 18321903]

## Item 24      Answer:   A

**Educational Objective:**  Diagnose chylothorax.

Chylothorax is drainage of lymphatic fluid into the pleural space secondary to disruption or blockage of the thoracic duct or one of its lymphatic tributaries. Malignancy is the most common cause of chylothorax, but trauma is the second most common cause. Chylothorax can present about 2 to 10 days after penetrating or non-penetrating trauma to the chest. The pleural fluid in chylothorax is usually milky but may also be serous or serosanguineous in malnourished patients with little fat intake. The pleural fluid triglyceride concentration in a chylothorax is typically greater than 110 mg/dL (1.24 mmol/L) and occurs in association with a low pleural fluid cholesterol concentration. If the triglyceride level is less than 50 mg/dL (0.56 mmol/L), chylothorax is unlikely. When the pleural fluid triglyceride concentration is between 50 and 110 mg/dL (0.56 and 1.24 mmol/L), a lipoprotein analysis should be done and the presence of chylomicrons would confirm the diagnosis in such cases.

Chylothorax can also occur in association with pulmonary tuberculosis and chronic mediastinal infections, sarcoidosis, lymphangioleiomyomatosis, and radiation fibrosis.

A lymphomatous pleural effusion is always a consideration in patients with a history of lymphoma; however, a lymphomatous pleural effusion typically has an elevated lactate dehydrogenase level (often greater than 1000 U/L). Parapneumonic effusion is usually associated with a neutrophilic pleocytosis. Patients with tuberculous pleural effusion usually present with a nonproductive cough, chest pain, and fever. Chest radiograph usually shows a small to moderate effusion.

**KEY POINT**

• The most common causes of chylothorax are cancer and trauma; other causes are pulmonary tuberculosis, chronic mediastinal infections, sarcoidosis, lymphangioleiomyomatosis, and radiation fibrosis.

**Bibliography**
Agrawal V, Doelken P, Sahn SA. Pleural fluid analysis in chylothorax. Chest. 2008;133(6):1436-1441. [PMID: 18339791]

## Item 25    Answer: E
**Educational Objective:**  Diagnose thymoma.

Up to 75% of patients with myasthenia gravis have thymic abnormalities, such as hyperplasia or tumor. Therefore, evaluation of patients with suspected myasthenia gravis should include CT scan of the chest. The CT image shows an anterior mediastinal mass, and the diagnosis of myasthenia gravis is supported by the findings of ptosis and the elevated acetylcholine receptor binding antibody (AChR-Ab). Myasthenia gravis is characterized by weakness with a predilection for various muscles, particularly the ocular, bulbar, proximal extremities, neck, and respiratory muscles. Symptoms of this condition are traditionally worsened by fatigue, exertion, a rise in body temperature, stress, and intercurrent infections. Approximately 30% to 50% of patients with thymoma have myasthenia gravis, and the tumors are most likely to be located in the anterior mediastinum.

An esophageal tumor or a neurolemmoma is typically a posterior mediastinal mass. Although sarcoidosis may be a cause of ptosis, it usually presents with symmetric hilar and middle mediastinal lymphadenopathy. Small cell lung cancer may cause a mediastinal mass and various neurologic syndromes, including Lambert-Eaton syndrome, but is not associated with an elevated AChR-Ab but rather with a serum anti–voltage-gated calcium channel antibody. Lambert-Eaton syndrome usually manifests with proximal upper- and lower-extremity weakness and symptoms of autonomic dysfunction (dry eyes and mouth, orthostatic hypotension, and bowel and bladder dysfunction).

**KEY POINT**
- **Thymomas may be associated with a paraneoplastic syndrome such as myasthenia gravis.**

**Bibliography**
Duwe BV, Sterman DH, Musani AI. Tumors of the mediastinum. Chest. 2005;128(4):2893-2909. [PMID: 16236967]

## Item 26    Answer: D
**Educational Objective:**  Recognize and treat malignant hyperthermia.

This patient likely has malignant hyperthermia, an inherited skeletal muscle disorder characterized by a hypermetabolic state precipitated by exposure to volatile inhalational anesthetics (halothane, isoflurane, enflurane, desflurane, sevoflurane) and the depolarizing muscle relaxants succinylcholine and decamethonium. Although malignant hyperthermia usually occurs at the time of exposure intraoperatively, it can occur several hours after the initial exposure and can develop in patients who were previously exposed to the drug

without any effect. Increased intracellular calcium leads to sustained muscle contractions with skeletal muscle rigidity and masseter spasm, tachycardia, hypercarbia, hypertension, hyperthermia, tachypnea, and cardiac arrhythmias.

Malignant hyperthermia is life-threatening unless treated promptly and aggressively. Supportive measures include hydration and decreasing the fever. Dantrolene, a skeletal muscle relaxant, is given as a bolus of 1 mg/kg intravenously and then 2 mg/kg every 5 to 10 minutes until the symptoms resolve. Response to dantrolene is not diagnostic of the disorder but is supportive if signs and symptoms resolve quickly. For those patients with a known history, pretreatment with dantrolene before the anesthetic agent is administered prevents the development of symptoms.

Alcohol sponge baths are generally not recommended as an augmentation of evaporative cooling in any hyperthermic patient, including malignant hyperthermia, owing to the possibility of substantial alcohol absorption through the skin. Furthermore, augmented cooling (typically accomplished with water misting and forced air circulation by fans) may result in shivering which can increase body temperature unless it is suppressed with benzodiazepine administration. Ampicillin-sulbactam might be a consideration if acute ascending cholangitis were suspected; however, this is unlikely only hours after an elective cholecystectomy. Furthermore, an infection cannot account for the patient's muscular rigidity. Corticosteroids would be effective treatment for an allergic reaction, but there are no symptoms suggesting an allergic reaction such as rash, urticaria, angioedema, or wheezing. Sodium nitroprusside is indicated in patients with hypertensive emergencies. However, this patient's blood pressure is elevated secondary to malignant hyperthermia, and treatment of the underlying disorder is the preferred therapy.

**KEY POINT**
- **Malignant hyperthermia is a life-threatening skeletal muscle disorder characterized by a hypermetabolic state precipitated by exposure to volatile inhalational anesthetics or depolarizing muscle relaxants.**

**Bibliography**
Hopkins PM. Malignant hyperthermia: advances in clinical management and diagnosis [erratum in Br J Anaesth 2001;86(4):605]. Brit J Anaesth. 2000;85(1):118-128. [PMID: 10928000]

## Item 27    Answer: D
**Educational Objective:**  Recognize indications for methacholine challenge testing in cases of suspected asthma.

This patient's history is consistent with, but not typical of, asthma. This presentation is sometimes referred to as cough-variant asthma. Asthma is often an episodic disease, with normal examination findings and spirometry between episodes. In such cases, a bronchial challenge test, such as with methacholine, can induce bronchoconstriction even when the patient is asymptomatic and spirometry is normal. Methacholine challenge testing is done by giving the patient increasing concentrations of methacholine by nebulization and performing spirometry after each dose until there is a greater than 20% decrease in $FEV_1$ from baseline. The methacholine dose that leads to a 20% decrease in the $FEV_1$ is known as the provocative concentration 20 ($PC_{20}$) and is calculated from a dose-response curve. In general, a $PC_{20}$ of less than 4 mg/mL is consistent with asthma. A $PC_{20}$ between 4 and 16 mg/mL suggests some bronchial hyperreactivity and is less specific for asthma. A $PC_{20}$ above 16 mg/mL is considered normal. The sensitivity of a positive methacholine challenge test in asthma is in the range of 85% to 95%. False-positive results can occur in patients with allergic rhinitis, chronic obstructive pulmonary disease, heart failure, cystic fibrosis, or bronchitis.

Bronchoscopy to evaluate the trachea could be helpful if an anatomic lesion is suspected. However, the symptoms in patients with such lesions are persistent or progressive rather than intermittent. Since this patient has intermittent symptoms, bronchoscopy is not indicated. Exercise echocardiography could help determine the presence of cardiac ischemia or myocardial dysfunction, the typical symptoms of which are dyspnea on exertion, chest tightness, or pain. Cough and wheezing can occur in coronary artery disease, particularly when associated with acute decompensation of the left ventricle, but this patient's intermittent episodes of cough and wheezing are provoked by an upper respiratory tract infection, making the diagnosis of coronary artery disease unlikely. Patients with rhinosinusitis have symptoms consisting of nasal congestion, purulent nasal secretions, sinus tenderness, and facial pain. Radiography, including sinus CT scan, is not indicated in the initial evaluation of acute sinusitis.

**KEY POINT**

- Methacholine challenge testing is most useful in evaluating patients with suspected asthma who have episodic symptoms and normal baseline spirometry.

**Bibliography**

Dicpinigaitis PV. Chronic cough due to asthma: ACCP evidence-based clinical practice guidelines. Chest. 2006;129(1 Suppl):75S-79S. [PMID: 16428696]

## Item 28    Answer:  A

**Educational Objective:** Recognize the role of inhaled corticosteroids in severe chronic obstructive pulmonary disease.

Regular use of inhaled corticosteroids in patients with chronic obstructive pulmonary disease (COPD) is associated with a reduction in the rate of exacerbations from 1.3 to 0.9 per year, and patients who have frequent exacerbations with more severe COPD benefit most. In six placebo-controlled trials in 1741 patients over 6 months, inhaled corticosteroids reduced exacerbations by 24%. Therefore, the GOLD guidelines recommend consideration of inhaled corticosteroids in patients whose lung function is less than 50% and those who have exacerbations. When inhaled corticosteroids are combined with a long-acting $\beta_2$-agonist, the rate of decline in quality of life and health status is significantly reduced and acute exacerbations are reduced by 25%; lung function is also improved and dyspnea is alleviated. There does not appear to be a dose response to inhaled corticosteroids in COPD, and the effects of combination therapy on mortality are uncertain.

Anticholinergic agents in COPD are especially useful when combined with short-acting or long-acting $\beta_2$-agonists. Tiotropium is effective in patients with stable COPD for up to 24 hours and should not be combined with short-acting anticholinergic agents, such as ipratropium. Mucolytic agents have little effect on lung function. The antioxidant *N*-acetylcysteine, a drug with both mucolytic and antioxidant action, did not reduce the number of exacerbations of COPD in a large prospective 3-year trial. Oral corticosteroids are not recommended for regular use in a long-term maintenance program because their use is not associated with superior outcomes compared with standard therapy and is associated with increased side effects.

**KEY POINT**

- Inhaled corticosteroids may offer significant benefit in patients with severe chronic obstructive pulmonary disease, with the benefit generally greater when an inhaled corticosteroid is combined with a long-acting $\beta_2$-agonist.

**Bibliography**

Celli BR. Update on the management of COPD [erratum in Chest. 2008;134(4):892]. Chest. 2008;133(6):1451-1462. [PMID: 18574288]

## Item 29    Answer:  C

**Educational Objective:** Manage a pulmonary nodule that is negative on CT enhancement study.

The attenuation coefficient of a pulmonary nodule is a measure of its density and is expressed in Hounsfield units. Enhancement after contrast reflects nodule vascularity and is an indicator of malignancy or active inflammation. A nodule that shows less than 15 Hounsfield units of enhancement on dynamic contrast study is highly likely to be benign; a multicenter study showed a 97% negative predictive value at a cutoff of 15 Hounsfield units.

Reevaluation of the nodule at 3 months would be appropriate given the low likelihood that this is a malignant nodule. Immediate evaluation with biopsy or surgical removal can be avoided because of the low likelihood that this is a malignant nodule. Lack of enhancement is not the same as a tissue diagnosis, and follow-up is appropriate whether or not the patient has risk factors for lung cancer.

**KEY POINT**

- **A nodule that is nonenhancing on dynamic CT contrast study is likely benign, and observation is appropriate.**

**Bibliography**

Gould MK, Fletcher J, Iannettoni MD, et al; American College of Chest Physicians. Evaluation of patients with pulmonary nodules: when is it lung cancer?: ACCP evidence-based clinical practice guidelines (2nd edition). Chest. 2007;132(3 Suppl):108S-130S. [PMID: 17873164]

## Item 30    Answer:  D

**Educational Objective:** Manage a patient on mechanical ventilation who fails a trial of extubation.

This patient has acute hypoxemic ventilatory failure and should be electively reintubated. The respiratory examination, large supplemental oxygen needs, and rising $P_{CO_2}$ suggest that he is at high risk for respiratory arrest. The most likely explanation for his failing a trial of extubation is insufficient recovery from his initial lung injury. Residual elevated dead space and poor lung compliance, coupled with loss of positive end-expiratory pressure after extubation, account for his deterioration in gas exchange.

Furosemide would not be indicated because there is little to suggest new-onset heart failure. Increasing supplemental oxygen is unlikely to reduce the patient's work of breathing or reverse the upward trend in $P_{CO_2}$. Shunt is the primary cause of hypoxemia in patients with the acute respiratory distress syndrome (ARDS), and placing the patient on 100% oxygen will likely only modestly improve hypoxemia.

Noninvasive positive-pressure ventilation (NPPV) may prevent postextubation respiratory failure if initiated immediately after extubation. Recent randomized studies have found no benefit, or even increased mortality, with the use of NPPV for patients failing a trial of extubation. Also, routine use of NPPV in patients with ARDS is not recommended.

The patient is alert and making vigorous respiratory efforts. Therefore, respiratory failure is unlikely to be the result of excessive sedation, and a trial of naloxone is unlikely to be efficacious.

**KEY POINT**

- **Noninvasive positive-pressure ventilation is potentially harmful in patients with hypoxemic respiratory failure who are failing a trial of extubation.**

**Bibliography**

Esteban A, Frutos-Vivar F, Ferguson ND, et al. Noninvasive positive-pressure ventilation for respiratory failure after extubation. N Engl J Med. 2004;350(24):2452-2460. [PMID: 15190137]

## Item 31    Answer:  D

**Educational Objective:** Evaluate pulmonary hypertension.

The patient's progressive dyspnea, hemodynamic symptoms during exercise, and physical findings suggest right ventricular dysfunction and pulmonary hypertension. Transthoracic echocardiography can confirm the presence of pulmonary hypertension and right ventricular dysfunction. Echocardiography is also useful to rule out left-sided heart disease and congenital heart disease as a cause of pulmonary hypertension. A ventilation/perfusion scan can also rule out potential causes. Typically, the ventilation/perfusion scan in pulmonary arterial hypertension is either normal or shows a scattered, "moth-eaten" perfusion pattern in the peripheral lung zones.

The patient has no evidence of bronchospasm. Exercise-induced asthma is unlikely because the symptoms begin immediately during mild exertion and subside rapidly upon rest. Furthermore, exercise-induced bronchospasm cannot explain the patient's clinical findings of pulmonary hypertension. Therefore, a methacholine challenge test is not indicated. Right-heart catheterization and pulmonary angiography might be necessary to confirm the diagnosis of pulmonary arterial hypertension but are not indicated before less invasive screening tests for pulmonary hypertension are done. Bronchoscopy and transbronchial lung biopsy may be indicated in patients with diffuse parenchymal lung disease, but this patient's chest radiograph is normal, making parenchymal lung disease unlikely.

**KEY POINT**

- **In patients with suspected pulmonary hypertension, transthoracic echocardiography can suggest the presence of pulmonary hypertension and evaluate cardiac causes of elevated pulmonary artery pressure.**

**Bibliography**

McGoon M, Gutterman D, Steen V, et al. Screening, early detection, and diagnosis of pulmonary arterial hypertension: ACCP evidence-based clinical practice guidelines. Chest. 2004;126(1 Suppl):14S-34S. [PMID: 15249493]

## Item 32    Answer:  D

**Educational Objective:** Manage excessive daytime sleepiness caused by insufficient sleep.

Evaluation of excessive daytime sleepiness consists of a careful history with inquiries into sleep duration and quality, daytime consequences of sleepiness, medical disorders, and medication or substance use.

Inadequate sleep duration is the most common cause of excessive daytime sleepiness and it can cause sleep paralysis. Sleep paralysis is a complete inability to move for 1 or 2 minutes immediately after awakening. Although sleep paralysis is one of the clinical characteristics of narcolepsy, it can occur in other conditions, including sleep deprivation. Although the adequate duration of sleep varies, most persons require about 8 hours of sleep each night. Patients with sleep deprivation generally describe a habitual sleep duration that is shorter than normal for most age-matched persons, and there may be a significant difference in nighttime sleep duration during weekends, with a longer "rescue" sleep. A trial of longer nighttime sleep duration is often all that is necessary to improve excessive daytime sleepiness.

Thyroid disease can cause central sleep apnea, which is more common in older persons and is very unlikely in this young man. Therefore, thyroid function tests would be unlikely to help in the management of his daytime sleepiness. Stimulant agents, such as modafinil, should not be used as a substitute for getting sufficient sleep. Sleep latency is the duration from getting into bed to the onset of sleep and is an objective measure of sleepiness. Polysomnography involves the measurement of several physiologic variables during sleep and is useful in the evaluation of excessive sleepiness. Neither polysomnography nor a multiple sleep latency test is required for the diagnosis of insufficient sleep syndrome.

**KEY POINT**

- Excessive daytime sleepiness is defined by a persistent or recurrent inability to both achieve and sustain alertness required to accomplish the tasks of daily living and is most commonly secondary to insufficient sleep.

**Bibliography**
Franzen PL, Siegle GJ, Buysse DJ. Relationships between affect, vigilance, and sleepiness following sleep deprivation. J Sleep Res. 2008;17(1):34-41. [PMID: 18275553]

## Item 33     Answer:  B

**Educational Objective:** Recognize poor inhaler technique as a possible cause of medication failure in asthma.

The best initial management approach for this patient is to have him demonstrate his inhaler technique. Patient education is a key component in asthma care. Studies have shown that patient education by the physician decreases the number of visits to the emergency department and improves asthma control. Improper technique in the use of inhalers is a major reason that patients do not respond well to medications. A clue suggesting poor inhaler technique includes the patient's rapid improvement in $FEV_1$ after the supervised use of a bronchodilator. Although there used to be one type of inhalation device (the metered-dose inhaler) with one technique that could be taught to the patient, there are now several new and different devices with significant differences in the technique needed for their use. Physicians should learn the proper technique for use of these inhalers before prescribing them to patients in order

to ensure proper technique to optimize drug delivery and effectiveness and to reduce side effects.

Adding a leukotriene modifying agent would be appropriate if the patient is effectively using the current medications. Oral prednisone would be appropriate for an exacerbation of poorly controlled severe persistent asthma. It would improve asthma control, but without proper education in the use of the inhaler, symptoms would most likely return when the corticosteroid dosage is tapered. Furthermore, oral corticosteroids have increased adverse effects. Simply having the patient return with a symptom and treatment log would not be expected to identify poor inhaler technique, although it would be helpful to assess compliance and symptom pattern.

**KEY POINT**

- Poor inhaler technique is a major reason why patients with asthma do not respond well to specific asthma therapy.

**Bibliography**
National Asthma Education and Prevention Program. Expert Panel Report 3 (EPR-3): Guidelines for the Diagnosis and Management of Asthma-Summary Report 2007 [erratum in J Allergy Clin Immunol. 2008;121(6):1330]. J Allergy Clin Immunol. 2007;120 (5 Suppl):S94-138. [PMID: 17983880]

## Item 34     Answer:  A

**Educational Objective:** Diagnose acute eosinophilic pneumonia.

This patient's dramatic presentation is typical of acute eosinophilic pneumonia, which must be differentiated from other causes of idiopathic acute respiratory distress syndrome. Treatment of respiratory failure due to acute eosinophilic pneumonia with intravenous corticosteroids is efficacious, with clinical improvement over 12 to 24 hours. If a patient does not respond to corticosteroid therapy, another diagnosis should be considered. Acute eosinophilic pneumonia is idiopathic, but it has been associated with inhaled environmental antigens. Recently, initiation of cigarette smoking has been linked to acute eosinophilic pneumonia in a Japanese population and in military recruits.

This patient does not have asthma or evidence of systemic vasculitis, making Churg-Strauss syndrome unlikely. Acute interstitial pneumonia, which occurs over 1 to 3 weeks, progresses to hypoxemic respiratory failure and is associated with fever, nonproductive cough, headache, myalgia, and a flu-like malaise. Chest radiograph shows diffuse, bilateral air-space infiltrates. Pathologically, a pattern of organizing diffuse alveolar damage is seen. Treatment is usually supportive, with intravenous pulse corticosteroids frequently used but of unproven benefit. Idiopathic acute interstitial pneumonia is a diagnosis of exclusion and would not be appropriate for this patient with eosinophilic pneumonia. *Mycoplasma* pneumonia may be culture-negative and present with respiratory symptoms. However, these symptoms rarely progress to respiratory failure and would not explain this patient's eosinophilia.

- Acute eosinophilic pneumonia may present as hypoxemic respiratory failure after 1 to 2 weeks of low-grade fever and systemic symptoms.

**Bibliography**

Uchiyama H, Suda T, Nakamura Y, et al. Alterations in smoking habits are associated with acute eosinophilic pneumonia. Chest. 2008;133(5):1174-1180. [PMID: 18263675]

## Item 35     Answer: B

**Educational Objective:** Treat pulmonary embolism.

The patient has an acute pulmonary embolism. In the absence of contraindications, the patient should be treated initially with intravenous or subcutaneous unfractionated heparin, low-molecular-weight heparin, or fondaparinux. Electrocardiographic abnormalities are present in 70% of patients with pulmonary embolism. Most common abnormalities are ST segment and T wave changes (49%). Cor pulmonale, right axis deviation, right bundle branch block, and right ventricular hypertrophy occur less frequently. T wave inversions in precordial leads may indicate more severe right ventricular dysfunction. This patient's electrocardiographic findings support the diagnosis of left ventricular hypertrophy/strain, most likely because of his essential hypertension.

Patients with hemodynamically unstable pulmonary embolism have a high mortality rate. The role of thrombolytic agents in pulmonary embolism is unclear. There are no clinical trials comparing thrombolytic agents with other forms of therapy for massive pulmonary embolism, and management decisions must therefore be made by inference from studies in stable patients. The Urokinase in Pulmonary Embolism Trial reported a short-term improvement in cardiac output and pulmonary pressure with thrombolytic therapy but no improvement in morbidity or mortality and increased bleeding. Acute pulmonary embolectomy is rarely warranted because medical therapy is successful, patient selection difficult, and the results of acute embolectomy unimpressive. However, if experienced surgical intervention is possible, embolectomy may be considered for a confirmed, massive embolism that fails to respond promptly to medical therapy. Mechanical clot dissolution has been performed in a small number of patients in cardiogenic shock secondary to massive pulmonary embolism. The mortality rate is high, and this intervention is not readily available in most institutions.

Placement of an inferior vena cava filter might be considered in a patient with a contraindication to anticoagulation, the onset of clinically important bleeding during anticoagulation, recurrent pulmonary embolism despite adequate anticoagulation, or in hemodynamically unstable patients.

- Unfractionated heparin, low-molecular-weight heparin, or fondaparinux is generally sufficient initial therapy for acute pulmonary embolism.

**Bibliography**

Kearon G, Kahn SR, Agnelli G, et al. Antithrombotic therapy for venous thrombolic disease : American College of Chest Physicians Evidence-Based Clinical Practice Guidelines (8th Edition). Chest. 2008;133(6 suppl):454S-545S. [PMID: 18574272]

## Item 36     Answer: B

**Educational Objective:** Evaluate an oxygen-dependent patient with obstructive lung disease before air travel.

Air travel is generally safe for patients with stable chronic respiratory disorders but can pose significant hazards for those who require continuous oxygen therapy for hypoxemia. Cabin air pressure for most commercial airplanes is maintained at about 4500 to 8000 ft above sea level, but the pressure can change significantly from flight to flight and from one airplane model to another. At a cabin pressure equivalent to 8000 ft above sea level, $P_{O_2}$ is expected to fall, potentially leading to hypoxemia and cardiac events in persons who require supplemental oxygen for hypoxemia. Therefore, using the same level of oxygen supplementation used at sea level may be inappropriate for many patients. Additional supplemental oxygen is recommended for patients whose predicted $P_{O_2}$ during flight is less than 50 to 55 mm Hg or oxygen saturation less than 85%.

In-flight $P_{O_2}$ can be predicted using published algorithms or determined by performing a hypoxia inhalation test. Prediction algorithms may fail to identify patients who will develop significant hypoxemia during air travel and, unlike the hypoxia inhalation test, cannot predict the development of cardiac events related to low oxygen levels. Simply increasing the level of oxygen supplementation runs the risk of underestimating the required oxygen demands during flight. The hypoxia inhalation test involves placing the patient in either a hypobaric chamber or having the patient breath a 15% oxygen mixture at sea level for at least 15 minutes with continuous pulse oximetry and electrocardiographic monitoring.

- Patients who require continuous oxygen therapy owing to chronic respiratory or cardiovascular disorders may not tolerate commercial air travel and should be assessed for the need for possible additional in-flight supplemental oxygen.

**Bibliography**

Seccombe LM, Peters MJ. Oxygen supplementation for chronic obstructive pulmonary disease patients during air travel. Curr Opin Pulm Med. 2006;12(2):140-144. [PMID: 16456384]

## Item 37     Answer: C
**Educational Objective:** Evaluate a patient for occupational asthma.

This patient likely has isocyanate-induced asthma caused by exposure to isocyanate-containing automobile paints. The most helpful piece of information to support the diagnosis of occupational asthma in this patient is an occupational history that substantiates direct or bystander exposure to isocyanate-containing paints with associated symptoms development. Although this man's job title may suggest such exposure, it is important to review the patient's daily job tasks to ascertain whether he is actually at risk for direct or bystander exposure to an isocyanate-containing product.

The significant reversible airflow limitation on spirometry in this patient is already compatible with a diagnosis of asthma, and a confirmatory methacholine challenge test is not necessary and potentially dangerous by provoking bronchospasm. CT scan of the chest would be indicated in a patient with possible parenchymal disease; this patient has obstructive airways disease. Skin prick testing to common aeroallergens would determine whether the patient is atopic; however, atopy is not a risk factor for the development of asthma from exposure to low-molecular-weight substances such as isocyanates. Review of Material Safety Data Sheets from the patient's workplace can be important in establishing a diagnosis of work-related illness, but only when reviewed with a clear understanding of what the patient does and to which products he is exposed.

### KEY POINT
- Reviewing a patient's occupational exposures, the job process and tasks, and substances involved in the patient's activities is necessary for an evaluation for possible occupational asthma.

**Bibliography**
Tarlo SM, Balmes J, Balkissoon R, et al. Diagnosis and management of work-related asthma: American College Of Chest Physicians Consensus Statement [erratum in Chest. 2008;134(4):892]. Chest. 2008;134(3 Suppl):1S-41S. [PMID: 18779187]

## Item 38     Answer: B
**Educational Objective:** Manage severe auto-positive end-expiratory pressure.

The patient's hypotension is the result of severe auto-positive end-expiratory pressure (PEEP). Patients with severe airflow obstruction are particularly vulnerable to developing auto-PEEP when receiving mechanical ventilation or bag-mask ventilation. This patient's high set respiration rate and tidal volume do not allow sufficient time for complete expiration before the next breath is delivered. The resulting elevation in intrathoracic pressure impairs venous return to the right heart and increases pulmonary vascular resistance, thereby reducing cardiac output and producing hypotension. Briefly disconnecting the patient from the ventilator allows for complete expiration, reduction in auto-PEEP, and recovery of cardiac output. The use of low tidal volumes and rates may result in acute respiratory acidosis, but this poses a lower risk to the patient than sustained severe auto-PEEP. This ventilator strategy is known as *permissive hypercapnia*.

The elevated airway pressures associated with auto-PEEP can also cause tension pneumothorax. However, the presence of bilateral breath sounds and absence of pneumothorax on chest radiograph effectively rule out tension pneumothorax. Therefore, inserting chest tubes would not be appropriate.

Cardiac tamponade and massive pulmonary embolism would be much less likely than severe auto-PEEP in a patient with severe airflow obstruction receiving mechanical ventilation with these ventilator settings. Therefore, thrombolysis and pericardiocentesis are not appropriate in this patient.

### KEY POINT
- Auto-positive end-expiratory pressure is relieved by allowing sufficient time for full expiration and aggressive treatment of airflow obstruction.

**Bibliography**
Blanch L, Bernabe F, Lucangelo U. Measurement of air trapping, intrinsic positive end-expiratory pressure, dynamic hyperinflation in mechanically ventilated patients. Respir Care. 2005;50[1]:110-123. [PMID: 15636649]

## Item 39     Answer: D
**Educational Objective:** Evaluate a solitary pulmonary nodule.

Evaluation of a pulmonary nodule should always begin by review of any previous images. The CT scan of the abdomen may show that the nodule was present but missed: evidence of growth would indicate a high likelihood of malignancy; evidence of shrinkage would indicate a high likelihood of a benign lesion. If the nodule was not present or not included on the previous CT images, CT chest evaluation is appropriate, and if a dynamic CT enhancement study shows no significant enhancement, then the nodule is likely benign.

18F-fluorodeoxyglucose positron emission tomography (FDG-PET) is generally done after CT of the chest. Lung cancers are metabolically active and take up FDG avidly, whereas benign pulmonary nodules do not. FDG-PET is most helpful in patients with a nodule 1 cm or larger and an intermediate probability of malignancy. MRI has a limited role in the evaluation of a pulmonary nodule; it is more expensive than CT, and CT can diagnose and stage lung cancer in a single examination. This patient is at significant risk for lung cancer because of his smoking history and the size of the nodule; therefore, more information to suggest it is benign (such as its presence unchanged on the old film, no enhancement on dynamic CT, or negative FDG-PET) would be desired before choosing to follow-up with

CT in 3 months. If the nodule shows significant uptake on FDG-PET, CT-guided biopsy or removal should be done.

**KEY POINT**

- Evaluation of a pulmonary nodule always begins by reviewing prior pertinent imaging studies.

**Bibliography**

Gould MK, Fletcher J, Iannettoni MD, et al; American College of Chest Physicians. Evaluation of patients with pulmonary nodules: when is it lung cancer?: ACCP evidence-based clinical practice guidelines (2nd edition). Chest.2007;132(3 Suppl):108S-130S. [PMID: 17873164]

## Item 40    Answer:   A

**Educational Objective:**  Manage a patient with a malignant pleural effusion and lung entrapment.

The development of severe, anterior chest pain during therapeutic thoracentesis is virtually diagnostic of an unexpandable lung with the development of significant negative intrapleural pressure. The anterior chest pain is quickly relieved by allowing air entry into the pleural space through the thoracentesis needle or catheter. In this situation, the patient is best managed with an indwelling catheter. The patient and his family are instructed to drain the pleural fluid when breathlessness ensues and to discontinue drainage immediately when anterior chest pain develops.

This patient has two distinct pathophysiologic causes of his pleural effusion: (1) fluid produced by the malignant involvement of the pleura primarily due to increased levels of vascular endothelial growth factor and (2) an unexpandable lung due to tumor involvement of the visceral pleura. Therefore, an indwelling catheter removes the "malignant fluid," and when this volume of fluid has been removed, further fluid removal (due to the unexpandable lung) results in a significant decrease in pleural pressure causing anterior chest pain. Talc pleurodesis will not be completely effective because all of the lung cannot expand to the chest wall to promote pleurodesis. A surgical procedure in a patient with advanced malignancy would not be the appropriate initial treatment, and furthermore, pleural abrasion would not promote effective pleurodesis with an unexpandable lung, which would require a decortication that would not be appropriate for this patient. Outpatient thoracentesis could be appropriate; however, it requires frequent trips to the hospital or clinic, which might be problematic for some patients. Radiation therapy is not indicated for lung entrapment from adenocarcinoma.

**KEY POINT**

- The development of severe, anterior chest pain during therapeutic thoracentesis is virtually diagnostic of an unexpandable lung with the development of significant negative intrapleural pressure.

**Bibliography**

Huggins JT, Sahn SA, Heidecker J, Ravenel J, Doelken P. Characteristics of trapped lung: pleural fluid analysis, manometry. and air

contrast chest computed tomography. Chest. 2007;131(1):206-213. [PMID: 17218577]

## Item 41    Answer:   A

**Educational Objective:**  Diagnose cyanide toxicity from sodium nitroprusside therapy.

Cyanide may cause toxicity through parenteral administration, smoke inhalation, oral ingestion, or dermal absorption. Sodium nitroprusside, when used in high doses or over a period of days, can produce toxic blood concentrations of cyanide. In most patients, cyanide release from sodium nitroprusside is slow enough that the body's innate detoxification mechanisms can eliminate the cyanide before it interferes with cellular respiration. However, patients with low thiosulfate reserves (for example, malnourished or postoperative patients) are at increased risk for developing symptoms, even with therapeutic dosing.

A severe anion gap metabolic acidosis, combined with a reduced arterial-venous oxygen gradient (less than 10 mm Hg due to venous hyperoxia), suggests the diagnosis of cyanide toxicity. Apnea may result in a combined metabolic and respiratory acidosis. The treatment of cyanide poisoning is empiric because laboratory confirmation can take hours or days. Treatment includes administration of both sodium thiosulfate and hydroxocobalamin.

Hepatic encephalopathy can cause confusion, respiratory alkalosis, and mild hypoxemia. Hypoxic-ischemic encephalopathy typically follows an obvious anoxic event such as cardiac arrest or drowning. This patient has no history of such a precipitating event. Wernicke encephalopathy is defined by confusion, ataxia, and ophthalmoplegia, but the full triad of findings is frequently absent. The first symptoms of alcohol withdrawal occur within 6 hours of the last drink and include tremors, diaphoresis, anxiety, headache, and gastrointestinal upset. None of these conditions are associated with an anion gap metabolic acidosis and a reduced arterial-venous oxygen gradient and are therefore unlikely causes of the patient's findings.

**KEY POINT**

- Sodium nitroprusside when used in high doses or over a period of days can produce toxic blood concentrations of cyanide.

**Bibliography**

Robin ED, McCauley R. Nitroprusside-related cyanide toxicity. Chest. 1992;102(6):1842-1845. [PMID: 1446499]

## Item 42    Answer:   B

**Educational Objective:**  Treat $\alpha_1$-antitrypsin deficiency.

$\alpha_1$-Antitrypsin (AAT) deficiency is associated with early-onset pulmonary emphysema, liver disease, and, rarely, skin disease. In suitable candidates, intravenous infusion of pooled human AAT is the most direct and efficient method of elevating AAT levels in plasma and lung interstitium.

Augmentation therapy is most effective in patients with an $FEV_1$ 35% to 60% of predicted and an $FEV_1/FVC$ ratio 30% to 65%. The selection criteria include:

- High-risk phenotype (Pi*Z [protease inhibitor Z])
- Plasma AAT levels below 50 to 80 mg/dL (0.5-0.8 g/L)
- Nonsmoker or ex-smoker
- Likely adherence to the protocol
- Airflow obstruction with spirometry
- Age at least 18 years

Estimated mean annual cost for patients receiving therapy is $40,000. Efficacy data are derived from observational (not randomized, controlled) trials that suggest that therapy retards the rate of $FEV_1$ decline. Pending further studies, expert groups recommend augmentation therapy for properly selected individuals. Aerosolized AAT augmentation is being studied and has many potential advantages compared with intravenous therapy. Augmentation therapy is not, however, recommended for patients without emphysema.

Lung transplantation is an option for patients with severe end-stage disease but is not indicated in this mildly symptomatic patient.

Certain hormonal drugs, such as danazol, tamoxifen, and progesterone, have been found to augment endogenous production of AAT. However, these drugs have had very limited success in increasing AAT levels to the point of having a clinical effect and are inferior to exogenous augmentation with AAT. The National Emphysema Therapeutic Trial of lung volume reduction surgery reported mixed results for patients with emphysema. Overall, lung volume reduction surgery appears to alleviate dyspnea and increase exercise capacity, lung function, and quality of life. Survival appears to be improved only in patients with upper lobe–predominant emphysema and low exercise capacity.

**KEY POINT**

- Intravenous augmentation therapy with an $\alpha_1$-antitrypsin (AAT) is the most direct and efficient means of elevating AAT levels in plasma and lung interstitium.

**Bibliography**

American Thoracic Society; European Respiratory Society. American Thoracic Society/European Respiratory Society Standards for the diagnosis and Management of Individuals with Alpha 1 Antitryspin Deficiency. Am J Respir Crit Care Med. 2003;168(7):818-900. [PMID: 14522813]

## Item 43    Answer:  C

**Educational Objective:** Recognize the importance of arterial blood gases in evaluating patients in status asthmaticus.

This patient is in status asthmaticus. She has not responded well to bronchodilator therapy and is at risk for respiratory failure. Pulse oximetry is a good screening and monitoring tool but is not a substitute for measuring blood gases. Oximetry would be in a normal range even when $Po_2$ has declined significantly because of the sigmoid shape of the oxygen dissociation curve, where the hemoglobin saturation reaches a flat part of the curve at $Po_2$ levels higher than 60 mm Hg. Measuring blood gases is essential to evaluate her ventilation and to direct management because decreased alveolar ventilation may not be reflected on pulse oximetry, particularly in patients receiving supplemental oxygen. In mild acute asthma exacerbations, the $Pco_2$ is decreased. With increasing severity of the attack, $Pco_2$ increases and reaches normal levels in moderate to severe attacks. Elevated $Pco_2$ is an ominous sign, indicating severe obstruction and risk of respiratory arrest.

A chest radiograph would be expected to show hyperinflation in acute severe asthma and can be very helpful to exclude other diagnoses or evaluate complications (for example, pneumothorax, atelectasis). After blood gases have been measured, a chest radiograph is the next most important step in evaluating this patient. Complete blood count with differential is not expected to change the management in most patients with acute asthma. Electrocardiography is likely to show sinus tachycardia and would not be expected to help in the management of this patient. Peak expiratory flow rate is unlikely to add useful information beyond what is gained from spirometry.

**KEY POINT**

- In patients in status asthmaticus, pulse oximetry is a good monitoring tool but is not a substitute for determining actual oxygenation by measuring arterial blood gases.

**Bibliography**

Shapiro JM. Management of respiratory failure in status asthmaticus. Am J Respir Med. 2002;1(6):409-416. [PMID: 14720028]

## Item 44    Answer:  A

**Educational Objective:** Manage a patient with severe sepsis.

Activated protein C (drotrecogin alfa activated) is a time-sensitive intervention that can improve survival in patients with severe sepsis at high risk of death. Improved survival has been demonstrated in patients with severe sepsis who have an APACHE score of 25 or greater. Patients with either a single failing organ system or an APACHE score less than 25 do not appear to benefit and are at risk of bleeding complications. Although activated protein C is an anticoagulant, when administered to patients with a platelet count between 30,000/µL (30 × 10⁹/L) and 50,000/µL (50 × 10⁹/L), there was a relative risk reduction in mortality of more than 30% in the Phase III PROWESS trial. Platelet counts below 30,000/µL are considered a relative contraindication. The patient is more than 12 hours out of surgery, with no ongoing active bleeding, a platelet count of 42,000/µL ($42 \times 10^9$/L), and a high risk of death; therefore, activated protein C is an excellent consideration.

Hyperglycemia is associated with poor clinical outcomes in critically ill patients. However, the benefit of tight glycemic control (≤110 mg/dL [6.1 mmol/L]) is controversial in critically ill postsurgical patients, and no benefit has been shown in critically ill medical patients.

Vasopressors are part of early goal-directed therapy if the mean arterial pressure is less than 65 mm Hg after initial adequate fluid resuscitation. The most commonly used vasopressor for septic shock is norepinephrine, a potent peripheral vasoconstrictor that reverses the endotoxin-induced vasodilation that is the hallmark of septic shock. Dopamine is also acceptable but is associated with more tachycardia and arrhythmia. Low-dose dopamine, however, is not indicated. A randomized controlled trial showed that there is no benefit from "renal doses" of dopamine on renal or other clinical outcomes in early renal dysfunction.

The goals of fluid resuscitation are a central venous pressure of 8 to 12 mm Hg, mean arterial pressure greater than 65 mm Hg, urine output greater than 0.5 mL/kg/h, and central venous oxygen saturation greater than 70%. Randomized controlled trials have shown no benefit to the use of colloid compared with crystalloid fluids.

**KEY POINT**

- Activated protein C has been shown to improve survival in patients with severe sepsis with an APACHE score of 25 or greater.

**Bibliography**

Bernard GR, Vincent JL, Laterre PF, et al; Recombinant human protein C Worldwide Evaluation in Severe Sepsis (PROWESS) study group. Efficacy and safety of recombinant human activated protein C for severe sepsis. N Eng J Med. 2001;344(10):699-709. [PMID: 11236773]

## Item 45    Answer:  C

**Educational Objective:** Recognize and treat anaphylactic shock.

Systemic allergic reactions are usually of acute onset and can involve multiple organ systems. Death may occur from refractory bronchospasm, respiratory failure with upper airway obstruction, and cardiovascular collapse. The pathogenesis consists of an IgE-mediated hypersensitivity reaction. The most common causes are foods, insect venoms, latex, and medications. Common skin manifestations include flushing, pruritus, urticaria, and angioedema. However, 10% to 20% of patients do not have cutaneous signs, and up to 80% of patients with food-induced anaphylactic reactions do not have any skin changes.

An "ABCD" approach is recommended including:

- Airway: Evaluate for airway compromise and consider endotracheal intubation or emergent cricothyroidotomy; oxygen
- Bronchospasm: Epinephrine intramuscular or subcutaneous (0.3-0.5 mL of 1:1000 solution); inhaled β-agonists
- Circulatory collapse: Aggressive fluid resuscitation; continuous epinephrine infusion; vasopressor infusion
- Drugs: Antihistamines; $H_1$-antagonist; $H_2$-antagonist; corticosteroids

This patient likely had an anaphylactic reaction to latex, which is contained in gloves, drains, and catheters. Repeated exposure leads to a higher risk of anaphylaxis. Reactions to latex can vary from mild with irritant contact dermatitis to an acute hypersensitivity reaction. Patients with a known latex allergy should wear a MedicAlert® bracelet and have an epinephrine auto-injector (EpiPen®) quickly accessible. All patients with moderate to severe symptoms regardless of the inciting agent should be closely monitored for at least 12 hours in the hospital, preferably in the intensive care unit for a possible late recurrence. Most patients who receive epinephrine therapy will not require intubation or an emergent cricothyroidotomy. Glucagon is not indicated in the treatment of anaphylaxis unless the patient is taking a β-blocker and is not responding to first-line treatment.

**KEY POINT**

- The most common causes of anaphylaxis are foods, insect venoms, latex, and medications.

**Bibliography**

Johnson RF, Peebles S. Anaphylactic shock: pathophysiology, recognition, and treatment. Semin Respir Crit Care Med. 2004;25(6): 695-703. [PMID: 16088511]

## Item 46    Answer:  C

**Educational Objective:** Diagnose lymphangioleiomyomatosis.

This patient presents with subacute respiratory complaints and high-resolution CT findings of diffuse cysts in the clinical context of a young woman with a spontaneous pneumothorax who is otherwise healthy and has never smoked. The diagnosis is most likely lymphangioleiomyomatosis (LAM), a rare disease that accounts for less than 1% of all cases of interstitial lung diseases and occurs nearly exclusively in women in their childbearing years. The histopathologic feature of pulmonary LAM is proliferation of atypical smooth muscle–like cells associated with cystic changes. LAM may occur in patients with multiorgan hamartomas and a diagnosis of the autosomal dominant neurocutaneous syndrome called tuberous sclerosis complex. LAM also may present as a sporadic form in which renal and lymphatic hamartomas occur without diagnostic criteria for the tuberous sclerosis complex. The sporadic form of LAM presents with pulmonary complications and occurs only in women. Spontaneous pneumothorax is the initial cause for presentation in 36% of cases. Physical examination is often normal. Crackles and digital clubbing are usually absent.

Many young women with LAM are initially thought to have emphysema. However, patients with LAM are much younger than those with emphysema and present with respiratory complications 86% of the time, which include pneumothorax, as in this case, and chylothorax. Although the HRCT appearance of emphysema may mimic LAM, the cystic air spaces that occur in LAM are more uniform in appearance and distribution. Testing for $\alpha_1$-antitrypsin deficiency may be appropriate to exclude emphysema in young, nonsmoking patients.

Idiopathic pulmonary fibrosis has a chronic or subacute onset, but typically occurs in older patients. HRCT findings typically show bibasilar reticular changes with honeycombing and an absence of ground-glass opacification.

Pulmonary Langerhans cell histiocytosis can present with spontaneous pneumothorax and nonspecific respiratory complaints. However, the HRCT findings, cysts accompanied by nodules, are distinct from those in LAM. In addition, pulmonary Langerhans cell histiocytosis occurs nearly exclusively in patients with a significant smoking history.

### KEY POINT

- **A pulmonary presentation including pneumothorax and abnormal chest imaging is the primary event leading to the diagnosis of lymphangioleiomyomatosis in most patients.**

**Bibliography**
Ryu JH, Moss J, Beck GJ, et al; NHLBI LAM Registry Group. The NHLBI lymphangioleiomyomatosis registry: characteristics of 230 patients at enrollment. Am J Respir Crit Care Med. 2006;173(1): 105-111. [PMID: 16210669]

## Item 47      Answer:  B

**Educational Objective:**  Prevent venous thromboembolism and pulmonary embolism in a hospitalized patient with renal insufficiency.

This patient is at substantial risk for venous thromboembolism because of her malignancy and her acute medical illness. Unfractionated heparin and low-molecular-weight heparins have been shown to reduce the risk of venous thromboembolism and are highly recommended for patients at moderate or high risk. Unfractionated heparin does not rely on normal renal function for clearance and would be an appropriate option in this patient.

Aspirin is not commonly recommended for the prevention of venous thromboembolism and has not been demonstrated by clinical trials to reduce the incidence of thromboembolism in most populations at risk. Low-molecular-weight heparins are renally cleared and would accumulate unpredictably in this patient with acutely worsening renal function. The same limitation is applicable to fondaparinux. Ultrasonographic surveillance for deep venous

thrombosis and subsequent treatment has not been shown to improve outcomes. Warfarin, especially at therapeutic doses, is not recommended as a first choice for prophylactic use in medical patients. Its long duration of action may be especially detrimental in medical inpatients who may need invasive procedures. In addition, it would take several days before the INR reached the therapeutic target.

### KEY POINT

- **Unfractionated heparin does not depend on normal renal function for clearance and is appropriate for prophylaxis of venous thromboembolism for patients with renal insufficiency.**

**Bibliography**
Geerts WH, Bergqvist D, Pineo GF, et al; American College of Chest Physicians. Prevention of venous thromboembolism: American College of Chest Physicians evidence-based clinical practice guidelines (8th Edition). Chest. 2008;133(6 Suppl):381S-453S. [PMID: 18574271]

## Item 48      Answer:  D

**Educational Objective:**  Screen for depression in a patient with severe chronic obstructive pulmonary disease.

Anxiety and depression are common in patients with chronic obstructive pulmonary disease (COPD). Dyspnea is a contributing factor to anxiety. Depression may be precipitated by the loss and grief associated with the disability of COPD. Depression also affects adherence to therapy. It is not easy to diagnose depression in patients with COPD because of overlapping symptoms. Dyspnea, fatigue, and altered sleep can occur both in depression and COPD. However, patients should be asked whether they have experienced depressed mood and anhedonia during the last month using the two-question model: "Over the past 2 weeks have you felt down, depressed, hopeless?" and "Over the past 2 weeks have you felt little interest or pleasure in doing things?" A positive response to either question should be followed-up with more detailed questioning to establish the diagnosis of a mood disorder.

This patient with several recent exacerbations and hospitalizations could benefit from pulmonary rehabilitation and has discontinued his participation. Therapy with antidepressants and exercise training are often effective in treating anxiety and depression and improving quality of life. The patient's oxygenation is adequate (oxygen saturation ≥88%) and, therefore, increasing the nasal oxygen is not indicated. In highly selected patients, lung volume reduction surgery and lung transplantation may improve lung function and quality of life but should not be considered in this patient before screening for depression.

### KEY POINT

- **Anxiety and depression are common in patients with severe chronic obstructive pulmonary disease.**

**Bibliography**
Hills K, Grist R, Goldstein RS, Lacasse Y. Anxiety and Depression in End Stage COPD. Eur Respir J. 2008;31(3):667-677. [PMID: 18310400]

## Item 49    Answer:  D

**Educational Objective:**  Manage systemic sclerosis–associated interstitial lung disease.

Approximately 50% of patients with systemic sclerosis who have pulmonary manifestations develop severe pulmonary involvement within the first 3 years of disease onset. In this patient, the high-resolution CT (HRCT) findings show minimal lung involvement (less than or equal to 20%) and are not diagnostic of active alveolitis; therefore, therapy is not indicated at this time. Follow-up and HRCT imaging and pulmonary function testing can determine whether this patient will benefit from systemic cytotoxic therapy. Pulmonary disease occurs in 70% of patients with systemic sclerosis and is the primary cause of death: 15% of affected patients develop severe restrictive pulmonary disease, with an associated 10-year mortality rate of 50%. Pulmonary fibrosis is more common in diffuse cutaneous systemic sclerosis than in limited cutaneous disease.

A recent study of interstitial lung disease in patients with systemic sclerosis showed that patients with extensive, but not moderate, alveolitis benefit from treatment with cyclophosphamide. FVC less than 70% of predicted was predictive of response to therapy. Goh and colleagues showed that clinicians' visual assessment of extent of lung disease on HRCT of less than 20% was highly predictive of survival at 120 months.

Open lung biopsy is not necessary to diagnose systemic sclerosis–associated interstitial lung disease unless HRCT features suggest an alternative diagnosis. Bronchoscopy with bronchoalveolar lavage is less invasive and may be appropriate in select cases to exclude infection or active alveolitis. There is no evidence that high-dose prednisone therapy is effective, and it is associated with an increased risk for scleroderma renal crisis.

**KEY POINT**

- **Pulmonary disease occurs in 70% of patients with systemic sclerosis and is the primary cause of mortality.**

**Bibliography**
Goh NS, Desai SR, Veeraraghavan S, et al. Interstitial lung disease in systemic sclerosis: a simple staging system. Am J Respir Crit Care Med. 2008;177(11):1248-1254. [PMID: 18369202]

## Item 50    Answer:  A

**Educational Objective:**  Evaluate a patient with positron emission tomography–CT–positive mediastinal nodes.

The patient likely has non–small cell lung cancer, and the likely clinical stage is IIIA because positron emission tomography (PET)–CT findings support mediastinal lymph node involvement despite the normal size of the nodes on CT. However, PET-CT positivity is not equivalent to a histologic diagnosis, and tissue is needed; therefore, referral for chemotherapy would be premature. The selection of a biopsy site should take into consideration the ability of the results to establish a tissue diagnosis and to stage the disease. The site for biopsy should be a lesion that has the potential to establish the highest disease stage in order to decrease the number of procedures for the patient. Therefore, the next step in management is to establish a diagnosis and pathologic stage with mediastinal lymph node sampling.

Endobronchial ultrasonography–guided node sampling is a less invasive means than mediastinoscopy (a surgical procedure) and has a high yield. A positive lymph node biopsy establishes advanced-stage disease, eliminates the need for surgical staging, and prompts referral to medical oncology. Endoscopic ultrasonography–guided sampling through the esophagus has shown similar results for accessible nodes and may be more available in some centers. A negative result at bronchoscopy or endoscopy would result in surgical staging of the mediastinum by mediastinoscopy or thoracotomy. CT-guided needle aspiration of the nodule would likely establish the diagnosis but not the stage, and a second procedure would be needed to stage the mediastinum.

**KEY POINT**

- **Endobronchial ultrasonography–guided and endoscopic ultrasonography–guided node sampling are less invasive alternatives to surgical staging of the mediastinum with mediastinoscopy in a patient with suspected lung cancer.**

**Bibliography**
Detterbeck FC, Jantz MA, Wallace M, Vansteenkiste J, Silvestri GA; American College of Chest Physicians. Invasive mediastinal staging of lung cancer: ACCP evidence-based clinical practice guidelines (2nd edition). Chest. 2007;132(3 Suppl):202S-220S. [PMID: 17873169]

## Item 51    Answer:  B

**Educational Objective:**  Recognize impending respiratory failure in a patient with an acute exacerbation of asthma.

Blood gas results must be correlated with a patient's clinical course. This patient's initial arterial blood gas results are consistent with acute respiratory alkalosis, which is typical in patients with an exacerbation of asthma. The return of $P_{CO_2}$ to normal on the repeat blood gas measurement may reflect rapid improvement after effective bronchodilator therapy but could also indicate impending respiratory failure. The patient's lack of symptomatic and objective improvement indicates the latter is the case, and she is at risk of rapid progression to severe respiratory acidosis. At this juncture, the patient is a suitable candidate for intubation and should be managed in the intensive care unit.

Patients with vocal cord dysfunction can present with wheezing and be misdiagnosed with an asthma exacerbation. However, vocal cord dysfunction is unlikely in this patient given her history of prior intubation for an asthma exacerbation, and direct laryngoscopy, which is used to diagnose vocal cord dysfunction, could precipitate respiratory arrest in the patient.

Benzodiazepines and other sedating medications should be used cautiously during asthma exacerbations because of the risk of precipitating respiratory arrest.

### KEY POINT

- A normal, slightly elevated, or rising $Pco_2$ may indicate impending respiratory arrest in patients with an asthma exacerbation.

**Bibliography**

National Heart, Lung, and Blood Institute. National Asthma Education and Prevention Program: Expert Panel Report 3: Guidelines for the diagnosis and management of asthma. www.nhlbi.nih.gov/guidelines/asthma/asthgdln.pdf. Published August 27, 2007. Accessed July 21, 2009.

## Item 52    Answer:  D

**Educational Objective:**  Evaluate obstructive sleep apnea.

Obstructive sleep apnea is more common in men than in women, and the prevalence increases with age and body weight. Common clinical features include excessive sleepiness, habitual snoring, witnessed apneas, awakenings with gasping or choking, insomnia, nighttime diaphoresis, morning headaches, nocturia, daytime fatigue, alterations in mood, and neurocognitive decline. Physical examination may reveal hypertension, excessive body weight, large neck circumference (greater than 43.2 cm [17 in] for men and greater than 40.6 cm [16 in] for women), nasal obstruction, tonsillar enlargement, low-lying palate, narrow oropharynx, macroglossia, or retro- or micrognathia.

Polysomnography is indicated for the diagnosis because clinical features and physical examination findings are neither sufficiently sensitive nor specific for the disorder. For some patients, respiratory events occur predominantly or exclusively during a supine sleep position.

Therapy for obstructive sleep apnea, which should be undertaken only after polysomnography, includes continuous positive airway pressure (CPAP), oral devices, and upper airway surgery. Positive airway pressure therapy is the most effective. Avoidance of alcohol, sedatives, and muscle relaxants is important, as is weight management. For some patients, the upper airway is most vulnerable to collapse during supine sleep; measures to prevent sleep in a supine position may be appropriate if the patient's

apnea-hypopnea index normalizes during sleep in a lateral or prone sleep position.

Supplemental oxygen is not a primary therapy for obstructive sleep apnea. Mandibular repositioners, the most commonly used oral devices, are contraindicated in persons with compromised or inadequate dentition (such as this patient) and should not be prescribed without a confirmed diagnosis of obstructive sleep apnea.

### KEY POINT

- Polysomnography is indicated to diagnose obstructive sleep apnea and assess its severity.

**Bibliography**

Morgenthaler TI, Kapen S, Lee-Chiong T, et al; Standards of Practice Committee; American Academy of Sleep Medicine. Practice parameters for the medical therapy of obstructive sleep apnea. Sleep. 2006;29(8):1031-1035. [PMID: 16944671]

## Item 53    Answer:  B

**Educational Objective:**  Begin step-down therapy in persistent asthma.

This patient with persistent asthma is doing well and her disease is well controlled. Therefore, her long-acting β-agonist should be continued at the current dose and the inhaled corticosteroid should be reduced from high-dose to moderate-dose to limit the risk of corticosteroid-related side effects (particularly osteoporosis), which increase significantly after the menopause. Although inhaled corticosteroids are generally safe in asthma, their long-term use, particularly at higher doses, can lead to osteoporosis, glaucoma, cataract, easy bruising, and suppression of the hypothalamic-adrenal axis. For many asthma outcomes, the dose-response curve for inhaled corticosteroids is relatively flat after reaching 400 µg/d of beclomethasone (or equivalent drug). Therefore, when a patient's condition is stable on inhaled corticosteroid therapy, lowering the dose should be considered.

Asthma control is better with the combination of a moderate-dose inhaled corticosteroid plus a long-acting β-agonist than with a high-dose inhaled corticosteroid without a long-acting β-agonist. Although the benefits of using a long-acting β-agonist in patients with asthma are well established, concern about increased asthma-related deaths led the U.S. Food and Drug Administration to mandate including a black box warning in the package insert for these drugs to warn patients about this possible risk. The National Asthma Education and Prevention Program's recent recommendations affirmed the practice of adding a long-acting β-agonist to the therapy for patients whose disease is not well controlled on moderate-dose inhaled corticosteroids.

Using a leukotriene modifying agent in place of an inhaled corticosteroid is an alternative approach in patients with mild to moderate persistent asthma. Therefore, in patients with persistent asthma, an inhaled corticosteroid is the first-line therapy, and a leukotriene receptor antagonist can be tried in patients who have recurrent corticosteroid-related side effects, who are unwilling to use inhaled corticosteroids regularly, or who have a strong preference for a medication in pill form rather than an inhaler. To minimize long-term side effects, patients should always be treated with the fewest medications at the lowest dose that adequately controls their disease. Therefore, follow-up at 3- to 6-month intervals is recommended to evaluate the patient and make step-wise adjustments to therapy as warranted.

**KEY POINT**

- In a patient taking high-dose inhaled corticosteroids as part of therapy for persistent asthma whose disease is stable, reducing the dose of corticosteroids should be considered to prevent therapy-related side effects.

**Bibliography**

National Heart, Lung, and Blood Institute. National Asthma Education and Prevention Program: Expert panel report III: Guidelines for the diagnosis and management of asthma. www.nhlbi.nih.gov/guidelines/asthma/asthgdln.htm. Published 2007. Accessed July 21, 2009.

## Item 54    Answer:  D

**Educational Objective:**  Treat an exacerbation of chronic obstructive pulmonary disease (COPD).

In moderate to severe exacerbations of chronic obstructive pulmonary disease (COPD), inhaled short-acting bronchodilators ($\beta_2$-agonists and anticholinergic agents) and systemic corticosteroids, antibiotics, and supplemental oxygen are the mainstays of treatment. In one trial of 100 patients with COPD, 16 responded to albuterol only; 17 responded to ipratropium only; and 47 responded to both. Corticosteroids improve lung function, reduce hospital stay, and lower rates of relapse and treatment failure. Antibiotic therapy has been shown to significantly reduce mortality, treatment failure, and sputum purulence in patients with exacerbations of COPD.

Noninvasive positive-pressure ventilation should be considered if patients have persistent hypoxemia and/or hypercapnia with a pH less than 7.35 and a $P_{CO_2}$ greater than 45 mm Hg and a respiration rate greater than 25/min despite maximal medical therapy. Exclusion criteria include respiratory arrest, cardiovascular instability, somnolence, impaired mental status, lack of cooperation, high risk of aspiration, recent facial or gastrointestinal surgery, craniofacial trauma, and extreme obesity. Patients who are hypoxemic need supplemental oxygen to achieve an oxygen saturation of 88% or greater.

The role of theophylline in COPD exacerbations is controversial. The conclusion from four trials with 169 patients was that theophylline therapy did not affect $FEV_1$ at 2 hours but slightly improved $FEV_1$ at 3 days. There were also increased rates of relapse and occurrence of tremor, palpitations, and arrhythmias. Long-acting $\beta_2$-agonists, such as salmeterol, have no role in the therapy of acute exacerbations of COPD.

**KEY POINT**

- Inhaled short-acting bronchodilators ($\beta_2$-agonists and anticholinergic agents), systemic corticosteroids, and antibiotics are the mainstay of treatment of exacerbations of chronic obstructive pulmonary disease in hospitalized patients.

**Bibliography**

Celli BK. Update on the Management of COPD [erratum in Chest. 2008;134(4):892]. Chest. 2008;133(6):1457-1462. [PMID: 18574288]

## Item 55    Answer:  A

**Educational Objective:**  Manage a parapneumonic pleural effusion.

Pleural infections often resolve with antibiotic therapy alone, but fibrinous organization and lung entrapment require invasive treatment in about 10% of parapneumonic effusions. Effusions at risk for loculation are called *complicated parapneumonic effusions*. Because clinical prediction is unreliable, thoracentesis should be done to assess the need for invasive treatment provided that the effusion can be clearly visualized on ultrasonography. This patient with presumed underlying chronic obstructive pulmonary disease had typical symptoms of an acute bacterial pneumonia with development of a parapneumonic effusion with septations, low pleural fluid pH, low glucose, and elevated lactate dehydrogenase level. All of these factors suggest that the patient will have a poor outcome without immediate pleural space drainage with either thoracostomy tube placement or a radiologically guided small-bore catheter. The evidence for use of fibrinolytic agents is still unclear, but in this situation, pleural space drainage is imperative and, with the ultrasonographic findings, a trial of a fibrinolytic agent is warranted before performing video-assisted thoracoscopic surgery (VATS). Intrapleural administration of fibrinolytic agents does not cause systemic thrombolysis. Early VATS or thoracotomy is the generally preferred approach for patients who are candidates for surgery and who have persistent sepsis and loculation.

The patient should not be discharged; he needs close follow-up for possible escalation of therapy. He should not be sent for surgery immediately without a trial of chest tube drainage with or without fibrinolytic therapy. If clinical improvement is not obvious by 3 days, surgical consultation should be initiated.

**KEY POINT**

- Immediate pleural space drainage, with or without fibrinolytic therapy, is indicated in a patient with acute bacterial pneumonia and a parapneumonic effusion with septations.

Bibliography

Sahn SA. Diagnosis and management of parapneumonic effusions and empyema. Clin Infect Dis. 2007;45(11):1480-1486. [PMID: 17990232]

## Item 56    Answer:  B

**Educational Objective:**  Manage sedation in a patient receiving mechanical ventilation.

A randomized controlled trial by Girard and colleagues in critically ill patients showed that intermittent bolus dosing of sedatives titrated against a validated sedation scale and with a daily spontaneous awakening trial with total cessation of sedatives yielded a 4-day reduction in intensive care unit (ICU) and hospital length of stay and an improvement in 1-year survival. In critically ill patients, this method allows enough sedation for comfort and reduces the likelihood of excess use of potent psychoactive medications, such as lorazepam. A sedative drip with propofol would also be a consideration, as long as sedation was interrupted daily. The newer-generation sedation scales are being widely adopted by ICUs to aid in drug titration and ease of communication. Therefore, sedation would be beneficial in this patient.

The use of sedation with intermittent paralytic agents as tolerated has the potential for increasing the risk of ICU-acquired weakness and paralysis without adequate sedation; this method is generally reserved for patients with severe ventilator dyssynchrony. Deep continuous sedation until the patient is extubated leads to unnecessarily prolonged and pronounced sedation. The notion of trying to "eliminate" memories from the ICU appears to be a risk factor for post-traumatic stress disorder, which occurs in about 15% to 20% of ICU survivors. Neuromuscular blockade with paralytic agents should be avoided unless absolutely necessary because of problems such as myopathy and prolonged paralysis.

**KEY POINT**

- Intermittent bolus dosing of sedatives titrated via a validated sedation scale plus a daily spontaneous awakening trial appears to be the superior method of delivering sedation in critically ill patients.

Bibliography

Girard TD, Kress JP, Fuchs BD, et al. Efficacy and safety of a paired sedation and ventilator weaning protocol for mechanically ventilated patients in intensive care (Awakening and Breathing Controlled trial): a randomised controlled trial. Lancet. 2008;371 (9607):126-134. [PMID: 18191684]

## Item 57    Answer:  C

**Educational Objective:**  Provide nutritional support to a malnourished patient in the intensive care unit.

Patients in the intensive care unit generally require 25 to 30 nonprotein kcal/kg/d and 1.0 to 1.5 protein kcal/kg/d to meet the energy expenditures associated with critical illness. This severely malnourished patient should receive approximately 1500 kcal (30 nonprotein kcal/kg/d) and 75 g protein (1.5 protein kcal/kg/d). The oral or enteral route is usually preferred. Albumin and prealbumin levels are indicators of visceral protein status. Albumin has a half-life of approximately 20 days. When albumin values are below normal levels, a sizeable amount of the serum pool has been lost. Generally, albumin is considered a late indicator of malnutrition. Albumin concentrations rise slowly during nutritional therapy (refeeding) and in patients recovering from stress. Reliable changes in albumin require at least 2 to 3 weeks of nutritional supplementation. Since albumin is formed in the liver, diseases of the liver cause the hepatocytes to lose the ability to synthesize albumin. Prealbumin is another protein status indicator. Prealbumin's short half-life of 2 days and small serum pool allow small changes in nutritional status to be identified in a short time frame. Low prealbumin levels result from either inadequate nutrition or inflammatory stress. Prealbumin levels less than 5 mg/dL (50 mg/L) indicate severe protein and calorie malnutrition. Prealbumin should be used as an indicator of nutritional improvement and as a measure of how well nutritional interventions are working. Prealbumin can be measured once or twice per week and used as a sensitive monitor of nutritional progress.

**KEY POINT**

- Patients in the intensive care unit require 25 to 30 nonprotein kcal/kg/d and 1.0 to 1.5 protein kcal/kg/d to meet the energy expenditures associated with critical illness.

Bibliography

Wernerman J. Guidelines for nutritional support in intensive care unit patients: A critical analysis. Curr Opin Clin Nutr Metab Care. 2005;8(2):171-175. [PMID: 15716796]

## Item 58    Answer:  A

**Educational Objective:**  Diagnose connective tissue disease–related lymphocytic interstitial pneumonia.

The diagnostic open lung biopsy specimen in this patient with Sjögren syndrome shows the histopathologic features of lymphocytic interstitial pneumonia (LIP), a rare form of interstitial lung disease (ILD) that may occur in one third of patients with ILD and Sjögren syndrome. Affected patients may develop ILD with known connective tissue disease, or ILD may be the presenting finding in a patient with undiagnosed connective tissue disease. Sjögren syndrome–associated ILD is not limited to LIP but may also present as usual interstitial pneumonia, nonspecific interstitial pneumonia, organizing pneumonia, and interstitial amyloidosis at open lung biopsy. In addition, finding LIP at open lung biopsy is not specific for Sjögren syndrome. Treatment is generally directed at the underlying connective tissue disease, but the severity of ILD is important in making treatment decisions.

Because this patient has Sjögren syndrome, the diagnosis of idiopathic LIP or any other idiopathic ILD, including idiopathic pulmonary fibrosis, is incorrect. Lymphoma, which develops in up to 5% of patients with Sjögren syndrome, is a rare cause of pulmonary interstitial infiltration in patients with Sjögren syndrome. The diagnosis of primary pulmonary lymphoma requires the pathologic demonstration of a monoclonal population of lymphocytes.

**KEY POINT**

- Lymphocytic interstitial pneumonia is detected at open lung biopsy in approximately one third of patients with Sjögren syndrome.

**Bibliography**

Parambil JG, Mers JL, Lindell RM, Matteson EL, Ryu JH. Interstitial lung disease in primary Sjögren syndrome. Chest. 2006;130(5): 1489-1495. [PMID: 17099028]

## Item 59        Answer:   C

**Educational Objective:**  Manage pulmonary hypertension.

This patient has signs and symptoms of pulmonary hypertension and a history of use of appetite suppressants, which have been associated with pulmonary hypertension. Echocardiography has ruled out the presence of cardiac diseases associated with pulmonary hypertension. Pulmonary function testing has ruled out parenchymal obstructive and restrictive lung diseases, and ventilation/perfusion scanning has ruled out chronic thromboembolic pulmonary hypertension. Right-heart catheterization will confirm the presence of pulmonary arterial hypertension, measure pulmonary vascular resistance, determine the magnitude of right ventricular dysfunction, and guide therapy.

High-resolution CT scan is useful for the evaluation of pulmonary parenchymal disease, but the absence of parenchymal abnormalities on chest radiograph and the normal pulmonary function tests make interstitial disease unlikely. This patient's physiologic testing discloses no evidence of lung parenchymal disease. Myocardial perfusion imaging can help detect compromised coronary flow. However, the echocardiographic findings can be explained by right ventricular overload and do not suggest acute coronary disease. Lung biopsy would add little to the diagnosis of pulmonary hypertension and entails a risk of bleeding in patients with pulmonary hypertension. Therapy with an angiotensin-converting enzyme (ACE) inhibitor may improve left ventricular function in patients with left ventricular systolic dysfunction. However, this patient's left ventricular dysfunction is attributable to compression from right ventricular hypertrophy and dilation. ACE inhibitors would not improve the pulmonary arterial resistance and might even cause dangerous decreases in this patient's blood pressure.

**KEY POINT**

- In patients with pulmonary hypertension, right-heart catheterization will confirm the presence of pulmonary arterial hypertension, quantify pulmonary vascular resistance, determine the magnitude of right ventricular dysfunction, and guide therapy.

**Bibliography**

McGoon M, Gutterman D, Steen V, et al; American College of Chest Physicians. Screening, early detection, and diagnosis of pulmonary arterial hypertension: ACCP evidence-based clinical practice guidelines. Chest. 2004;126(1 Suppl):14S-34S. [PMID: 15249493]

## Item 60        Answer:   E

**Educational Objective:**  Recognize that routine screening for lung cancer is not recommended.

Screening for early-stage lung cancer is not now recommended by any methodology, including spiral CT scan, chest radiography, sputum cytology, or 18F-fluorodeoxyglucose (FDG)-PET scan. No method has been shown to reduce death from lung cancer. Screening for lung cancer with spiral CT scanning detects 60% or more of incident cancers in stage I. However, the false-positive rate (number of benign nodules detected) for spiral CT lung cancer screening is high and may result in patient anxiety and unnecessary invasive testing. Recent large, single-arm observational studies of spiral CT screening show that about 60% to 85% of incident cancers (detected after the baseline scan) are stage I and that the survival rate is better than that of historical unscreened cohorts. However, this finding alone does not prove that lung cancer screening is effective. Proof of efficacy for a lung cancer screening test would be a reduction in the mortality rate among those screened compared with a comparable group at risk who were not screened. Although survival results may be provocative in an observational study, they are subject to bias. The survival rate may be dramatically improved without actually resulting in a reduction in deaths from lung cancer. Because of lead-time bias, length-time bias, and overdiagnosis, a randomized, controlled trial is generally accepted as the definitive means of establishing efficacy for a screening test. Various screening studies now under way are randomized trials that might answer the question of the efficacy of screening for lung cancer.

The American Cancer Society does not recommend testing for early lung cancer detection in asymptomatic persons. However, the Society historically has recognized that patients at high risk of lung cancer because of significant exposure to tobacco smoke or occupational carcinogens may decide to undergo testing for early lung cancer on an individual basis after consultation with their physicians.

**KEY POINT**

- Results from single-arm observational studies of spiral CT screening for lung cancer show that survival results with screening are improved over historical controls, but there is no proof of reduction of the mortality rate.

**Bibliography**

Smith RA, Cokkinides V, Brawley OW. Cancer screening in the United States, 2008: a review of current American Cancer Society guidelines and cancer screening issues. CA Cancer J Clin. 2008;58(3): 161-179. [PMID: 18443206]

## Item 61    Answer:  B

**Educational Objective:**  Manage hypoxemia in a patient with the acute respiratory distress syndrome.

The patient has severe hypoxemic respiratory failure from the acute respiratory distress syndrome (ARDS). The primary cause of hypoxemia is shunt, which will not correct with breathing 100% oxygen. Increasing positive end-expiratory pressure (PEEP) improves gas exchange by recruiting flooded and collapsed alveoli. Recruitment may also reduce subsequent ventilator-induced lung injury. However, excess PEEP can cause lung injury by overdistending alveoli and reducing cardiac output. The National Institutes of Health ARDS Network ALVEOLI study randomized patients to high levels of PEEP (starting at 12 cm $H_2O$) versus low levels (starting at 5 cm $H_2O$). Despite greater acute improvements in oxygenation with higher levels of PEEP, there was no difference in the mortality rate between the groups. In another trial, the high-PEEP group, in which the PEEP was uniformly titrated up to plateau pressure of 28 to 30 cm $H_2O$, spent fewer days on the ventilator than the low-PEEP group but overall mortality was not decreased. In this patient, oxygenation is inadequate, and it would be appropriate to increase PEEP.

Increasing the respiration rate is inappropriate because increasing ventilation does not correct hypoxemia resulting from shunt. Increasing the tidal volume is not as effective as increasing PEEP, and the use of higher tidal volumes is associated with increased mortality in patients with acute lung injury. Use of paralytic agents is generally reserved for ARDS patients with hypoxemia refractory to maximal ventilator support or temporarily in patients with marked ventilator dyssynchrony. Paralytic agents can improve oxygenation by reducing oxygen consumption but pose a risk of intensive care unit–acquired weakness and require aggressive sedation.

### KEY POINT

- **Increasing positive end-expiratory pressure is first-line therapy in acute respiratory distress syndrome patients with severe hypoxemia.**

**Bibliography**

Mercat A, Richard JC, Vielle B, et al; Expiratory Pressure (Express) Study Group. Positive end-expiratory pressure setting in adults with acute lung injury and acute respiratory distress syndrome: a randomized controlled trial. JAMA. 2008;299(6):646-655. [PMID: 18270353]

## Item 62    Answer:  C

**Educational Objective:**  Recognize theophylline toxicity.

This patient requires a thorough physical examination and diagnostic studies, including electrocardiography, a comprehensive metabolic profile, and measurement of the serum theophylline level. She may require urgent hospitalization.

The initial step should be to stop theophylline. Various medications influence theophylline metabolism in the liver, leading to increased serum levels (for example, ciprofloxacin, cimetidine, erythromycin, allopurinol, and zileuton) or decreased levels (for example, rifampin, phenobarbital, and ethanol). Ciprofloxacin can increase the serum theophylline level several-fold, potentially resulting in theophylline toxicity. Theophylline clearance is also decreased in the elderly and in those with heart failure or liver disease. The target serum theophylline level should be between 8 and 12 µg/mL (44.4 and 66.6 µmol/L) to limit its side effects. Many patients have side effects from theophylline (tremor, palpitations) at high therapeutic levels (15 to 20 µg/mL [83.2 to 111 µmol/L]). Higher levels lead to nausea, vomiting, arrhythmia, and seizures and can result in death. Despite theophylline's ease of use, low cost, and mild anti-inflammatory activity, its regular use in the management of asthma is not recommended because of its limited bronchodilatory activity and narrow therapeutic range.

Local side effects of inhaled corticosteroids include oral candidiasis and dysphonia. Systemic effects include suppression of the hypothalamic-adrenal axis, reduced growth velocity in children, osteopenia, skin thinning, and increased risk for cataracts or glaucoma. Common adverse effects of inhaled β-agonists include tachycardia, palpitations, tremors, and hypokalemia. Concomitant use of a fluoroquinolone antibiotic does not increase the incidence of adverse effects from inhaled corticosteroids or β-agonists, and stopping these medications could significantly worsen the patient's asthma. Drug-induced pancreatitis is relatively uncommon and difficult to substantiate but seems not to be related to the use of commonly prescribed asthma control medications or fluoroquinolone antibiotics. Finally, pancreatitis is typically associated with abdominal pain in addition to nausea and vomiting.

### KEY POINT

- **Various medications influence theophylline metabolism in the liver, leading to increased serum levels and potential toxicity (for example, ciprofloxacin, cimetidine, erythromycin, allopurinol, and zileuton) or decreased levels (for example, rifampin, phenobarbital, and ethanol).**

**Bibliography**

Shakeri-Nejad K, Stahlmann R. Drug interactions during therapy with three major groups of antimicrobial agents. Expert Opin Pharmacother. 2006;7(6):639-651. [PMID: 16556082]

## Item 63    Answer:  A

**Educational Objective:**  Recognize $\alpha_1$-antitrypsin deficiency as a possible cause of early-onset chronic obstructive pulmonary disease.

This patient may have $\alpha_1$-antitrypsin (AAT) deficiency, a clinically underdiagnosed disorder that primarily affects the lungs but also the liver and, rarely, the skin. AAT protects against proteolytic degradation of elastin, a protein that promotes elasticity of connective tissue. The normal plasma concentration of AAT is 150 to 350 mg/dL (1.5 to 3.5 g/L). Patients with plasma levels lower than 50 to 80 mg/dL (0.5 to 0.8 g/L) have severe deficiency. In the lungs, severe deficiency of AAT predisposes to early-onset chronic obstructive pulmonary disease, especially panacinar emphysema, which involves the lung bases. This patient is younger than 45 years and has bilateral basilar emphysema, and, therefore, AAT deficiency must be ruled out.

High-resolution CT scan is not helpful in the diagnosis of AAT deficiency, although it may be useful in evaluating the extent of the disease.

The sweat chloride test is a screening test for cystic fibrosis. Nearly 10% of patients diagnosed with cystic fibrosis are older than 18 years. Of these patients, gastrointestinal symptoms and infertility are the most common presenting problems. In cystic fibrosis lung disease, chest radiography typically shows hyperinflation and accentuated bronchovascular markings, appearing first in the upper lobes, followed by bronchiectasis and cyst formation. This patient's age, presenting symptoms, and chest radiograph findings make cystic fibrosis unlikely.

A flow-volume loop, which includes forced inspiratory and expiratory maneuvers, is indicated for patients with unexplained dyspnea and can detect upper airway obstruction that cannot be diagnosed with spirometry. However, this patient has no physical findings suggestive of upper airway obstruction (for example, stridor), and even if such findings were present, they would not explain the patient's findings on chest radiography.

**KEY POINT**

- Patients with severe α₁-antitryspin deficiency are predisposed to early-onset chronic obstructive pulmonary disease, especially panacinar emphysema, which involves the lung bases.

**Bibliography**

American Thoracic Society; European Respiratory Society. American Thoracic Society/European Respiratory Society Standards for the diagnosis and Management of Individual with Alpha 1 Antitryspin Deficiency. Am J Respir Crit Care Med. 2003;168(7):818-900. [PMID: 14522813]

## Item 64    Answer:  E

**Educational Objective:** Evaluate acute abdominal pain.

The term *acute abdomen* refers to sudden and severe abdominal pain less than 24 hours in duration. Rebound tenderness and severe diffuse abdominal pain are suggestive of an acute abdomen with peritonitis. Pain that is acute in onset generally points to acute inflammatory, infectious, or ischemic causes. Upper abdominal pain is usually of gastric, hepatobiliary, or pancreatic origin, whereas pain in the lower abdomen originates from the hindgut and genitourinary

organs. All patients with abdominal pain should have measurements of serum amylase and lipase to evaluate for acute pancreatitis.

Although an abdominal CT scan is usually necessary for a definitive diagnosis of acute abdominal pain, initial screening with supine and upright abdominal radiographs to look for air-fluid levels, suggestive of a perforated viscus, should be done.

Chest radiograph and supine and upright abdominal radiographs should be obtained in every patient with significant acute abdominal pain to exclude bowel obstruction or perforation or intrathoracic processes (for example, pneumonia, pneumothorax, or aortic dissection) that can present as abdominal pain. This patient's history of diverticulitis suggests possible diverticular rupture. An elevated leukocyte count may suggest an intra-abdominal infection or abscess, but the onset is usually not abrupt. Based on its relatively low cost, convenience, and noninvasive nature, ultrasonography has been utilized as a diagnostic tool for acute diverticulitis. However, the examination remains operator-dependent and in the absence of well-designed prospective comparative studies, it remains a second-line diagnostic tool. Colonoscopy is not indicated in a patient with acute peritoneal signs and has the potential to worsen the situation by causing a perforation of inflamed bowel wall.

**KEY POINT**

- Although an abdominal CT scan is usually necessary for a definitive diagnosis of acute abdominal pain, initial screening with supine and upright abdominal radiographs to look for air-fluid levels, suggestive of a perforated viscus, should be done.

**Bibliography**

Cartwright SL, Knudson MP. Evaluation of acute abdominal pain in adults. Am Fam Physician. 2008;77(7):971-978. [PMID: 18441863]

## Item 65    Answer:  D

**Educational Objective:** Manage end-stage idiopathic pulmonary fibrosis.

This patient has had gradual worsening of idiopathic pulmonary fibrosis and has not responded to immunosuppressive therapies. He now has severe respiratory distress and either needs ventilatory support or initiation of palliative care. Patients with pulmonary fibrosis requiring admission to the intensive care unit for respiratory failure have a very poor prognosis, with in-hospital mortality rates of 61% and post-discharge rates of 92% by 2 months. This patient has no evidence of respiratory infection and has failed to respond to previous appropriate treatment, and he should be informed of his poor prognosis and offered the option to initiate palliative care. End-of-life care should be discussed with all patients with idiopathic pulmonary fibrosis, ideally in the outpatient setting with family present and when there is no urgency to intervene.

Mechanical ventilation would be reasonable provided that the patient understands his poor prognosis and wishes to continue with aggressive treatment. Initiation of noninvasive positive-pressure ventilation is not an effective means to avoid mechanical ventilation in patients with pulmonary fibrosis. Noninvasive ventilation may delay the need for intubation and ventilation, but it would not improve this patient's poor prognosis.

Methylprednisolone is commonly given to patients with idiopathic pulmonary fibrosis and worsening respiratory distress, but there is no evidence that treatment of such patients with respiratory failure is beneficial, and methylprednisolone is unlikely to reverse this patient's need for more urgent management of respiratory failure.

### KEY POINT

- **Patients with idiopathic pulmonary fibrosis who require intensive care unit admission for respiratory failure have a very poor prognosis.**

**Bibliography**

Saydain G, Islam A, Afessa B, Ryu JH, Scott JP, Peters SG. Outcome of patients with idiopathic pulmonary fibrosis admitted to the intensive care unit. Am J Respir Crit Care Med. 2002;166(6):839-842. [PMID: 12231494]

## Item 66      Answer:  C

**Educational Objective:**  Treat inadequately controlled persistent asthma.

This patient has persistent asthma, which is defined as having asthma symptoms 2 or more days per week or 2 or more nights per month. Patients with persistent asthma should be treated with daily corticosteroid therapy. When asthma is not adequately controlled on low- or moderate-dose inhaled corticosteroid therapy, adding a long-acting β-agonist (salmeterol or formoterol) has been shown to be superior to doubling the dose of the corticosteroid for improving asthma control and quality of life. The concerns about increased asthma-related deaths in patients using a long-acting β-agonist led the U.S. Food and Drug Administration to include a black box warning in the package insert for these drugs. The National Asthma Education and Prevention Program (NAEPP) expert panel guidelines in 2007 affirmed the recommendation of adding a long-acting β-agonist in patients whose disease is not controlled with an inhaled corticosteroid but advised against using a long-acting β-agonist as a single controller therapy.

Theophylline and leukotriene-modifying drugs are third-line agents that should be considered in patients who remain symptomatic despite the addition on a long-acting β-agonist to the corticosteroid therapy. Long-acting anticholinergic drugs are beneficial in patients with chronic obstructive pulmonary disease; however, their role in management of asthma is not defined.

### KEY POINT

- **In patients with persistent asthma not adequately controlled with daily low- or moderate-dose inhaled corticosteroids, adding a long-acting β-agonist improves asthma control and quality of life.**

**Bibliography**

Ni Chroinin M, Greenstone IR, Danish A, et al. Long-acting beta2-agonists versus placebo in addition to inhaled corticosteroids in children and adults with chronic asthma. Cochrane Database Syst Rev. 2005;(4):CD005535. [PMID: 16235410]

## Item 67      Answer:  E

**Educational Objective:**  Confirm the clinical diagnosis of acute pulmonary embolism.

This patient is at high risk for pulmonary embolism because of his recent hospitalization, cancer, and nephrotic syndrome. A positive ventilation/perfusion scan would confirm the diagnosis of pulmonary embolism in this patient with a high pretest probability for the condition, especially in the absence of parenchymal lung defects on chest radiograph.

The probability of pulmonary embolism is very high based on this patient's presentation that included chest pain, dyspnea, recent hospitalization and surgery, and active cancer and a protein-losing nephropathy. A negative D-dimer test would not be sufficient evidence to rule out a pulmonary embolism under these circumstances, and a high D-dimer level would add little to the diagnostic work-up. Decreased antithrombin III levels may result from nephrotic syndrome, and levels are lowered during acute thrombosis, especially during treatment with heparin. Therefore, measuring antithrombin III would add little to the accuracy of the diagnosis of pulmonary embolism or have any implication for immediate management decisions. Lower extremity ultrasonography can disclose asymptomatic deep venous thrombosis in a small percentage of patients presenting with symptoms of pulmonary embolism. However, the yield is relatively low and ventilation/perfusion scanning would have a much higher degree of accuracy. CT angiography is an acceptable modality to diagnose acute pulmonary embolism but requires a significant amount of contrast infusion, which would be contraindicated in a patient with an elevated serum creatinine level.

### KEY POINT

- **Ventilation/perfusion scanning is an appropriate noninvasive test to diagnose acute pulmonary embolism.**

**Bibliography**

Anderson DR, Kahn SR, Rodger MA, et al. Computed tomographic pulmonary angiography vs ventilation-perfusion lung scanning in patients with suspected pulmonary embolism: a randomized controlled trial. JAMA. 2007;298(23):2743-2753. [PMID: 18165667]

## Item 68     Answer:   B

**Educational Objective:** Evaluate a patient with non–small cell lung cancer.

Positron emission tomographic (PET) scanning has been shown to be cost effective in the preoperative management of patients with non–small cell lung cancer. Randomized studies evaluating the addition of PET to the standard workup found that the procedure identifies advanced disease and precludes unnecessary thoracotomy in approximately 1 in 5 patients. PET-CT has been shown to have higher sensitivity and specificity for assessing lung cancer stage than CT and PET done separately. PET-CT may not be widely available but will likely completely replace PET alone. Current guidelines identify low-risk patients for surgery based upon preoperative spirometry. An $FEV_1$ greater than 2.0 L (or greater than 80% of predicted) identifies low-risk patients for pneumonectomy, whereas an $FEV_1$ greater than 1.5 L is low risk for lobectomy. Measurement of $D_{LCO}$ is generally reserved for patients who have an acceptable $FEV_1$ but also have exertional dyspnea or coexistent interstitial lung disease. Patients with preoperative results for $FEV_1$ and $D_{LCO}$ that are both greater than 80% of predicted do not need further physiologic testing. The patient has no limitation to walking and adequate pulmonary function, and, therefore, quantitative perfusion lung scan would not be needed. Surgical consultation is probably premature before staging the tumor and determining its resectability. A dynamic CT enhancement study is helpful in the evaluation of indeterminate nodules but would not be expected to add helpful information in the patient with an established diagnosis.

### KEY POINT

- **Positron emission tomography (PET) scanning (or PET-CT if available) is helpful in the preoperative evaluation of patients with known or suspected non–small cell lung cancer.**

**Bibliography**

Silvestri GA, Gould MK, Margolis ML, et al; American College of Chest Physicians. Noninvasive staging of non-small cell lung cancer: ACCP evidenced-based clinical practice guidelines (2nd edition). Chest. 2007; 132(3 Suppl):178S-201S. [PMID: 17873168]

## Item 69     Answer:   A

**Educational Objective:** Manage ventilator settings in a patient with the acute respiratory distress syndrome.

The patient has developed the acute respiratory distress syndrome (ARDS) complicating aspiration pneumonia. A lung-protective ventilator strategy should be used to reduce the risk of ventilator-induced lung injury by minimizing alveolar overdistention. A randomized controlled trial in patients with acute lung injury compared ventilation with tidal volumes of 6 mL/kg and 12 mL/kg ideal body weight and found an absolute mortality reduction of 8% in the low-tidal-volume group.

The cause of the patient's bilateral infiltrates is ARDS rather than poorly responding pneumonia. His fever curve and right lower lobe infiltrate have improved, and he has minimal secretions. A change in antibiotic therapy is not indicated.

Noninvasive positive-pressure ventilation (NPPV) would not be appropriate. He is sedated and has rapidly deteriorating gas exchange. Furthermore, ARDS is not rapidly reversible, and previous trials of NPPV in patients with ARDS have not shown a mortality benefit.

Recent trials have found no advantage to using pulmonary artery catheters compared with central venous catheters for fluid management in acute lung injury.

### KEY POINT

- **A lung-protective ventilator strategy employing low tidal volumes reduces mortality in patients with the acute respiratory distress syndrome.**

**Bibliography**

Ventilation with lower tidal volumes as compared with traditional tidal volumes for acute lung injury and the acute respiratory distress syndrome. The Acute Respiratory Distress Syndrome Network. N Engl J Med. 2000;342(18):1301-1308. [PMID: 10793162]

## Item 70     Answer:   C

**Educational Objective:** Recognize and treat hypothermia.

Hypothermia is a significant and common problem among elderly people because of such factors as impaired shivering. Normal body temperature is 35.6 °C (96.1 °F) to 36.8 °C (98.3 °F) in the elderly. Medications may also predispose the elderly to hypothermia.

There are three types of rewarming techniques: passive external rewarming, active external rewarming, and active internal core rewarming. Passive rewarming (use of blankets and insulation) and active external rewarming techniques (warm blankets, heating pads, radiant heat, warm baths, forced warm air) are indicated for mild hypothermia with temperatures from 33.9 °C (93.0 °F) to 36.1 °C (97.0 °F). The same maneuvers can be used for moderate hypothermia except that only the truncal areas should be externally rewarmed. Heat applied to the arms and legs forces cold blood back toward the heart, lungs, and brain, causing the core body temperature to decrease, which can worsen the preexisting hypothermia. In this patient with severe hypothermia (temperature less than 30.0 °C [86.0 °F]), active internal rewarming measures should be considered, such as warmed intravenous fluids, warm and humid oxygen, peritoneal lavage, and extracorporeal rewarming. Complications of rewarming include rhabdomyolysis, compartment syndromes, disseminated intravascular coagulation, pulmonary edema, and acute tubular necrosis.

- In patients with severe hypothermia (temperature less than 30.0 °C [86.0 °F]), active internal rewarming measures using warmed intravenous fluids, warm and humid oxygen, peritoneal lavage, and extracorporeal rewarming should be considered.

**Bibliography**
Epstein E, Anna K. Accidental hypothermia. BMJ. 2006;332(7543): 706-709. [PMID: 16565126]

## Item 71    Answer:  A
**Educational Objective:**  Manage severe chronic obstructive pulmonary disease.

This patient has severe (GOLD stage III) chronic obstructive pulmonary disease (COPD) defined as $FEV_1/FVC$ <70% and $FEV_1$ 30% to 50% of predicted with or without chronic symptoms (cough, sputum production). Treatment for this patient includes support for his smoking cessation, short-acting bronchodilators as needed, and regular treatment with one or more long-acting bronchodilators, as well as an inhaled corticosteroid, along with pulmonary rehabilitation.

Oral corticosteroids are not recommended for regular use in a long-term maintenance program because there has been no consistent evidence of efficacy or superiority compared with other agents that have fewer adverse effects. Low-dose theophylline reduces exacerbation in patients with COPD but does not increase post-bronchodilator lung function significantly. High-dose theophylline is an effective bronchodilator but due to its potential toxicity inhaled bronchodilators are again preferred. Leukotriene modifiers, such as montelukast, are not recommended in COPD. Many studies have evaluated leukotriene modifiers in COPD, but the improvement in lung function and symptoms with these agents is modest at best.

Two recent long-term studies of more than 11,000 patients have evaluated treatment for patients with GOLD stages II to IV. The TORCH study and the UPLIFT study showed that in patients with COPD, combination therapy with bronchodilators and an inhaled corticosteroid improved quality of life and pulmonary function without significant adverse effects. Patients enrolled in pulmonary rehabilitation programs benefit with respect to both exercise tolerance and symptoms of dyspnea and fatigue. The minimum length of an effective rehabilitation program is 2 months, but the longer the program continues, the more effective the results are.

- Treatment of GOLD stage III chronic obstructive pulmonary disease includes short-acting bronchodilators as needed and regular treatment with one or more long-acting bronchodilators with an inhaled corticosteroid and pulmonary rehabilitation.

**Bibliography**
Global Initiative for Chronic Obstructive Lung Disease. Global Strategy for the Diagnosis, Management and Prevention of Chronic Obstructive Pulmonary Disease. www.goldcopd.org/Guidelineitem .asp?l1=2&l2=1&intId=2003. Published January 2009. Accessed July 21, 2009.

## Item 72    Answer:  A
**Educational Objective:**  Recognize and manage imatinib mesylate–induced lung disease.

This patient has drug-induced lung disease caused by imatinib mesylate. The most important management step in treatment of drug-induced lung disease is immediate withdrawal of the offending agent. Diagnosis of drug-induced lung disease requires a high index of suspicion. This patient developed new-onset respiratory symptoms and radiologic changes (mixed alveolar and interstitial pattern) that were temporally associated with initiation of imatinib mesylate to treat chronic myeloid leukemia. Exclusion of underlying infectious causes by bronchoalveolar lavage in this patient is an important diagnostic step. The findings of peripheral blood eosinophilia and organizing pneumonia on bronchoscopic lung biopsy are nonspecific but support drug-induced lung injury caused by imatinib mesylate.

This patient has no evidence for respiratory infection on bronchoalveolar lavage, and antibiotic or antiviral therapy is not needed. Deep venous thrombosis and pulmonary embolism are always a possibility in patients with underlying malignancy. However, this patient's CT chest findings and biopsy results are most consistent with drug-induced lung disease, and initiation of heparin anticoagulation would not be appropriate.

- The most important management step in treatment of drug-induced lung disease is immediate withdrawal of the offending agent.

**Bibliography**
Ohnishi K, Sakai F, Kudoh S, Ohno R. Twenty-seven cases of drug-induced interstitial lung disease associated with imatinib mesylate. Leukemia. 2006;20(6):1162-1164. [PMID: 16598305]

## Item 73    Answer:  B
**Educational Objective:**  Monitor for delirium in the intensive care unit.

The Confusion Assessment Method for the Intensive Care Unit (CAM-ICU) is an instrument for nurses and physicians to use in evaluating a patient for delirium; the assessment takes less than 1 minute and is recommended for routine monitoring of all mechanically ventilated patients. The CAM-ICU, a well-validated and highly reliable method now translated into more than 10 languages, is widely used for monitoring delirium in ICU patients. The prevalence of delirium in most studies of mechanically ventilated patients is between 50% and 80%. ICU delirium has been shown to be an independent predictor of ICU and hospital length of stay, cost of care, cognitive status at hospital discharge, and 6-month mortality. The agitated, hyperactive subtype of delirium is much less common than the "quiet," hypoactive subtype, which is generally associated with a lower likelihood of survival.

The Beck Depression Inventory II consists of 21 items to assess the intensity of depression in clinical and normal patients. The Mini-Mental State Examination (MMSE) is a 30-point questionnaire that is used to screen for cognitive impairment. It is commonly used to screen for dementia. It is also used to estimate the severity of cognitive impairment at a given time and to follow the course of cognitive changes in a patient over time.

The diagnosis of delirium is a clinical one, and there are no laboratory tests, imaging studies, or other tests that can provide greater accuracy than the CAM-ICU algorithm. Specifically, a head CT scan and metabolic profile will not establish the diagnosis of delirium as effectively as CAM-ICU.

**KEY POINT**

- **The Confusion Assessment Method for the Intensive Care Unit (CAM-ICU), a clinical instrument for use in evaluating a patient in the intensive care unit for delirium, takes less than 1 minute and is recommended for all mechanically ventilated patients.**

**Bibliography**
Ely EW, Shintani A, Truman B, et al. Delirium as a predictor of mortality in mechanically ventilated patients in the intensive care unit. JAMA. 2004;291(14):1753-1762. [PMID: 15082703]

## Item 74     Answer: D

**Educational Objective:** Manage hypoventilation caused by opioid overdose.

The patient's acute ventilatory failure is most consistent with hypoventilation resulting from opioid intoxication. In pure hypoventilation, the alveolar-arterial difference is normal. The alveolar-arterial difference equals $[(PiO_2 - PcO_2/0.8) - PO_2]$ where $PiO_2$ is the partial pressure of oxygen in inspired air. $PiO_2$ equals the atmospheric pressure (760 mm Hg at sea level) minus the partial pressure of water (47 mm Hg at 37.0 °C) times the fraction of inspired oxygen (0.21). This patient's alveolar-arterial difference $[(150 - 80/0.8) - 40]$ is 10 mm Hg, which is normal for the patient. The normal alveolar-arterial gradient increases with age and can be estimated in patients breathing ambient air using the following equation: $[2.5 + (0.21 \times age\ in\ years)]$.

Improved alertness after administration of naloxone confirms opioid intoxication. Naloxone has a short half-life and is typically given as a continuous intravenous infusion. If the response to naloxone is inadequate, endotracheal intubation would be appropriate.

Hypoxemia in asthma exacerbations is caused by ventilation/perfusion mismatch, which is associated with elevation of the alveolar-arterial difference. Patients with an asthma exacerbation typically present with a respiratory alkalosis; respiratory arrest without first coming to medical attention would be unusual in a hospitalized patient.

Continuous positive airway pressure would not likely offer sufficient ventilation in this hypoventilating patient. The bilevel pressures used in noninvasive positive pressure ventilation might provide adequate ventilation but would be high risk in this patient with a depressed level of consciousness. Patients with a pulmonary embolism typically present with respiratory alkalosis and elevated alveolar-arterial difference, which is not consistent with this patient's findings. Therefore, intravenous heparin and CT angiography are not indicated.

**KEY POINT**

- **Continuous naloxone infusion is used to treat opioid intoxication.**

**Bibliography**
Peris LV, Boix JH, Salom JV, Valentin V, Garcia D, Arnau A. Clinical use of the arterial/alveolar oxygen tension ratio. Crit Care Med. 1983;11(11):888-891. [PMID 6627959]

## Item 75     Answer: B

**Educational Objective:** Diagnose exercise-induced asthma.

Exercise-induced asthma (EIA) occurs in nearly 90% of patients with asthma who exercise at sufficient intensity and is more common with exercise in cold, dry air. Exercise challenge testing (to greater than 85% of maximal predicted heart rate) with postexercise spirometry confirms the diagnosis. An exercise challenge test has a high specificity for the diagnosis when the fall in $FEV_1$ after exercise is 15% or greater. Airway obstruction after exercise peaks in 5 to 15 minutes and resolves in 20 to 30 minutes. Prophylaxis with short-acting inhaled β-agonists, such as albuterol, 5 to 10 minutes before exercise, prevents EIA in more than 80% of patients. With appropriate management, patients with EIA need not limit their involvement in sports.

Measurement of lung volumes and diffusing capacity for carbon monoxide is helpful in evaluating patients with suspected parenchymal lung diseases but is not likely to help in the evaluation of this patient given the symptoms and normal chest radiograph. Allergy skin test could be done in this patient at some point, and if positive, would support the diagnosis of asthma because most patients with asthma have allergies. But many patients with allergies do not have asthma; therefore, skin testing alone will not provide an explanation for the patient's symptoms. Checking resting arterial blood gases would have a very low yield in this young and otherwise healthy patient with a normal chest radiograph and spirometry.

**Bibliography**

Parsons JP, Mastronarde JG. Exercise-induced asthma. Curr Opin Pulm Med. 2009;15(1):25-28. [PMID: 19077702]

## Item 76      Answer:  B

**Educational Objective:**  Recognize a patient at risk for chronic obstructive pulmonary disease.

The patient's lung function as measured by spirometry does not fall into any of the Global Initiative on Obstructive Lung Disease (GOLD) stage classifications for chronic obstructive pulmonary disease (COPD). He is, however, at risk for COPD because of his smoking history and chronic cough and sputum production. The only definitive diagnosis of COPD is by spirometry. At-risk patients used to be classified as having GOLD stage 0 disease. The current staging system of GOLD is as follows:

**GOLD Stage**

At risk

    Normal spirometry

    Chronic symptoms (cough, sputum production)

I. *Mild*

    $FEV_1/FVC$ <70%

    $FEV_1$ ≥80% of predicted

II. *Moderate*

    $FEV_1/FVC$ <70%

    $FEV_1$ 50% to 80% of predicted

III. *Severe*

    $FEV_1/FVC$ <70%

    $FEV_1$ 30% to 50% of predicted

IV. *Very Severe*

    $FEV_1/FVC$ <70%

    $FEV_1$ <30% of predicted *or* <50% of predicted plus chronic respiratory failure

The outcome for treating at-risk patients is not yet clear. This population of patients is largely underdiagnosed. Because they are younger and mostly active smokers, detection at this stage may provide an opportunity for early intervention and initiating a smoking cessation program. About 15% of long-time smokers develop clinically significant COPD. Patients who quit smoking have a reduced decline in pulmonary function.

This patient does not have asthma. There is no evidence of bronchospasm, atopy, or airflow hyperreactivity or reversibility.

**Bibliography**

Maleki-Yazdi MR, Lewczuk, Haddon JM, Choudry N, Ryan N. Early Detection and Impaired quality of Life in COPD Stage O a pilot study. COPD. 2007;4(4):313-320. [PMID: 18027158]

## Item 77      Answer:  D

**Educational Objective:**  Evaluate pulmonary hypertension and chronic thromboembolic pulmonary hypertension.

The patient has chronic symptoms and echocardiographic evidence of pulmonary hypertension. Her history of acute pulmonary embolism raises the possibility of chronic thromboembolic pulmonary hypertension (CTEPH). Patients with CTEPH often present with unexplained progressively worsening dyspnea, especially dyspnea on exertion, in the absence of (or out of proportion to) pulmonary parenchymal disease. The predisposing acute pulmonary embolism may have been asymptomatic or undiagnosed, and, therefore, only about 50% of patients have a history of clinically detected pulmonary embolism. Ventilation/perfusion scanning can help determine whether the patient's pulmonary hypertension is due to obstruction of large pulmonary arteries (as is characteristic of CTEPH) or to widespread obstruction of the small pulmonary vasculature.

Pulmonary angiography can confirm the diagnosis of CTEPH and determine whether the large-vessel obstruction is amenable to surgical endarterectomy. Pulmonary arteriographic findings in CTEPH are very different from those in acute pulmonary embolism. In acute pulmonary embolism, intraluminal filling defects and abrupt vessel "cutoffs" are diagnostic. In CTEPH, however, the embolic material has been organized into the arterial wall itself, and angiography shows gradual tapering of the lumen, whereas the presence of webs and luminal irregularities give evidence of the body's ineffectual attempts at recanalization. However, screening for CTEPH with a ventilation/perfusion scan should take precedence over the more invasive pulmonary angiography as the next diagnostic test.

Coronary artery disease would be unlikely to result in isolated right ventricular hypertrophy and right atrial enlargement. Therefore, coronary angiography is not indicated. Endocardial biopsy might elucidate the cause of a diffuse cardiomyopathy. However, this patient's findings are specific to the right ventricle and suggest chronic strain and hypertrophy.

- Patients with chronic thromboembolic pulmonary hypertension often present with dyspnea on exertion without (or out of proportion to) pulmonary parenchymal disease.

**Bibliography**

Fedullo PF, Auger WR, Kerr KM, Rubin LJ. Chronic thromboembolic pulmonary hypertension. N Engl J Med. 2001;345(20): 1465-1472. [PMID: 11794196]

## Item 78    Answer:  D

**Educational Objective:** Diagnose and stage advanced lung cancer.

In the evaluation of a patient with suspected lung cancer, obtaining a tissue diagnosis is critical for treatment planning and determining prognosis. Staging the cancer and determining whether the patient is a candidate for resection are also important parts of the evaluation. In this patient, determining whether the supraclavicular node is involved with non–small cell cancer should be done, and the next step in the evaluation would be to sample the lymph node; this would likely establish both a diagnosis and that the patient has advanced unresectable disease.

As the clinical stage is already suggesting an advanced stage of disease, positron emission tomography (PET)–CT would not be needed for staging if the supraclavicular node is positive. A positive PET-CT in the supraclavicular lymph nodes would not obviate the need for node sampling. Biopsy of the mass or hilar lymph nodes by either CT guidance or bronchoscopy would establish the diagnosis but not the stage and would not determine resectability.

- In the evaluation of possible lung cancer, obtaining a tissue diagnosis and staging for lung cancer should be done simultaneously.

**Bibliography**

Silvestri GA, Gould MK, Margolis ML, et al; American College of Chest Physicians. Noninvasive staging of non-small cell lung cancer: ACCP evidenced-based clinical practice guidelines (2nd edition). Chest. 2007;132(3 Suppl):178S-201S. [PMID: 17873168]

## Item 79    Answer:  C

**Educational Objective:** Recognize the diagnostic value of pleural fluid amylase value and amylase isoenzymes in the diagnosis of a pleural effusion.

A pleural fluid amylase concentration greater than the upper limits of normal for serum amylase or a pleural fluid to serum amylase ratio greater than 1.0 suggests the following diagnoses: pancreatic disease (either acute pancreatitis or pancreaticopleural fistula), malignancy (most commonly adenocarcinoma of the lung), and esophageal perforation. Finding salivary isoamylase in pleural fluid virtually excludes acute pancreatitis and pancreaticopleural fistula. As the patient has not had an endoscopic procedure, particularly esophageal dilation, and has had no chest pain, fever, chills, severe vomiting, and retching, it would be highly unlikely that he had barogenic esophageal perforation. The pleural fluid amylase level was relatively low compared with values frequently over 100,000 U/L in the setting of a direct communication between a pancreatic pseudocyst and the pleural space with a pancreaticopleural fistula. Therefore, finding a high salivary isoamylase concentration in pleural fluid in the absence of esophageal perforation increases the likelihood of malignancy, most commonly adenocarcinoma of the lung because adenocarcinoma cells produce a salivary-like isoamylase.

- An elevated pleural fluid amylase level suggests that the cause of the pleural effusion is pancreatic disease, esophageal perforation, or malignancy.

**Bibliography**

Villena V, Perez V, Pozo F, et al. Amylase levels in pleural effusions. A consecutive unselected series of 81 patients. Chest. 2002;121(2): 470-474. [PMID: 11834659]

## Item 80    Answer:  C

**Educational Objective:** Recognize the neuroleptic malignant syndrome.

The neuroleptic malignant syndrome can result from administration of neuroleptic agents, such as haloperidol. Acute and abrupt withdrawal of antiparkinsonian medications may also precipitate the syndrome and may be the cause for this patient's symptoms. The pathogenesis of this syndrome results from dopamine $D_2$ receptor antagonism. Muscular rigidity and altered mental status occur early, followed by hyperthermia, hypertension, tremors, fever, dysphagia, diaphoresis, myoclonus, and autonomic dysfunction. Criteria for the diagnosis of neuroleptic malignant syndrome are based on clinical features, although elevations in serum potassium, creatine kinase, and lactate dehydrogenase levels and a metabolic acidosis are common. The mortality rate is 10% to 20%, although the rate is generally higher in patients who develop severe muscle necrosis and rhabdomyolysis.

The first sign of serious heat stroke is the absence of sweating and warm and dry skin. This patient's diaphoresis makes heat stroke unlikely.

Malignant hyperthermia is an inherited skeletal muscle disorder characterized by a hypermetabolic state precipitated by exposure to volatile inhalational anesthetics (halothane, isoflurane, enflurane, desflurane, sevoflurane) and the depolarizing muscle relaxants succinylcholine and decamethonium. Findings include sustained muscle contractions with skeletal muscle rigidity and masseter muscle spasm, tachycardia, hypercarbia, hypertension, hyperthermia, tachypnea, and cardiac arrhythmias. This patient's history does not include exposure to drugs responsible for malignant hyperthermia, making this diagnosis unlikely.

The serotonin syndrome is caused by use of selective serotonin reuptake inhibitors. Distinguishing features include shivering, hyperreflexia, myoclonus, and ataxia. The diagnosis of serotonin syndrome is less likely in the absence of evidence that the patient was taking a selective serotonin reuptake inhibitor drug.

**KEY POINT**

- **The neuroleptic malignant syndrome can result from administration of neuroleptic agents and abrupt withdrawal of antiparkinsonian medications.**

**Bibliography**

Adnet P, Lestavel P, Krivosic-Horber R. Neuroleptic malignant syndrome. Br J Anaesth. 2000;85(1):129-135. [PMID: 10928001]

## Item 81      Answer:  E

**Educational Objective:** Begin step-up therapy for asthma.

This patient with previously well-controlled asthma has had "loss of control" after having had a respiratory tract infection. A short course of an oral corticosteroid (for example, prednisone 0.5 mg/kg daily for 5 to 7 days) can resolve the asthma symptoms and enable the patient to regain control of her disease. It is unclear whether doubling (or even quadrupling) the dose of inhaled corticosteroids is an effective strategy in place of oral corticosteroids.

Antibiotics are generally not recommended for acute respiratory infections in asthma because most of these infections are viral. There are some data to suggest that atypical bacteria (for example, *Mycoplasma* or *Chlamydia*) may contribute to acute asthma exacerbations or persistence of symptoms after a respiratory tract infection. However, at this time the routine use of antibiotics in patients with an asthma exacerbation is not recommended.

Nebulized therapy at home should be reserved for patients who cannot use a metered-dose inhaler appropriately. Even though nebulized bronchodilator therapy can be more effective in reversing bronchoconstriction than metered-dose inhaled bronchodilators, nebulized therapy should not be used as a substitute for oral corticosteroid therapy in patients with asthma exacerbations. Adding a leukotriene-modifying agent can be considered in patients who cannot or will not take oral corticosteroids; however, leukotriene receptor antagonists are less potent anti-inflammatory agents than corticosteroids and are not effective in patients with significant exacerbations. Adding a long-acting β-agonist would be reasonable in this patient if her symptoms persist after the oral corticosteroid therapy, but the persistence and severity of the patient's current symptoms suggest that there is ongoing airway inflammation and that a systemic corticosteroid is warranted.

**KEY POINT**

- **A short course of oral corticosteroids may help restore asthma control in previously well-controlled patients who have developed unstable disease as a result of a respiratory tract infection.**

**Bibliography**

National Heart, Lung and Blood Institute. Expert Panel Report 3 (EPR3): Guidelines for the Diagnosis and Management of Asthma. www.nhlbi.nih.gov/guidelines/asthma/asthgdln.htm. Published August, 2007. Accessed July 27, 2009.

## Item 82      Answer:  B

**Educational Objective:** Manage progressive idiopathic pulmonary fibrosis.

Lung transplantation is the only therapy that improves survival in patients with idiopathic pulmonary fibrosis (IPF), and referral to a transplant center should be considered for all eligible patients with the disorder. Patients referred for transplantation should be free of significant other organ dysfunction, be younger than 65 years, have acceptable nutritional status, and have a satisfactory psychosocial profile and support system.

IPF is a relentlessly progressive form of interstitial lung disease, with a median survival from diagnosis of 3 to 4 years. No medical therapy has shown survival benefit in randomized, placebo-controlled clinical trials. Current options to manage patients with IPF include (1) referral of eligible patients for transplantation, (2) referral of interested patients for clinical research trials, (3) observation with supportive care and no medical therapy, and (4) a trial of corticosteroid therapy with or without a cytotoxic agent in an educated patient aware of the risks of unproven therapy.

Treatment of patients with immunosuppressive therapy including prednisone and cytotoxic agents, such as azathioprine, has not been shown to improve survival in IPF. A recent, large clinical trial investigating interferon-γ in patients with IPF was stopped early because of lack of benefit and a trend toward worsening outcome in patients treated with interferon-γ.

*N*-acetylcysteine has not been shown to improve the mortality rate in patients with IPF. Addition of *N*-acetylcysteine to prednisone and azathioprine may modestly improve lung function or protect against the cytotoxic effects of azathioprine. The effect of *N*-acetylcysteine monotherapy in IPF is not known and a large National Institutes of Health–sponsored clinical trial is currently underway to investigate these issues.

**KEY POINT**

- **Lung transplantation in eligible patients is the only therapy known to improve survival in patients with idiopathic pulmonary fibrosis.**

**Bibliography**

Daniels CE, Ryu JH. Treatment of idiopathic pulmonary fibrosis. Semin Respir Crit Care Med. 2006;27(6):668-676. [PMID: 17195143]

## Item 83     Answer:  A

**Educational Objective:**  Recommend risk-reduction procedures for a patient with chronic obstructive pulmonary disease undergoing elective surgery.

There is good evidence supporting routine lung expansion with incentive spirometry and deep-breathing exercises to prevent postoperative pulmonary complications in patients with chronic obstructive pulmonary disease. No particular pulmonary expansion modality has been found to be clearly superior to the others.

The data suggest that there is a moderate increase in risk for postoperative pulmonary complications among current smokers. There is also evidence suggesting that at least 2 months of smoking cessation reduces postoperative pulmonary risk. A brief period of abstinence does not improve perioperative pulmonary outcomes, and smokers who tried to decrease cigarette use shortly before surgery are more likely to develop a postoperative pulmonary complication than those who continued smoking. The preoperative consultation can certainly be used to reinforce the benefits of smoking cessation and even to consider delaying elective surgery in patients who are ready to quit, but smoking cessation 1 week prior to the planned surgery is unlikely to be helpful in preventing postoperative pulmonary complications.

Right-heart catheterization has not been found to prevent postoperative pulmonary complications. Evidence on prophylactic systemic corticosteroids before surgery for the prevention of postoperative pulmonary complications is insufficient to make a recommendation. Using leukocyte-depleted blood in transfusions has not been found to prevent postoperative pulmonary complications.

### KEY POINT

- Routine lung expansion with incentive spirometry and deep-breathing exercises has been shown to prevent postoperative pulmonary complications.

**Bibliography**

Qaseem A, Snow V, Fillerman N, et al; Risk assessment for and strategies to reduce perioperative pulmonary complications for patients undergoing noncardiothoracic surgery: a guideline from the American College of Physicians. Ann Intern Med. 2006:144(8):575-580. [PMID: 16618955]

## Item 84     Answer:  D

**Educational Objective:**  Manage chronic obstructive pulmonary disease exacerbation with noninvasive positive-pressure ventilation.

The patient is having a moderate to severe exacerbation of chronic obstructive pulmonary disease (COPD) and should be placed on noninvasive positive-pressure ventilation (NPPV). A landmark study found that NPPV reduced the need for intubation, the length of hospital stay, and the mortality rate in such patients. Suitable candidates for NPPV include patients with moderate to severe dyspnea, use of accessory respiratory muscles, respiration rate greater than 25/min, and pH less than 7.35 with $Pco_2$ greater than 45 mm Hg. Contraindications to NPPV include impending respiratory arrest, cardiovascular instability, altered mental status, high aspiration risk, production of copious secretions, and extreme obesity, as well as surgery, trauma, or deformity of the face or upper airway.

Intubation is inappropriate because the patient is not in respiratory arrest and is a suitable candidate for NPPV. However, if the patient's condition deteriorates or does not improve after 1 to 2 hours of NPPV, intubation should be considered. Most patients with exacerbations of COPD are usually easily oxygenated on low levels of inspired oxygen. Excessive oxygen supplementation can worsen carbon dioxide retention during a COPD exacerbation. Therefore, oxygen should be titrated to maintain a saturation of approximately 90%; increasing the nasal oxygen to 5 L/min is not indicated at this time.

Methylxanthines are generally not recommended for the treatment of acute exacerbations of COPD because they are not more effective than inhaled bronchodilators and corticosteroid therapy but can cause nausea and vomiting.

### KEY POINT

- Noninvasive positive-pressure ventilation should be initiated early in the course of moderate or severe exacerbations of chronic obstructive pulmonary disease unless there is a specific contraindication to use of noninvasive ventilation.

**Bibliography**

Quon BS, Gan WQ, Sin DD. Contemporary management of acute exacerbations of COPD: a systematic review and meta-analysis. Chest. 2008;133(3):756-766. [PMID: 18321904]

## Item 85     Answer:  E

**Educational Objective:**  Recognize and treat pheochromocytoma.

Acute pheochromocytoma hypertensive crises may occur before or during an operation, and patients require intravenous treatment with rapidly acting drugs such as sodium nitroprusside, phentolamine, or nicardipine. Sodium nitroprusside is typically preferred because of its rapid onset of action and short half-life.

Oral captopril and oral nifedipine are too slow acting and their blood pressure effect too unpredictable to be useful in the treatment of this patient. Metyrosine inhibits catecholamine synthesis, but this drug is generally used preoperatively in patients who cannot tolerate α- and β-adrenergic blockade. It must be administered 3 to 4 days before surgery and therefore is not indicated for treatment of a hypertensive crisis. The use of a β-blocker, either orally or intravenously, is contraindicated in a patient with a hypertensive crisis from pheochromocytoma because unopposed α-adrenergic activity may actually worsen the blood pressure.

- **Hypertensive crisis from pheochromocytoma is typically treated with sodium nitroprusside, phentolamine, or nicardipine.**

**Bibliography**

Pacak K. Preoperative management of the pheochromocytoma patient. J Clin Endocrinol Metab. 2007;92(11):4069-4079. [PMID: 17989126]

## Item 86      Answer:  A

**Educational Objective:**  Recognize contraindications to therapy with activated protein C.

All the contraindications for therapy with activated protein C (APC, drotrecogin alfa activated) therapy refer to bleeding risk. Heme-positive upper gastrointestinal aspirate or fecal occult blood testing in the absence of active bleeding (often present in intensive care unit patients) is not a contraindication to APC, but this patient's moderate upper gastrointestinal bleeding is a contraindication. As a rule of thumb, when systemic heparin is contraindicated, APC is also contraindicated.

A low platelet count (or elevated INR) is evidence of coagulopathy, which is a good reason to give APC (relative risk reduction of greater than 30%) as long as the platelet count is greater than $30,000/\mu L$ ($30 \times 10^9/L$) and the INR is 3.0 or less. An active malignancy that would predict less than 1 month of survival was an exclusion in the PROWESS study of the efficacy and safety of APC, and such patients were not investigated because they often have do-not-resuscitate orders early in severe life-threatening acute illness such as sepsis. In this case, a history of colon cancer in remission would not be a contraindication.

- **Activated protein C has anticoagulant properties, and evidence of active bleeding is a contraindication to its use in patients with sepsis.**

**Bibliography**

Bernard GR, Vincent JL, Laterre PF, et al; Recombinant human protein C Worldwide Evaluation in Severe Sepsis (PROWESS) study group. Efficacy and safety of recombinant human activated protein C for severe sepsis. N Eng J Med. 2001;344(10):699-709. [PMID: 11236773]

## Item 87      Answer:  D

**Educational Objective:**  Diagnose allergic bronchopulmonary aspergillosis.

Allergic bronchopulmonary aspergillosis (ABPA) is a rare (occurring in 1% to 2% of patients with asthma), but important, complication in patients with asthma. These patients develop humoral and cell-mediated immune responses to *Aspergillus fumigatus* in their airways, leading to persistent inflammation, airway damage with development of central bronchiectasis, and eventually pulmonary fibrosis. Features of the disorder include moderate to severe persistent asthma, expectoration of brown sputum that contains *Aspergillus* organisms, bronchiectasis and radiologic abnormalities (infiltrate, mucous plugging), elevated levels of serum total IgE (typically greater than 0.1 mg/dL [1.0 mg/L]), a positive skin test to *A. fumigatus*, and eosinophilia. Treatment often requires the use of systemic corticosteroids. A skin test to determine the presence of allergic response to *Aspergillus* is an important first step in evaluating patients with ABPA because essentially all patients with ABPA have a positive skin test. However, many patients with a positive skin test do not have ABPA, and therefore, the positive predictive value of the skin test is low. A negative skin prick test followed by negative intradermal skin test virtually excludes the diagnosis of ABPA, provided that the tests were done using optimal extracts and technique. If the skin test is positive, the next diagnostic step is measurement of serum total IgE. ABPA is excluded if the serum total IgE concentration is less than 0.1 mg/dL (1.0 mg/L). If skin testing for *Aspergillus* is not available, measuring serum total IgE may be an efficient way to pursue the diagnosis.

Bronchoscopy is an invasive procedure that is not indicated unless an alternative diagnosis (for example, a superimposed opportunistic infection) is suspected. Positron emission tomography may reveal increased uptake in the lungs due to ongoing pulmonary inflammation, but the information is unlikely to be specific or helpful in making a diagnosis in this patient and adds significant cost. A methacholine challenge test would be positive in patients with asthma regardless of the presence of ABPA. The test is not recommended in patients with symptomatic airway obstruction or $FEV_1$ less than 70% because of the risk of severe airway obstruction. The sweat chloride test is a screening test for cystic fibrosis, which leads to central bronchiectasis and chronic pulmonary infection with frequent exacerbations. However, the symptoms of cystic fibrosis typically start in childhood and rarely present for the first time at age 55 years and do not include eosinophilia, unless complicated by ABPA. Patients with cystic fibrosis are, however, at significant risk for ABPA, with most studies showing a prevalence of approximately 10%.

- **The characteristic features of allergic bronchopulmonary aspergillosis include moderate to severe persistent asthma, bronchiectasis and chest radiographic abnormalities, elevated serum IgE level, eosinophilia, and a positive skin test to *Aspergillus fumigatus*.**

Bibliography

Agarwal R. Allergic bronchopulmonary aspergillosis. Chest. 2009; 135(3):805-826. [PMID: 19265090]

## Item 88     Answer:   C

**Educational Objective:** Prescribe smoking cessation therapy in a patient with chronic obstructive pulmonary disease.

This patient has already used a nicotine patch unsuccessfully. However, using the high-dose patch again but in combination with another therapy, such as nicotine replacement with gum or spray, gives the best long-term cessation rate.

Bupropion has been shown to be effective in smoking cessation and is generally well tolerated. However, seizures occur in approximately 0.1% of patients who take the drug, and the risk appears to be higher in patients with a preexisting seizure disorder, anorexia nervosa, or bulimia. This patient has a history of seizure disorder, and, therefore, bupropion is contraindicated.

Varenicline can be used for smoking cessation, and the patient should try to stop smoking 1 week after starting varenicline. The common side effects are nausea and abnormal dreams. The U.S. Food and Drug Administration (FDA) has issued information regarding post-marketing reports of suicidal thoughts and erratic/aggressive behavior in patients who have taken varenicline. Many cases suggest new-onset depression, suicidal ideation, and emotional/behavioral changes within days to weeks after treatment initiation. It is not clear whether these effects are related to the drug itself or to the effects of smoking cessation. In this patient with a history of major depression and suicidal ideation, varenicline would not be indicated. In 2008, the FDA reported that it is increasingly likely that varenicline is associated with serious neuropsychiatric symptoms. There are also reports of patients experiencing drowsiness that affects their ability to drive or operate heavy machinery. The investigation by the FDA is ongoing.

**KEY POINT**

- A high-dose nicotine patch in combination with another antismoking therapy, such as nicotine replacement therapy (gum and/or spray), is the most effective therapy for smoking cessation.

Bibliography

Clinical Practice Guideline Treating Tobacco Use and Dependence 2008 Update Panel, Liaisons, and Staff. A Clinical Practice Guideline Treating Tobacco Use and Dependence: 2008 update. A US Public Health Service Report. Am J Prev Med. 2008;35(2):158-176 [PMID: 18617085]

## Item 89     Answer:   B

**Educational Objective:** Diagnose sarcoidosis.

This patient has radiographic features suggesting sarcoidosis, with mediastinal, hilar, and pulmonary parenchymal involvement and mild hypercalcemia. There is no definitive diagnostic test for sarcoidosis. Diagnosis is established by demonstrating histopathologic evidence of noncaseating granulomas in a compatible clinical setting with supportive imaging and exclusion of diseases with similar histopathologic findings. Patients with suspected sarcoidosis should have tissue biopsy performed on accessible lesions to confirm the diagnosis. Fiberoptic bronchoscopy with transbronchial lung biopsy is the initial procedure when suspecting sarcoidosis and has a reported diagnostic yield of 46% to 90%. The addition of transbronchoscopic needle aspiration of mediastinal lymph nodes and bronchoalveolar lavage to transbronchoscopic lymph node biopsy increases the diagnostic sensitivity of bronchoscopy and helps to exclude competing diagnoses. If available, endobronchial ultrasonography–guided transbronchoscopic needle aspiration of abnormal lymph nodes is a low-risk procedure with a reported sensitivity of 85% for sarcoidosis.

Bone marrow biopsy occasionally shows noncaseating granulomatous inflammation in patients with systemic sarcoidosis but should not be considered the next diagnostic test in this patient because the diagnostic yield is low in a patient with no hematologic abnormalities. Although fungal disease is a diagnostic consideration, fungal serologies, such as *Histoplasma* antibody testing, are not specific.

Mediastinoscopy remains the gold standard for undiagnosed mediastinal lymphadenopathy, but it has higher morbidity and cost than bronchoscopy with parenchymal and mediastinal biopsies. If bronchoscopy is not diagnostic, mediastinoscopy may be the next appropriate test. Observation and follow-up chest radiograph in 6 months of suspected cases of sarcoidosis is occasionally appropriate. For instance, patients presenting with typical findings of Löfgren syndrome (erythema nodosum with hilar lymphadenopathy and migratory arthralgia) is highly specific for sarcoidosis, has a good prognosis for spontaneous improvement, and may be carefully observed without treatment. However, this patient does not have findings suggesting Löfgren syndrome.

**KEY POINT**

- Patients with suspected sarcoidosis should have tissue biopsy of accessible lesions to confirm the diagnosis.

Bibliography

Garwood S, Judson MA, Silvestri G, et al. Endobronchial ultrasound for the diagnosis of pulmonary sarcoidosis. Chest. 2007;132(4): 1298-1304. [PMID: 17890467]

## Item 90     Answer:   C

**Educational Objective:** Manage chronic thromboembolic pulmonary hypertension.

This patient has echocardiographic evidence of pulmonary hypertension and evidence on ventilation/perfusion scanning of regional perfusion defects suggestive of chronic thromboembolic pulmonary hypertension (CTEPH). Pulmonary angiography is typically performed next and can confirm the diagnosis and determine whether the large-vessel obstruction is amenable to surgical therapy. The definitive therapy is pulmonary thromboendarterectomy, which is performed only in centers with special expertise in the preoperative evaluation, surgery, and postoperative therapy for these patients.

CTEPH is a progressive disease that causes significant mortality if not evaluated and treated in a timely manner. Although CTEPH is a complication of acute pulmonary embolism, the disease is due to a combination of organized intra-arterial scarring and a secondary small-vessel reaction. Acute anticoagulation with heparin followed by chronic warfarin therapy or thrombolysis would do little to reverse the disease. Bosentan may have a role in the treatment of patients with CTEPH in whom surgery is not possible. However, bosentan therapy is controversial and would not relieve the primary cause of the pulmonary artery obstruction. It would not be appropriate to use this controversial treatment instead of referral for definitive treatment by pulmonary thromboendarterectomy.

### KEY POINT

- **The definitive therapy for chronic thromboembolic pulmonary hypertension is pulmonary thromboendarterectomy.**

**Bibliography**
Fedullo PF, Auger WR, Kerr KM, Rubin LJ. Chronic thromboembolic pulmonary hypertension. N Engl J Med. 2001;345(20):1465-1472. [PMID: 11794196]

## Item 91          Answer:  D

**Educational Objective:**  Recognize a paraneoplastic syndrome associated with small cell carcinoma.

Paraneoplastic neurologic disorders are associated with systemic malignancy but are not related to direct tumor involvement or to other toxic or metabolic, infectious, or vascular complications of cancer. Paraneoplastic sensory neuropathy is commonly associated with lung carcinoma (particularly small cell carcinoma) but may develop in patients with other malignancies. The neurologic syndrome precedes the diagnosis of cancer in most patients. Paraneoplastic sensory neuropathy manifests with progressive paresthesias, profound sensory ataxia, and multimodality sensory loss. Such patients usually have limited-stage small cell lung carcinoma at presentation. The ANNA-1 antibody is the most common antibody present in a sensory neuropathy associated with small cell carcinoma. Paraneoplastic neurologic syndromes are uncommonly associated with the other cell types of lung cancer or other tissue malignancies.

### KEY POINT

- **The ANNA-1 antibody is the most common antibody present in a sensory neuropathy due to small cell lung carcinoma.**

**Bibliography**
Maddison P, Lang B. Paraneoplastic neurological autoimmunity and survival in small-cell lung cancer. J Neuroimmunol. 2008;201-202:159-62. [PMID: 18667241]

## Item 92          Answer:  B

**Educational Objective:**  Manage poor tolerance of ventilator weaning.

Ventilatory support in patients with chronic ventilatory failure should be targeted to match the baseline $P_{CO_2}$. At baseline, the patient has a chronic respiratory acidosis, but his $P_{CO_2}$ normalized while he was receiving mechanical ventilation. Subsequent reversal of his renal compensation prevented a sustained period of metabolic alkalosis. However, he cannot sustain a $P_{CO_2}$ of 40 mm Hg during trials of spontaneous breathing, resulting in acute respiratory acidosis and difficulty with ventilator weaning. The $P_{CO_2}$ is inversely proportional to alveolar ventilation. Reducing the ventilator rate from 15/min to 10/min will result in a roughly proportional increase in $P_{CO_2}$ to his baseline of 60 mm Hg.

The patient otherwise is a good candidate for weaning in that he is requiring only a modest amount of ventilator support and has minimal secretions. The patient's oxygen desaturation during his weaning trial is mild, and the primary problem is respiratory acidosis.

Anxiety and agitation can complicate ventilator weaning in good candidates. However, this typically manifests when sedation is reduced. This patient is alert, oriented, and doing well while receiving full ventilator support, which makes it unlikely that an increase in sedation will expedite weaning.

The patient's critical illness and exposure to systemic corticosteroids place him at risk of intensive care unit (ICU)–acquired weakness. However, he has a strong cough, is moving all extremities, and has been critically ill for only 3 days. ICU-acquired weakness develops in approximately 25% of ICU patients receiving mechanical ventilation for at least 7 days.

### KEY POINT

- **Excessive ventilation can cause difficulty weaning in patients who otherwise require only modest ventilator support.**

**Bibliography**
Koh Y. Ventilatory management in patients with chronic airflow obstruction. Crit Care Clinics. 2007;23(2):169-181. [PMID: 17368164]

## Item 93          Answer:  E

**Educational Objective:**  Diagnose and manage cough-variant asthma.

The patient has cough-variant asthma. A trial of inhaled albuterol could help control the patient's symptoms and confirm the diagnosis. The most common causes of chronic cough are asthma, postnasal drip syndrome (chronic sinusitis-rhinitis), and gastroesophageal reflux disease (GERD). Bronchoscopy and chest CT play no role in diagnosing cough due to these three causes. The diagnosis of cough-variant asthma is suggested by the presence of airway hyperresponsiveness and confirmed when cough resolves with asthma therapy.

Sensitivity to cold air is a clinical marker of airway hyperresponsiveness that can be confirmed with a methacholine challenge test. The methacholine challenge test has a negative predictive value of nearly 100% in the context of cough; this test is extremely useful in ruling out asthma, but because it has a poor positive predictive value, it is not very useful in patients with high prior probability of airway hyperresponsiveness. There is little about the character and timing of chronic cough due to GERD that distinguishes it from other conditions; in addition, it often can be "silent" from a gastrointestinal standpoint. However, the patient failed to benefit from 3 months of empiric gastric acid suppression therapy for GERD; therefore it is reasonable to rule out cough-variant asthma before pursuing 24-hour esophageal pH monitoring.

The patient does not have postnasal drip, purulent nasal secretions, sinus congestion, or other symptoms to suggest chronic or recurrent sinusitis and has not responded to treatment. Therefore, CT scan of the sinuses is not necessary. If the patient does not respond to albuterol, eosinophilic bronchitis should be considered as the cause of chronic cough, and bronchoscopy should be done to confirm that diagnosis.

**KEY POINT**

- **The diagnosis of cough-variant asthma is suggested by the presence of airway hyperresponsiveness and confirmed when cough resolves with a trial of inhaled albuterol.**

**Bibliography**
Abouzgheib W, Pratter MR, Bartter T. Cough and asthma. Curr Opin Pulm Med. 2007;13(1):44-48. [PMID: 17133124]

## Item 94        Answer:  A

**Educational Objective:**  Refer a patient with severe chronic obstructive pulmonary disease for lung transplantation.

Patients with homogenous emphysema, an $FEV_1$ not greater than 20% of predicted, and $D_{LCO}$ not greater than 20% of predicted have a median survival of 3 years and should be considered for lung transplantation. This patient is a candidate for transplantation. Functional capacity and quality of life are improved after lung transplantation, but the effect on overall survival is mixed.

The National Emphysema Therapeutic Trial of lung volume reduction surgery reported mixed results on patient outcomes. For patients with very reduced lung function ($FEV_1$ less than 20%), low $D_{LCO}$ (less than 20%), and diffuse disease, the

mortality rate was greater with surgery than with medical therapy. However, in patients with predominant upper lobe emphysema and low baseline exercise tolerance, functional capacity and survival improved. Patients with homogeneous emphysema, $FEV_1$ less than 20% of predicted, and $D_{LCO}$ less than 20% of predicted have high mortality rates with lung volume reduction surgery. This patient did not benefit from 6 months of pulmonary rehabilitation and is unlikely to benefit from additional rehabilitation. Patients with severe chronic obstructive pulmonary disease, daytime hypercapnia, and nocturnal oxygen desaturation despite supplemental oxygen might benefit from the use of nocturnal assisted ventilation, but this patient does not have nocturnal desaturation.

**KEY POINT**

- **Patients who have emphysema, an $FEV_1$ not greater than 20% of predicted, and homogeneous disease on high-resolution CT or $D_{LCO}$ not greater than 20% should be considered for lung transplantation.**

**Bibliography**
Patel N, DeCamp M, Criner GJ. Lung transplantation and lung volume reduction surgery versus transplantation in chronic obstructive pulmonary disease. Proc Am Thoracic Soc. 2008; 5(4):447-453. [PMID: 18453354]

## Item 95        Answer:   D

**Educational Objective:**  Manage drug-induced organizing pneumonia.

This patient has organizing pneumonia, which is likely caused by treatment with pegylated interferon alfa. Organizing pneumonia is a nonspecific reparative reaction that can occur in infections, connective tissue diseases, drug reactions, and radiation-induced lung injury. The presentation and radiographic findings depend on the cause of the organizing pneumonia. Organizing pneumonia presenting without an identifiable cause is termed cryptogenic organizing pneumonia (COP, formerly called idiopathic bronchiolitis obliterans organizing pneumonia). Patients with COP often present with such systemic symptoms as fever and weight loss. The typical radiographic presentation of COP is bilateral migratory patchy alveolar infiltrates. Organizing pneumonia can present radiographically as a distinct nodule or nodules indistinguishable from malignancy. Focal organizing pneumonia is typically positron emission tomographic (PET) scan–positive, and, therefore, PET does not differentiate focal organizing pneumonia from malignancy. Pegylated interferon alfa has been reported to cause drug-induced lung injury with several histopathologic patterns, including organizing and granulomatous lung disease. When a drug is suspected of causing pulmonary toxicity, it should be stopped whenever reasonable. Treatment with corticosteroids may benefit this patient with systemic symptoms.

Bronchoscopic biopsy provides diagnostic tissue, and resection is not needed. Although fungal infection could cause a similar clinicoradiographic presentation, this patient has had multiple biopsies and cultures that failed to show fungal infection; therefore, antifungal therapy is not needed. Observation and follow-up CT in 3 months would not be appropriate. Failure to recognize and treat drug-induced lung disease leads to continuous or progressive symptoms while the offending agent is continued.

**KEY POINT**

- Organizing pneumonia is a nonspecific reparative reaction that can occur in infections, connective tissue diseases, drug reactions, and radiation-induced lung injury.

**Bibliography**

Maldonado F, Daniels CE, Hoffman EA, Yi ES, Ryu JH. Focal organizing pneumonia on surgical lung biopsy: causes, clinicoradiologic features, and outcomes. Chest. 2007:132(5):1579-1583. [PMID: 17890462]

## Item 96      Answer:  B

**Educational Objective:**  Treat severe pulmonary arterial hypertension.

This patient has severe pulmonary arterial hypertension. Intravenous epoprostenol can have an immediate and substantial beneficial effect in such patients. However, because of the complexity and risk associated with epoprostenol therapy, it is best used in a center with special expertise in the evaluation and treatment of pulmonary arterial hypertension.

There is no evidence of hemodynamically significant acute thromboembolism in this patient, and thrombolytic medications would not affect the mechanisms causing pulmonary arterial hypertension. By increasing intrathoracic pressure and limiting venous return, mechanical ventilation may in fact worsen the patient's hemodynamic status and should be reserved for when the patient is truly in respiratory failure. Only a minority of patients (approximately 6%) with pulmonary arterial hypertension respond well to calcium channel blockade. In this patient, with preexisting hemodynamic instability, calcium channel blockade should be avoided. The ventilation/perfusion scan that disclosed no regional perfusion defects essentially ruled out chronic thromboembolic pulmonary hypertension, and pulmonary thromboendarterectomy is, therefore, not indicated.

**KEY POINT**

- Intravenous epoprostenol can have an immediate and substantial beneficial effect in severe pulmonary arterial hypertension, but it is best used in a specialized center.

**Bibliography**

Badesch DB, Abman SH, Simonneau G, Rubin LJ, McLaughlin VV. Medical therapy for pulmonary arterial hypertension: updated ACCP evidence-based clinical practice guidelines. Chest. 2007; 131(6):1917-1928. [PMID: 17565025]

## Item 97      Answer:  C

**Educational Objective:**  Evaluate metastatic lung nodules.

This patient has multiple pulmonary nodules, and metastatic disease would lead the differential diagnosis. A CT-guided needle biopsy would likely establish the diagnosis and would have significantly higher yield for nodules of this size than would bronchoscopy. There are reported yields of about 90% for nodules of 1 to 2 cm with transthoracic needle aspiration and less that 50% for bronchoscopy.

Video-assisted thoracoscopic nodule resection would also establish the diagnosis but by a more invasive means than needle aspiration. Because of the number and bilateral nature of the nodules, primary resection would not be pursued for treatment. Positron emission tomography–CT would likely show these nodules to be 18F-fluorodeoxyglucose (FDG)-avid, but this finding would not obviate the need for tissue diagnosis or alter the stage.

**KEY POINT**

- Transthoracic needle aspiration has high yield for evaluation of pulmonary nodules 1 to 2 cm in diameter.

**Bibliography**

Gould MK, Fletcher J, Iannettoni MD, et al; American College of Chest Physicians. American College of Chest Physicians. Evaluation of patients with pulmonary nodules: when is it lung cancer?: ACCP evidence-based clinical practice guidelines (2nd edition). Chest. 2007;132(3 Suppl):108S-130S. [PMID: 17873164]

## Item 98      Answer:  A

**Educational Objective:**  Facilitate weaning from mechanical ventilation.

Increasingly, protocol-driven care is being integrated into the routine management of patients in the intensive care unit. This approach has proven to be especially effective in weaning patients from mechanical ventilation. A randomized controlled trial found a protocol that paired sedation reduction and spontaneous breathing trials resulted in fewer days of mechanical ventilation, earlier discharge from the intensive care unit, and earlier hospital discharge compared with daily spontaneous breathing trials alone.

One randomized study found early extubation of 50 patients with exacerbation of chronic obstructive pulmonary disease directly to noninvasive positive-pressure ventilation shortened stays in the intensive care unit and improved survival. However, these benefits were not duplicated in subsequent studies, and this approach is suitable only for highly selected patients with acute-on-chronic respiratory failure rather than this patient with acute respiratory failure.

Increasing supplemental oxygen beyond 50% will not expedite weaning. Patients requiring more than 50% supplemental oxygen are generally not considered candidates for weaning. Daily, rather than every other day, trials of spontaneous breathing reduce the duration of mechanical ventilation.

This patient requires modest ventilator support, and her condition is improving. The anticipated duration of invasive mechanical ventilation is brief, and tracheostomy is not routinely indicated in such cases. Limited evidence suggests early tracheostomy can improve outcomes in patients receiving invasive mechanical ventilation, but there is no consensus on the selection criteria and timing of early tracheostomy.

**KEY POINT**

- Daily spontaneous breathing trials and daily sedation reduction both reduce the duration of mechanical ventilation, and combining the two is superior to daily breathing trials alone.

**Bibliography**

Girard T, Kress J, Fuchs B, et al. Efficacy and safety of paired sedation and ventilator weaning protocol for mechanically ventilated patients in intensive care (Awake and Breathing Controlled trial): a randomised controlled trial. Lancet. 2008;371(8607):126-34. [PMID: 18191684]

## Item 99      Answer:  A

**Educational Objective:** Manage severe sepsis with aggressive fluid resuscitation.

The patient has severe sepsis presumptively from pyelonephritis. Aggressive fluid resuscitation with resolution of lactic acidosis within 6 hours would have a beneficial effect on this patient's survival. Resuscitation of the circulation should target a central venous oxygen saturation ($S\text{c}\text{v}\text{o}_2$) or mixed venous oxygen saturation ($S\text{v}\text{o}_2$) of at least 70%. Other reasonable goals include a central venous pressure of 8 to 12 mm Hg, a mean arterial pressure of at least 65 mm Hg, and a urine output of at least 0.5 mL/kg/h. In patients such as the one presented, this often translates into administration of 5 to 6 L of fluid. Timing of resuscitation matters to survival. In a landmark study by Rivers and colleagues, early goal-directed therapy that included interventions within the first 6 hours to maintain a $S\text{c}\text{v}\text{o}_2$ of greater than 70% and to resolve lactic acidosis resulted in higher survival rates than more delayed resuscitation attempts. Over the first 72 hours, patients in the control arm received the same quantity of fluid for resuscitation, but they had a significantly higher likelihood of dying by discharge or at 60 days.

Crystalloid is given much more frequently than colloid, and there are no data to support routinely using colloid in lieu of crystalloid. Blood transfusion may be part of resuscitation for anemic patients in shock, but maintaining hemoglobin levels above 12 g/dL (120 g/L) is not supported by evidence. In stable patients who are not in shock, a transfusion threshold of 7 g/dL (70 g/L) is an acceptable conservative approach. There are no data to support that maintaining a lower $P\text{co}_2$ or using a pulmonary artery catheter would help to increase survival in this patient.

**KEY POINT**

- In patients with severe sepsis, early goal-directed therapy within the first 6 hours to maintain a central venous or mixed venous oxygen saturation of greater than 70% and to resolve lactic acidosis improves survival compared with more delayed resuscitation attempts.

**Bibliography**

Rivers E, Nguyen B, Havstad S, et al; Early Goal-Directed Therapy Collaborative Group. Early goal-directed therapy in the treatment of severe sepsis and septic shock. N Engl J Med. 2001;345(19):1368-1377. [PMID: 11794169]

## Item 100      Answer:  B

**Educational Objective:** Recognize and treat organophosphate poisoning.

This patient likely has organophosphate poisoning. Organophosphates are a diverse group of chemicals used in both domestic and industrial settings that include insecticides, nerve gases (soman, sarin, tabun, VX), ophthalmic agents (echothiophate, isoflurophate), and antihelmintics (trichlorfon). Exposure to organophosphate insecticides may occur by dermal, gastrointestinal, inhalational, and intravenous routes. Organophosphate insecticides inhibit both cholinesterase and pseudocholinesterase activities. The inhibition of cholinesterase activity leads to accumulation of acetylcholine at synapses, causing overstimulation and disruption of neurotransmission in both the central and peripheral nervous systems. Signs and symptoms of organophosphate poisoning include muscarinic effects, nicotinic effects, and central nervous system effects peripherally at muscarinic receptors and nicotinic receptors. Muscarinic manifestations include excessive salivation, diarrhea, vomiting, hypersalivation, respiratory distress with bronchorrhea and bronchospasm, abdominal pain, depressed level of consciousness, and muscle fasciculations. The muscarinic signs of organophosphate poisoning can be recalled with the help of the mnemonic DUMBELS—Defecation, Urination, Miosis, Bronchorrhea/Bronchospasm/Bradycardia, Emesis, Lacrimation, Salivation. Nicotinic manifestations include increased muscle weakness, skeletal muscle fasciculations, and respiratory failure secondary to diaphragmatic paralysis. Central nervous system effects include altered mental status and seizures. Organophosphate insecticide poisoning is a serious condition that requires rapid diagnosis and treatment.

Pralidoxime (2-PAM) reactivates acetylcholinesterase and can reverse the muscle weakness, paralysis, and respiratory depression of organophosphate toxicity. Although atropine treats the bronchorrhea, it does not reverse the muscle weakness or respiratory depression. Amyl nitrite, sodium nitrite, and sodium thiosulfate are used to treat cyanide toxicity and are ineffective in the treatment of organophosphate poisoning. The most common early clinical manifestations of cyanide poisoning include headache and confusion, coma, tachypnea, tachycardia, and skin flushing. Excessive salivation, wheezing, and bronchorrhea do not occur. An anion-gap metabolic acidosis typically occurs as well as a low arterial-venous oxygen gradient as a result of hyperoxygenation of the venous blood.

**KEY POINT**

- Pralidoxime (2-PAM) reactivates acetylcholinesterase and can reverse the muscle weakness, paralysis, and respiratory depression of organophosphate toxicity.

**Bibliography**
Peter JV, Moran JL, Graham P. Oxime therapy and outcomes in human organophosphate poisoning: an evaluation using meta-analytic techniques. Crit Care Med. 2006;34(2):502-510. [PMID: 16424734]

## Item 101      Answer:  C
**Educational Objective:**  Diagnose vocal cord dysfunction.

Vocal cord dysfunction (VCD) can mimic asthma. However, in contrast to asthma, the symptoms often begin and end abruptly and do not usually respond to inhaled β-agonists. Symptoms often include throat or neck discomfort, inspiratory wheezing, and anxiety. Many affected patients have asthma as well as VCD, thus complicating the diagnosis. VCD can occur during exercise, in which case it must be distinguished from exercise-induced asthma. An important difference between asthma and VCD is that airflow limitation in asthma is mainly during expiration, whereas in VCD the limitation occurs mainly during inspiration. Flow volume loops document the inspiratory and expiratory flow by recording the flow while the patient inhales as deeply as possible and then exhales as much as possible. An inspiratory cut-off in flow (flattening of the inspiratory portion of the flow loop) with relatively preserved expiratory flow indicates an extrathoracic variable obstruction that is typical in patients with VCD. However, flow volume loops may be normal when the patient is asymptomatic between episodes.

Another confirmatory test for VCD is laryngoscopy at the time of symptoms that reveals abnormal adduction of the vocal cords on inspiration. Management should target predisposing factors, mainly postnasal drip and gastroesophageal reflux disease. Even after controlling these problems, many patients continue to have episodes and require additional approaches, including speech therapy, relaxation techniques, and antianxiety medications. Chest radiograph, CT scan of the neck, and thyroid function tests would not add any additional diagnostic information in this patient with VCD.

**KEY POINT**

- Vocal cord dysfunction is diagnosed by flow volume loops showing an inspiratory cut-off in flow with relatively preserved expiratory flow indicative of an extrathoracic variable obstruction.

**Bibliography**
Ibrahim WH, Gheriani HA, Almohamed AA, Raza T. Paradoxical vocal cord motion disorder: past, present and future. Postgrad Med J. 2007;83(977):164-172. [PMID: 17344570]

## Item 102      Answer:  D
**Educational Objective:**  Recognize chronic obstructive pulmonary disease as a cause of weight loss.

Severe chronic obstructive pulmonary disease (COPD) can cause systemic effects including unexplained weight loss, skeletal muscle dysfunction, increased cardiovascular morbidity and mortality, increased risk for type 2 diabetes mellitus, osteoporosis, fractures, and depression. Unexplained weight loss occurs in about half of the patients with severe COPD, mostly due to the loss of skeletal muscle mass. Unexplained weight loss carries a poor prognosis in COPD independent of other indicators, such as $FEV_1$ or $Pco_2$.

Although the weight loss of malignancy is a possibility in this patient, the absence of gastrointestinal symptoms or other localizing symptoms, the normal cancer screening tests within the last year, and the patient's history of severe COPD make the cachexia of COPD the most likely cause in this patient. The patient's spirometry indicates severe COPD and aggressive management of COPD is necessary. Evaluation for depression is also indicated.

The mechanisms underlying these systemic effects are unclear; they are probably interrelated and multifactorial, including inactivity, systemic inflammation, tissue hypoxia, and oxidative stress. Increases in concentrations of inflammatory mediators indicating peripheral blood cell activation also have been found throughout the body and may mediate some of these systemic effects.

**KEY POINT**

- Severe chronic obstructive pulmonary disease can cause systemic effects including unintentional weight loss; skeletal muscle dysfunction; and increased risk of cardiovascular disease, osteoporosis, and depression.

**Bibliography**
Agusti A, Soriano JB. COPD as a systemic disease. COPD. 2008; 5(2):133-138. [PMID: 18415812]

## Item 103      Answer:  D
**Educational Objective:**  Recognize smoking-related interstitial lung disease.

Although the current American Thoracic Society/European Respiratory Society classification of interstitial lung disease (ILD) lists respiratory bronchiolitis interstitial lung disease (RB-ILD) as an idiopathic ILD, it is causally linked to smoking. Diagnosis of RB-ILD requires the clinical context of a patient with a significant smoking history. Respiratory bronchiolitis, which is also called smoker's bronchiolitis, is common among smokers and is thought to be responsible for the reduction in air flow in young, otherwise healthy smokers. The histopathologic diagnosis of respiratory bronchiolitis is made when pigmented macrophages accumulate in the bronchioles and peribronchiolar alveolar spaces. The difference between respiratory bronchiolitis and RB-ILD is poorly defined in the literature, but the diagnosis of RB-ILD is appropriate when patients have clinical and radiographic evidence of ILD in addition to airway disease. Pulmonary function testing typically shows a mixed obstructive–restrictive pattern with a slightly reduced diffusing capacity for carbon monoxide but in some cases, testing may be normal or associated with only an increase in the residual volume. Histopathologically, RB-ILD is usually associated with a greater degree of peribronchiolar fibrosis if lung biopsy is obtained. The most important treatment intervention is smoking cessation. Although previous reports suggest clinical improvement can be expected in patients who quit smoking, a recent study by Portnoy and colleagues reported clinical improvement in less than one third of RB-ILD patients who quit smoking.

Although smoking is associated with an increased relative risk for other ILDs, including idiopathic pulmonary fibrosis, RB-ILD is causally linked to inhalation of tobacco smoke, whereas cryptogenic organizing pneumonia, idiopathic pulmonary fibrosis, and nonspecific interstitial pneumonia are not. Finally, these disorders are typically associated with restrictive physiology without evidence of airflow obstruction, which is an important point in distinguishing these diseases from RB-ILD.

**KEY POINT**

- Diagnosis of respiratory bronchiolitis interstitial lung disease requires the clinical context of a patient with a significant past or current smoking history.

**Bibliography**

Portnoy J, Veraldi KL, Schwarz MI, et al. Respiratory bronchiolitis interstitial lung disease: long-term outcome. Chest. 2007;131(3);664-671. [PMID: 17356078]

## Item 104   Answer:   E

**Educational Objective:**  Determine readiness for extubation among patients receiving invasive mechanical ventilation.

This patient has clinically improved and tolerated a trial of spontaneous breathing. However, he still is requiring frequent suctioning and would, therefore, be at high risk for failing a trial of extubation. It is particularly important to consider the burden of secretions in patients with impaired cough, such as this patient with neuromuscular weakness. This case emphasizes the importance of addressing whether the patient needs the ventilator and whether the patient needs the endotracheal tube before extubation.

Improvement in the radiographic appearance of pneumonia typically lags substantially behind clinical improvement. Therefore, the appearance of chest radiographs does not routinely influence the time course of ventilator weaning.

The patient's rapid shallow breathing index (RSBI) during a trial of spontaneous breathing indicates that he is ready to breathe independent of the ventilator. The RSBI (respiration rate/tidal volume) in this patient is 20/min/0.5 L or 40 breaths/min/L; values less than 105 breaths/min/L have been shown to be predictive of extubation success.

The patient has adequate oxygenation on 40% supplemental oxygen. Patients with supplemental oxygen needs less than 40% to 50% are considered suitable candidates for weaning.

**KEY POINT**

- Patients requiring frequent suctioning or with impaired ability to clear secretions are not suitable candidates for extubation even if they do not require mechanical ventilatory support.

**Bibliography**

Yang KL, Tobin MJ. A prospective study of indexes predicting the outcome of trials of weaning from mechanical ventilation. N Engl J Med. 1991;324(21):1445-1450. [PMID: 2023603]

## Item 105   Answer:   B

**Educational Objective:**  Manage hyperglycemia in a critically ill patient.

Glucose control in critically ill patients is now practiced widely. Hyperglycemia is believed to contribute to various physiologic derangements, such as inflammation and coagulopathy, that should be controlled in the septic patient. The exact range and goal for target glucose levels have been controversial, with previous studies suggesting that intensive glucose control (a target level of 80 to 110 mg/dL [4.4 to 6.1 mmol/L]) reduced mortality. However, in a recent large, international, randomized trial (the NICE-SUGAR study), intensive glucose control increased mortality among adults in the intensive care unit; a conventional blood glucose target of less than or equal to 180 mg/dL (10.0 mmol/L) resulted in lower mortality than did a target of 81 to 108 mg/dL (4.5 to 6.0 mmol/L).

Continuous intravenous insulin is the most effective method for adequate glycemic control in these patients. Subcutaneous regular insulin based on a sliding scale and intermediate-acting or long-acting basal insulin do not offer the best acute titration of glucose in intensive care unit patients who may have volatile glucose levels. Furthermore, current guidelines emphasize the need to reconsider the widespread use of regular insulin sliding scales, which often result in labile glucose control, as the sole antihyperglycemic therapy in hospitalized patients. Instead, more active, physiologic insulin regimens are advisable.

**KEY POINT**

- Continuous intravenous insulin is the most effective method for adequate glycemic control in critically ill patients.

**Bibliography**

Finfer S, Chittock DR, Su SY, et al; NICE-SUGAR Study Investigators. Intensive versus conventional glucose control in critically ill patients. N Engl J Med. 2009;360(13):1283-1297. [PMID: 19318384]

## Item 106     Answer:   C

**Educational Objective:**  Diagnose the reactive airways dysfunction syndrome.

Many chemicals are irritants to the respiratory tract, affecting both the upper and lower airways. Asthma occurring after an acute, high-level exposure to an irritant is called the reactive airways dysfunction syndrome (RADS). Respiratory tract irritants reported to cause RADS include chlorine and its derivatives (hydrochloric acid, chlorine dioxide, phosgene), acids, ammonia, bromine, bleaches, isocyanates, formaldehyde, pyrolysis products contained in smoke, and aromatic hydrocarbons in sealants. RADS follows a single, accidental inhalation of high levels of a nonspecific respiratory irritant in patients who typically do not have a history of asthma. Within minutes of exposure, the patient develops cough, wheezing, dyspnea, and chest tightness. Symptoms persist even after the exposure has stopped and may last for years. The diagnosis is based on history and confirmed by a positive methacholine challenge test. Methacholine challenge testing can be done safely in patients with asthma provided that appropriate guidelines are followed and that the $FEV_1$ is greater than 70% of predicted. Pharmacologic management is similar to that of other forms of asthma. Avoidance of nonspecific asthma triggers is often helpful.

Exposure challenge with chlorine poses an unnecessary risk of severe attacks and would not be indicated in this patient. Histologic features of RADS include epithelial desquamation, submucosal inflammation, and thickening of the basement membrane. However, bronchial biopsy is not necessary for the diagnosis or management of the patient's symptoms. Spirometry before and after work is not helpful in cases of accidental exposure to irritants because these exposures are not likely to happen on a daily basis; therefore, these measurements, which are used in other forms of occupational asthma, are not useful in the diagnosis of RADS.

**KEY POINT**

- **The reactive airways dysfunction syndrome follows a single, accidental inhalation of high levels of a nonspecific respiratory irritant in patients who typically do not have a history of asthma; the diagnosis is confirmed by a positive methacholine challenge test.**

**Bibliography**

Dykewicz MS. Occupational asthma: current concepts in pathogenesis, diagnosis, and management. J Allergy Clin Immunol. 2009;123(3):519-528. [PMID: 19281900]

## Item 107     Answer:   E

**Educational Objective:**  Implement vaccination strategy for a patient with chronic obstructive pulmonary disease.

Annual influenza vaccination is recommended in patients with chronic obstructive pulmonary disease (COPD) regardless of their age. In the general population, annual influenza vaccination is recommended in persons 50 years of age or older.

If this patient received influenza and pneumococcal vaccination 1 year ago, he needs only influenza vaccination. Pneumococcal vaccination is recommended for all adults older than 65 years and for younger patients who are active smokers or who have various disorders, including COPD and asthma, that increase their risk for invasive pneumococcal disease. Influenza vaccination is also recommended for pregnant women whose last two trimesters coincide with the influenza season (late December through mid-March). The main vaccine used in the United States is a trivalent inactivated virus, but an intranasally administered vaccine from a trivalent live attenuated virus is also available for patients aged 5 to 49 years who are not pregnant, immunosuppressed, or living with an immunosuppressed person. Because of the patient's age, the most appropriate vaccination is the trivalent killed influenza vaccination.

A single revaccination with pneumococcal vaccine is recommended in adults older than 65 years if they were vaccinated more than 5 years previously at a time when they were less then 65 years of age and in immunosuppressed patients 5 years or more after the first dose. Patients with COPD who received their first pneumococcal vaccination after age 65 years do not need revaccination.

**KEY POINT**

- **Influenza vaccination is recommended annually for all patients with chronic obstructive pulmonary disease regardless of age.**

**Bibliography**

MMWR. Recommended Adult Immunization Schedule. www.cdc.gov/mmwR/PDF/wk/mm5641-Immunization.pdf. Published January 9, 2009. Accessed on August 6, 2009.

## Item 108     Answer:   C

**Educational Objective:**  Evaluate pulmonary hypertension in a patient with sarcoidosis.

There are many causes for worsening dyspnea in a patient with end-stage interstitial lung disease, but this patient's presentation of subacute worsening dyspnea with lower extremity swelling, fatigue, and anorexia suggests that he has developed pulmonary hypertension. Pulmonary hypertension is a frequent cause of worsening dyspnea in patients with interstitial lung disease, and a report of patients with sarcoidosis referred for lung transplantation demonstrated that 73.8% had pulmonary hypertension by right heart catheterization. Transthoracic echocardiography is a useful diagnostic test for suspected pulmonary hypertension. The test can assess for valvular disease, evaluate right atrial and ventricular enlargement and function, and estimate right ventricular systolic pressure.

The diagnosis of pulmonary hypertension is usually confirmed by right-heart and pulmonary artery catheterization. However, this invasive test is not typically the first diagnostic test to evaluate pulmonary hypertension.

This patient has no clinical or radiographic features to suggest community-acquired respiratory infection.

Although he is immunosuppressed, he is treated with trimethoprim-sulfamethoxazole as prophylaxis against *Pneumocystis jirovecii* infection. Therefore, bronchoscopy with bronchoalveolar lavage should not be the next diagnostic test.

Venous thromboembolic disease should always be considered in patients with dyspnea. However, this patient's dyspnea has been progressing over the past 4 weeks, a course that is not typical for pulmonary embolism. Finally, this patient has an existing condition that can account for the presence of pulmonary hypertension; therefore, ventilation/perfusion scan would be premature at this time.

**KEY POINT**

- **Pulmonary hypertension is a frequent cause of worsening dyspnea in patients with interstitial lung disease.**

**Bibliography**

Ryu JH, Krowka MJ, Pellikka PA, Swanson KL, McGoon MD. Pulmonary hypertension in patients with interstitial lung diseases. Mayo Clinic Proc. 2007;82(3):342-350. [PMID: 17352370]

## Item 109      Answer:   C

**Educational Objective:** Manage a patient with acute hypoxemic respiratory failure who fails to respond to noninvasive positive pressure ventilation.

Noninvasive positive-pressure ventilation (NPPV) reduces intubation rates and improves mortality rates in immunosuppressed patients with acute hypoxemic respiratory failure. Patients with acute respiratory failure whose condition does not stabilize within the first 1 to 2 hours of a NPPV trial should undergo elective intubation rather than incur the risk of subsequent respiratory arrest requiring emergent intubation. The patient's respiratory status remains tenuous 2 hours into a trial of NPPV as evidenced by severe hypoxemia, accessory respiratory muscle use, and an elevated respiration rate.

This patient is already receiving 100% supplemental oxygen on NPPV; the elimination of positive end-expiratory pressure with removal of NPPV would place the patient at risk of further deterioration in oxygenation. This patient should remain on NPPV right up to the time of intubation because some limited data suggest that NPPV provides better oxygenation than bag-mask ventilation in hypoxemic patients being prepared for intubation.

Sedation could precipitate respiratory arrest in this patient. Reduced level of consciousness is a relative contraindication to NPPV, and sedation should be used cautiously. In addition, there is little to suggest that excess ventilatory drive or anxiety is independently contributing to her persistent respiratory distress.

**KEY POINT**

- **Patients with acute respiratory failure who do not respond after a 1- to 2-hour trial of noninvasive positive-pressure ventilation should undergo elective intubation.**

**Bibliography**

Baillard C, Fosse JP, Sebbane M, et al. Noninvasive ventilation improves preoxygenation before intubation of hypoxic patients. Am J Respir Crit Care Med. 2006;174(2):171-177. [PMID: 16627862]

## Item 110      Answer:   B

**Educational Objective:** Recognize and manage the propofol infusion syndrome.

This patient has the propofol infusion syndrome, and the drug should be discontinued and replaced by fentanyl and midazolam. The propofol infusion syndrome is a rare and often fatal syndrome originally described in critically ill children undergoing long-term propofol infusion at high doses. The syndrome has recently been reported in adults, mostly in patients with acute neurologic illnesses or acute inflammatory diseases complicated by severe infections or even sepsis and who are receiving catecholamines and/or corticosteroids in addition to propofol. The main features of the syndrome consist of cardiac failure, rhabdomyolysis, severe metabolic acidosis, and renal failure associated with hyperkalemia. Central nervous system activation with production of catecholamines and corticosteroids, and systemic inflammation with cytokine production are priming factors for cardiac and peripheral muscle dysfunction. High-dose propofol, but also supportive treatments with catecholamines and corticosteroids act as triggering factors. At the subcellular level, propofol impairs free fatty acid utilization and mitochondrial activity. The syndrome can be lethal if not identified early, and caution should be exercised when using prolonged (more than 48 h) propofol sedation at doses greater than 75 µg/kg/min, particularly in patients with acute neurologic or inflammatory illnesses. In these cases, alternative sedative agents should be considered immediately, and monitoring of the plasma levels of troponin I, creatine kinase, and myoglobin should be undertaken. There is no need to obtain a CT scan of the head, which would pose added risk of transport for the patient.

Beyond immediate discontinuation of the drug, the treatment of propofol infusion syndrome is supportive. Supportive treatment may ultimately include bicarbonate infusion, hemodialysis, treatment of heart failure, and cardiac pacing for profound bradycardia. There is no indication for intravenous heparin at this time. Plasmapheresis has no role in managing the propofol infusion syndrome.

**KEY POINT**

- **The propofol infusion syndrome in adults occurs primarily in patients with acute neurologic or acute inflammatory diseases complicated by severe infection or sepsis and who are receiving catecholamines or corticosteroids in addition to propofol.**

**Bibliography**

Fong JJ, Sylvia L, Ruthazer R, et al. Predictors of mortality in patients with suspected propofol infusion syndrome. Crit Care Med. 2008; 36(8):2281-2287. [PMID: 18664783]

## Item 111     Answer:   C

**Educational Objective:** Recognize bronchial hyperresponsiveness in patients with hay fever.

Airway responsiveness to methacholine is increased in patients with hay fever, smoking, bronchitis, chronic obstructive pulmonary disease, and cystic fibrosis, as well as after viral infections. The severity of airway hyperresponsiveness is most pronounced in patients with asthma. No specific asthma therapy is needed for asymptomatic bronchial hyperresponsiveness. This patient may benefit from therapy for hay fever, with nasal corticosteroids with or without antihistamines.

There is no evidence that the patient has bronchial asthma, and, therefore, treatment with albuterol, inhaled corticosteroids, and long-acting β-agonists is not indicated. There is also no need for a repeat methacholine challenge test because no therapy is needed for the mildly abnormal response in asymptomatic patients.

### KEY POINT

- No specific therapy is needed for asymptomatic bronchial hyperresponsiveness.

**Bibliography**

Hewitt DJ. Interpretation of the "positive" methacholine challenge. Am J Ind Med. 2008;51(10):769-781. [PMID: 18702111]

## Item 112     Answer:   C

**Educational Objective:** Recognize and evaluate complications of obstructive sleep apnea.

This patient has evidence of mild to moderate pulmonary hypertension. Her body habitus and long-standing history of fatigue and daytime sleepiness raise the possibility of obstructive sleep apnea, a contributing factor or cause of the pulmonary hypertension. Therefore, a full polysomnography would be appropriate in this patient. Identification and treatment of coexisting obstructive sleep apnea may improve the outcome of pulmonary arterial hypertension. In addition to weight loss, continuous positive airway pressure therapy at nighttime improves quality of life, cognitive function, and symptoms of daytime sleepiness. Initiating therapy without a diagnostic evaluation is not indicated.

Right-heart catheterization may be appropriate at some point in the evaluation of this patient, but noninvasive testing to rule out secondary causes of pulmonary hypertension should be done first. Although pulmonary arterial hypertension was at one time a relentless disease, many effective treatment options exist for this patient, and evaluation for lung transplantation would be inappropriate.

### KEY POINT

- The presence of pulmonary arterial hypertension should prompt an evaluation for associated conditions, such as obstructive sleep apnea and connective tissue diseases.

**Bibliography**

McGoon M, Gutterman D, Steen V, et al; American College of Chest Physicians. Screening, early detection, and diagnosis of pulmonary arterial hypertension: ACCP evidence-based clinical practice guidelines. Chest. 2004;126(1 Suppl):14S-34S. [PMID: 15249493]

## Item 113     Answer:   B

**Educational Objective:** Treat health care–acquired methicillin-resistant *Staphylococcus aureus* pneumonia.

The patient has had a good clinical response to treatment for methicillin-resistant *Staphylococcus aureus* (MRSA) pneumonia and, therefore, does not need antibiotic therapy beyond 7 to 9 days. The patient's residence in a nursing home and chronic hemodialysis place her at risk for infection with resistant organisms, including MRSA and *Pseudomonas aeruginosa*, and she received appropriate empiric coverage for health care–associated pneumonia. Now that MRSA has been isolated from her sputum, empiric coverage for other organisms should be discontinued. In the absence of bacteremia, it appears treatment for MRSA pneumonia can be safely limited to approximately 8 days. Patients with *P. aeruginosa* pneumonia appear to have a greater risk of recurrent infection when antibiotic therapy is limited to 8 rather than 15 days.

### KEY POINT

- Most causes of health care–associated pneumonia, including ventilator-associated pneumonia, require only approximately 8-day antibiotic courses.

**Bibliography**

Guidelines for the management of adults with hospital-acquired, ventilator-associated, and healthcare-associated pneumonia: Official statement of ATS and IDSA 2004. Am J Respir Crit Care Med. 2005;171(4):388-416. [PMID: 15699079]

## Item 114     Answer:   C

**Educational Objective:** Treat gastroesophageal reflux disease complicating persistent asthma.

Gastroesophageal reflux disease (GERD) is common in patients with asthma. Obesity is also associated with an increased prevalence of GERD, which may lead to acute airway hyperresponsiveness and an exacerbation of asthma. Because of the patient's increased nocturnal symptoms, a trial of gastric acid suppression with a proton pump inhibitor is warranted. Additional measures to reduce gastric acid and GERD include elevating the head of the bed and refraining from eating and drinking 2 hours before bedtime. Certain foods (tomatoes, chocolate, caffeinated beverages) promote acid reflux and should be avoided.

Increasing the inhaled corticosteroid dose is not appropriate because the patient has good daytime control, suggesting that a factor specifically exacerbating her bronchospasm at night is present. Furthermore, increasing the corticosteroid dose is likely to lead to a repeated episode of oral thrush. Increasing the β-agonist dose is also inappropriate because the approved dose is fixed and such an increase could cause difficulty sleeping.

The use of an allergen-impermeable bedcover as a main intervention to reduce exposure to house dust mites is not very effective in patients with asthma. It has been proposed that its use as part of a vigorous approach to reduce environmental allergen exposure might be of some benefit in allergic patients with difficult-to-control asthma.

**KEY POINT**

- **In patients with asthma who have increased nocturnal symptoms despite adequate daytime control, a trial of gastric acid suppression therapy is warranted.**

**Bibliography**
Frye JW, Vaezi MF. Extraesophageal GERD. Gastroenterol Clin North Am. 2008;37(4):845-858. [PMID: 19028321]

## Item 115    Answer:  B
**Educational Objective:** Monitor respiratory status of a patient with neuromuscular weakness.

In patients with neuromuscular weakness and tenuous respiratory status, serial measurement of vital capacity is an effective method to anticipate the need for mechanical ventilatory support before the onset of respiratory arrest. Patients with vital capacity under 15 to 20 mL/kg, unable to generate more than 30 cm $H_2O$ of negative inspiratory force, or with declining values are at high risk of ventilatory failure requiring invasive mechanical ventilation. Patients with bulbar dysfunction may not be able to accurately perform bedside spirometry and are at increased risk of rapid deterioration due to acute aspiration events.

Measuring arterial blood gases is inappropriate because carbon dioxide retention is typically a sign of impending respiratory arrest and is therefore not optimal for identifying patients best managed with elective, rather than emergent, intubation.

Continuous monitoring of oxygen saturation is inappropriate because the patient could develop life-threatening respiratory acidosis before oxygen desaturation if she were receiving supplemental oxygen. Desaturation is also a relatively late finding suggestive of impending respiratory arrest.

The rapid shallow breathing index is used to assess patients during ventilator weaning but not in this clinical context. Furthermore, the index requires measurement of the patient's tidal volume, which is not routinely obtained in patients who are breathing without invasive or noninvasive ventilatory support.

**KEY POINT**

- **Patients with neuromuscular weakness and tenuous respiratory status should be monitored with serial measurement of vital capacity.**

**Bibliography**
Mehta S. Neuromuscular disease causing acute respiratory failure. Respir Care. 2006; 51(9):1016-1021. [PMID: 16934165]

## Item 116    Answer:  A
**Educational Objective:** Diagnose delirium in a mechanically ventilated patient.

This patient has the most common manifestation of delirium in the intensive care unit (ICU), which is hypoactive or "quiet" delirium. Delirium is a form of acute brain dysfunction that occurs in 50% to 80% of ventilated patients in the ICU. It is associated with a threefold higher rate of death by 6 months, much longer lengths of ICU and hospital stay, higher costs, and a 10-fold higher rate of chronic cognitive deficits after survival. It can be diagnosed quickly using the Confusion Assessment Method for the Intensive Care Unit (CAM-ICU), which takes less than a minute in most patients. The four cardinal features of the diagnosis are (1) acute onset or fluctuations in mental status over a 24-hour period, (2) inattention, (3) disorganization of thinking, and (4) an altered level of consciousness at the time of the evaluation. Patients are defined as delirious if they are positive for features 1 and 2 and either 3 or 4. This patient has features 1, 2, and 3: she is having fluctuations in her mental status as evidenced by the Richmond Agitation Sedation Scale, is inattentive as evidenced by her inability to do the random letter A test, and cannot correctly answer simple questions that require organization of her thinking. Hallucinations may be a symptom of delirium, but they are not required for the diagnosis. She is not hyperactive or in "distress," which is also not required for the diagnosis of delirium.

The patient has no signs of acute focal neurologic findings, which are characteristic of stroke. Dementia is an acquired chronic impairment of memory and other aspects of intellect that impedes daily functioning and is not compatible with this patient's acute fluctuating mental status. Psychosis is a disturbance in the perception of reality, evidenced by hallucinations, delusions, or thought disorganization. The patient denies hearing or seeing things that are not there, making psychosis unlikely.

**KEY POINT**

- **The cardinal features of delirium are (1) acute onset or fluctuations in mental status over a 24-hour period, (2) inattention, (3) disorganization of thinking, and (4) an altered level of consciousness at the time of the evaluation.**

**Bibliography**
Ely EW, Shintani A, Truman B, et al. Delirium as a predictor of mortality in mechanically ventilated patients in the intensive care unit. JAMA. 2004;291(14):1753-1762. [PMID: 15082703]

# Index

Note: Page numbers followed by f and t denote figures and tables, respectively. Test questions are indicated by a Q.